MEASURING READING COMPETENCE

A Theoretical–Prescriptive Approach

MEASURING READING COMPETENCE
A Theoretical–Prescriptive Approach

STEVEN SCHWARTZ
University of Queensland
St. Lucia, Queensland, Australia

PLENUM PRESS • NEW YORK AND LONDON

Library of Congress Cataloging in Publication Data

Schwartz, Steven.
  Measuring reading competence.

  Bibliography: p.
  Includes index.
  1. Reading—Ability testing. 2. Reading—Research. 3. Individualized reading in-
struction. I. Title.
LB1050.46.S38   1984   371.2'6   84-17953
ISBN 0-306-41749-9

©1984 Plenum Press, New York
A Division of Plenum Publishing Corporation
233 Spring Street, New York, N.Y. 10013

Printed in the United States of America

For Tricia

'TIS THE GOOD READER THAT MAKES THE GOOD BOOK.'
— RALPH WALDO EMERSON

PREFACE

This book concerns measuring reading skills. It is not meant to be a comprehensive survey of reading research or a review of all possible approaches to reading measurement (although considerable attention is given to both subjects). Instead, the purpose of this book is to present a coherent, theoretically based approach to measuring reading competence.

The ability to measure a phenomenon is an important prerequisite for scientific analysis. As Lord Kelvin said, "One's knowledge of science begins when he can measure what he is speaking about and express it in numbers." Unfortunately, not just any numbers will do. Presently available reading tests provide their users with a plethora of numbers—age levels, percentiles, grade equivalents—but their scientific value is questionable. The problem is that there is more to scientific measurement than merely assigning numbers to arbitrarily chosen behaviors. Scientific measurement occurs only within the confines of a theory, and most reading tests are atheoretical.

Recent years have witnessed an explosive growth in reading research. Although there are still many unanswered questions, important decoding skills, language competencies, and cognitive structures underlying reading have been identified and are beginning to be understood. A tentative model of reading, based on recent research findings, is presented in this book. The model is used to demonstrate how theoretically meaningful measures of reading competence may be developed from a cognitive theory of reading. These measures go beyond the mere description of common reading tests; they permit the examiner not only to say that someone is having difficulties learning to read but also to suggest what might be done about the problem. As indicated by this book's subtitle, such measures are both theoretically based and prescriptive.

Several preliminary reading decoding and comprehension measures and their development are described in this book. These measures are not meant to be final test versions; further development is clearly necessary. To help readers who wish to get involved in this work, instructions and computer programs for the reading measures are also included. Thus, readers with access to a microcomputer can try out the measures for themselves.

The book consists of nine chapters. The first chapter is an introduction to the topics covered in the book. Chapter 2 is a historical and conceptual overview of reading research. Chapter 3 describes several popular approaches to measuring reading skills and reviews the current state of the art. In Chapter 4, a tentative reading model based on recent research is developed. Chapters 5 and 6 trace the development of encoding and comprehension measures, respectively, from theory to practical instruments. Chapter 7 shows how the measures may be used to develop individualized instruction programs. Future test development and improved teaching techniques are the subject of Chapter 8. Descriptions of the computer programs underlying the tests appear in Chapter 9. The chapter's goal is to make the measures available to those educators with even modest computing facilities. For this reason, the programs have been written to be as general as possible. Nevertheless, they will have to be modified in order to run on computers other than the Cromemco system for which they were written.

This book is written for the professional educator, teacher, counselor, reading specialist, reading student, and anyone else concerned with reading. I have assumed that readers are familiar with current educational practices and research methods, but it is not necessary to be an expert in either field to follow the book's various discussions. New terms are explained and research techniques are described in detail.

At various times in doing the research for this book, I have been aided by grants from the National Institute of Mental Health (U.S.A.), the Educational Research and Development Committee (Australia), and the Australian Research Grants Scheme. My students and colleagues have been of invaluable help in collecting and analyzing data, researching articles, criticizing earlier drafts, and doing the various chores that go into writing a book. I am particularly grateful to Tim Griffin, Christine Butler-Smith, and Tim Wiedel for collecting much of the data reported in this book. I am also indebted to Judy Brown, who wrote the computer programs described in Chapter 9. Finally, I must express my gratitude to my family, who put up with a lot.

STEVEN SCHWARTZ

CONTENTS

ix

PART V. TECHNICAL SPECIFICATIONS

PART I

INTRODUCTION

CHAPTER 1

THE PROBLEM WITH READING TESTS

The ability to read is an invaluable asset in our modern, technologically oriented society. Given the importance of reading and of identifying those who will have difficulty learning to read, it is no surprise that many attempts have been made to develop practical measures of reading skills. Today, there are dozens of commercially available reading tests that may be used to determine who is having trouble learning to read. Indeed, it seems that reading tests have probably reached the maximum predictive power attainable given the usual restrictions on time and expense. Unfortunately, this concentration on predictive validity (predicting who will have trouble learning to read) has overshadowed attempts to examine reading competence at a more theoretical level. The purpose of this book is to begin to redress the balance by showing how theoretically meaningful reading measures may be developed.

It is customary at this point for authors of books on reading to define just what they mean by reading. To avoid what has often become a sterile debate, this book takes an eclectic view. Reading, in the present context, is the name given to all of the processes involved in getting meaning from print or writing. It is not just decoding print into speech, nor is it just being able to get meaning from print—it is both. Moreover, reading processes may vary with the nature of the material being read and one's purpose (study or pleasure). In summary, reading is not a single skill; it is a dynamic, flexible set of cognitive processes.

OPERATIONALISM AND UNDERSTANDING

Until relatively recently, test constructors have not emphasized to test users that the scores derived from traditional norm-based reading tests are not typical of scientific measures. Scores on norm-based tests, unlike measures of physical

3

characteristics such as height or weight, are not direct trait measures. They are indicators of rank order or the relative standing of an individual in a given population. (If a similar approach were taken to the measurement of height, a value of 100 would be assigned to anyone of average height regardless of whether the population is one of pygmies or giants.)

Relativistic measures have sometimes been justified by appeals to operationalism. For example: Intelligence is what the intelligence test measures. In the reading domain, operationalism takes the following form: If a reading test exhibits systematic relationships to other data believed to reflect reading ability, then the test is a valid reading measure. Operationalism, by itself, probably provides a sufficient rationale when a test's purpose is purely technological (predicting whether a child will learn at grade level, for example). Operationalism, alone, however, is not a substitute for understanding the underlying nature of the reading process. In most branches of science, it is taken for granted that measures reflect some basic theoretical framework. The important point to be made about traditional, norm-based reading tests is that they are largely atheoretical.

The lack of a sound theoretical basis means that reading tests are of rather limited use in practical situations. To discover that a child has difficulty interpreting short paragraphs or replacing missing words in sentences (both tasks appear frequently in reading tests) is not to understand what caused the child's problem in the first place. Nor do traditional measures necessarily tell the teacher what to do about a child's problem. That is, they do not provide the information necessary to tailor-make instructional materials for the needs of a specific child. For this reason, traditional tests have been severely criticized by teachers and educators (Fry, 1976; Gurney, 1978; Newkirk, 1975). To be truly diagnostic and prescriptive, tests must be based on a theory of reading.

NORM-REFERENCED VERSUS CRITERION-REFERENCED TESTS

At this point, the knowledgeable reader might be thinking: All this may be true for traditional, norm-based tests, but what about criterion-referenced tests? Do not they solve the problem? The answer, in most instances, is unfortunately *no*.

Glaser's (1963) original distinction between norm-referenced and criterion-referenced tests was based on their different goals. Norm-referenced tests rank subjects relative to a population. Criterion-referenced tests, on the other hand, measure whether an individual has reached some stated level of competence. (For instance, a criterion-referenced test may be designed to determine whether a student has mastered long division.)

In recent years, increasingly fine distinctions have been made among criterion-referenced tests so that today we have "domain-referenced," "objectives-referenced," "competency," "proficiency," "mastery," and "diagnostic" tests. Sometimes these distinctions are difficult to grasp. For instance, Pyrczak (1979) defines a domain-referenced test as one in which "the tasks are based on a systematic analysis of the specific subskills underlying a broad skill area called a domain" (p. 74). He defines a diagnostic test as "a test that measures skills that are thought to be independent and provides a score for each skill" (p. 74). Clearly, there is considerable overlap in these two approaches.

No doubt criterion-referenced tests play a vital role in educational evaluation (see Berk, 1980, for a review of the current state of the art). Nevertheless, as pointed out by Farr and Roser (1974), criterion-based measures can be just as empirical and atheoretical as the norm-based variety. In fact, norm-based tests can serve as criterion-based tests and vice versa. It is not their questions that differentiate them, but their scoring procedures. Perhaps an example would help.

Smith, Smith, and Brink (1977) have created a compendium of criterion-referenced reading tests they call STARS. These tests require students to read paragraphs and answer questions about them, fill gaps in sentences from a set of possible words, find synonyms, and so on. All of these tasks appear on norm-referenced tests as well. The only difference (and it is not as large as many educators appear to believe) is that Smith *et al.* set competency standards whereas norm-based tests compare students with the average performance in a population. There is no reason why the same tests cannot be used as both a norm- and a competency-based measure. In fact, Smith *et al.* present tables that permit just that.

Because competency-based measures ask the same questions and tap the same skills as norm-based tests, they are no more likely than norm-based tests to reflect a coherent theoretical framework. It is not scoring that is at issue here but how test items are chosen in the first place. These matters are explored further in the next section.

VALIDITY AND THEORY

To a large extent, test constructors rely on face validity to justify including a question on a test. For example, Smith *et al.* devote over 50 pages in their book to discussing the validity of STARS. A large part of this discussion is devoted to showing that the tasks included correspond to "psychological and linguistic considerations" (p. 12). This is done by describing their tasks and showing how—on their face at least—they appear to tap linguistic skills. But how do we know that the tests really measure the skills they are supposed to measure? And how do we know that these are the important skills involved in reading? Smith *et al.* answer this question by providing some evidence (albeit limited) that their measures are related to other indices of reading ability; many test constructors provide no evidence at all. The same reliance on face validity is found among developers of instructional materials. Readers and workbooks are often developed by including what *appears* useful and needed for beginning readers (copious illustrations, for instance) often without any data supporting the validity of their assumptions (Willows, Borwick, & Hayvren, 1981).

It is not my intention to argue that reading tests do not tap certain basic components of the reading process. Their substantial predictive validity indicates that they do. My point is that although the tests tell us that people differ in their ability, they tell us very little about the nature of these individual differences.

A great deal of research in cognitive and educational psychology (and neurology) over the past 20 years has been devoted to explicating the component skills underlying reading. This research has been largely ignored by test constructors. It would appear that a schism has developed between test makers and those engaged in the experimental study of the reading process. As a result, measures of reading competence (whether norm- or competency-based) tend to be atheoretical, empirical efforts.

Modern studies of cognition based on an information-processing point of view have attempted to develop working models of how people think. The goal has been to extend a data processing analogy to a variety of mental abilities and, by implication, to the human intellect as well. Information-processing models have the virtue of being clearly stated and open to empirical test. Unfortunately, experimentalists have been primarily concerned with developing general (nomothetic) laws applicable to all and have not, with certain notable exceptions, paid much attention to the problem of individual differences. The main object of this book is to pull together the fields of reading measurement and the study of cognitive processes by showing how theoretically meaningful tests may be developed from cognitive models of reading. These tests measure both what one can do in an absolute sense as well as what one can do relative to others. Such tests also have considerable practical usefulness, as they not only define what aspects of the reading process are potentially modifiable but they also indicate how such modifications may be obtained.

ORGANIZATION OF THIS BOOK

This book is divided into five parts. The first is this introduction. The second part, which consists of Chapters 2 through 4, provides the background for the tests developed later. Chapter 2 reviews some of the history of reading research and theory. The diverse backgrounds of researchers (they come from psychology, education, neurology, ophthalmology, linguistics, and pediatrics) is shown to have produced a multiplicity of theories and constructs. Moreover, because researchers in the various disciplines tend to pursue independent research programs, they are often unaware of what researchers in other disciplines are doing. In a very real sense, the reading field can be said to be suffering from too many independent researchers and too little interdisciplinary communication. Chapter 3 is a review and critique of various approaches to measuring reading competence. Although reading tests include many different tasks, these tasks are rarely related to a particular theory. Most tests are purely empirical instruments and are of little use in helping teachers devise instructional programs. Chapters 2 and 3 provide the background for the model of reading competence described in Chapter 4. Based on a review of psychological, medical, and educational research into the reading process, a tentative model of reading is developed in Chapter 4. This model is referred to throughout the remainder of the book.

Part III consists of two chapters describing the development and characteristics of a preliminary set of theoretically based reading tests. The tests described in Chapter 5 are concerned with decoding; those dealing with comprehension are discussed in Chapter 6. The rationale behind the tests, the skills they are supposed to measure, and evidence for their reliability and validity are presented. Although the tests are usable in their present form, they are not meant to be final versions. Further refinements are not only possible, they are necessary.

Part IV, "Testing and Instruction," also contains two chapters. The first, Chapter 7, shows how the measures can be used to produce individualized instruction. Here the benefits of theoretically based measures become obvious, as the same tasks used to test reading competence may also be used to provide skilled practice for those whose reading competence is lagging behind. Chapter 8 is devoted to possible future developments in automated testing and instruction.

Part V consists of a single chapter in which the technical details of the tests are described. No longer will these measures remain the sole property of laboratory-based psychologists; anyone working in an educational setting with a microcomputer facility can use them. Although the specifications for the computing system (the present tests are all automated) and the hardware necessary to implement the tests are presented in some detail, producing the total package on a computing system other than the one we use is likely to require at least some modifications. For this reason, the programs were written in the popular BASIC language.

SUMMARY

Reading is a crucial skill in today's society. Although much effort has gone into devising measures of reading competence, a great deal of this effort has been atheoretical. Although traditional tests can identify children with reading problems, they usually do not provide sufficient information to design intervention programs. The present book represents an attempt to show how information-processing theories of the reading process and psychometrics can be linked to provide a rationale for test construction. Tests designed this way would not only describe a child's reading problems but also suggest what to do about them. In this chapter, the important issues of validity and theoretically based tests were discussed. The present approach was outlined, and the remainder of the book was introduced.

PART II

THE CURRENT SCENE

CHAPTER 2

Reading Research and Theory

HISTORY AND PRESENT STATUS

The overwhelming importance of reading in our society is a fairly recent phenomenon. Prior to the Industrial Revolution, reading was considered a luxury reserved for the upper classes and church officials. The working classes were either not taught to read or they were taught only enough to permit them to recognize and respond to familiar materials such as the catechism (Resnick & Resnick, 1977). In the eighteenth and nineteenth centuries, industrialization and the rise of democratic governments in France and in America created the need for an educated population to do a variety of new skilled jobs and to carry out the duties of citizens in a democracy. Mass education lead to a concern for those who were falling behind and, in time, for measures of cognitive skills. Medical science also made great strides in the nineteenth century. Anatomical and physiological investigations into the visual and neural systems led to speculations about their role in reading disorders. Researchers continue to be active in these areas today.

In addition to medicine and education, psychology developed as a science in the nineteenth century. Much early experimental psychology was concerned with reading. Indeed, reading was one of the most active research areas of experimental psychology until the early 1940s, when psychology embraced a rather narrow behaviorism that relegated much reading research to the "mentalistic" category of taboo topics. Psychologists left reading research to educators, linguists, and physicians until the late 1960s, when interest in cognitive matters revived. Today, reading is one of the liveliest areas in experimental psychology.

11

Contemporary reading research and theory reflect the influence of education, psychology, linguistics, and medicine. To appreciate the current situation, it is worthwhile reviewing how some common theories and research techniques developed during the past century. The following discussions are not meant to be exhaustive. Instead, the goal is to highlight significant issues that have relevance for reading measurement today.

INSTRUCTIONAL INFLUENCES ON READING MEASUREMENT AND RESEARCH

Mass education brought with it the need to develop suitable instructional methods. Unprecedented numbers of school children, some from backgrounds very different from their teachers, had to be taught academic skills, often in just a few short years. The early nineteenth century was also an age of optimism about mankind's perfectibility. The revolutions in France and America were looked on as the dawning of a democratic age—the age of the common man. All these factors had important effects on education. For the next 200 years, educational theorists and researchers devoted most of their efforts to three problems: how to teach reading (and what instructional materials to use), what skills a child needs to have in order to learn to read, and how to measure reading competence. Reading tests are addressed in Chapter 3. Here we review the history of the other two research areas.

INSTRUCTIONAL TECHNIQUES AND MATERIALS

Today, as in the past, teachers use a variety of methods to help their students learn to read. These methods fall into two general categories: those that emphasize meaning and those that focus on decoding. Decoding approaches to reading instruction assume that the primary task in learning to read is discovering the relationship between sounds and letters and building up from these to syllables and, finally, words. In contrast, a meaning-emphasis approach to reading instruction stresses the relationship between whole words and their meaning. The "look-and-say" method is an example of a meaning-emphasis approach, whereas phonics training is primarily concerned with decoding.

Although emphases vary, and educational fads come and go, virtually all teachers use a combination of meaning-emphasis and decoding-emphasis approaches. This does not mean that an emphasis on one type of approach or another does not make a difference. It is just that the irregular nature of sound–letter correspondences in English (letters are not always pronounced the same way), and the visual similarity of many words, make any single approach difficult to sustain. Nevertheless, many have tried.

In prerevolutionary America, the *New England Primer* (reprinted in 1967) set the standard for reading materials. It began with the alphabet and soon progressed to nursery rhymes. Although meaning training was involved, much emphasis was given to learning to recite whole passages, sometimes by rote. *McGuffey's Eclectic Primer* (1881) came next and was soon to become one of the most popular readers ever produced. Millions of American school children learned to read with it. Its most distinctive feature was little numbers above each letter indicating the appropriate pronunciation. Although teachers were free to use a variety of teaching methods, the numbers clearly gave *McGuffey's Primer* a decoding (specifically, a phonics) emphasis.

Decoding remained the most popular instructional method through the early part of the twentieth century. The major objective of reading instruction at that time was fluency, which was achieved then, as now, by drill and practice (Diederich, 1973).

The rise of Gestalt psychology in the 1930s, brought a change to reading instructional practices. The Gestaltists emphasized the cognitive operations involved in perception. Rather than passive receptors of sensory stimulation, the Gestalt psychologists viewed people as active constructors of their own perceptions. Studies of visual illusions indicated the many ways that our brains influence what we see. According to Gestaltists, the constituents of a particular stimulus were less important than how individuals interpreted them ("the whole is more than the sum of its parts"). Among reading educators, Gestalt psychology was taken to support a whole-word as opposed to the more analytic decoding approach to reading instruction. For twenty years, meaning-based instruction prevailed but not without some challengers. Bloomfield (1942), for example, pointed out that the words used in most meaning-based programs were chosen because they are familiar and meaningful to children. Such words (*coat, stove,* and *fight,* for example) are unlikely to be regular in terms of pronunciation. From Bloomfield's viewpoint, greater generalization and progress would come from using words, at least early in reading instruction, with more regular pronunciations (for example, *pen* or *hen*). Although Bloomfield's (and others') suggestions were not totally ignored, it was not until 1955 and the publication of Rudolph Flesch's book *Why Johnny Can't Read* that the pendulum began to shift back toward a decoding emphasis. The pendulum was pushed even further along by Chall (1967).

Flesch's book was a polemic that captured the public's imagination; Chall's contribution was more scholarly. She reviewed the existing literature comparing meaning- and code-emphasis approaches to instruction and concluded that a code emphasis is superior—at least in early reading instruction. Although studies conducted since 1967 have tended to substantiate Chall's conclusions (Chall, 1979; Guthrie, Samuels, Martuza, Seifert, Tyler, & Edwall, 1976), it should be noted that research in this area is notoriously difficult to conduct. The main problem is that classifying instructional practices as either "meaning" or "code" emphasis ignores the differences within each group. Code-emphasis programs may use special alphabets like the *Initial Teaching Alphabet* (Southwell, 1973) or the conventional alphabet. Meaning-based programs use basal readers, but so too do many code-emphasis programs. As Beck (1981), who reviewed this area, notes, "a variety of procedures, some of which may be inappropriate, go under the same label" (p. 73).

Research is also made difficult because materials designed for early reading instruction differ in more than just their choice of words or sentences. They also differ in their story content, readability, printing format, illustrations, and even in the size of their pages. Unfortunately, the influence of these various factors has not received a great deal of research attention, and their interaction with instructional techniques is presently unknown. The literature review by Willows *et al.* (1981) found that the design of early reading materials (the number and type of new words, for example) is often based more on intuition than research data. Indeed, what research data are available (on the effects of illustrations, for instance) actually contradict intuition. More illustrations do not necessarily help children learn new words, nor do they always increase interest in the text.

Studies comparing different instructional methods assume that the methods can be differentiated clearly. In practice, however, instructional methods, and the materials used with a particular instructional method, may differ on many dimensions. In some cases, materials designed to be used in a meaning-emphasis program may actually be more similar to materials used in decoding programs than to other meaning-based materials. Clearly, meaningful comparisons between instructional approaches require precise specification of the procedures and materials involved in each. Such specification is often difficult to achieve in large-scale empirical research. For this reason, most studies are vulnerable to methodological criticism (House, Glass, McLean, & Walker, 1978). Thus, despite many expensive research efforts and a number of reviews favoring code-emphasis approaches (Beck, 1981; Chall, 1979), proponents of meaning-based programs have by no means disappeared.

Global comparisons of instructional techniques have probably gone about as far as they can go. Future progress is more likely to result from more sophisticated research seeking to determine which particular techniques are best for which children using which materials. Phrasing the research question in this manner recognizes the many similarities among supposedly different techniques (as well as the differences among supposedly similar ones). It also introduces the notion of individual differences. It has always been unreasonable to assume that a single technique is best for all children. Individual differences have, of course, not been totally neglected by those interested in instruction. Individualized reading programs have been developed (see Harris & Sipay, 1980, for some examples). With the decreasing cost of computers, we should see increasing use of computer-aided reading instruction to individualize the learning process. The testing approach described in this book was developed to assist the development of individualized instruction by providing individualized diagnostic data. Future trends are certain to emphasize individual differences instead of generalizations supposedly applicable to everyone. Concern with individual differences is also likely to alter the traditional concept of reading readiness.

THE SKILLS NECESSARY FOR READING

The notion behind the reading readiness concept is that because children mature at different rates and undergo different learning (and cultural) experiences, they will also differ in the age at which they will be "ready" to profit from reading instruction. In the past, this emphasis on individual differences has not always translated into individualized instructional practices. For many years, the readiness concept was actually used to argue that reading training should be delayed until the primary grades for all children!

The nineteenth century was not only a time of rapid industrialization, it was also a romantic age. Romanticism in education meant idealizing the past, particularly Rousseau's innocent "noble savage." Thus, it was no surprise that when a boy was found near the woods in Aveyron, France, in 1880, he would become the center of a great deal of popular attention. Jean Itard, a French psychologist, undertook the "wild boy's" (as the child came to be called) education.

Itard was largely unsuccessful—the child failed to learn more than rudimentary skills—but Itard's efforts brought popular and professional attention to the mentally retarded and lead to the establishment of institutions devoted to helping them. Itard's work produced much theorizing about the nature of learning and the interaction of innate and experiential factors in learning. These theories produced an interest in early childhood education that would soon see kindergartens established in Europe and America.

An important force in the development of early childhood education was Pestalozzi (1895), whose goal was to develop a philosophy and method of education that would reflect the ideas of the great French philosopher Rousseau. For Pestalozzi, the goal of education was the development of the child's innate perceptual and cognitive powers. Pestalozzi was an early advocate of what came to be known as "discovery methods" of teaching. Pestalozzi recommended field trips and lots of practical activities as the way to get children to "discover" the world around them. The notion that children should become active participants in their own education was in great contrast to earlier ideas and it soon won wide appeal. Froebel (1903) instituted them in his first kindgarten and so did many other educators throughout Europe. Froebel also popularized the idea that children vary in their maturational rate and pattern and that they become "ready" to learn to read at their own individual speed.

The first American kindergarten was established in Boston in 1860. This private venture was followed by public school kindergartens in 1873. The new century saw public kindergartens established nationwide along with freely available primary schools. A consequence of mass education was the early realization that, despite the valiant efforts of teachers and schools, not all children were learning academic skills such as reading with equal proficiency. The need to design curricula suited to various children lead inexorably to the need to measure children's abilities. Indeed, much of the early impetus to the development of mental tests and the study of child development came from the need to understand why some children had difficulty learning to read. Although many reasons were advanced, one that appealed to many educators (in part because it did not blame instructional techniques) is that children were just not ready to read in the early primary grades.

Dewey (1898) and Patrick (1899) both argued that physiological and anatomical data supported their view that reading and writing should not be taught in the early primary school years. Although the term *readiness* did not actually catch on for some years, Dewey's ideas grew in popularity, if not actual practice. By the 1930s, research on readiness began to appear in professional journals (see Morphett & Washburne, 1931, for example). More recently, researchers have tended to take a position opposite to Dewey's pushing forward the age for beginning reading instruction (Downing & Thackray, 1971), so that today, television series such as Sesame Street attempt to convey reading fundamentals to preschoolers.

The major goal of readiness research and theory is to identify the important factors involved in beginning reading. Writers have implicated anywhere from 4 to 64 factors, and, to some extent, the various lists are arbitrary. Nevertheless, there is some commonality among the various lists. Physiological factors (cerebral laterality, vision, hearing, sex differences); social-environmental factors (cultural background, bilingualism); emotional factors (mental illness, motivation for learning, unconscious conflicts); and intellectual factors (intelligence, reasoning, linguistic development, and information-processing skills) are the ones most often thought to be important contributors to reading readiness.

It was realized rather early that reading readiness measures must be independent of reading itself. Otherwise, the readiness construct degenerates into a pure tautology: A child who fails to learn how to read is not ready, and we know this because he fails to learn.

To avoid this, researchers generally develop reading readiness measures based on those factors deemed important determinants of learning to read (physiological, emotional, social-cultural, intellectual). They administer these measures to children usually in kindergarten or first grade. Sometime later—a few months to a few years—they test the same children for reading achievement and compare the two sets of findings. High correlations between the two data sets are taken to indicate the important influence of whatever factors were measured in the readiness tests on learning to read. Although the logic of this technique is not without its faults (correlation, we cannot be too often reminded, does not necessarily mean causation), it remains the most common approach to readiness research. The need for caution in correlational research may be illustrated by considering the example of sex differences.

Many studies conducted over the past 50 years have found that girls learn to read before boys and maintain their superiority at least through the primary grades. In one large-scale study (Dykstra & Tinney, 1969), over 3,200 children were compared in four different American states. The authors found girls superior both in readiness and later reading, concluding that the girls had more advanced visual and auditory discrimination abilities than the boys. Many theorists have interpreted these sex differences as supporting the theory that boys and girls differ physiologically or, at least, that they mature at different rates (see Dwyer, 1973, for a review). But the relationship between sex and reading achievement is purely correlational. That is, the relationship could have been produced by a third variable. Dwyer (1973), for instance, argues that the sex difference is culturally produced. It is, she says, an artifact of male and female sex roles. Reading is seen as a "feminine" activity and the male sex role interferes with school performance.

Dwyer's explanation for sex differences in reading ability is supported by studies done in cultures where reading is not viewed as feminine. In Finland, for example, Viitaniemi (1965), found boys are superior to girls in learning to read. As can be seen, a correlation between two items of information can be open to several interpretations, making research in the field of reading readiness an often controversial enterprise. Some of these controversies are addressed later in this chapter in the discussions of neurophysiological and psychological research and theory.

The correlational nature of readiness research means that interpretations must be cautious, but it does not mean that the research is not worthwhile. Patterns of correlational findings may often converge on a single interpretation— and patterns are beginning to develop. Hundreds of readiness research studies have been conducted during the past 50 years. The outcome of this research has been a number of widely available reading readiness tests many of which will be described in Chapter 3. This large body of research has also produced a great deal of information about the relationships among various factors and reading achievement.

As already noted, the majority of readiness studies correlate scores on either standardized or *ad hoc* readiness tests with scores on standard reading tests given sometime later. Sometimes several readiness measures are compared (Lesiak, 1977, for instance). In general, the findings of these studies support the predictive validity of both standardized and *ad hoc* readiness measures, although the level of prediction does vary with the measures used and the children studied (Clay, 1979; Goodman & Wiederholt, 1973; Kapelis, 1975; Lundburg, Olaffson, & Woll, 1980; Newcomer & Magee, 1977; Satz & Friel, 1978; Speer & Lamb, 1976; Wallbrown, Wallbrown, Engin, & Blaha, 1975; White & Jacobs, 1979).

Some researchers have expanded the scope of readiness research by including factors such as classroom behavior (Feshbach, Adelman, & Fuller, 1977), teacher ratings (Glazzard, 1979), self-concept (Miles, Forman, & Anderson, 1973), visual-recognition memory (Benenson, 1974) and even finger localization (Lindgren, 1978) in their readiness batteries. The predictive validity of these "extra" factors tends to vary across studies. As with the standard tests and the *ad hoc* measures, the actual level of predictive validity obtained depends on the subject sample, the length of time between the initial testing and follow-up, and the specific measures used. Despite these variable findings, there is little doubt that readiness measures do predict later achievement. The level of prediction, although far from perfect, does reach respectable levels in some studies (correlation coefficients above .70 are not uncommon). There are more important questions, from the viewpoint of this book. Do the tests permit educators to understand why some children fail to learn to read and do the tests tell educators what to do about reading failure? For most readiness tests, the answer is no.

With few exceptions (see Chapter 3), readiness tests do not tell educators and teachers what they must know in order to develop remedial programs. Teachers need to know what reading materials are most useful for a child at a particular stage of learning to read, how much practice and drill a child requires, and what form the practice should take. To provide this information, tests must be more than predictive; they must be based on a theory of the reading process. Unfortunately, like most reading tests, reading readiness measures are atheoretical.

INSTRUCTIONAL INFLUENCES ON READING RESEARCH: CURRENT STATUS

Research on instructional materials, teaching techniques, and readiness is being carried out in many centers today. In contrast to the past, today's researchers are moving away from simple questions such as which reading program (code or meaning emphasis) is "best," toward more complicated, but realistic, questions such as what type of child is most likely to benefit from various types of instructional programs? Similarly, it is being realized that reading readiness measures are only useful to the extent that they help educators to plan specific instructional programs. It is not enough to identify those who will have difficulty learning to read; tests should also suggest remedial measures. A method for developing such useful tests is the main subject of this book.

In addition to educators, in the area of reading research, neurologists, pediatricians, and others interested in neurology have been influential. Their work is addressed in the next section.

NEUROPHYSIOLOGICAL AND NEUROANATOMICAL INFLUENCES ON READING MEASUREMENT AND RESEARCH

For over 100 years, and continuing today, physicians and other medical researchers have been studying children and adults who fail to learn to read. The subjects of this research are generally labeled *dyslexic*; their reading problems are usually not attributable to low intelligence or to obvious environmental causes (such as poor teaching).

Although the term *dyslexia* is used frequently, particularly by physicians, its definition is decidedly unclear. Some writers use the term to refer to reading disabilities that originate in a central nervous system defect (Lerner, 1971); others demand that "dyslexics" have no known brain deficit (Critchley & Critchley, 1978). Some writers use the term as a synonym for *poor readers* (Money, 1962).

The World Federation of Neurology has defined developmental dyslexia as

> a disorder manifested by difficulty in learning to read despite conventional instruction, adequate intelligence and socio-cultural opportunity. It is dependent upon fundamental cognitive disabilities which are frequently of constitutional origin. (Cited in Critchley, 1970, p. 11)

This definition, although seemingly explicit, never defines its terms. It assumes that everyone knows what conventional instruction, adequate intelligence, and sociocultural opportunity are. It also assumes that we can separate experiential from constitutional problems. It is essentially a definition by exclusion. Once all other possible sources of reading disability are ruled out dyslexia is what is left.

In recent years, the term *reading disability* appears to have replaced *dyslexia* at least among nonmedical writers (Harris & Sipay, 1980). Unfortunately, this substitution of terms has not solved the definitional problem. The main difficulty is that the meaning of terms like *illiteracy, reading disability, dyslexia,* and so on vary with the context in which they are measured. For example, some high school students can perform well enough on standardized tests to score at or just below grade level, but they cannot follow the written instructions on an income tax form nor can they use a dictionary adequately. Such individuals are called *functionally illiterate*, and, in the United States, they make up more than 10% of the population (Education Commission of the States, 1977). Whether or not this population is considered reading disabled or even dyslexic depends to a large degree on which measure (the standardized reading test or the functional tests) are taken to indicate reading ability.

The definition of who is reading disabled will vary not only with the tests used but also with the motivation of the tested population to do well on tests, the person administering the tests, and so on. This is why estimates of the prevalence of reading disability can vary by 400% even in what is supposed to be the same population (Klasen, 1976; Weinschenk, 1970)!

Ignoring these definitional problems (as many teachers and clinicians have) can be dangerous. For one thing, it almost guarantees that subject samples will not be homogeneous. It is more than likely (as will be shown) that at least some of the disagreements in the medical literature are due to the heterogeneous populations used in the various studies.

WORD BLINDNESS

The most important figure in nineteenth century neurolinguistics was Paul Broca, who, along with others, noted the left cerebral hemisphere location for the damage underlying the language disorder known as *expressive aphasia* (Broca, 1861). Patients suffering from expressive aphasia can comprehend language but have trouble producing coherent speech. Broca was one of the first to report a separation of function between the left and right cerebral hemispheres. It was also one of the first *scientific* demonstrations (the phrenologists had been active long before Broca) of a connection between anatomy and function. Shortly after Broca's discovery, Carl Wernicke (1874) described several other left hemisphere brain sites involved in language functioning.

Broca's work represents a milestone in neurological history. Following his reports, it was only a matter of time before researchers began to look for a relationship between specific brain lesions and reading disorders. Déjerine (1892) described several "alexias" (reading disabilities due to brain damage), and other reports soon followed. The notion that brain damage can produce reading disabilities similar to aphasia soon became well established.

Although reading problems can be produced by brain lesions, it is worthwhile noting that the correlation between brain injury and specific reading disorders is not nearly as close as many writers appear to believe. Traumatic brain injuries result in swelling, which dissipates over time. As the swelling is reduced, the tissue surrounding the injury can change position and actually alter the brain's shape. (This process is known as accommodation.) The typical aphasic patient has extensive tissue damage and a highly individualistic pattern of tissue accommodation. It is for this reason that similar language impairments may arise from different patterns of tissue damage. Indeed, there is little evidence that any single cortical lesion will always produce the same pattern of acquired dyslexia (Penfield & Roberts, 1959).

Despite these ambiguities, many psychologists, physicians, and others interested in language have adopted a naive "psycho-anatomical" viewpoint (as described by Brain, 1961). These writers assume a cortical "center" for every speech or reading function. Hence, recognizing visually presented words takes place in the "visual word center" and linking sound with visual codes takes place in the "phonological coding center." Psycho-anatomy is often combined with circular reasoning, so that an inability to perform a function is interpreted as evidence for damage to a particular center. Examples of such reasoning will be given later in this section. For now, it is sufficient to note that, although most cases of aphasia involve left hemisphere damage, it is not presently possible to identify specific cortical lesions for specific reading subskills. There is, in fact, no *a priori* reason to believe that brain areas corresponding to the specific subskills postulated in theories of reading even exist.

Another dubious line of reasoning is the direct generalization of hypotheses drawn from observing brain-injured patients to those without brain damage. The typical sequence goes something like this: brain injury can produce reading problems, so those with reading problems must have brain damage too. This was the line taken by Morgan (1896), who published the case of a boy who, despite obvious academic talent in other areas, seemed unable to learn to read. Generalizing from cases of acquired aphasia, Morgan thought that the parts of the brain found damaged in cases of alexia (mostly the left angular gyrus) were "undeveloped" in this boy. Similar observations and conclusions were reached by Hinshelwood (1895, 1917). Hinshelwood (1917) summarized the field of dyslexia in his book *Congenital Word Blindness,* which set the theoretical stage for many years to come. In this book, Hinshelwood explicitly stated that at least some reading problems are due to an "inherent aphasia" or "word blindness" that is analogous to acquired aphasia. In other words, those with reading disabilities suffer from a form of brain damage that makes it difficult for them to connect the printed word with either sound or meaning. As there has never been evidence for anatomical damage in the majority of reading-retarded children, Hinshelwood's word blindness has usually been assumed to reflect "developmental immaturity" (dyslexics have immature nervous systems) rather than actual tissue damage.

Developmental delay also figured importantly in the writings of Samuel Orton. Orton, who worked in an Iowa "mental" clinic, noted that the reading-disabled children he saw had a typical behavior pattern. He claimed that they frequently reversed letters in reading and writing and also appeared to be left handed (or at least ambidextrous) more often than normal readers. Orton summed up his position in what has come to be known as "the Orton credo."

> My theory of the obstacle to the acquisition of reading in children of normal intelligence which results in the varying grades of reading disability is a failure to establish the physiological habit of working exclusively from the engrams of one hemisphere. As

a result, there is incomplete elision of one set of antitropic engrams and there results confusion as to the direction of reading which serves as an impediment to facile associative linkage with the auditory engrams which, during the learning years at least, carry the meaning. (Orton, 1966, p. 96)

In plain English (not one of Orton's strong points), Orton believed that dyslexia is the result of a failure to develop cerebral dominance. Orton's theory was derived from his notion that visual inputs are registered simultaneously in both hemispheres, but in the nondominant hemisphere (usually the right), the visual percept is actually reversed! According to Orton, the dominant hemisphere normally suppresses this reversed image; but in those people with incomplete dominance, competition between the hemispheres leads to reading problems. Orton called this problem "strephosymbolia" or "twisted symbols"; he felt that it often appears as incomplete handedness or mixed dominance (crossed eye and hand preferences).

Orton's theory implies that there are two visual "images" processed separately and "projected" in literal form onto the visual areas of each hemisphere. These images are then "observed" by some homunculus, who normally ignores one in favor of the other. Orton's notion is pictured in Figure 1.

Unfortunately, this is not how the visual system operates. As everyone familiar with Hubel and Wiesel's work (1968) knows, cells in the primary visual

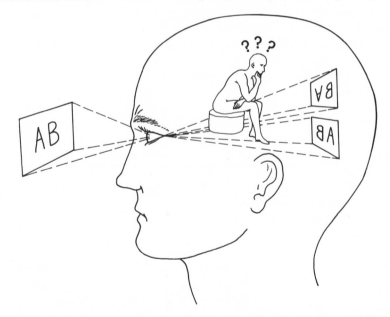

FIGURE 1. Orton's theory, a particularly naive form of psycho-anatomy, asserts that incomplete dominance confuses readers, who must interpret different "pictures" projected into each cerebral hemisphere.

cortex respond to specific stimulus characteristics. But these feature detectors do not construct visual images in each cortex (let alone reversed images). In actuality, images from the two eyes are ultimately superimposed in the visual cortex because nerve impulses from both eyes (and visual fields) impinge on the same cells. Indeed, this arrangement makes it possible for us to assign depth to the perceived scene. Furthermore, studies of patients who have had their cerebral hemispheres surgically disconnected have not found reversed images in either of the patients's disconnected hemispheres (Gazzaniga, Bogen, & Sperry, 1962). Finally, there is some doubt about how common reversed letters really are in reading-disordered children. After reviewing the literature, Critchley and Critchley (1978) conclude that such reversals are quite rare.

Despite its lack of hard, scientific support, Orton's theory became very popular, and the Orton Society remains active today. Many modern researchers have rejected Orton's theory (of reversed images in the nondominant hemisphere) while continuing to believe that reading disability is related to faulty cerebral dominance. Indeed, rather than fading away, the hemispheric laterality literature (particularly in relation to reading disability) appears to be growing at an accelerating rate. Despite the negative tone of this discussion, it is important to keep in mind that nothing said here should be taken as implying that studying brain-damaged patients is not worthwhile. Neuropsychological research has not only produced new hypotheses but has also permitted the testing of theories developed to explain the behavior of normal readers. Modern neuropsychological researchers avoid many of the pitfalls of psycho-anatomy by focusing on processes rather than brain structures. That is, previously literate adults who have incurred brain injury (through cerebrovascular accidents, wounds, or closed head injury) are not assumed to have lost specific brain "centers" but to have lost specific information-processing abilities (which are not given a single cerebral location).

The technique favored by neuropsychologists is the analysis of patients' reading errors. Few patients ever lose the ability to read entirely; they read some words correctly and make errors on others. Often, these errors exhibit characteristic patterns. A patient may say "hat" for "cat" or even "dog" for "cat." Analyses of these errors can reveal how the patients (and perhaps nonpatients) process information while reading.

Neuropsychologists are particularly sensitive to dissociations—an impairment in one aspect of a reading skill with normal functioning on another aspect of the same skill. Such dissociations can reinforce information-processing theories by demonstrating the physiological independence of theoretical constructs.

Beginning with a paper by Marshall and Newcombe (1973), neuropsychological researchers have identified several syndromes of acquired dyslexia (Patterson, 1981). Deep dyslexia or phonemic dyslexia is the most carefully studied. *Deep dyslexia* is characterised by great difficulty in using phonological cues to read. These patients cannot "sound out" nonsense syllables or unfamiliar words. If pressed, they will produce a word that looks similar to the target word (*lake* for *dake*). Patients suffering from deep dyslexia find it easier to read nouns than function words and make numerous visual, semantic, or derivational errors. Clinical observations, research data, and theoretical models of deep dyslexia are reviewed by Coltheart, Patterson, and Marshall (1980). Several other syndromes of acquired dyslexia were described by Patterson (1981) and are depicted in Table 1.

Although not without controversy (see Henderson, 1981), observations of patients suffering from acquired dyslexia do seem to reveal characteristic dissociations (Patterson, 1978, 1979, 1981). Most often these dissociations are taken to support a "two-route" theory of reading. That is, deep dyslexic patients who can read most common words but have difficulty reading nonwords or irregularly spelled words are thought to have lost the ability to read phonologically (by sounding out) but can still go directly from print to a word's meaning and sound (the visual route). This work will be explored further in Chapter 4.

Modern neuropsychological research has progressed a long way from the psycho-anatomy of "word blindness" and Orton's brand of naive perceptual materialism. Today, the emphasis is on identifying the processes involved in normal reading and examining the fate of these various processes in patients with cerebral injuries. Because this neuropsychological research requires functional measures that are based on theories of normal reading, it is quite congenial with the approach followed in this book. For this reason, neuropsychological research will be encountered again in later chapters.

Although our understanding of the reading process has undoubtedly benefited from the study of acquired dyslexia, it should not be assumed that all those who have difficulty learning to read also have brain damage similar to that found in acquired dyslexia. Although there are some similarities between developmental and acquired dyslexia (Aaron, Baxter, & Lucenti, 1980; Jorm, 1979), there are substantial differences as well (Baddeley, Ellis, Miles, & Lewis, 1982; Byrne,

TABLE 1. Syndromes of Acquired Dyslexia[a]

Syndromes	Symptoms
Phonemic (deep) dyslexia	Cannot read nonwords, makes semantic errors
Phonological dyslexia	Difficulty reading nonwords or function words
Déjerine's syndrome (Letter-by-letter dyslexia)	Can only read by first identifying each letter
Semantic (surface dyslexia)	Difficulty reading irregularly spelled words

[a]Adapted from "Neuropsychological Approaches to the Study of Reading" by K. E. Patterson, 1981, *British Journal of Psychology, 72,* 151–174. Copyright 1981 by the British Psychological Society.

1981). At present, there seems to be no way to decide whether developmental and acquired dyslexia are more alike than they are different. Moreover, there are enough differences among even acquired dyslexics who are supposed to have the same syndrome (see Henderson, 1981) to insure that the debate will probably remain unsettled.

Although it is not possible to say that acquired and developmental dyslexia derive from the same roots, we have learned much about the normal reading process from studying the errors made by those suffering from various reading disorders. This information, as will be shown, has proved helpful in developing reading tests. A much larger literature dealing with faulty dominance or "lateralization" among those with reading problems has produced far less useful information. The reasons for this are addressed in the next section.

CEREBRAL LATERALIZATION

The notion behind the lateralization literature is that reading problems are related to differences in cerebral organization—specifically in faulty cerebral dominance. Assertions about group differences in brain organization are not new. Descartes, for example, felt that the direction in which the pineal gland points (in some individuals it points left, in others right, and in others up and down) influences behavior. Today, researchers and theorists focus on differences between the cerebral hemispheres. We have already encountered Orton's (1966) hypothesis. His theory, as we have seen, had several flaws. Current theories also have serious shortcomings. In order to appreciate these problems, it is first necessary to understand how laterality researchers operate.

Researchers looking for laterality differences among reading groups adopt the following logic:

1. Distinct reading groups may be identified.
2. Reading groups perform differently on some behavioral or physiological task.
3. The task reflects differences in the degree of lateralization of one or more cortical processes.
4. The two groups, therefore, differ in laterality.

For this logic to proceed, certain conditions must be met. First, the reading groups must be identifiable. (Different definitions of reading disability across studies may give rise to different findings.) Second, the laterality task must be reliable; otherwise high within-group variance will make between-group comparisons impossible. Finally, the laterality tasks must be valid indicators of cerebral organization. Unfortunately, research on the role of laterality in reading has failed to meet any of these requirements.

Identifiability of Reading Groups

We have already seen that the definition of dyslexia is by no means universally agreed on. Researchers have been left to develop their own idiosyncratic definitions, which, as a consequence, differ from experiment to experiment. In some experiments, good and poor readers are identified by their performance on standardized reading tests (although not the same tests); in others, children with varying types of learning disorders are compared. The upshot of this lack of definitional precision is that attempts to compare different reading groups on laterality measures are difficult to interpret. That is, a failure to find laterality differences among groups may be caused by their not existing in the first place or it may result from using the wrong definition of laterality. By the same token, when differences are found, it is unclear what characteristics of the group are responsible for them.

Reliability of Laterality Indices

Researchers have used many laterality measures in attempting to relate reading problems to differences in laterality. These measures include handedness, dichotic listening, electroencephalograms (EEGs), perceptual differences between right and left, ear and face temperature, preference for music or speech, and patterns of performance on "verbal" and "spatial" intelligence tests. Few of these measures are reliable enough to differentiate between groups. Take handedness, for instance. How subjects are classified on handedness depends to a considerable degree on how handedness is measured. For example, "preference measures" (which hand does the subject prefer?) do not give the same result as skill measures (which hand is more skillful? Lake & Bryden, 1976). Depending on which measurement technique is adopted, different individuals will be assigned to each group. Even using purely hand preference, results depend on how many activities are tested. These problems are merely compounded when we also try to compare *eyedness, footedness* (yes, footedness has also been related to reading; see Porac & Coren, 1981), or mixed dominance (e.g., crossed eye–hand preferences). Perhaps, then, it is no surprise that literature reviews (see Benton, 1975, for example) find no differences between normal and disabled readers in eye or hand preferences.

Other laterality indices fare no better. For over 70 years (see Ruediger, 1907), psychologists studying perceptual asymmetries have been asking subjects to identify or otherwise react to visual stimuli presented either to the right or left of a central fixation point. Although this literature has grown large and complicated, one thing seems clear—the findings are highly variable. Sometimes performance is best when "verbal" stimuli are presented to the right visual field; at other times, the left visual field has the advantage (Jonides, 1979; Schwartz

& Kirsner, 1982). Visual field asymmetries not only shift from one task to another (Geffen, Bradshaw, & Wallace, 1971) but also from one subject to another (Kroll & Madden, 1978) and even from trial to trial in the same subject (Schwartz & Kirsner, 1982).

Similar variability may be found in dichotic listening (Berlin, 1977). Blumstein, Goodglass, and Tratter (1975) reported test–retest reliability coefficients for dichotic asymmetry scores to be .21 for vowels and .74 for consonants. About one-third of their normal adult subjects showed reverse asymmetries for vowels and consonants their second time through the task (Blumstein *et al.,* 1975). Lateral eye movements, EEGs, and other laterality indices have similar low reliabilities (Ehrlichman & Weinberger, 1978; Feurstein, Ward, & Le Baron, 1979). Because unreliable tests are less likely to reveal group differences (because of high measurement error) than reliable tests, studies that compare measures differing in reliability may produce spurious results. Even finding a reliable laterality index will not solve all the problems in laterality research. No index of group differences, no matter how reliable, is useful as a measure of laterality unless it can be shown that the task is related to underlying brain asymmetry. Validity has yet to be demonstrated for most tasks.

Handedness is a good example. Researchers looking for differences in the incidence of left-handedness or for "crossed-dominance" (left handedness and right eyedness, for instance) have estimated handedness in various groups. Even for the "same" groups, these estimates often disagree (compare Dean, Schwartz, & Smith, 1981, with Kershner, 1978, for example). One must suspect substantial sampling error in many of these reports. Moreover, even if handedness could be reliably measured there is some doubt about what it would mean insofar as laterality is concerned. Although it is true that 95% of right-handers have language localized in the left cerebral hemisphere, about two-thirds of left-handers show the same pattern (Annett, 1975).

The situation is no better for other laterality indices. Dichotic listening, for example, is influenced by intensity level, frequency, signal-to-noise ratio, and the asynchrony between competing stimuli (Berlin, 1977). It also depends on the type of stimuli used (Berlin, 1977). Any or all these factors can produce changes in ear advantage independent of lateral asymmetries in brain function.

Visual half-field experiments are equally problematic. Schwartz and Kirsner (1982) found that verbal ability (and by inference, reading ability) interacted with visual field in a letter-matching experiment. Similar results had been reported earlier (Kroll & Madden, 1978) and had been interpreted as reflecting different lateralization patterns in subjects of different verbal ability levels. Schwartz and Kirsner, on the other hand, found that these visual asymmetries could be altered by manipulating stimulus probability and that the verbal ability differences did not reflect underlying differences in laterality but merely differences in cognitive capacity. Schwartz and Kirsner also found that traditional patterns of visual field advantages could be found even when the visual fields are defined horizontally rather than vertically from the midline. This also suggests that visual field asymmetries in behavior may not be related to underlying brain asymmetries.

Handedness, dichotic listening, and visual half-field tasks are the most common indices of laterality in the "group differences" literature. As can be seen, their validity as measures of lateralization is questionable. The situation is worse for less common measures like performance on intelligence tests. A high verbal test score is by no means a measure of "left" hemisphere superiority. Even in split-brain patients, the right hemisphere retains some language ability (Zaidel, 1978) and most "spatial" tasks can also be performed by the left hemisphere (Gazzaniga & Le Doux, 1978).

This discussion does not exhaust the available "laterality" measures that have been used to demonstrate group differences. EEG measures (Ornstein, Herron, Johnston, & Sueencionis, 1979) and other indices have also been used. Their validity may prove to be higher than those described here. For the present, however, it seems necessary to conclude in agreement with Naylor (1980) and Young and Ellis (1981) that no clear demonstration of a cerebral asymmetry disorder in the reading disabled has yet been found.

One aspect of laterality theorizing that has not yet been mentioned is the explanation of some symptoms of deep dyslexia as evidence for the right cerebral hemisphere taking over reading (Coltheart, 1980). Although there does seem to be considerable ability to read in the right hemisphere (Hécaen, 1978; Zaidel, 1978), this hypothesis has met with some opposition (Besner, 1981; Henderson, 1981). At present, there is insufficient knowledge to settle the question of how the right hemisphere (or the left, for that matter) actually reads.

Despite conflicting results and obvious interpretive problems, laterality studies continue to be a growth industry. At present, these studies have contributed little to our ability to measure reading competence.

VISUAL DEFECTS AND READING

Because print must be seen to be read, it is obvious that children with severe (uncorrected) visual handicaps will have difficulty learning to read. Many researchers have assumed that the reverse is also true. That is, children who have difficulty learning to read must have a visual defect. Not only is such an assumption untenable on purely logical grounds, it also—as we shall see—lacks research evidence in its support.

The literature on visual defects and reading disability has not always displayed the dispassionate discussion of facts that is supposed to characterize scientific research. Often, those who feel they have found a cause or cure for "dyslexia" proclaim their findings in an exhortative rather than scientific manner.

Differences of opinion about what research data actually mean can be quite dramatic in this field.

Stack (1980–1981), for example, quotes the combined committee of the American Academy of Pediatrics, Academy of Ophthalmology and Otolaryngology, and the American Association of Ophthalmology: "No peripheral eye defect will produce dyslexia and associated learning difficulties" (p. 65).

Optometrists, on the other hand, believe there is a link between visual problems and reading disability. Compare the following statement of the Australian Optometrical Association made in a report to Parliament (1976) with the statement quoted above: "There is considerable evidence that some children with learning problems have abnormal visual characteristics . . . and evidence that abnormal visual characteristics negatively influence the learning process in some children" (p. 409).

Given this point of view, it is not surprising that most work in the visual defect area has been performed by optometrists (with the aid of psychologists and teachers). Because each writer focuses on a particular defect, it is not easy to summarize the field. Nevertheless, it is possible to characterize the general optometric approach.

The beginning is usually the identification of a population of reading disabled subjects. These subjects are generally called *dyslexic,* although exactly what this term means differs from study to study. Next, the dyslexic population is screened for visual defects. If any are found, they are taken to be the "cause" of that subject's (and perhaps all poor readers') reading disability. The possibility that the visual disorder is actually the result rather than the cause of reading problems is rarely considered. Yet, for many visual defects, this is not at all unlikely.

Many different forms of visual defects have been implicated in reading disability. Refractive errors (near- or farsightedness, astigmatism) can usually be corrected with glasses and, therefore, present only a minor problem for reading (providing the individual wears his or her spectacles). Of much more interest to optometrists are the binocular fusion errors called *phorias.* The person with a phoria has eyes that point in slightly different directions so that an image does not fall on corresponding points on the retina of both eyes. *Exophoria* is a tendency for one or both eyes to move outward: in *esophoria* one or both eyes turn inward. An extreme example of a phoria is *convergent strabismus* (cross-eye) in which the defect is quite obvious. Accommodation and convergence problems (focusing the eye's lens) and rare problems such as *aniseikonia* (different size optical images in the retina of each eye) have also been implicated as causes of reading problems.

Having isolated a visual defect in some proportion of a reading-disabled sample, the last step is to present a "cure" for reading disability based on correcting the visual problem. Cures include exercises to increase eye–hand coordination, walking a wooden beam while staring at a target (another coordination exercise), following a swinging target with both eyes, patching one eye and many other similar interventions (see Dunlop & Dunlop, 1981; Frostig, 1972; and Spache, 1981).

There have been some attempts to evaluate these programs, and some writers look favorably on them (Spache, 1981). Unfortunately, the quality of much of this research is very poor. Control groups are often missing or not carefully chosen to match the experimental group, and correlational findings are often taken to be causal.

Lawson (1968) and Keogh (1974) critically reviewed the literature on optometric training programs and concluded that various methodological and logical defects make it impossible to draw conclusions about the effectiveness of these programs. It appears that things are not much improved today. Dunlop and Dunlop (1981), for example, reported on 132 children who underwent their "orthoptic" treatment (which consists of putting a patch on one eye).

> Reversals decrease, and writing, previously very untidy, becomes neat and readable; reading improves in speed and fluency; the spelling improves. . . . The child becomes a happy, welcome member of the family and the class. (p. 116)

These remarkable results are unsupported by control groups, objective measures, or independent evaluations. Such studies are, unfortunately, the norm rather than the exception in this field of research.

Sometimes the logic behind studies is very difficult to accept. Brod and Hamilton (1973), for instance, used an aniseikonic lens to disturb binocular functioning and found (not surprisingly) that the presence of such a lens led to a decrement in reading performance. They took this finding as evidence that binocular instability may hinder reading performance. This is similar to arguing that if children cannot read with blindfolds on that reading disability may be caused by early wearing of blindfolds!

Not all research in the area of visual problems is uncontrolled or uninterpretable. Careful researchers have found relationships between specific visual defects and reading disorders. Stein and Fowler (1982), for example, found poor eye movement control among "dyslexics," and Nyman and Laurinen (1982) found poor spatial vision among their dyslexic sample. There is also clear evidence that eye movements during reading are less systematic among reading disabled than among normal readers (Lester, Benjamin, & Stagg, 1978). It seems reasonable to believe that at least some children who evidence reading disabilities do so because of some visual defect. But it seems equally likely that for a great many reading-disabled children, visual disorders are the result rather than a cause of reading disability. As Critchley (1970) argues, children who have not grasped the syntax and other codes of the language may be expected to be erratic in eye movement patterns because they have not learned to use the structure of the language to serve as a cue for fixations. The correlational nature of most of the research in the area of visual defects and reading disability makes it very difficult to tell what is cause and what is effect. (The possibility that both reading and visual problems are the result of some third cognitive problem also cannot be ruled out.)

In addition to visual defects, the role of perceptual distortion in reading disability has also proven controversial (see Fletcher & Satz, 1979, and Vellutino, 1979). Here, again, it is difficult to tell which came first, perceptual distortion or reading disability, or whether both reading and perceptual problems are due to some third factor.

A central visual process that has been receiving attention recently is the perception of contrast and visual persistence (Badcock & Lovegrove, 1981). Visual persistence (continued visibility of a stimulus after the stimulus is no longer present) appears to be greater for reading disabled than for other children. This is particularly true when the visual stimuli are composed solely of low-frequency information (see Figure 2 for an example of what is meant by spatial frequency).

If these findings are supported by further research, they may point to a difference in central (cortical) visual processing between poor and average readers. A difference at the level of cortical mechanisms would be not only interesting

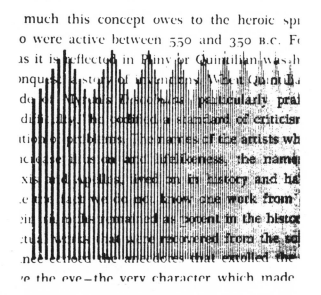

FIGURE 2. High spatial frequency (finely detailed) gratings and low spatial frequency (coarse) gratings mask different aspects of print. The masking effect is greatest when the frequency of the gratings coincides with the frequency of the underlying print. (From "What Does Visual Perception Tell us About Visual Coding" by Stewart Anstis, which appeared in M. S. Gazzaniga and C. Blakemore (Eds.), *Handbook of Psychobiology,* New York: Academic Press, 1975. Reprinted with the permission of the publisher and the author.)

in itself, it would also reinforce a view proposed by James Hinshelwood almost a century ago:

> The optical aspect of vision has long been studied with great attention. The anatomy, physiology, pathology, and physics of the eye have been investigated with the greatest care. The cerebral or mental aspect of vision, however, has not received the same attention. Yet the brain contributes quite as much to each visual act as the eye. . . . We are apt to forget that we see with our brains as well as our eyes. (Cited in Pirozzolo, 1979, p. vii)

NEUROPSYCHOLOGICAL AND NEUROANATOMICAL INFLUENCES ON READING RESEARCH: CURRENT STATUS

Neurological and physiological theories concerning the origin of reading disabilities have been around for over a century. Indeed, many of the theories— and "treatments" based on these theories—propounded by optometrists and neurologists today are indistinguishable from those of the nineteenth century. For the most part, neurological theories depend on an analogy between the defects observed in brain-damaged (aphasic, alexic) patients and those who show reading disability but no obvious brain damage—hence, the search for deviant cerebral asymmetry among poor readers. There is some value in this approach. By pointing out how some brain-damaged individuals differ in their information processing from other (normal) readers, neuropsychologists have been able to provide support for information-processing theories of reading. The neurological approach is not without its difficulties, however. The most obvious problem is that brain-damaged patients may compensate for their affliction by adopting new cognitive strategies different from those ordinarily used by normal readers.

Optometrical theories (concerning the role of phorias, for instance) also rely on a logic that may prove difficult to substantiate. Just because some individuals with severe visual problems may have difficulty learning to read does not mean that all (or even most) poor readers have such problems. A further difficulty with the optometrical approach is its naive view of perception. Reversed letters and words are thought to confuse readers, but this can only be true if some homunculus views these letters projected in their reversed orientation on the brain's "screen." But this is ridiculous. Words are not "projected" onto the brain nor is there a homunculus to be confused. Subjects have been found to adapt to all sorts of visual distortions, even to wearing glasses that turn the whole visual world upside down (Ewert, 1930; Kolers, 1975, 1976).

Some visual deficiencies may be present in poor readers just because they are poor readers. This seems particularly true of eye movement patterns, which appear very sensitive to reading strategy and reading ability (Carpenter & Daneman, 1981). So close is the relationship between eye movements and reading ability, that eye movements will reappear later in this book where cognitive reading models and evaluation methods are discussed. For now, it must be concluded that with the possible exception of eye fixation patterns, the neurological, neuroanatomical, and physiological literature have not been directly concerned with measuring reading competence. Hypotheses drawn from this literature, however, have guided research into reading. Some of this research will be reviewed in later chapters.

PSYCHOLOGICAL INFLUENCES ON READING MEASUREMENT AND RESEARCH

Modern psychological research into reading is reviewed in detail later in this book. This section, therefore, deals mainly with historical trends and themes.

EXPERIMENTAL PSYCHOLOGY

As an experimental science, psychology began life in the nineteenth century. Almost from the beginning, reading was an important area of study. Indeed, many of the topics currently being researched by experimental psychologists were also avidly studied in the 1880s. One reviewer (Venezky, 1977) called the period from 1880 to the early 1900s "the golden years of reading research" (p. 340). These golden years were reviewed extensively by Woodworth (1938) and Huey (1968).

Many of today's important psychological topics were first investigated in the late nineteenth century. Take eye movements, for example. Questions such as the length, duration, and direction of eye movements in reading were studied by Buswell (1920) and Erdmann and Dodge (1898). Dodge (1900) was concerned with perception during eye movements. Ruediger (1907) took this work a bit further by concentrating on foveal versus nonfoveal perception. This work is clearly the forerunner of present-day eye movement investigations (Carpenter & Daneman, 1981; Rayner, 1977).

Reading speed was studied by Dearborn (1906), who showed that speed changed with changes in materials. This work combined with findings by Quantz (1897, 1898) indicating that words can be seen before they are read were actually early investigations of what today would be called the "eye–voice" span (Levin, 1979).

Even present-day notions of automaticity and divided attention (see Shiffrin & Schneider, 1977) were foreshadowed by work done early in the century. Pinter's (1913b) studies were particularly interesting as they used the dual-task methodology (LaBerge, 1981) to show that reading can become fairly automatic and that it can proceed without articulation.

The question of whether words are recognized as whole shapes independent of their constituent letters is an important one for modern researchers (Umansky

& Chambers, 1980). It was also studied in the nineteenth century (Pillsbury, 1897).

Although it should be clear that many of today's important research questions were also studied 100 years ago, it would be incorrect to conclude that experimental psychologists are merely repeating experiments whose results are already known. Measurement techniques are much improved today; modern laboratory equipment provides accuracy that was not available 100 years ago. Perhaps most important of all, modern theories of reading (see Chapter 4) are richer and more consistent than those available during the golden years. These more elaborate theories permit research results to be more truly cumulative, each study building on the results of earlier ones.

In addition to questions of perception and decoding, today's experimental psychologists are also concerned with linguistic influences on reading. This is particularly apparent in studies concerned with text processing and meaning. Much of this work will be reviewed in Chapter 4.

INSTRUCTIONAL PSYCHOLOGY

At the end of the present century, experimental psychology and education were seen as closely allied fields (see Glaser, 1982, for a historical review of instructional psychology). John Dewey (1900) and Edward Thorndike (1923) were both influential in forging a link between the two fields, although from different perspectives. Thorndike was a strict associationist who saw most learning tasks in terms of complicated stimulus–response chains. Dewey, on the other hand, resisted associationism in favor of more global (holistic) teaching methods.

Experimental psychology and education began to drift apart during the 1920s and remained mostly separate until World War II. Psychology during this period was largely concerned with its development as a natural science largely along strict behaviorist grounds. During this period, most applied work was rejected as not scientific. Two exceptions to this split between psychology and education were the fields of psychometrics and clinical psychology.

Advances in psychometrics during the period from 1920 to 1950 are discussed below and in Chapter 3. It should only be noted here that many advances in measuring reading and other competencies were made during this period. These advances (see Cronbach, 1957) were made more or less independently of the mainstream of experimental psychology.

Clinical psychologists, too, remained interested in educational problems. Their work was largely with special or disabled populations and the object (given the spirit of the times) was to come to a psychodynamic understanding of a child's learning problem. The flavor of this approach can be gained from the psychoanalytic interpretation of reading disability produced by Blanchard (1946).

World War II brought about the beginning of a rapprochement between experimental and instructional psychology. The work at first focused on skill learning in man–machine systems (Broadbent, 1973) but soon expanded to include virtually all areas of teaching and learning.

Cognitive models are dominant in instructional psychology today, although behavior modification in the classroom is also popular—particularly when a single skill is being taught (Kazdin, 1975; Ross, 1976). Cognitive research and theory is discussed in detail in Chapter 4.

PSYCHOMETRICS

The history and development of reading tests is described in Chapter 3. To a large degree, these reading tests grew from work on intelligence tests.

Galton (1862/1962), Darwin's cousin, was one of the first scientists to investigate individual differences in mental functioning. Convinced of the heritability of human traits and influenced by the philosophical notion that all knowledge comes through the senses, Galton theorized that those individuals considered to be the most knowledgeable also possessed the most acute senses. He began his investigation by designing numerous tests that measured simple sensory discriminations (visual acuity and tone discrimination, for example). But his attempts to measure cognitive ability through perceptual-motor tasks did not succeed in differentiating the gifted from the moronic. In retrospect, it is easy to see that Galton's theory was wrong. His attempts to measure intellectual prowess were undermined by the much greater extent to which he was measuring motor and sensory functioning.

Interest in intelligence was revived as a subject for psychology by the work of Alfred Binet at the beginning of the twentieth century. Binet's early work on human abilities closely resembled that of Galton; he also was concerned largely with physical attributes and simple sensory discriminations. It was not until he was commissioned by the French government to study mental deficiency in the Paris school system that Binet's work took a more practical turn. Binet temporarily abandoned the theoretical approach of Galton and turned from investigating the "elements" of human ability to the development of an overall index of intellectual functioning. The only theoretical assumption Binet made was that the relative mental ability of an individual (with respect to others in a population) was constant over time. Binet realized that to produce a socially useful instrument, his tests had to tap various aspects of intelligence, for example, the knowledge of facts, reasoning, and language ability. One of his most far-reaching contributions was his assumption that the types of tasks used to measure intellectual ability need only satisfy the criteria of agreeing with current and future academic success. Thus, any task was considered useful if it could be shown to predict later academic accomplishments. In 1905, Binet completed his first test, which consisted of 30 items reflecting a child's ability to understand and reason with objects common to his cultural environment. Test items were clustered by age levels and increased in difficulty from those that could easily be solved by the very young to those that were difficult for the average adult. In a later revision, Binet introduced the concept of mental age, which was defined as the highest age level at which a child could perform adequately.

Binet's test of intelligence had a tremendous impact and strongly influenced the field of applied psychology and the study of children. His method of discriminating those children who could benefit from normal school experiences from those who lacked the capacity to advance was rapidly emulated by psychology clinics, the armed forces, and industry. The success of Binet-type tests in various settings greatly increased the influence of applied psychology in subsequent human-ability research. Since Binet's day, efforts to improve the predictive power of IQ tests have succeeded to an impressive degree. Indeed, we have probably reached the maximum predictive power attainable, given the usual restrictions on time and expense. This concentration on predictive validity has, however, overshadowed attempts to explicate the theoretical construct.

The atheoretical nature of intelligence tests has led to their frequent misuse. They have been used to label national and racial groups inferior and otherwise serve political ends (Kamin, 1974). Misuse, of course, is caused as much by the social climate as by test practitioners and designers. For example, the depression of the 1930s and, earlier, the immigration waves of the late nineteenth and early twentieth centuries frightened many people who feared their jobs would be lost to cheaper labor. As a result, in some quarters, "scientific proof" of the inferiority of this or that immigrant group was eagerly welcomed.

Psychometric technology spurred on by the widespread acceptance of intelligence and personality tests became increasingly sophisticated. Multivariate statistical techniques and advances in test theory were applied not only to intelligence tests but also to tests of academic competencies such as reading. Both norm-referenced and criterion-referenced measures were developed, but, as already noted in Chapter 1, these tests were (and remain) largely atheoretical devices.

LEARNING DISABILITIES

The past 30 years have seen the differentiation into subcategories of children who have trouble in school. Instead of considering all such children to be mentally retarded, subgroups of children with specific problems have been identified (with varying degrees of precision).

There are several currently used definitions of learning disabilities. The most commonly used definition, however, is the one developed by the National Advisory Committee on Handicapped Children. This definition reads as follows:

Children with specific learning disabilities exhibit a disorder in one or more of the basic psychological processes involved in understanding or in using spoken or written language. These may be manifested in disorders of listening, thinking, talking, reading, writing, spelling or arithmetic. They include conditions which have been referred to as perceptual handicaps, brain injury, minimal brain dysfunction, dyslexia, developmental aphasia, etc. They do not include learning problems which are due primarily to visual, hearing or motor handicaps, to mental retardation, emotional disturbance or environmental disadvantage. (Cited in Schwartz & Johnson, 1981, p. 283)

The definition of learning disabilities given above, although a useful guide, presents several theoretical and practical problems. Some of these problems are due to our ignorance about important factors in learning. For example, the definition states that learning disabilities stem from "a disorder in one or more of the basic psychological processes involved in learning." At present, however, these processes are largely unknown, and this part of the definition has no definite referent. Another problem is the insistence that learning disabilities not be secondary to sensory dysfunction, mental retardation, or cultural deprivation. As these conditions are often present in children with difficulties in learning, the definition suggests that it is possible to determine whether, for a particular child, a learning disability is related to, independent of, or interacting with another particular defect. In practice, however, the tools do not at present exist to tell us, for example, whether a child's reading problem is independent of his cultural deprivation or caused by it or whether the two interact in some complex fashion. Myers and Hammill (1976) suggest that if we adhere strictly to the definition embodied in the act, only a "well behaved child with a high IQ from a middle-class home who has a severe reading problem . . . is a clearcut case of learning disability" (pp. 9–10). Although this view may seem overly critical, it does appear that in actual practice the "official" definition is frequently ignored and children with difficulties in learning, whatever their background, are considered to be learning disabled.

The medical model is, not surprisingly, a popular one in the field of learning disabilities. Early demonstrations of the relationship between brain damage and difficulties in learning have led to what must be considered a crude form of tautological reasoning. That is, because some brain-damaged individuals have learning disabilities, the converse has also been assumed to be true. Hence, diagnoses of minimal brain damage are made on the basis of perceptual, cognitive, and learning disabilities. Alternative models of learning disabilities are certainly possible, however. For example, some learning disabilities may be considered to be the result of inadequate reinforcement histories, and others may be the outcome of poor information-processing strategies. At present, the fairest thing to say is that any conclusions concerning the underlying nature of learning disabilities are premature, given our current knowledge.

PSYCHOLOGICAL INFLUENCES ON READING RESEARCH AND MEASUREMENT:
CURRENT STATUS

Psychological research into reading, a major preoccupation of psychologists at the turn of the century, decreased markedly during the long behaviorist era. With the exception of psychometrics, there was little basic psychological research into instruction or reading between 1920 and World War II. After the war, the situation began to change; today, reading research is one of the most active fields of psychological research.

Several traditions can be seen in psychological research. One is basic experimental investigations into decoding, memory for prose, and text processing. The second is psychometrics, and the third is the problems of clinical populations and the reading disabled. Each of these research areas has produced findings relevant to reading measurement. The relationship between the measurement of reading competency and psychological research and theory will be further elaborated in Chapters 3 and 4.

Summary

This chapter reviewed many areas of reading research emphasizing historical trends that have influenced (or for some reason failed to influence) reading measurement techniques. Not surprisingly, research on curriculum and instruction was found to be both important and controversial. At least some of the controversy in the field is due to the way in which research questions are formulated. Today, the trend is away from trying to discover which reading program (code versus meaning emphasis, for instance) is best and toward more realistic questions such as what type of child is most likely to benefit from what type of instructional program. Similarly, reading readiness measures will become more practically useful when they not only predict who will have trouble learning to read but also suggest proper remedial measures. The design of such tests is the main subject matter of this book.

Neurologists, neuroanatomists, and optometrists along with psychologists and others interested in the physiological basis of reading have been active in reading research and treatment for the past 100 years. Their primary concern has been children labeled dyslexic, a label whose meaning is not always clear. Research in this area has looked for similarities between dyslexics and patients with known brain damage, particularly those patients suffering from aphasia. There has also been great interest in discovering deviant lateral asymmetry among the reading disabled—an enterprise that has thus far proven quite futile. At least one group of neuropsychologists has investigated the behavior of brain-damaged patients in an attempt to validate psychological theories of reading. This approach, while not without its difficulties, will be discussed more extensively in Chapter 4. The research on neurophysiology and medical approaches has not had a great impact on designing reading measures. A possible exception is the work of optometrists and others who believe that visual and peripheral processes play a role in reading disability. There are by now, a fair number of visual tests and treatments, but their validity remains undemonstrated.

After an active start, psychologists put aside reading research in favor of the "pure" behavioristic studies of the mid-twentieth century. Since World War II, however, reading research has come back into its own. Psychologists have studied the perceptual and cognitive processes involved in decoding print, the influence of language on decoding and comprehension, and the influence of social and emotional factors on reading. Psychologists interested in psychometrics along with their collaborators in education have devoted much effort to developing reading measures. These efforts are described more fully in Chapter 3.

It is fair to conclude, after reviewing this wide area of research, that reading research and theory is becoming increasingly psychological and methodologically sophisticated. Individual differences in children's learning styles are being related to instructional techniques and the components of cognitive processing are being studied at more fundamental levels. Unfortunately, reading measures have so far failed to keep up. To a large extent, they remain atheoretical empirical devices. The reasons for this state of affairs and the current state of the reading measurement art are the subject of the next chapter.

CHAPTER 3

READING TESTS TODAY

It is perfectly possible to teach children to read without administering a single reading test. Moreover, reading tests are not always useful in teaching or as fair to minority groups as some writers would prefer (Farr & Roser, 1974; Fry, 1976; Gurney, 1978; Levine, 1976; Newkirk, 1975; Rowley, 1980). Nevertheless, many teachers and curriculum designers have found tests to aid reading instruction (Vincent & Cresswell, 1976). For example, teachers are continually monitoring their students' performance in order to determine what classroom exercise should come next and which students need extra tutoring. These evaluations can be done subjectively by the teacher but not without introducing a source of bias. That is, different teachers may use different standards to judge reading competence. Reading tests ensure that all students are being evaluated in the same manner. Because they are repeatable and comparable across situations, reading tests permit children or even whole schools to be compared with outside standards. Such comparisons make it possible to determine whether a particular school or individual is falling behind and needs additional attention. Reading tests also provide a standard for evaluating new teaching techniques. Some "diagnostic" tests measure performance on several reading subskills, thereby indicating a child's strengths and weaknesses.

Clearly, there is a place in teaching for good reading tests. It is no surprise, therefore, that there have been many attempts to design such tests. Standardized, norm-referenced reading tests are almost as old as intelligence tests (see Pinter, 1913a, for an early reading comprehension test). Criterion-referenced tests are not as old but nearly as common. Clearly, no single book, let alone a solitary chapter, can hope to describe all available reading tests. Instead, the present chapter has more attainable goals—an explanation of how reading tests are constructed along with an examination of several examples of the current state of the art. The first topic addressed is test evaluation and the standards by which tests should be judged are described. This is followed by a review and evaluation of test construction techniques. In the final two sections of this chapter, the standards for test evaluation are applied to several currently popular types of tests. The strengths and weaknesses of the various tests are noted and lessons drawn for how practical tests may be designed.

WHAT MAKES A GOOD TEST?

A reading test that no one has ever heard of (because I just made it up) is the Schwartz Shoe-Size Reading Inventory, henceforth known as the SSSRI. The test is based on my observation that well-nourished children are both bigger and do better in school than malnourished children. Administration of the test is simple. A measuring instrument like the one found in shoe stores is used to measure the individual's foot. The shoe size obtained by this procedure is the test's raw data. Shoe-size measurements ordinarily yield very high "inter-rater" agreement. That is, two people measuring shoe size usually come up with the same answer.

Another important fact about shoe size is that although it changes with age, children tend to remain in their same position relative to the population. In other words, children with average shoe sizes at age 6 tend also to be average at age 12. Similarly, children with big feet early in life tend to remain above average in shoe size as they grow older. This characteristic—the tendency to remain in the same relative position in a population—is an important one for mental tests, as it makes prediction possible. We simply predict that children with low scores (small feet, in this case) will continue to have low scores in the future.

Another nice thing about the shoe-size test is that population norms are readily available from shoe manufacturers, who have collected shoe-size data from enormous samples. These norms makes it very easy to find out how a particular child compares with others. Once we have gathered the raw data of our test, all we need do is look at the population norms and see how our subject compares. There is even a method for getting "reading-age" scores from the shoe-size test.

One simply assigns the mean shoe size in any age group, a "reading age" equal to the age of that particular group. For example, among 12-year olds, the mean shoe size is assigned a reading age of 12. Large shoes sizes are assigned higher reading ages; smaller shoes sizes are given lower reading ages. Because shoe sizes are distributed along a normal, bell-shaped curve, reading ages are also normally distributed.

Perhaps an example would help clarify how the test works. Let us say we measure a hypothetical 12-year-old's foot and find it to be size 6. We consult the shoe manufacturer's norms and find that the average 12-year old has a size 4 foot with a standard deviation of 1 size. Our child's foot is two standard deviations above the mean, a size achieved by only 2.5% of the population, and average for 15-year olds. We thus assign this child a reading age of 15. This procedure may sound a bit odd and perhaps even arbitrary, but it is the technique used in most norm-referenced tests. (Because there is no particular shoe size children should aspire to, the SSSRI is clearly a norm-referenced rather than a criterion-referenced test.)

In summary, the SSSRI is easy to administer (different examiners tend to arrive at the same raw score) and it possesses extensive norms. There is even a small but consistent relationship between body size and intelligence (Broman, Nichols, & Kennedy, 1975). But is the SSSRI a good test? To answer this question, we must first establish what good tests are like. Several characteristics of good tests are described in the following discussion.

GOOD TESTS ARE RELIABLE

According to the American Psychological Association's *Standards for Educational and Psychological Tests* (1974), reliability refers to the consistency and stability of a test's score. It is usually expressed in the form of a correlation coefficient with 0 indicating no reliability and 1 meaning perfect reliability. Reliability can be determined by testing an individual on two versions of the same test (alternate-forms reliability) or by testing subjects on two occasions with the same test (test–retest reliability). It is also sometimes possible to divide a test in half and to compare the results on one half with the results on the other (split-half reliability). In some instances, reliability may be estimated by an "item analysis" in which the relationship between each test item and the total score is calculated.

Each method for estimating reliability is prone to different types of errors. For instance, test–retest reliability will be reduced if test administration procedures differ on the two testing occasions. This source of error is eliminated by the split-half procedure, which requires only a single testing session. However, the latter procedure effectively uses "tests" that are only half as long as those evaluated by the test–retest technique. Shorter tests, by themselves, can reduce reliability. Some error sources (scoring errors, for example) are present in both test–retest and split-half situations. Although it is possible to measure the contribution of the various error sources statistically, most reliability studies settle for merely reporting the correlation between two test administrations or split-half correlations from a single session. If statistical techniques (other than correlation coefficients) are used at all, they are generally aimed at "correcting" correlation coefficients for the use of a short version of the test in split-half studies. These corrections (see Cronbach, 1970) produce higher reliabilities than those actually obtained using the split-half technique.

An important point to emphasize is that different reliability measures have slightly different meanings. For example, to apply the alternate forms technique to the SSSRI, we would merely compare the size of left and right feet. Although many people have two slightly different sized feet, the overall alternate forms reliability for shoe size is likely to be quite high. If we use the test–retest method and measure the foot on two separate occasions, we will find that children's feet grow between the two test administrations. This does not, of course, mean the test is unreliable. Children also answer more questions correctly on intelligence tests as they grow older. Although the child's raw score changes, reliability will still be high if the child's relative standing in the population remains unchanged. This is because correlations are mainly sensitive to rank order. All that is necessary to get a high correlation between two test administrations is that children with the highest score the first time around continue to have the highest score on the second testing and that the middle and low scorers also maintain their relative positions. We have already seen that this is true of shoe size. Because both alternate forms and test–retest reliability is likely to be high for shoe size, we have every reason to conclude that the SSSRI is reliable.

Sometimes, test constructors report a statistic called "inter-rater reliability." This refers to the level of agreement between two examiners testing the same subject. As already noted, with an objective test like the SSSRI, inter-rater agreement is likely to be almost perfect—there is very little error in measuring shoe size. In more subjective situations (reading comprehension tests, for instance, where examiners have to decide whether children really understood what they have read), inter-rater agreement may be less than perfect. Clearly, tests with low inter-rater agreement are not of much use. In fact, inter-rater agreement is a prerequisite for any test. It is important to keep in mind, however, that inter-rater agreement is no substitute for test reliability. A test may have perfect inter-rater agreement and virtually zero split-half or test–retest reliability.

There are times, of course, when we want tests to show a relative change in standing. For example, if we are comparing a new reading curriculum with the old curriculum, we hope to find that those instructed in the new manner will increase their reading test scores more than those following the old curriculum. As it turns out, this is not an easy comparison to make with unreliable tests. For one thing, low-scoring children will do better on a second administration simply as a result of a statistical phenomenon called "regression to the mean." (Scores on unreliable tests tend to gravitate toward the population mean.) There is also some improvement to be expected merely on the basis of practice and familiarity with the test. There have been several attempts to devise statistical methods for measuring change on reading tests (Carpenter, Gray, & Galloway, 1974; Farr, 1970b), but all depend on tests being reliable in the first place.

Although it is clear that tests must be reliable, there is some debate about how reliable a test must be to be useful. This question was addressed as long ago as 1927 by Kelley (reprinted in Kelley, 1965), who published some guidelines still useful today. Kelley's recommendations appear in Table 2. As can be seen, Kelley's advice varies depending on the purpose for which the test will be used. In general, higher reliabilities are required for making judgments about individuals than about groups. Modern researchers have come up with rather similar recommendations (National Foundation for Educational Research, 1977).

Although both norm-referenced and criterion-referenced tests must be reliable, correlation statistics may not be the best way to estimate the reliability of criterion-referenced tests. Correlations require variability among scores, but criterion-referenced tests tend to produce scores that "bunch up" at the high end. For these tests, therefore, reliability is often estimated by the number of subjects who pass on repeated administrations of the test (see Schell, 1981, for other methods of estimating the reliability of criterion-oriented tests).

To summarize, reliability is a test characteristic that may be measured in several ways, each with its benefits and drawbacks. Inter-rater agreement is not the same as test reliability; both are necessary. Finally, the reliability level required of a test depends on the purpose for which the test will be used. Although the data have not actually been collected, the SSSRI could be expected to possess inter-rater agreement as well as high reliability. But these qualities alone do not make the SSSRI an ideal reading test. It must also possess validity, the subject discussed next.

GOOD TESTS ARE VALID

Even perfectly reliable tests are useless if they do not reflect the traits they are supposed to measure. In other words, the shoe-size test may be reliable and easy to administer, but if it does not measure reading ability, it can hardly be

TABLE 2. Reliability and Testing Goals[a]

Comparison	Testing goal	Minimum necessary reliability
Group	Reading level	.50
Group	Changes in reading level	.90
Individual	Reading level	.94
Individual	Changes in reading level	.98

[a]Adapted from "Interpretation of Educational Measurements" by T.L. Kelley, in *Measurement and Evaluation in Educational Psychology and Guidance* by G.S. Adams (Ed.), 1965, New York: Holt, Rinehart, & Winston. Copyright 1965 by Holt, Rinehart, & Winston.

considered a reading test. The extent to which a test measures the trait it is supposed to measure is known as its validity. Validity is a necessary characteristic of both norm- and criterion-referenced tests. On the face of it, the SSSRI does not seem valid. After all, no reading behavior is involved in its administration. From a psychometric point of view, the SSSRI is said to lack content validity.

Content Validity

A teacher planning a final exam in mathematics would not consider including questions requiring students to conjugate French verbs, nor would a geography test normally include questions on chemical reactions. The general rule for any test of scholastic achievement or aptitude is that the test contain items that reflect the skill in question. A vocabulary test, for example, should require subjects to identify words, and a mathematics test must measure ability to complete mathematical problems.

But even a vocabulary test that requires students to define words may lack content validity if the words do not represent the population of words that students should know. A test made up of the single item "introspect," for instance, would produce low scores for most primary school children. Does this mean primary school children are all deficient in vocabulary skills? Hardly. To permit this conclusion, the test must contain a representative sample of the words primary school children are expected to know. The test should also contain enough items to give children several opportunities at various difficulty levels.

Content validity is clearly necessary if a test is to be used to estimate a subject's mastery of one or more of the skills underlying reading. The SSSRI does not appear to be useful for this purpose. This does not mean that the test is invalid. Whether a test is valid depends on what it is used for. Although the shoe-size test has little or no content validity, it may still be useful for predicting reading performance. That is, it may still have some predictive or concurrent validity.

Criterion-Oriented Validity

Whenever a test is used to predict performance on some other measure or at some future time, it is being validated against a criterion. When the criterion is some other test or behavior that occurs in the present, validity is said to be concurrent. When the criterion to be predicted is in the future, validity is said to be predictive. Criterion-oriented validity is not limited to one type of test. Both norm-referenced and criterion-referenced tests may be related to performance in other situations.

Concurrent validity is important when a test is being used to estimate performance on a related test or behavior. The usual reason for using a test this way is that the related behavior is too time-consuming or expensive to test directly. The shoe-size test, which takes only a few seconds to administer and yields a reading-age score, would save a lot of time in measuring reading if it could be shown to possess concurrent validity.

Predictive validity differs from concurrent validity only in that the criterion is measured some time in the future rather than the present. Many reading tests, particularly tests of reading readiness, are validated this way. Typically, tests are administered early in a child's school career and correlated with reading performance in later years. The better the correlation, the more valid the measure. A valid measure has practical value because it can be used to identify young children who will need extra coaching later in their school years.

Criterion-oriented validity, like reliability, is generally expressed as a correlation coefficient. Although it is conceivable that a test can have a validity of 1, most common reading tests report validities in the .6 to .7 range. It should be obvious that a test's correlation with a criterion can never be higher than a test's correlation with itself given on another occasion. Therefore, reliability sets a ceiling for validity. In other words, as far as criterion-oriented validity is concerned, unreliable tests are by definition invalid. Although the data have not been collected, there is no *a priori* reason why the SSSRI cannot have both predictive and concurrent validity. The test may also be useful theoretically, as it represents an indirect measure of the underlying construct *health*.

Construct Validity

Reading ability and most other intellectual skills are adversely affected by poor health (see Schwartz and Johnson, 1981). To the extent that the SSSRI measures malnutrition or poor health, the test is measuring a possible underlying determinant of reading ability. The value of a test as a measure of an underlying trait is known as a test's construct validity. Construct validity can be assessed only by examining the relationships of various tests and observations. Continuing with the present example, construct validity can be demonstrated for the SSSRI if it can be shown that shoe size correlates with other measures of health status (medical exams and so on) *and* these various measures predict reading ability. From a theoretical viewpoint, construct validity may well be the most important type of validity. It is also the rarest and is hardly ever mentioned in the manuals of popular tests.

To summarize, the SSSRI, a norm-referenced test, has little or no content validity, but it may have concurrent and predictive validity if it can be shown to correlate with other measures of reading ability. The test may also have construct validity to the extent that it taps an underlying factor influencing reading ability. Its construct validity is likely to be very weak, however, in Western cultures where malnutrition is rare and good health is common. In Third World countries, on the other hand, its construct validity and even its criterion-oriented validity may be much higher. This fact makes clear an important point about any test. Tests are designed to be used in a particular population and society. Even tests as objective as shoe size will have different validities in different settings.

A test with high reliability and high validity for the purpose for which it was designed (prediction, scholastic attainment, and so on) will obviously be preferred to a test that does not have these characteristics, but these are not the only qualities looked for in tests. Several others are described in the next section.

READING TESTS SHOULD BE PRACTICAL

As already noted, a reading test should be reliable, and it should also be valid for the purpose for which it will be used. (A test designed to evaluate an individual's improvement after undergoing a remedial reading course may not be valid for predicting third-grade reading skill when given to a group of first graders.) Even tests that meet these two basic requirements may not be used if they are not also practical.

"Practical," in the testing context, refers to how easily a test can be administered, scored, and interpreted. An excellent test with high reliability and validity will never become widely used if it takes two days to administer and a week to interpret. This does not mean that only simple tests like the SSSRI ever become popular. There is, instead, a trade-off between reliability and validity on the one hand and practicality on the other. Test users appear willing to sacrifice some ease in administration for greater reliability and validity but only up to a point. Beyond this point, practicality may outweigh reliability and validity as a factor in test popularity (Cronbach, 1970).

Tests must also be appropriate. That is, they should possess what is usually known as "face validity." A lack of face validity is the biggest drawback facing the SSSRI. If a test appears silly or if it lacks plausibility, it is unlikely to become popular. Neither teachers nor students will take it seriously. In truth, face validity is not a very accurate determiner of value. Nineteenth century phrenologists claimed to be able to measure character and intelligence by examining the size of bumps on the skull—a procedure with a great deal of face validity, at least at the time. Nevertheless, a test without face validity will have a difficult time being accepted by the educational community. The most popular tests, then, are those that are valid for a particular purpose, reliable, practical, and appealing in their face validity.

IS THE SSSRI A GOOD TEST?

All of the criteria necessary to evaluate tests have now been introduced. It remains to be seen how well the shoe-size test fares. Although no data were gathered, it is reasonable to assume that its alternate-forms reliability (compare left and right feet) is very high as is its test–retest reliability. Inter-rater agreement is also very high. The SSSRI is obviously useless as a criterion-referenced test because its content validity is essentially zero. But it may have some small success in predicting reading scores on other tests to the extent that it reflects the underlying theoretical construct "poor health." Whether poor health is an important determiner of reading ability varies across societies. Finally, although the test is quite practical, it has virtually no face validity. All in all, the SSSRI is not likely to be adopted as a reading test by many school districts. In the next sections, reading test construction methods and reading tests themselves will be examined. The ways in which these depart from those of the SSSRI will be emphasized; similarities will also be noted. Although virtually all tests are superior in content validity to the SSSRI, many will be found only marginally more useful.

CONSTRUCTING READING TESTS

In most areas of everyday life, measurement is a relatively straightforward matter. If we want to know the temperature, we merely consult a thermometer. Scales are readily available for measuring weight, and we have already seen that shoe size presents no particular measurement problem. Measuring educational and psychological traits is not quite so easy.

To measure something, there must first be some agreement as to what the something is. For most psychological and educational traits, no such agreement exists. Reading competence, for instance, has been defined in many different ways. These definitions are so different, no single measurement technique could hope to suffice. Instead, different tests have been developed to cope with the various definitions. Today, there are hundreds of different reading tests available with no clear agreement as to which tests are "best" in a particular situation. How such a situation developed is the main theme of this section. Because all efforts to create reading tests begin with some conception of the skills involved in reading, methods for determining reading skills are addressed first. This is followed by an overview of testing techniques, a discussion of standardization methods, and finally a brief look at the way tests are interpreted.

WHAT SHOULD READING TESTS MEASURE?

Reading is a complicated activity. It involves recognizing words, phrases, and sentences; abstracting meaning, drawing inferences, and gleaning information. Reading can be silent or oral, fast or slow, fluent or halting. How do test designers decide which aspect of reading to measure? Three main approaches to this question may be identified: logical analysis, statistical techniques, and theoretical deductions.

Logical Analyses

Logical analyses are nothing more than statements by test experts about what skills are necessary for reading. Typically, these analyses conclude that reading requires skills such as word recognition, sentence comprehension, fluency, and many more. Traxler (1970) reviewed several dozen logical analyses and identified 49 differently named reading skills. Interestingly, Traxler could not find 49 different tests for measuring these skills. Instead, the same test was used (by different experts, of course) to measure supposedly different reading skills. Not surprisingly, Traxler concluded that some writers were using different names to refer to the same skill. A similar but opposite problem was highlighted by Farr (1970a), who examined commonly available tests and found 50 different tests, each purporting to measure reading comprehension.

Clearly, logical analyses of the skills underlying reading produce varying results across experts. This does not mean that they are without value. Indeed, as a first step in identifying reading subskills, it is difficult to see how they can be replaced. Although logical analyses continue to be popular today as a means of identifying reading skills (Clay, 1979; Smith, Smith, & Brink, 1977; also see Pumfrey, 1977, for a review), the skills identified have been relegated to the status of hypotheses rather than conclusions. That is, theorists hypothesize the skills underlying reading, but their suggestions are put to the test by means of the statistical method, factor analysis.

Statistical Techniques

Factor analysis is a statistical technique designed to reveal regularities among tests. It was originally developed as an aid to researchers attempting to define intelligence (Thurstone, 1947) and was viewed as mainly an exploratory technique. That is, factor analysis was seen as a "useful tool in hypothesis formation rather than hypothesis testing" (Humphreys, 1962, p. 475). Factor analysis, in the reading context, is a means of determining relationships among skill measures to identify independent reading subskills. Using factor analysis, it is possible to reduce the large number of skills identified by logical analysis to a manageable few.

An investigator wishing to use factor analysis begins by selecting those tests believed to cover the entire range of reading skills. The tests may come from logical analyses of reading or from reading theories or both. In addition to a representative set of tests, factor analysis also requires a representative subject sample. Because reading tests are designed to be applied to virtually every person in a population, the sample must be representative of the population at large. The tests are administered to the members of the sample and scores on each test are correlated with scores on every other test. The result is a correlation matrix, the raw data of the factor analysis.

There are many factor analytic techniques (each based on a different mathematical model); but in every case, the output of a factor anlaysis is two matrices: a factor pattern and a factor structure. The factor pattern contains a set of numbers called factor loadings. These loadings weight each factor in predicting test scores. The factor structure is the correlation between each test and the factors. When factors are uncorrelated, the structure and pattern coefficients are identical. Multiplying the pattern matrix by the structure matrix (actually, the transpose of the structure matrix) will reproduce the original correlation matrix if all factors are included. But all factors are rarely left in the solution, as this would make the solution no simpler than the original correlation matrix and nothing will have been accomplished. Instead, the less important factors are excluded. This makes for a simpler solution but at the expense of reproducibility. That is, with fewer factors, it becomes more difficult to reproduce the original correlation matrix. Inevitably, factor analyses leave some of the variability in the original correlation matrix unexplained.

To be of any value, factor analyses must involve fairly large subject samples. They must also contain a representative selection of tests. (These tests, of course, must be both reliable and valid.) If any important skills are omitted, the whole factor analytic solution will be suspect. The problem is that researchers are rarely sure what the important skills are before performing the factor analysis. In fact, one of the reasons for performing a factor analysis in the first place is to identify the subskills necessary for reading. It is a paradox. Factor analysis is being used to reveal the important subskills in reading, but unless tests tapping these skills are included in the original battery (before the factor analysis is done), the whole enterprise is doomed to failure.

Because factor analysis depends so strongly on the tests administered and on the type of statistical technique chosen, researchers using different tests and techniques have reached rather different conclusions about reading subskills. Reviews of factor analytic attempts to identify reading subskills (Farr, 1969; Lennon, 1962; Pumfrey, 1977) routinely point out the variability in factor analytic findings. Nevertheless, the approach remains popular (Kingston, 1977). Given the difficulties involved in deciding which tests to include in a factor analysis, perhaps the best way is to base the choice on a theory of reading.

Theoretical Deductions

Over the years, there have been many attempts to develop psychological and psycholinguistic theories of reading. Goodman and Goodman (1979), for example, present a theory in which reading is viewed as a language process to be mastered very much like learning to speak. On the other hand, Gibson and Levin (1975) emphasize perceptual learning and the ability to decode printed stimuli. More recent theories, based on information-processing models of cognition, are described in Chapter 4. Although these theories have been important generators of research, they have not generally been applied to devising reading tests. An exception, however, is the *Illinois Test of Psycholinguistic Abilities* (ITPA), developed by Kirk, McCarthy, and Kirk (1968).

The ITPA was developed from a theory of the communication process. The theory makes strong assumptions about what skills are necessary for effective communication; each subskill is evaluated by a different subtest of the ITPA. For example, the communication theory makes a distinction between skills at the "representational" and "automatic" levels. Representational skills include the ability to understand verbal questions and commands, the ability to express oneself verbally, the ability to understand visual symbols, and other "higher level" communication skills. Automatic skills include the ability to fill in parts of a word omitted by the tester, the ability to blend sounds to make a word, short-term memory capacity, and other "lower level" cognitive skills. Each of these skills is measured separately by the ITPA. Although not primarily designed as a reading test, the ITPA contains similar items to those appearing on many reading readiness measures (Pumfrey, 1977).

The ITPA has not escaped criticism (Carroll, 1972), but it does illustrate a valuable approach to defining reading subskills. That is, the designers of the ITPA deduced the important subskills from their theory. Tests like the ITPA that are developed from theories have important advantages over atheoretical tests in that they can be linked with teaching programs designed to improve specific skills. That is, theoretically based tests are not only descriptive, they can also be diagnostic provided the theory on which they are based is adequate. Sometimes, the theoretical approach to defining reading subskills is combined with factor analysis to test both the adequacy of the theory and the test. In this combined procedure, the theoretically derived test is administered to a representative sample and then every subtest is correlated with every other subtest. A factor analysis performed on the resulting correlation matrix should reveal whether the various subtests are measuring independent contructs. Evidence for independence supports both the test and the theory from which it is derived. Results indicating that the subtests are not independent reveal deficiencies in the theory as well as the test. In this way, feedback from the factor analysis improves both our understanding of the reading process and our test procedures. A combination of theoretical and factor analytic approaches was adopted for the research described in Chapters 5 and 6.

Defining Reading Skills: Summary

The history of reading research is filled with attempts to define reading subskills (see Samuels, 1976, for a historical perspective). Many of these attempts have been futile because they depend solely on logical analyses that differ from writer to writer. Factor analysis, a useful procedure for determining regularities in mental test data, is no real help without some guidelines as to what tests to include in the first place. The best way to decide which skills to measure is to rely on a theory of reading. Theoretically important skills can then be measured and factor analyses used to determine whether the skills are independent. Deciding what to measure is an important first step in test construction, but it is only the beginning. Having decided what to measure, the test constructor is then faced with designing reliable and valid measures of the various skills. Methods of skill measurement are discussed in the next section.

METHODS OF SKILL MEASUREMENT

There are literally dozens of different ways to measure any reading subskill. In some ways, the diversity of possible measures is a good thing, as it makes it possible to devise alternate test forms. A difficulty arises, however, when the various tests disagree. The problem is determining which method is best. The difficulties involved in measuring reading subskills were reviewed by Farr (1969). Since then, a fair amount of progress has been made, but some of the problems pointed out by Farr still remain. Consider reading vocabulary, for example.

Most reading tests include some measure of vocabulary, but exactly how vocabulary is measured differs greatly from test to test. Sometimes, testees are expected to use words in a sentence. In other tests, the examinee is expected to give a synonym for a word, and in still others, an antonym is required. Tests also differ in the extent to which memory is a factor (multiple-choice versus recall tests, for instance), in their time constraints, and in the number of words tested. Fifty years ago, Kelley and Krey (1934) identified 26 different approaches to testing vocabulary. Today's list would be even longer. Moreover, there does not appear to be any rationale for choosing one measurement technique rather than another. Test constructors sometimes seem to choose a particular measurement technique more or less by whim.

The differences among even commonly used tests can be quite dramatic. The *Nelson–Denny Reading Test* (Nelson, Denny, & Brown, 1960), for example, consists of 100 items, each followed by a partial definition. The task is to choose from among five alternatives the word that best completes a definition. All 100 items must be completed in 10 minutes. The *Gates–MacGinitie Reading Test* (Gates & MacGinitie, 1965) requires examinees to complete 50 items in 15 minutes by choosing the best synonym from among five alternatives. On the surface, at least, these tests appear to be tapping rather different skills. But even if performance on the two tests is correlated, the greater emphasis on speed in the *Nelson–Denny* could well produce a different finding from the *Gates–MacGinitie*. It has become commonplace to distinguish between the power and speed components of mental tests (Schwartz, Griffin, & Brown, 1983). In many situations, these are quite separate determiners of test scores. In other words, it is possible to find students who answer questions correctly but very slowly and others who are both accurate and fast. To the extent that a test requires speedy responding, it will favor the fast students but may not actually reflect the slow students' knowledge. Clearly, choosing a test with a severe time constraint over one with only a minimum time constraint should be determined by one's theory of reading, not by whim. Although the *Nelson–Denny* and *Gates–MacGinitie* are norm-referenced tests, the same diversity of measurement techniques is found among criterion-referenced tests.

Another serious problem with vocabulary tests in which words are presented in isolation is the lack of linguistic context. In actual reading, words appear in sentences and paragraphs. The context provides important cues as to what a word means. Indeed, a word's meaning changes with the context in which it is found (compare "The baby buggy" with "The buggy baby," for example). By testing words in isolation, many vocabulary tests fail to reflect real reading behavior.

Despite their different techniques, most vocabulary measures correlate with one another, usually in the range .7 to .8 (Farr, 1969). Although this means the various tests are largely tapping the same thing, it does not mean that the "thing" they are measuring is vocabulary. For example, vocabulary tests also correlate in the range .7 to .8 with comprehension tests that are supposed to be measuring a different skill. Such findings call into question the validity of vocabulary tests. Their reliability has also been shown to be highly variable and to be strongly influenced by guessing strategies (Farr, 1969).

Vocabulary is not the only skill that can be measured in more than one way. Comprehension, pronunciation, and even reading speed have been measured using many different techniques. The various measures do not always yield similar results, and the choice of one over the other often boils down to a matter of convenience. There is an alternative, however. Tests can be chosen on a theoretical basis. Just as the skills to be measured may be derived from a theory of reading, so too can measurement techniques be derived. As an example, reading theories that emphasize language and the importance of meaning require vocabulary to be measured in the context of a sentence or a paragraph rather than in isolation. Such theories would also value accuracy over speed. Theoretically derived measures can be evaluated experimentally and by factor analysis to determine their relationship to other measures and their construct validity. The goal of such an enterprise would be to develop tests that not only have adequate psychometric qualities but that are interpretable in the context of a particular reading theory. Needless to say, different theories may well give rise to different tests, but the ultimate value of any test will be determined by how well it reflects the theoretical construct it was designed to measure.

Having decided what to measure and how to measure it (remember, both decisions are best based on a psychological theory of reading), the test constructor must next collect data and devise some sort of scoring procedure that either permits comparisons across individuals for norm-referenced tests or permits skill mastery to be measured for criterion-referenced tests. Normally, this is accomplished by standardizing the tests.

Most reading tests are norm referenced. They are intended to permit students to be compared with their peers. Because test constructors usually intend their measures to have wide applicability, they must first administer their test to a sample of people representative of the entire population. The performance of this sample is used to determine the mean and distribution of test scores. In effect, the performance of this sample will constitute the "norm" to which individuals will be compared. Clearly, the constitution of the normative sample is a crucial determinant of a test's value. If for some reason only very able readers were included in the sample, then the mean score would be very high, and future testees will be held to an unreasonable standard. Their performance would look worse than if the sample had been more representative of the population.

There are a variety of ways to construct a normative sample for reading tests (see Vincent & Cresswell, 1976, for a description of several). Samples can be randomly selected or chosen to meet certain predetermined characteristics (so many boys, girls, ethnic minorities, and so on). Whatever technique is used, the final sample will always be a less than perfect reflection of the entire population. In general, sampling error decreases as the size of the sample increases. Many commercial reading tests have very large normative samples. *The Stanford Diagnostic Reading Test* (Karlsen, Madden, & Gardner, 1966), for example, used a normative sample of 15,000 students across various American states; most samples, however, are much smaller. Even tests with norms based on large samples can lose their usefulness if the norms are not updated from time to time. Changes in the culture and in society mean that the date when a test's norms were first developed is an important factor in its present usefulness. If the standard of reading achievement goes up as it appears to have done in Great Britain (Start & Wells, 1972), tests normed long ago will show too many children to be above average. A decreasing standard of achievement would produce the opposite effect.

The process of collecting data from a representative sample is called standardizing the test. The test will become a standard to which future testees can be compared. Before this can happen, however, the test constructor must provide a scale on which such comparisons can be made.

The "raw" scores of a reading test (the number of words correctly identified, the time in seconds required to read a paragraph, and so on) are difficult to interpret in isolation, particularly for norm-based tests. Is a score of 70 words out of 100 correctly identified a good vocabulary score or a mediocre one? The answer depends on how the normative group performed. Similarly, it is difficult to compare an individual's performance on two different tests using just raw test scores. The comparison process is greatly facilitated by transforming the raw scores achieved by the normative sample and by the individual subject to more easily comparable numbers. Of these, perhaps the simplest is percentiles.

A testee's percentile score is his or her relative standing expressed in percentage terms. A child who scores better than 90% of the children in the normative sample is given a percentile score of 90. A percentile score of 50 is equal to the mean score of the normative sample. Most children score close to the 50th percentile, and only a few score at the extremes. In practice, this means that a small change in raw score means a bigger percentile change for those near the middle of the range than for those at the extremes. This effect can be seen in Figure 3, where percentile scores are plotted against test scores for a hypothetical reading test. As may be seen, a 10 point increase in raw score in the

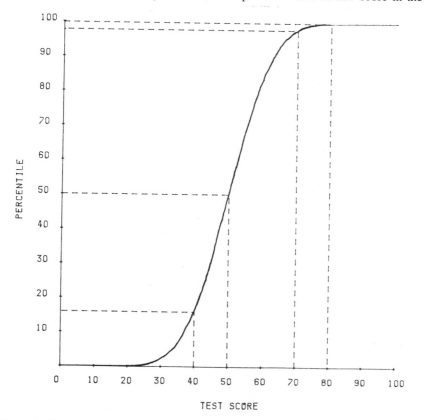

FIGURE 3. The relationship between percentile and raw scores. Note that the same change in raw score means different percentile changes, depending on where in the distribution the change occurs.

middle of the range (from 40 to 50, say) results in more than a 30 point increase in percentile rank, whereas a 10 point increase at the high end of the scale (from 70 to 80, for instance) results in less than a 2 point change in percentiles. Because percentiles mean different things at different parts of the score distribution, they cannot be added, substracted, or otherwise treated mathematically.

Stanine scores are similar to percentiles but may be somewhat misleading, as they involve dividing the entire range of scores into nine "bands." The two extreme bands may be of any size, but the seven inner bands is each one-half a standard deviation. The middle band (where the average score is found) is given a stanine score of 5 and the others range from 1 at the low to 9 at the high end.

When comparing across tests, it is often useful to have a score that permits different test results to be expressed in comparable terms. The easiest such score to calculate is the z score. The formula for calculating z scores is: $z = (X - \overline{X})/SD$ where X is the individual's reading test score, $\overline{X}$ is the raw mean, and SD is the standard deviation of raw reading-test scores. If an individual achieves a score of 30 on a test with a mean of 20 and a standard deviation of 5, the resulting z score is 2. In practice, z scores are rarely used by test constructors. Instead, the preference is for "standard" scores, which are nothing more than z scores where 100 is used to represent the mean and the standard deviation is arbitrarily set at 15. In the example just given, the standard score equivalent of the z score of 2 is 130 (two standard deviations above the mean). Actually, when a test's scores are normally distributed, standard scores can easily be translated into percentiles because there is a direct relationship between the normal distribution, percentiles, and standard scores. For example, a standard score of 130 is equal to a percentile of 97.9.

In addition to the scores described thus far, two other types of scores are sometimes used on reading tests: reading ages and reading quotients. As noted earlier in this chapter, a reading age is nothing more than the mean score achieved by children of a particular age. Therefore, if the mean score on a vocabulary test for 13-year-old boys is 40, then anyone who scores a 40 will be assigned a reading age of 13. Reading-age scores are popular among teachers and many educators, but they are not without their problems. First, it is necessary to continually update norms as next year's 13-year olds may know more than last year's. Second, it is difficult to interpret scores above or below average because being "a year behind" means different things at different ages. This is because reading does not develop at uniform rates. There is a vast improvement in skills between grades 1 and 3, but only a small improvement between grades 9 and 11. Thus, the child who is 2 years advanced in grade 1 cannot be considered equal to the child who is 2 years advanced in grade 9. Reading ages are easily prone to misinterpretation (see Rowley, 1980, for a description of how serious these misinterpretations can be).

It should also be noted that so-called reading quotients derived by dividing the reading age by the chronological age and multiplying by 100 overcome none of the problems of reading age scores and add a few more. Consider what happens to the child who achieves the highest score possible on the test, say a reading age of 18. If a 9-year-old child achieves this score, the reading quotient is 200; but when he or she is 18 and receives the same perfect reading age score of 18, the reading quotient is only 100; and when he or she is 36, the reading age will be merely 50. These scores are clearly worthless. They should not be substituted for the standard scores described above, nor should the two be confused. Standard scores, like reading quotients, both have means of 100, but that is where the similarity ends.

Although it is perfectly possible for users to calculate standard scores or percentiles themselves (so long as the test constructor provides the mean and standard deviation of scores), most tests come complete with tables of norms. All the user must do is administer the test, look up the raw score in a table, and find the standard score equivalent. Tables of norms are typically found in commercial tests, and some tables are quite elaborate. Users should keep in mind, however, that norms alone do not mean a test is reliable and valid. Extensive norms are available for the shoe-size test courtesy of the shoe manufacturers, but we would not want to take this fact as evidence of the SSSRI's validity.

Even though they do not compare an individual with a normative group, criterion-oriented tests must also be concerned with norms. This is because criterion-oriented tests all set some standard for adequate performance. If the standards that children are required to meet are not based on the average performance of children, it is difficult to know whether these standards are reasonable and realistic.

The test construction process is now complete. We followed the path of the test constructor from deciding what to test to deciding how to tests it and finally to deciding how performance on the test should be described. There is now only one remaining step—deciding what test scores mean.

INTERPRETING READING TEST SCORES

The following quotation comes from a review of the *Developmental Reading Tests* by Fry, which appeared in the *Sixth Mental Measurements Yearbook* (1965):

> The directions for administering and scoring are clear. The printing is good. Graphic profiles of subtest scores are printed on the front of each booklet. In fact, in most respects, the *Developmental Reading Tests* "look" like well-made standardized tests and this is perhaps what is so insidious. The teacher follows the directions, the students mark the booklet, the tests are scored, and Johnny gets a reading grade of 1.9. What on earth does this mean? (pp. 294–295)

This reaction is all too common among reading test users. Tests are administered; scores are obtained; but the translation of the various scores into some sort of action on the part of the teacher is by no means straightforward. There is sometimes no clear relationship between the purpose for which a test is given and the test outcome. The final job of a test constructor, therefore, is to show how and in what circumstances the test should be used.

Reading tests may be administered for several different purposes. Sometimes, school administrators wish to evaluate how well children at various schools are progressing. For this purpose, norm-referenced tests are used to compare each school with the population norms. The same tests may be used to compare individual students with the normative group. But the results of these comparisons are difficult to interpret and may give rise to misinterpretations. For example, Haney and Madaus (1978) describe the reaction of various government officials in New York and Connecticut when minimum competency standards for high school graduation were first being introduced. In New York, where a 9th grade reading age was suggested, one official was quoted as saying, "What about twelfth grade?" (p. 468). In Connecticut, where a reading age equivalent to 7th grade was proposed, a school board member said, "We're paying for twelve years of schooling but only getting seven years" (p. 468). These statements reveal a complete misunderstanding of how reading ages (and standard scores) are calculated. Because 12th grade reading age will by definition apply to the average performance of students in that year, one-half of all students could be expected to do worse and one-half better. The result of setting a 12th grade reading standard for high school graduation is that one-half the students are *guaranteed* not to graduate.

Misunderstandings about what norm-based reading tests actually measure are really not surprising. Reading age scores appear to tell the examiner something about how well a student can read, when, in fact, they do nothing of a kind. In a society where standards are low, the average reader will be able to read far less than in a society in which the reading standard is high. In each society, however, average children will receive the same standard or age-equivalent score. Criterion-referenced tests are an attempt to get around the limitations of the norm-referenced variety. Instead of comparing children with group norms, children are being measured in regard to a criterion of mastery. The tests purport to tell the user whether the child has mastered certain reading skills.

It is obviously possible to design tests that are purely norm-referenced. The SSSRI is one. Even if the shoe-size test were found to be a valid predictor of reading achievement, it would clearly be useless as a diagnostic or mastery instrument because it reveals no information about where a child's strengths and weaknesses are to be found. As noted in Chapter 1, however, most tests are capable of being both norm and criterion referenced, and many publishers provide both types of scores for their tests.

Although criterion-referenced tests do provide information about the mastery of specific reading skills, their usefulness still depends on how closely the skills they measure reflect those actually involved in reading. The role of theory cannot be overemphasized in both types of tests. Even criterion-referenced tests are of limited usefulness for teachers if the skills they measure do not reflect those necessary for reading.

CONSTRUCTING READING TESTS: SUMMARY

Constructing a reading test means making a series of crucial decisions. First, the test designer must decide what skills to measure. This decision can be based on a logical analysis of the skills involved in reading, or it can be based on a psychological theory of the reading process (or both). The independence of various skills can be assessed by factor analysis and by experimentation. The second decision the test designer must make is how to measure the various reading skills. There are many ways to measure each reading skill, and often test constructors seem to choose one or another simply by whim. Theories of reading are often helpful in making measurement choices because they specify important test variables (speed versus accuracy, for instance). The next step in test development is specifying how the test will be scored. Several different scores have been used, and sometimes a test yields more than one type of score. As scores may sometimes be misunderstood by the public (and even by educational professionals), test designers must also indicate when their tests should be used and how they should be interpreted.

So far, this chapter has been concerned with what makes a good test and how tests are constructed. In the next sections, the focus is on specific types of tests.

FORMAL READING TESTS: TYPES AND USES

There are hundreds of commercially available English reading tests, and more are being published all the time. Test reviews may be found in the series *Reading Tests and Reviews*, edited by Buros (1975 is the most recent volume), and in books by Vincent and Cresswell (1976), Harris and Sipay (1980), and Pumfrey (1976). A review of secondary school reading tests may be found in Olsen (1975). Because test reviews are readily available, there is no attempt in the present section to review all or even most reading tests. Instead, the goal of this discussion is to illustrate the various types of tests currently in use.

A number of schemes have been proposed for classifying reading tests. Reading tests have been dichotomized as group versus individual, silent versus oral, norm versus criterion referenced, readiness versus achievement, timed versus untimed, diagnostic versus attainment, decoding versus comprehension, formal versus informal, and standardized versus nonstandardized tests. Each of these dichotomies has some value in differentiating tests, but few tests fall neatly into a single category. As already noted, norm-referenced tests may also be criterion referenced. Similarly, diagnostic tests may also provide an indication of attainment. Despite the inevitable ambiguity in any classification scheme, some organization is necessary to help keep the present discussion from wandering around aimlessly. The classification scheme adopted here represents an extension of one proposed by Pumfrey (1977). In this system, tests are characterized on three dimensions: the information they gather (and the way they gather it); the interpretations they allow (normative, mastery, or both); and how tests relate to instructional goals (when to start reading instruction, how to improve comprehension, how to increase reading speed, and so on). This three-way classification scheme will be used to structure the present discussion of formal tests. Only commercially available tests are considered. In the next section of this chapter, informal and other tests will be described.

INFORMATION GATHERED BY READING TESTS

Most reading tests attempt to measure one or more of the following skills: vocabulary, comprehension, reading speed, and decoding. As already mentioned, reading tests often use quite different methods to measure what is supposed to be the same skill. In addition, without providing any validity data for their assumption, test constructors tend to assume that their tests measure the skill they are supposed to measure. It cannot be overemphasized that all tests (even criterion-referenced tests) must be valid tests of the skill they purport to measure. The following discussions give specific examples of how several reading subskills are measured by currently popular reading tests.

Vocabulary

Vocabulary skill is measured in many different ways. It is sometimes tested by having testees select a synonym for a given item from several alternatives as on the *Gates–MacGinitie Reading Test* (Gates & MacGinitie, 1965). The *Diagnostic Reading Tests* (Committee on Diagnostic Reading Tests, 1966), on the other hand, require examinees to select, from several alternatives, the word that best fits a definition. Still another method, used by the *Woodcock Reading Mastery Tests* (Woodcock, 1973), has examinees demonstrate their vocabulary knowledge by completing a four-word analogy (for example: Up-Down: High-_____). Yet another method is used by the *Nelson-Denny Reading Test* (Nelson, Denny, & Brown, 1960), which requires subjects to choose the one word from several alternatives, that best completes an item's definition. Further examples of vocabulary measurement techniques can be found in Harris and Sipay (1980).

As can be seen, there is little consistency among tests concerning how vocabulary (also called "word knowledge" and many other things) should be measured. Moreover, this inconsistency is not limited just to norm-referenced tests. The tests described in the preceding paragraphs include both norm- and criterion-referenced tests, timed and relatively untimed tests, and both group and individual tests. The failure to present any theoretical rationale for the choice of measurement techniques makes it very difficult to decide how the various testing approaches relate to reading theories. To take but a simple example, presenting single vocabulary words in isolation ignores the importance of context in both language and reading. Any reading theory that emphasizes natural language processing would find such an approach to vocabulary measurement quite inappropriate.

Although the various methods for studying vocabulary (Farr, 1969) are correlated, these correlations are not high enough to ensure that vocabulary as conceived in the various tests is actually a unitary ability. It may be the case that several subskills underlie what test constructors have referred to as vocabulary. This point will be returned to in Chapter 4.

Comprehension

Comprehension is another skill typically measured by reading tests. The history of reading comprehension tests from their beginnings early in this century up to 1970 was reviewed by Farr (1970a). He concluded that although reading comprehension tests were becoming increasingly more sophisticated psychometrically, they were not making the same degree of theoretical progress. In fact, today's reading comprehension tests are largely just variations of those used in the early 1900s.

According to Farr, prior to the development of reading tests, comprehension was assessed by determining how well a reader's purpose for reading was fulfilled. That is, reading and following directions correctly was considered *prima facie* evidence of comprehension. Unfortunately, with the development of formal reading tests, the importance of reading purpose was largely forgotten. The reason for this is that early reading comprehension tests were influenced by intelligence tests. Test constructors considered reading comprehension a psychological trait like intelligence that was essentially the same across all conditions.

The earliest reading comprehension test (Pinter, 1913a) required subjects to write down as much as they could recall of a short passage after having read it. This "reproduction" method is still used in the *Durrell Analysis of Reading Difficulty* test (Durrell, 1955) except reproduction is oral rather than written. Pinter's test was never actually published. The first published reading tests were similar to present group verbal-ability tests such as the *Scholastic Aptitude Test*. These tests had subjects read short paragraphs and answer questions about what they read, a technique that is still in common use.

Reading comprehension tests were further refined in the 1920s with the addition of time limits and new measurement techniques. For example, instead of answering questions about what they had read, subjects taking *Monroe's Standardized Silent Reading Test* (Monroe, 1919) were required to read a paragraph and then choose from among several alternatives the phrase that is correct given the information in the paragraph. A similar technique is used by the *Gates–MacGinitie Test* (Gates & MacGinitie, 1969).

Further developments in the 1920s and 1930s included true-false comprehension questions and tests that require subjects to pick out the word in a sentence that changes the sentence's intended meaning. More recent refinements include tests in which words are missing from sentences and paragraphs, and the examinee is required to choose the correct word from among several alternatives. Another version of this technique is the cloze procedure, in which words are omitted from sentences, and the subject must fill in the appropriate word without any alternatives to choose from. An example of the cloze technique appears in Chapter 5.

Despite their methodological differences, virtually all comprehension tests attempt to judge how well subjects can discern what the test constructor is getting at—a quality Farr refers to as "thought-getting" (1970a, p. 5). Little or no attention is given to relating reading purpose to comprehension.

Criticisms of reading comprehension tests have appeared more or less constantly since the tests were first introduced. The extent to which comprehension tests merely measure a general factor of intelligence, how much the tests measure logical inference as opposed to restating the facts in a paragraph, and whether it is possible to answer comprehension questions solely on the basis of prior knowledge without actually reading the selections are all questions debated by test proponents and critics (see the Buros series for the flavor of this debate).

In the years since World War II, reading comprehension measures have burgeoned. One development of these years is the growing view that reading comprehension is actually a complex skill made up of various subskills. This view has brought with it an attempt to measure the subskills supposedly underlying reading comprehension. The *Prescriptive Reading Inventory* (CTB/McGraw-Hill, 1974), for instance, measures literal comprehension, interpretive comprehension, and critical comprehension, each of which is assumed to be a different skill. As far back as 1970, Farr was able to find 50 differently named comprehension subskills (not counting the three just mentioned), and today there are even more. Research on these subskills is described in some detail in Chapter 4 and will not be repeated here except to note that there is little evidence that the various subskills actually exist.

Comprehension measures are in much the same state as vocabulary tests. As is the case for vocabulary, there does not seem to be any theoretical rationale for choosing one type of comprehension measure over another. Thus, there is no way to determine which measurement approach is best, how much prior knowledge should be permitted to influence comprehension, and so on. There have been several recent experimental attempts to apply psychological theories to the development of comprehension measures. Daneman (1982), for example, explains the rationale for a measure of comprehension based on short-term memory capacity. Chapter 6 contains a description of one method for developing a comprehension test based on psychological theory.

Reading Speed

Most reading tests are timed. For some tests, the time limit seems more a matter of the tester's convenience than anything else. That is, some time limits are set just to make certain that the testing session is over quickly. In other tests, however, time is a matter of interest in its own right. Such tests usually provide some indication of reading speed. The importance of reading speed is a matter of some debate. Some experimenters have found reading speed related to measures of reading comprehension (Jackson & McClelland, 1979, for example), whereas other studies fail to find such a relationship (see Farr, 1969, for a review). Even if they are sometimes related, reading speed and reading comprehension are clearly not the same thing. Consider, for example, what Henderson (1982) calls the *bar mitzvah* effect. Jewish boys are routinely taught to recite a portion of the Torah fluently and quickly without actually understanding a word they are saying. The relationship between reading speed and comprehension also depends on whether reading speed is measured orally or silently. The former is much more dependent on verbal fluency then the latter.

Many reading tests that include speed measures—the *Neale Analysis of Reading Ability* (Neale, 1958), for example—also include a "comprehension check" so that speed and comprehension can be related. But just how the relationship should be interpreted is not always clear. For example, on some reading tests, reading "rate" is calculated by multiplying reading speed times the comprehension score. This procedure is thought to serve as a "correction" for the bar mitzvah-type effect (reading without understanding) and is similar to the way typing tests are corrected for errors. As Farr (1970a) points out, the problem with this approach is that most readers can always get a few comprehension questions correct solely on the basis of prior knowledge or guessing. To see the problem this poses for reading rate measures, imagine two subjects who are required to read a 1,500 word essay. Subject 1 reads the essay in 10 minutes and achieves a speed score of 150 words per minute. If this same subject scores 80% on the comprehension test, the corrected "reading rate" is 120. Subject 2, on the other hand, who merely pretends to read for a minute before claiming to have read the essay, gets a reading score of 1,500 words per minute. Now, if subject 2, through a combination of prior knowledge and guessing, achieves a comprehension score of 25% (which, after all, is merely chance performance on a four-alternative multiple-choice test), this subject will receive a rate score of 375, compared with the first subject's 120. The correction, therefore, really does not work. It is still possible to achieve a high reading speed without comprehension.

Reading speed, like vocabulary and comprehension, frequently appears on formal reading tests, often without any theoretical rationale for why it is there, how it should be measured, and what it means. This does not necessarily mean that reading speed is unimportant. In fact, a type of speed measure will be presented in Chapter 5. This speed measure derives its importance from the theoretical framework from which it was developed. In addition, it is not subject to the "correction" problem that plagues typical reading speed measures.

Decoding

Many reading tests include measures of what is called decoding. Unfortunately, decoding does not always mean the same thing in different tests. Although the term *decoding* usually refers to the ability to read individual words aloud using the correct pronunciation, on some tests it can also mean the ability to attach meaning to a word. In tests designed to judge whether a preschool-aged-child is "ready" to read, decoding may not involve reading at all. For example, the *Clymer–Barrett Pre-Reading Battery* (Clymer & Barrett, 1967) tests such skills as letter recognition, auditory and visual discrimination, and visual-motor coordination in the belief that each of these skills is a precursor of the decoding skills required in beginning readers.

Even when test constructors agree that decoding is the ability to read words aloud, they may still disagree about how decoding should actually be measured. Letter recognition, the pronunciation of syllables and other letter groups, and the fluency with which words are read have all been used to measure decoding on one test or another. In tests designed for beginning readers (as opposed to prereaders), the most common approach to decoding is the graded word-reading test in which testees are required to read aloud a list of increasingly difficult words. This approach is very common in Great Britain, where many reading tests include graded word recognition, but similar measures are also found in American tests such as the *Botel Reading Inventory* (Botel, 1978), the *Doren Diagnostic Reading Test* (Doren, 1964), and the *Woodcock Reading Mastery Tests* (Woodcock, 1973).

The procedure by which the words were graded is usually described in test manuals (although not always in much detail) as are some criteria for determining when a word has been read correctly. Nevertheless, graded word-reading tests have been criticized on several grounds (Vincent & Cresswell, 1976). Perhaps the major criticism leveled against this measurement approach is that words are read in isolation rather than in context as in normal reading. Although true, the importance of this criticism depends on the purpose of the test and the theory from which the test is derived. As discussed in Chapters 4 and 5, there may be times when reading words in isolation is a useful measurement technique. Another criticism of graded word-reading tests is that the norms determining what words are more difficult than others may change with time, requiring frequent renorming of the test.

This last criticism is really aimed at the norm-referenced variety of graded word-reading test in which the last word read is taken as indicating the examinee's standing in comparison with the normative sample. It is also possible to develop a criterion-referenced word-reading test in which the goal is not to compare an individual with others but to determine whether the examinee has the decoding skills necessary to read everyday material (Pumfrey, 1977; Vincent & Cresswell, 1976). Such a test can be constructed by consulting frequency counts of words appearing in typical books and articles (Pumfrey, 1977, provides a list of 26 such frequency counts in English, pp. 189–190). Of the thousands of English words, a few hundred account for most of the words in children's reading (McNally & Murray, 1962). Thus, a criterion-oriented word-reading test would simply determine how many of these common words a child is able to read. Examples of tests using this approach are the *Basic Sight Word Test* (Dolch, 1942) and the *Mastery Test* (Sipay, 1970).

Although they go under many different names, the skills described in the preceding paragraphs (vocabulary, comprehension, speed, and decoding) are the most commonly measured reading subskills. Various methods are used to measure these subskills, often with no theoretical rationale for why one method has been chosen over another. There are, of course, noncognitive factors that can also influence reading performance. Personality variables, motivation, socioeconomic background, teacher effectiveness, and many other factors can influence whether a child has difficulty learning to read (Farr, 1969; Harris & Sipay, 1980). There are even tests that attempt to measure these "attitudinal" variables (Pumfrey, 1976). Although attitudinal factors may be important determiners of reading performance (Roettger, Szymczuk, & Millard, 1979), they will not be addressed in this book.

As noted in the classification scheme described earlier, the skills measured by a test make up only one dimension along which tests may be characterized. A second dimension is the interpretations a test allows. This dimension is discussed next.

INTERPRETATIONS PERMITTED BY READING TESTS

Tests are used for many purposes, but there are really only two types of interpretations open to test users. Tests can either be interpreted normatively by comparing an individual (or individuals) with group norms, or they can be interpreted as indicating how closely a testee's performance approximates a criterion. In other words, tests are either norm- or criterion-referenced. Within each of these categories, there are several subcategories. For example, some norm-referenced tests are intended to be diagnostic. These tests are designed to indicate where an individual stands relative to a normative group on several subskills presumed to underly reading competence. Other norm-referenced tests (the shoe-size test is an example), are designed to make overall competence judgments without any diagnostic interpretation. Criterion-referenced tests also differ from one another both in the skills they measure and their criteria for demonstrating competence.

Norm-referenced tests are older and more common than criterion-referenced tests, at least among those available commercially. But as the book of test reviews edited by Schell (1981) indicates, commercial criterion-referenced tests are not exactly rare. Indeed, the trend is to provide both norm- and criterion-referenced scoring procedures for the same tests, thus blurring the distinction between the two (again, see Schell, 1981). In the present discussion, the emphasis is on how well either type of measure fulfills its goals, given the requirements for tests outlined earlier in this chapter.

With very few exceptions, norm-referenced test constructors recognize the need for norms and devote considerable attention to selecting large, appropriate normative samples. Some criterion-referenced tests, however, ignore norms entirely. Without norms, however, it is impossible to determine whether the criteria adopted by the test constructor to indicate mastery are realistic. For example, the *Botel Reading Inventory* (Botel, 1978) requires testees to achieve a score of 70% to 80% correct on a "Word Opposite Test" to demonstrate mastery. But where did this criterion come from? Can most children achieve this level? Without norms (or a theoretical rationale for that matter), one cannot tell whether the scoring procedures of either norm-referenced or criterion-referenced tests are realistic.

The importance of test reliability is recognized by most test constructors. It is very rare for a commercial reading test not to provide evidence for its reliability in the manual accompanying the test (but see the *Classroom Reading Inventory*, Silvaroli, 1976, for an exception). Reading subtest reliabilities range from .60 to .80. For whole tests, reliabilities of .95 and higher have been reported. According to Kelley (1965), whose work was described earlier, these figures mean that not all tests are useful for all testing purposes. Some tests have reliabilities high enough to permit the evaluation of individual differences and change, but most do not. These latter tests may be useful only for group comparisons.

As already noted, a major problem with both criterion- and norm-referenced tests is their failure to provide any rationale for their testing procedures. This is less of a problem for nondiagnostic tests because (as in the shoe-size test), they are not attempting to describe what a subject knows or how an individual compares with others on any subskill. Because criterion-referenced tests (and remember, these are often just norm-referenced tests scored differently) claim to indicate how closely a subject approaches some criterion of skilled performance, their value hinges on demonstrating that the criterion is an important one. In essence, the question comes down to one of validity. For nondiagnostic, norm-referenced tests, validity involves showing a relationship between scores on the test and some other measure presumed to reflect reading ability. For criterion-referenced tests, validity means demonstrating that the criterion really is tapping an important aspect of reading competence. This type of validity can be demonstrated in several ways. For instance, behavior at the criterion level can be shown to predict progress in a standard reading program. Alternatively, criterion performance can be shown to reflect reading in a limited domain. For example, in the example given earlier, the ability to read most common words aloud can be shown to determine fluency in reading children's books. No matter how they are measured, all tests should be reliable and valid.

Many test constructors have taken what can best be described as a cavalier attitude toward validity. The manual of the *Woodcock Reading Mastery Tests* (Woodcock, 1973), for example, provides two types of validity data. Content validity is demonstrated merely by asserting that test items are drawn from the "reading domain." Construct validity is "demonstrated" by showing that two versions of the test correlate more with one another than with other measures. Clearly, there is little in either of these two demonstrations to help the reader decide whether the test is valid. The *Individualized Criterion-Referenced Tests* (Educational Development Corporation, 1976), although field tested on hundreds of thousands of students, reports correlations with an unnamed norm-referenced test as the only evidence for validity. (It is not even clear why a criterion-referenced test should correlate with a norm-referenced one.)

Although many commercially available tests do provide adequate norms as well as evidence for reliability and validity (see the test review collections cited above), virtually none attempt to provide any but the weakest theoretical rationale for the skills they test and the measures they use. This failure leaves it up to the teacher to decide what it means when a child does well on one measure of comprehension and poorly on another.

So far, the discussion has focused on test content and test interpretations; the final part of this section examines tests from the viewpoint of instructional goals.

Tests and Instructional Goals

One of the main reasons for using tests is the belief that they assist teaching. According to Pumfrey (1977), reading tests can be used to diagnose reading difficulties, measure reading progress, and aid in matching teaching materials and methods to a particular child. In practice, however, few reading tests can really be used in this fashion. Nondiagnostic, norm-referenced tests (like the shoe-size test) are of no value in reading instruction, as they provide no information about a child's strengths and weaknesses. Diagnostic norm-referenced and criterion-referenced tests are better, but their usefulness is limited by their lack of theoretical rigor. That is, poor performance on subskill measures is unrelated to any theory of reading. Thus, it is unclear why a child performs poorly on a particular test and what to do about it.

Consider reading-readiness tests, for example. "Readiness to read" is an old and well-accepted notion in the reading literature (de Hirsch, Jansky, & Langford, 1966). The basic idea is that children must develop various cognitive and language competencies before they can be expected to learn to read. By administering reading-readiness tests, teachers hope to determine whether a particular child should be assigned to reading instruction or whether prereading skills must be developed further. Although there is nothing wrong with the logic behind reading-readiness tests—there must be some skills necessary to learning how to read or even infants would be reading—in practice they have not always proven useful. The problem once again can be traced to lack of theory. Readiness tests are based on the notion that the necessary prereading skills are known and can be measured. In truth, however, these skills have always been controversial and remain so. In Chapter 2, it was noted that earlier in this century, Dewey and his colleagues (Dewey, 1898) felt that children were not ready to read until well into their primary school years; today many children begin reading instruction prior to entering school. Clearly, some of the skills thought necessary by Dewey turned out not to be crucial. The same may be true of the skills measured by current reading readiness tests.

There are several commercial reading-readiness tests available along with many specific tests (eyesight, eye–hand coordination, and even finger localization ability; Lindgren, 1978) that are supposed to be related to readiness to read. Among the specific tests are a number designed to measure "visual perception." The *Frostig Developmental Test of Visual Perception* (Frostig, 1963), is one such test. Children are measured on such skills as eye–motor coordination, figure–ground discrimination, and spatial relationships. If children do poorly, there is a training program that can be used to improve scores. (The program consists of giving children practice on items very similar to those on the test.) Diagnosis of perceptual skills followed by the training program allegedly leads to improved readiness for reading. Unfortunately, despite ample opportunity, the validity of the Frostig test for this purpose has never been demonstrated. Other perceptual tests (for example, the *Visual Motor Gestalt Test*, Bender, 1946) face similar criticisms when they are used as measures of reading readiness.

Tests designed specifically to measure reading-readiness skills generally include a battery of subtests. The *Clymer–Barrett Pre-Reading Battery* (Clymer & Barrett, 1967), for example, has seven subtests measuring such things as the ability to recognize the letters of the alphabet, auditory discrimination (the ability to tell one sound from another), the ability to copy a sentence, and a rating scale that includes ratings of the child's "emotional development," "social skills," and "work habits." The manual says little about what a poor subtest score means and even less about what to do about it. The *Gates–MacGinitie Reading Tests: Readiness Skills* (Gates & MacGinitie, 1968) shares several subtests with the *Clymer–Barrett* but also has several of its own, including a test of the ability to "follow directions" and "auditory blending." The *Metropolitan Readiness Tests* (Hildreth, Griffiths, & McGauvran, 1966) include a test of "numbers" and an optional "draw-a-man" test. In addition to these well known tests, other readiness tests include subtests of "rhyming," "comprehension," and even of "learning rate." Clearly, there is a great diversity among test constructors about which skills reflect reading readiness. Without a clear-cut theory about how children learn to read, such diversity is to be expected.

Diagnostic tests designed to give the teacher information about areas in which a child needs extra help are also quite variable in the skills they measure and the methods they use (see Schell, 1981). One result of this diversity is that a child's pattern of strengths and weaknesses depends upon the particular test used to assess reading competence. Again, the problem is the lack of an adequate theory of reading underlying most tests.

FORMAL READING TESTS: SUMMARY

This section described currently available commercial reading tests along three dimensions. First, tests were seen to vary in their content and in the ways they measure reading skills. (There are few differences between norm-referenced and criterion-referenced tests in their content or testing techniques.) Second, although tests are designed for either norm-referenced or criterion-referenced interpretations (or both), they are often inadequate for either purpose. For example, some tests lack norms. Norms are necessary to determine how well an individual's performance compares with that of the population and *also* to determine whether mastery criteria are realistic. Reliability is often not high enough for the comparisons test constructors wish to make, and validity is an issue that many tests fail to confront in an adequate manner. Finally, the relationship between tests and instructional goals is tenuous. Tests designed for the same instructional purpose (reading readiness, for example) often measure completely different skills in different ways. Many of these problems can be traced back to the empirical nature of most reading tests. The lack of a theory is responsible for much of the variability among tests. Without a theory to guide them, test constructors have relied on "logical analyses," face validity, and other less satisfactory methods of test validation.

If formal tests often fail to meet the criteria for good tests, do informal and experimental methods fare any better? The next section of this chapter attempts to answer this question.

INFORMAL READING INVENTORIES AND OTHER READING TESTS

The reading tests described in the previous section are all commercially available and most are standardized. Although these tests are widely known and used in many schools, they are (as was noted) only of limited use in day-to-day teaching. It is frequently impossible for teachers to draw any specific instructional references from commercial tests. For this reason, most teachers develop their own informal assessment methods. These methods can be quite diverse. For example, library usage, outside reading activities, and self-evaluations of reading have all been used at one time or another as informal reading tests (Farr, 1969). Sometimes, curriculum developers include suggestions for informal reading assessment. For instance, in their *Framework for Reading*, Dean and Nichols (1974) include checklists and test items that permit teachers to determine a child's progress through the curriculum. Each test is tied to a specific suggestion for remediation. There are even commercially available checklists (Larsen, Mastropier, Harris, & Wainright, 1966).

Perhaps the most popular informal assessment technique is what has come to be called the Informal Reading Inventory. This technique requires children to read a graded series of paragraphs and to demonstrate their comprehension of each. The point at which comprehension breaks down is taken to indicate a child's "reading level."

A second trend in informal measurement has no universally agreed upon name but for the purposes of this discussion will be called experimental methods. This approach involves empirical demonstrations that certain cognitive tasks are related to reading competence. Usually, but not always, the tasks involved are chosen for theoretical reasons. That is, the tasks are supposed to reflect some aspect of a theory of reading.

In this section, both Informal Reading Inventories and experimental reading assessment methods will be described and evaluated. As in the previous section, the emphasis will be on each testing technique's usefulness in aiding children to learn to read.

INFORMAL READING INVENTORIES

The Informal Reading Inventory (usually known simply as the IRI) is a commonly used assessment instrument. It consists of a graded series of passages usually about one paragraph long, which the child is required to read aloud. The teacher keeps track of mispronunciations, omissions, and other reading errors and also asks questions designed to measure the child's comprehension of each passage. Over the years, IRIs have grown to also include vocabulary tests, silent-reading tests, checklists, measures of reading-related abilities (the ability to use a table of contents, for example) and many other tests as well. Although commercial reading inventories are available (see Harris & Sipay, 1980, for a description of eight commercial inventories), most IRIs are constructed by the classroom teacher entirely from classroom materials.

Although IRIs can be used at any stage in a child's school career, the performance expected of a child differs from one level to the next. Young children are obviously not held to the same standard as older ones, but exactly what standard should be used is not at all clear. Moreover, because IRI scoring is quite subjective, scores lack reliability.

IRIs usually involve recording a child's errors in oral reading. The theoretical rationale for this is given by Goodman (1973), and a great deal of effort has gone into teaching teachers to record different types of reading errors. Unfortunately, there is a fair amount of disagreement about how specific errors should be interpreted and what to do about them (Ekwall, 1974; Packman, 1972). It is even possible to argue that oral reading errors are not terribly important if children can demonstrate comprehension of what they have read.

There is no doubt that IRIs are popular among teachers, and the reason for their popularity is easy to understand. The tests are easy to administer, and they provide useful information—the match between a child's reading skill and specific instructional materials. Despite their obvious appeal, IRIs have all the problems of standardized tests plus a few more. The first and most obvious problem with IRIs is their arbitrary choice of reading materials. Depending on the passages chosen for testing, a child may be placed at "different" reading levels. Similarly, IRIs using identical materials but different criteria for comprehension can assign the same child to different reading levels.

A more basic problem with IRIs is defining just what is meant by reading level. In fact, some attempts have been made to define different "reading levels" for different purposes. Pumfrey (1977), for example, distinguishes four reading levels. The *independent level* is reached when a child reads a passage with 99%

to 100% accuracy and 90% to 100% comprehension. Reading at the independent level indicates mastery and competence of the passage. Reading at the *instructional level* is reflected by 95% to 98% accuracy and 70% to 89% comprehension. Readers at this level can benefit from systematic instruction at the difficulty level represented by the passage. The *frustration level* is measured by accuracy under 95% and comprehension below 70%. Too much reading at this level could prove damaging to the child's motivation to learn to read. The final level, *capacity level*, is not really a measure of reading level at all. Instead, it is reflected by the ability to comprehend 75% of the material read orally by the teacher. It is designed to gauge oral language ability, which is supposed to be an indicator of reading ability.

Although Pumfrey's scheme (actually, these levels were not invented by Pumfrey; they have been used by educators for many years) appear logical, it really only compounds the difficulties. The percentages recommended are entirely arbitrary and depend on scoring procedures that can vary across IRIs. Moreover, the materials used and the way questions are asked will have a strong influence on the scores achieved. For many writers, the whole notion of reading levels is unnecessary (Lowell 1970; Powell, 1971). These writers argue that informal tests should be just that, informal ways of observing and describing how children read. Reading levels, they maintain, give IRIs a spurious statistical accuracy which they do not actually possess.

A great deal of effort has gone into comparing IRIs with standardized reading tests. The purpose behind this research is not always clear. Typically, researchers have attempted to show that standardized tests can predict the reading level as determined by an IRI (see Johns, Garton, Schoenfelder, & Skriba, 1977, for a bibliography of such studies). Clearly, in these studies, the IRI is taken as the criterion and standardized tests are examined to see how closely they approach it. The results of these studies are mixed. Some seem to indicate that standardized tests overestimate the reading level (McCracken, 1962), whereas others find the two types of tests produce similar levels (Burgett & Glaser, 1973). As already noted, however, different types of "levels" (frustration, capacity, and so on) have been identified. Perhaps standardized reading tests are related to only one such level and not others. Attempts to determine which of the various levels standardized tests are related to have failed to find any consistent relationships between standardized test scores and any instructional level (Sipay, 1964).

Because standardized reading tests are rarely designed to indicate appropriate instructional levels and because IRIs are often constructed from classroom reading materials, it is no surprise that the two tests often disagree. Different IRIs disagree as well. It does not seem logical to judge standardized tests by how well they predict a criterion they were not designed to predict. This research merely underscores the point made several times earlier—standardized tests are of limited usefulness to the classroom teacher.

Although the discussion thus far has concentrated on IRIs, other informal reading measures have also received research attention. Teacher rating scales and even an individual's self-ratings have been shown to correlate with the findings of both standardized reading tests and IRIs (Farr, 1969). It was inevitable that someone would try to incorporate all the various techniques into a single measure. One attempt to do this is Clay's *Diagnostic Survey* (1979). This test is designed to uncover reading difficulties in 6-year olds. The survey includes various informal methods as well as test materials for which some limited New Zealand norms are provided. The *Diagnostic Survey* includes informal analyses of childrens' oral reading behaviors, their errors, and even their motor movements during reading. It also includes a letter identification task and various other tests for which norms are provided.

Informal reading tests are popular among educators because they yield information directly relevant to reading instruction. Nevertheless, informal methods are not without their problems. The most significant of these problems is the arbitrary nature of the materials used. Different materials can lead to placing students in different levels. Nevertheless, IRIs are a step in the right direction—at least they offer practical advice to test users. Another approach to measuring reading competence makes use of methods derived from experimental psychology. These experimental methods are described next.

EXPERIMENTAL APPROACHES TO MEASURING READING COMPETENCE

Educational and psychological experiments concerning reading are by no means rare. Many of these experiments are described in Chapter 4. The present discussion is limited to examples of experiments specifically concerned with measuring reading competence.

By far the majority of research effort has been devoted to correlating various psychological skills with reading measures. In the case of reading readiness, this approach has involved administering a host of tests to prereaders and waiting to see how well these various tests predict reading performance as measured by a standardized test at some future time. Sometimes the predictor tests are chosen for theoretical reasons (because they measure skills thought necessary by some theory of reading). Sometimes no rationale is given for including a specific test. De Hirsch *et al.* (1966), for example, administered 37 tests to their kindergarten sample (which, by the way, consisted of only 53 children). Among these tests were a measure of throwing, tying a knot, and figure drawing, as well as tests of word recognition, vocabulary, and other typical reading skills. They found 19 of their measures to correlate with reading performance some years later, although except for traditional reading skills (letter naming, for instance), the correlations were quite modest. They made no attempt to factor analyze their data (with the small sample this was probably wise), but many of their tests were correlated. Their procedure has been repeated many times but not surprisingly, despite the large number of studies, no consensus has yet been reached about the best predictors of reading competence.*

Attempts to incorporate psychological measures directly into reading tests are rarer than readiness studies but not completely unknown. For example, several studies have attempted to define the frustration level of IRIs by using polygraphs to measure physiological activity as children read or attempt to answer comprehension questions (Davis & Ekwall, 1976; Ekwall, Solis, & Solis, 1973). The logic behind this approach is that frustration produces physiological responses in the child that can serve as a criterion for when a child is reading at the frustration level. Some studies use skin electrical conductance as the physiological criterion of frustration (Rugel, 1971), others use different physiological measures. Although the findings of such studies provide construct validity for the notion of frustration level, they are of limited usefulness in practical classroom measurements of reading competence. Nevertheless, such experiments do represent an attempt to include theoretical formulations in measurement.

Some experiments have gone even further and attempted to develop reading measures based on theories of reading. Again, much of this work comes from the field of reading readiness. The typical approach is to develop a theory of the skills required in reading, devise a measure of each skill, and then see how well the measures correlate with reading scores on a standardized test given some time in the future. For example, Rosner and Simon (1971), starting from the notion that the ability to differentiate language sounds is an important precursor to learning to read, developed the *Auditory Analysis Test*, which consists of 40 words varying from one to four syllables. Each word is said aloud by the examiner, who then asks the child to repeat the word and then to repeat it again omitting one sound. The words were selected so that eliminating one phoneme resulted in another word (cow[boy], for example). The test was found to be difficult for children in kindergarten but to get progressively easier as children got older. What's more, test scores correlated highly with a standardized achievement test of "language arts." In fact, the *Auditory Analysis Test* was a better predictor of reading achievement than an IQ test. This finding appears to agree with those of other researchers (e.g., Rogers, 1980) who have also reported that knowing the sounds of letters is an important reading skill.

The experimental approach not only permits reading measures to be validated, it also serves the equally important function of disconfirming incorrect theoretical ideas. Benenson (1974), for example, hypothesized that visual memory is an important skill in reading acquisition because children are required to

---

*These authors later performed a study using a much larger sample and with more detailed analyses. This latter study, reported in Jansky and De Hirsch (1972) remains the most ambitious attempt to date to predict reading failure.

remember what letters and words look like. But when she examined visual memory in young children and correlated their performance with reading scores later in the year, she found that there was no relationship between the two measures. Assuming that her test was a valid measure of visual memory, Benenson's experiment demonstrates that her theory is not correct.

A more recent approach to reading measurement derived from psychological theory is described by Daneman (1982). Daneman's interest is in measuring reading comprehension. She reasons that because comprehension depends on drawing inferences, relating the subject being read to past information, comparing different parts of the passage, and so on, comprehension requires substantial memory capacity. Thus, she devised a measure of working memory capacity that, if she is correct, should underly comprehension ability. The correlations between her measure and standardized comprehension measures are fairly high, giving support to both her test and her theory. As will be seen in Chapter 6, a related approach to measuring reading comprehension is used in the present book.

A theoretical approach to reading measurement that has not been mentioned so far is represented by the work of Sticht (1979). The premise underlying Sticht's approach is that reading is one of two ways of gaining meaning from language; the other is through hearing (or auding, in Sticht's terminology). In early childhood, auding is superior to reading; but as the child becomes more proficient, the two skills tend to converge. Several measures have been developed to compare auding and reading. One such measure is the *Literacy Assessment Battery (LAB)*, devised by Sticht and Beck (1976). This test was designed to determine whether there is a discrepancy between the ability to understand orally presented and written language among adults. A commercial test using a similar technique is the *Diagnostic Reading Scales* (Spache, 1972), in which oral comprehension is used to measure reading potential. The highest graded passage a child is able to comprehend orally with 60% accuracy is said to be the level the child could read at if she or he were not experiencing difficulties. The logic of this approach has been explicated by Crowder (1982) and is inherently appealing. It goes something like this: If an individual shows poor comprehension performance in both auding and reading, the person does not have a reading problem *per se* but may have a problem in "comprehending" or may just never have been exposed to proper language models. Only when there is a discrepancy between auding and reading can a reading problem be inferred.

Most reading tests do not access auding, so from Crowder's viewpoint, they are difficult to interpret, as it is not clear whether a poor score represents a reading problem or a general language comprehension one. Although the logic seems clear, this position entails several assumptions for which comprehensive data is lacking. For example, is it true that good readers have auding and reading scores that coincide? Crowder (1982) presents the relationship between the two skills as a straight line (at least after primary school age). This implies that for "normal readers," auding and reading produce similar scores. Although this makes sense, it would be nice to have data to show that this is so. Comparing two tests (in this case, an auding and reading test) also presents special problems that must be resolved before the tests can be used in the way suggested by Sticht and Crowder. First, the tests must be equally reliable. Otherwise, the unreliable test may produce spurious differences that cannot be replicated. Second, the tests must have equal discriminating power. If one test is much easier than the other, differences between reading and auding will be produced purely for psychometric reasons. (See Chapman & Chapman, 1973, for a detailed discussion of the problems involved in comparing performance on two tests.) Although an interesting approach, the auding–reading distinction requires further work before it will be usable in everyday settings.

In this section, informal reading inventories and experimental reading measures were discussed. Although IRIs are appealing to teachers, they have many of the same problems as standardized tests. Experimental tests in which the tasks are chosen purely empirically are also of limited usefulness, but those based on theories hold some promise. Such tests not only make it possible to validate the theory on which they are based but also permit the design of theoretically based instructional interventions. The theoretical approach is illustrated in the following chapters.

SUMMARY

This chapter began by introducing the criteria by which tests are evaluated. Reliability, validity, and practicality were discussed and several ways of measuring each were illustrated. A purely empirical instrument based on shoe size was shown to possess many of the qualities of a good test, even though it was valueless as an aid to reading instruction.

Reading-test construction was seen to require a series of decisions. Test constructors must decide what skills to measure, how to measure them, how to represent test performance (that is, what scores to use), and what the scores mean. Each of these decisions means choosing from among many possible alternatives. Typically, these choices are made arbitrarily, on the basis of the tester's convenience. The result—an arbitrary group of motley tests that use different methods to measure what are supposed to be the same skill and the same method to measure what are supposed to be different skills. Some tests fail to provide adequate norms (some provide no norms at all), although without norms it is impossible to judge whether a test's scoring criteria are realistic. Finally, the reliability and validity of many reading tests are inadequate for the purposes for which they were designed.

The deficiencies of many formal tests have driven educators to informal testing methods. Although many informal measures appear more practical and more relevant to everyday teaching concerns than formal tests, most informal tests possess all of the problems of formal ones plus a few of their own (subjective scoring, for instance).

Testing techniques derived from theories of reading have the potential to overcome many of the problems associated with reading tests. Moreover, theoretically derived tests permit theories to be confirmed or disconfirmed and usually suggest ways in which teaching may be adapted to a particular child's problems. The remainder of this book is devoted to illustrating how such theoretically based reading tests may be developed.

INFORMATION-PROCESSING SKILLS IN READING

An information-processing model of reading has much in common with general information-processing models of memory and cognition. Each model has its unique features, but all share many characteristics as well. A schematic outline of a general information-processing model appears in Figure 4.

As depicted in Figure 4, information-processing models are usually stated in terms of a series of "stores" (see Broadbent, 1971, for examples). Incoming information is first held in one of several sensory-specific buffer stores. These buffer stores have large capacities to hold information, but the information held within them decays rapidly and is lost unless some attention is paid to it. The result of paying attention is that information is passed on to a limited-capacity short-term memory store where it is either "rehearsed" or displaced by new information. Rehearsal can mean nothing more than repeating the information to oneself as one does when trying to keep a telephone number in mind long enough to dial it, or it can refer to more complicated short-term memory strategies. Information retained for longer periods is transferred to a more-or-less permanent long-term memory store, where capacity is apparently limitless and forgetting is the result of an inability to retrieve stored information.

The physical reality of the various stores is highly doubtful; they can easily be conceived to be stages or "levels of analysis" (Craik, 1973) without doing much damage to the model or the present description. The levels-of-analysis view sees cognitive processing as passing through a series of "levels" beginning with superficial, physically based codes (color, size, and so on) and proceeding to deeper, meaning-based codes. In reading, a shallow processing-level would

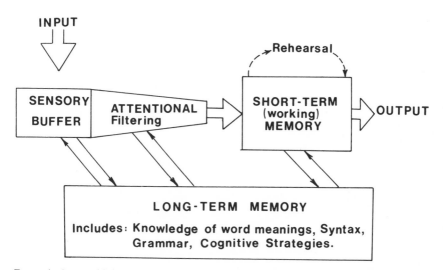

FIGURE 4. A general information-processing model. Sensory information is held briefly in a sensory specific buffer store before it is placed in short-term memory. Cognitive manipulations take place in short-term memory as does simple rote "rehearsal." Long-term memory is a large information repository whose stored rules and strategies can affect cognition at all stages in the information-processing sequence.

consist of identifying the stimuli as typed or hand-written, whereas a deep level of analysis might represent the text as a business letter requesting payment.

Information-processing models usually posit two broad dimensions along which intellectual functioning may be described. The first dimension, memory structure, refers to processes that are "wired in" to the "hardware" of the brain. These remain fairly constant across situations. The second dimension, control processes, refers to cognitive processes that vary from person to person and across situations. These dimensions are usually elaborated as follows.

MEMORY STRUCTURE

Three structural components are typically identified: the sensory register or buffer store, the short-term memory store, and the long-term memory store. Information is thought to flow from the environment through the sensory system where it is held only briefly (half a second to a second or so) in the sensory register. Information is then transferred to the short-term memory store, which has a limited capacity. The short-term memory store is the central processing unit of the information-processing system; it is where cognitive work gets done, and it is also sometimes known as "working memory." Selected information (the influence of attention and set are felt here) is transferred from the short-term memory store to the long-term memory store, which has a virtually unlimited capacity. Long-term memory serves as the information repository of the information-processing system. Little is known about the actual information structure of long-term memory, but it is obvious that the organization of information in long-term memory determines whether a particular bit of information is easy or difficult to retrieve.

CONTROL PROCESSES

The various strategies and techniques used in solving problems and in processing information are collectively known as "control processes." Among the most important control processes are the coding strategies used in short-term memory. Such processes include "chunking" related items together, rehearsal, and so on. Search and decision rules are also important control processes, particularly as they affect finding information in the long-term memory store. In general, control processes can be thought of as roughly equivalent to a computer program, the software that tells a computer what to do with the information it is about to receive. Memory structure is more like the machine itself, the hardware that actually performs the data processing.

Information-processing models of cognition not only view the organism as a sort of computing system in which information from the environment is assumed to pass through a series of stores (or encoding stages), but they also view each stage as involved in the active recoding of its input. These recodings take place in the light of past experience and depend on knowledge already present in long-term memory. For example, perception is influenced by what one expects (based on past experience) to occur in a situation. Thus, one's knowledge about the world affects the way the world is perceived (as in visual illusions, for instance). Previous knowledge also determines how information is stored and how new problems are approached. Information processing, therefore, is an interaction between "bottom up" or "data driven" processes that depend on the nature of the stimulus input and "top down" or "conceptually driven" processes that depend on information, strategies, and expectancies learned over time and stored in long-term memory.

In the present chapter, this basic model of cognition will be expanded to account for many of the phenomena involved in reading. The chapter begins with a discussion of reading from an information-processing perspective. The volume of books and articles on this subject makes an exhaustive review impossible. Instead, the focus will be on themes that continually occur in the literature. Each theme concerns an important theoretical question. These themes are explicated in the first part of this chapter. The second two sections contain discussions of some sources of individual differences in reading ability: first in terms of individual differences in decoding print and second in terms of comprehending what is read. These sources of individual differences are incorporated into a general reading model in the final section of this chapter. This model will serve as the basis for test development in the following chapters.

READING FROM AN INFORMATION-PROCESSING PERSPECTIVE

Reading has received an enormous amount of attention from cognitive scientists. Just about every aspect of the reading process has come under scrutiny. Fortunately, these studies have concentrated on specific themes such as identifying the "unit" of reading, identifying reading "pathways," and examining the role of language awareness in reading. These themes are reviewed in this section.

WHAT IS READ IN READING?

The basic unit of reading (letter features, letters, syllables, words, or clauses) has been a controversial issue for many years. Because resolving this issue has obvious implications for how reading should be taught, this question has received substantial research attention.

Different researchers use different definitions, so it is first necessary to make clear what is meant by a *unit*. In the physical sciences, a unit can be something as tiny as an electron or as gigantic as a galaxy. It is not size that defines a unit; it is the level of abstraction. Once a particular unit level has been established, there is no further need to be concerned with its constituent parts or smaller units. If we define galaxies as our unit, then we can ignore individual planets. Similarly, if a musical chord is our unit, we need not be concerned with individual notes. In the reading area, the result is similar. If letters are chosen as the unit, we can ignore the lines and features that constitute them. If words are the unit, then letters can be ignored.

Virtually all researchers agree that, at least where nonword letter series are concerned, processing takes place letter by letter. Some theorists have claimed that the letter is also the unit of normal reading (Gough, 1972). Others have conceptualized words as the basic reading unit (Osgood & Hoosain, 1974), and still others have nominated spelling patterns as the basic reading unit (Gibson, 1965).

The seminal research finding in this area dates back around 100 years to Cattell (1886), who demonstrated that short, familiar words can be read as easily as single letters and that letters are more easily recognized in words than in nonword letter strings. These results suggest that a word's individual letters are processed simultaneously (in parallel). Support for Cattell's view also comes from experiments by Reicher (1969) and Wheeler (1970), who briefly exposed words or letters to subjects using a tachistoscope. They asked their subjects to judge whether a subsequently presented "probe" letter appeared in the original word. They found subjects were better able to recognize a letter when it appeared in a word than when it appeared alone or in a pseudoword made up of a meaningless string of pronounceable letters. Some researchers have concluded that this finding (known as the "word superiority effect") is evidence that words, rather than letters, are the basic unit in skilled reading.

Johnson (1975), for example, advanced a hierarchical model of reading in which words are identified before any of their component letters. He based his model on the results of matching tasks in which two stimuli (*CHAIR-CHAIR*) were presented quickly and subjects had to decide whether they were the same or different. He found subjects able to match two words faster than they could match a single letter with the first letter in a word (*C-CHAIR*). Johnson concluded that letters are identified by first recognizing the whole word and then breaking it down into its constituent letters. Some aspects of matching tasks, however, are open to different explanations.

For example, Chambers and Forster (1975), in an attempt to explain why *different* matches are sensitive to the length of the words presented (longer words take longer to tell apart), whereas *same* matches are insensitive to length, proposed a "race model" in which letters are distinguished first, followed by letter clusters, and finally words. This model is precisely opposite to Johnson's (1975), and makes different predictions about word frequency.

Because words are identified first in Johnson's model, he would expect a word-frequency effect both when two words are matched and when a letter is matched to a word's first letter. The frequency effect is simply that common words are identified (and therefore matched) faster than rare words. Chambers and Forster (1975), on the other hand, would expect a word-frequency effect only when words are matched. Experiments by Umansky and Chambers (1980) supported the race model. But the story does not end here.

Healy and her colleagues (see Healy, 1981, for a review), using a detection task in which subjects were asked to read a prose passage and circle every instance of a target (say, the letter *t*), found that subjects missed more *t*s in common words (*the*, for instance) than in rare words such as *thy*. Healy hypothesized that targets in easy words were missed because they are processed as whole-word units, whereas rare words are processed at the component-letter level. Healy concludes that there is no single reading unit. Instead, there appear to be varying levels of reading units (letters, syllables, words, and even phrases). These units may be processed simultaneously or interactively (the results of one analysis feeding information to another analysis). The reading unit employed at a particular time appears to depend on reading skill (Samuels, LaBerge, & Bremer, 1978) and the nature of what is being read (Estes, 1975). Sometimes, multiple units may be employed in reading a single word (Drewnowski & Healy, 1980).

Clearly, any model of reading must include the ability to encode units at various levels and to share information among levels. Consequently, these skills will be incorporated into the model presented in the last section of this chapter.*

READING PATHWAYS

Much theorizing about the reading process proceeds from the assumption that there are several reading "routes" or "pathways." In the visual route, a word's (or other unit's) physical representation is thought to access directly its meaning in long-term memory. In contrast, the reader who uses the phonemic or phonological route first transforms the graphemic (print) representation of the word (or other unit) into a "phonological code" (in effect, the reader "sounds it out"). This phonological code is then used to access meaning in long-term memory.

The visual route is thought to make it possible to read "exception" words that are not pronounced according to the typical pronunciation rules (*knight*, for instance). The existence of the visual route is also used to explain how the reader can speed-read faster than subvocal pronunciation would appear to permit.

The phonemic route, which involves applying "grapheme-to-phoneme" (print-to-sound) conversion rules to print, is used to explain the ability to read pseudowords like "dake" and "bappy." Both routes appear to be necessary for skilled reading (Bradshaw, 1975; Meyer, Schvaneveldt, & Ruddy, 1974). The reality of the two routes is further supported by the observation that some adult brain-damaged patients who have lost the ability to sound out print may still be able to read (Coltheart, 1980).

The relative importance of the two routes to skilled reading is unclear. Some research findings indicate that good readers are very sensitive to phonological information (Barron, 1981a); other findings seem to suggest that sentences can be read and recalled even while simultaneously performing an unrelated vocalization task designed to interfere with phonemic coding (Baddeley & Lewis, 1981).

Some writers have questioned the reality of the two-route model. Henderson (1981), for example, has noted that for "exception" words to be read via the visual route, there must be some way of knowing that they are exception

---

*As it is typical practice among reading teachers to refer to the word as the basic reading unit, there will be occasions later in this book (during discussions of word decoding, for instance) when the notion of multiple units is de-emphasized. This is not a lapse on the part of the author, but merely evidence of the paucity of educational literature on units lower than the word.

words in the first place. That is, these words must be classified as exceptions before they are even read. But this seems impossible. On the other hand, if all exception words were attempted through the phonological route first, mispronunciations in oral reading would be common and they are not. It would seem, then, that the only way mispronunciations are avoided is be accessing phonological codes *after* meaning is accessed (Barron, 1981b). In other words, the visual route leads to a word's (or other unit's) meaning in long-term memory, where associated with its meaning are the rules for that unit's pronunciation. This is the position taken by Glushko (1981), who goes even further than Henderson, suggesting that there are no consistent "spelling-to-sound" rules in English and, therefore, no such thing as exception words. Glushko bases his argument on the results of studies that show pseudowords resembling real exception words take longer to read than pseudowords that are not similar to any exception word. For example, he found that the pseudoword "bint," which resembles the "exception" word "pint," took longer to read than the pseudoword "bink," which resembles the real word "pink"—a word in which the "i" sound is pronounced normally. Glushko took results like this to mean that pseudowords are not pronounced by merely applying some abstract set of spelling-to-sound rules to each letter. Instead, pseudowords appear to be pronounced in the same manner as real words. That is, words and pseudowords are pronounced by comparing their visual appearance with already known words sharing similar graphemic (print) characteristics. Thus, the two reading routes may actually be one route with a unit's physical appearance accessing both its meaning and pronunciation in long-term memory.

Although the reality of the two reading pathways may be problematic, there is no argument that new words are frequently encountered and that good readers have little trouble pronouncing them. Frederiksen (1978) has even found pseudoword decoding to be a good predictor of reading ability. For this reason, the reading model presented here assumes that skilled readers can decode words and pseudowords using both graphemic and phonological codes. However, the codes are not necessarily conceived of as separate pathways, they can just as easily be thought to be two types of information stored together in long-term memory.

LANGUAGE KNOWLEDGE AND READING

Up to this point, the discussion has concentrated on the cognitive processes involved in decoding print—in categorizing into units the ink on the printed page. Decoding has been presented as a process that proceeds in a linear fashion from print to meaning. In some reading theories, decoding is viewed as largely one directional; the influence of language knowledge on reading is largely ignored. Gough (1972), for example, presented a model in which readers were conceived to be largely passive information processors who decode print in a serial and hierarchical fashion beginning with the registration on the retina of the image of the ink on the page and working up to letters, words, phrases, and so on. Models of this type are called "bottom up" or "data driven" because they view reading as essentially a one-directional process proceeding from low (print) to high (meaning) levels of abstraction.

Bottom-up theories, although superficially plausible, have difficulty explaining certain classes of reading errors. For example, many of the oral reading errors made by beginning readers consist of substituting a word for a related word that is semantically and syntactically appropriate to the context (Goodman & Goodman, 1979). Someone who substitutes the word *little* for the word *small* must be doing more than merely decoding print. Such errors suggest that readers are actively engaged in using what they know about language and the context of what they are reading to construct a meaning from the text as they go. The inferential processes that readers use to construct this meaning are called "top down" or "conceptually driven" to distinguish them from the bottom-up processes discussed so far.

There are other lines of evidence that also point to the importance of top-down processes in reading. For example, it has been found to be easier to pronounce a word in context than in isolation (Frederiksen, 1981). Also, semantic "priming" with a related word has been shown to make it easier to decide whether a letter string is actually a word (Antos, 1979). The semantic context in which a word appears has also been found to be an important influence on what a word is taken to mean (Tulving & Thompson, 1973). Metalinguistic awareness (the ability to reflect on and characterize language rules) is another language factor that has been found to be related to reading ability (Tunmer & Herriman, 1983).

Now, it goes without saying that reading cannot be a totally top-down process or there would be no need for printed text at all; a blank page would suffice! For this reason, the trend in reading theories appears to be toward an interactive approach in which top-down and bottom-up processes combine to determine what is read (Rummelhart, 1977; Lesgold & Perfetti, 1981; Stanovich, 1980).

Interactive models are exemplified by theories using eye movements as their main data source (Just & Carpenter, 1980). Readers have been found to make longer eye movement pauses at points in the text where processing loads are greatest (for example, at infrequent words, when integrating data from several sources, or when making inferences at the end of sentences). Eye movements during reading are also controlled by such factors as the spaces between words and line length. Thus, top-down processes controlled by one's knowledge of the language interact with bottom-up processes influenced by the physical properties of the text to control eye movements.

The present model adopts the interactive view. It includes bottom-up, top-down, and interactive processes at different points in the reading sequence.

READING COMPREHENSION

Because the purpose of reading is to extract meaning from print, it is puzzling that reading comprehension has been relatively neglected by researchers, who have preferred instead to concentrate on decoding skills. The reason for this neglect is probably the broad nature of the skills involved in comprehending text. To a large extent, reading comprehension requires mature reasoning. To understand texts, the reader must be able to infer cause–effect relations, prove hypotheses, infer implications, make value judgments, use logic, and understand abstract ideas. None of these skills is really specific to reading; they are used in practically all intellectual endeavors (understanding spoken messages, films, and so on). None of these abilities is yet fully understood; but attention is now being paid to reading comprehension, and progress is being made.

Several studies have shown that subjects asked to recall printed passages include in their recall related information that did not actually appear in the original passage (Dooling & Christiaansen, 1977; Reder, 1979). These studies illustrate clearly that reading comprehension involves inferences beyond the information actually appearing in the printed text. Interestingly, it is not known whether these inferences are made during reading (and are therefore part of the reading process) or at the time of recall (Fredericksen, 1981; Kintsch, 1974; Singer, 1976; Spiro, 1977).

Inferences drawn from a text may be influenced by the purpose for which the text is read (Spiro, 1977) and the very structure of the text. Passages with a clearly stated theme and a sequential structure are most likely to produce inferences (Thorndyke, 1977). Kintsch (1974) and Kieras (1979) have shown that text comprehension is a matter of deriving and relating propositions drawn from the text. These propositions consist of abstractions of the text's main ideas. If the text does not specify how these propositions should be linked, then the reader must supply these links through inference. Texts with a large number of propositions and few specified links are more difficult to read than texts with fewer propositions or more explicit links.

To a substantial degree, drawing inferences means using prior knowledge to make sense out of what is being read. This knowledge is often applied using a *schema* (Adams & Collins, 1979). A schema is a prototype knowledge structure (buying a car, going to a party) that can be applied to specific situations. Schemas serve as "advance organizers" (Ausubel, 1968) to help readers interpret the material they are about to read. In other words, a text suggests a certain schema that can then be used to help build a mental representation of the text's meaning. This mental representation is then used to draw inferences even about missing information.

Studies have shown that when subjects are actually given prepared schemas, the schema will strongly influence what they recall from a subsequently read passage (Pichert & Anderson, 1977). Some schemas are so well developed, they have been said to have their own "story grammars," which convey the meaning of a story to a reader much as deep structure sentence rules convey the meaning of a sentence (Rummelhart, 1975). When passages have been purposely constructed to violate these grammars (say, by providing information in a non-standard sequence), readers have difficulty recalling or making sense out of them (Stein & Glenn, 1979).

Rosenshine (1980) summarized the comprehension skills included in popular reading tests and texts. He also reviewed correlational and factor analytic studies of comprehension skills. Although he concluded that the evidence for discrete, independent comprehension skills is still weak, his review does provide an idea of the kinds of skills generally associated with comprehension. These include

1. Recalling word meanings
2. Drawing inferences
3. Finding answers to questions
4. Following the structure of a passage
5. Recognizing a writer's purpose, attitude, or mood.

These skills are fairly broad. They can be broken down into subskills. For example, drawing inferences from a text involves being able to understand the individual words in their text context, recognizing the event sequence, and the ability to unite cause and effect. As already noted, these subskills are highly intercorrelated as are the main comprehension skills listed above. The possibility that there is only one general skill involved in comprehension or reasoning cannot at present be rejected. The model developed here is based on the assumption that although there may be several comprehension subskills, these have not yet been identified. Comprehension, therefore, must be considered a complex but single skill.

RESEARCH FROM AN INFORMATION-PROCESSING PERSPECTIVE: INTERIM SUMMARY

The research described thus far suggests that there is no single basic reading unit. The reading unit depends on the type of material being read, the purpose for reading, and the reader's skill. The literature also suggests that units at various levels can be linked directly to meanings (and phonological codes) stored in long-term memory without the need for phonological recoding (sounding out). Both decoding and comprehension appear to be guided by an interaction between hypotheses and inferences drawn from the semantic content of the text (and one's knowledge of the languge and the topic) combined with bottom-up processes.

To this point, the discussion has focused on reading processes common to all readers. But the present book is concerned with measuring differences among readers. The next two sections of this chapter review the evidence for individual differences in reading skills from an information-processing viewpoint. First, differences in decoding skills are discussed. This is followed by a discussion of comprehension differences.

SOURCES OF INDIVIDUAL DIFFERENCES: DECODING SKILLS

Reading tests include a variety of tasks that have been shown to distinguish good from poor readers. These tasks, unfortunately, have generally been chosen for empirical rather than theoretical reasons. That is, they have been chosen because they predict reading performance on some criterion, not because they help explicate the nature of the reading deficit. There is, however, a substantial literature concerned with individual differences in decoding skills from an information-processing viewpoint. Decoding skills are those that permit the reader to recognize printed text, pronounce words, and ultimately access meaning. In other words, decoding skills are those necessary to process individual letters, words, and other small units. In the present discussion, decoding skills will also be considered to include processes necessary to understand sentences as well. The extraction of meaning from paragraphs and larger prose passages as well as the ability to make inferences from what is read will be considered in a later section when comprehension skills are discussed.

SHORT-TERM MEMORY DIFFERENCES BETWEEN SKILLED AND UNSKILLED READERS

Several writers have noted a relationship between reading ability and short-term memory (Jorm, 1983a; Morrison, Giordani, & Nagy, 1977). Jorm (1983a) suggests that the problem is one of storage—poor readers have difficulty storing material in short-term memory for further processing.* As already noted, short-term memory is given several important functions in information-processing models of cognition. It is seen as a work space, as a temporary storage area, the executive that controls the system's information flow, and the site of selective attention (see Baddeley & Hitch, 1974). Difficulties in the ability to store information in short-term memory can result from inefficient storage strategies (a control-process problem), smaller short-term memory capacity among poorer

---

*Unless otherwise noted, references to good and poor readers refer to distinctions made on the basis of standardized tests.

readers (a structural difference), or some combination of both. There is evidence for all three problems among poor readers.

Images of the printed page enter the information-processing system as brief visual images lasting about one-fourth of a second before they are replaced by images from the next eye fixation. These brief visual images must be attended to or the information contained in them will be lost (Gough, 1972; Neisser, 1967). Although some writers have said that poor readers have difficulty processing information in this sensory stage (called "iconic memory"), studies designed specifically to assess this stage of information processing (e.g., Morrison *et al.*, 1977) have found no differences between good and poor readers.

The quality of the image in iconic memory is determined by the physical quality of the visual stimulus (brightness, contrast, duration). Degrading the stimulus (by reducing contrast, for instance) will also degrade the iconic image (Neisser, 1967). Manipulations that degrade the text do affect poor readers more seriously than skilled readers (Lesgold & Roth, 1981), but the site of this influence is probably in a posticonic memory stage in which partial information is used to complete words. It is important to note that manipulations that affect access to long-term memory codes (substituting rare for common words, for instance) also differentiate between reading groups (Becker & Killion, 1977), but the effect of this manipulation is independent of stimulus degrading. The two manipulations exert independent influences on reading.

Memory access will be discussed in a later section. For now, suffice it to say that poor readers begin to show their problem early in the information-processing sequence. They seem to be able to transfer information from iconic memory at a rate equal to good readers, but degrading the information in this store has a greater effect on them than on skilled readers.

Several studies (Bauer, 1977; Spring & Capps, 1974; Torgeson & Goldman, 1977) have concluded that poor readers fail to "rehearse" material in short-term memory. A failure to rehearse is an example of a control-process deficit. Poor readers either do not have the ability to use rehearsal or they have not developed a strategy that tells them when using such a control process would be worthwhile.

Another sort of strategy deficit was reported by Wong, Wong, and Foth (1977), who found poor readers less likely to develop mnemonic strategies to help organize their memory and aid subsequent recall than good readers. For example, when learning a list of words, it is more efficient to group related words together to assist recall; poor readers fail to do this. Wong *et al.* concluded that poor readers were "inactive learners" who engaged in fewer strategies (including rehearsal) than proficient readers.

Evidence that poor readers may also have a structural short-term memory deficit in addition to their control-process deficit comes from memory-span studies in which poor readers were found to recall fewer items than good readers

(Senf & Freundl, 1972; Valtin, 1973), although these findings are not always easy to replicate (Guyer & Friedman, 1975).

Some researchers see the short-term memory deficit in poor readers as an interaction or trade-off between short-term memory's storage and executive functions. Daneman & Carpenter (1980), for example, had subjects read aloud a series of sentences and then recall the final word of each sentence. They found the number of final words recalled to correlate highly with reading comprehension measures. They concluded that poor readers were inefficient information-processors who did not develop a strategy for storing final words and thereby limited the amount of information they could store in short-term memory. These findings indicate that the structural deficit may actually be secondary to the control-process deficit.

The research discussed so far has focused on short-term memory itself without regard to the type of information being operated on. There is, however, evidence that reading skill is particularly related to short-term memory strategies for dealing with information about the order of stimulus events. It should be recognized that separating item from order information in short-term memory is a controversial activity (Crowder, 1979). For one thing, poor item retention will necessarily result in poor order retention because order is determined, in part, by the number of items recalled. This difficulty may be minimized, however, by careful scoring (taking into account the total number of items recalled) or by thoroughly familiarizing subjects with all of the items (Healy, 1974).

In a series of studies, Koppitz (1970, 1973, 1975) reported the development of a measure of sequential memory skills that appears to differentiate between average and reading-disabled children of equal intelligence (as measured by intelligence tests). Koppitz's task, named the Visual-Aural Digit-Span Test, is composed of four subtests (visual-oral, visual-written, aural-oral, and aural-written) that assess the ability to recall digit sequences when presentation and response modes are systematically varied. In her studies, Koppitz found the tests involving visual-digit presentation showed the most consistent relationship to reading and school learning ability.

Koppitz (1973) considers her test to be a measure of short-term memory capacity as well as a measure of sensory integration. She explains the particularly strong relationship between the visual-oral subtest and oral reading skill by pointing out that both involve the visual perception of symbols and the oral recall of what is being perceived.

The relationship between memory for order or sequence and reading ability was also noted by Bakker (1967, 1970), who found that poor readers had difficulty perceiving and retaining the temporal order of verbal items. Similarly, Blank, Weider, and Bridger (1968) found reading-disabled children unable to "assimilate" verbal temporal-order patterns.

More recent studies reinforce the relationship between order-information recall and reading skill (Mason, Pilkington, & Brandau, 1981; Singer, 1979; Tallal, 1980). Using a variety of different procedures, these studies demonstrated poor retention of order information for below average as compared with more skilled readers. Lunzer (1978) even produced data indicating that the ability to reproduce a visual sequence at age 6 is highly correlated with initial progress in learning to read.

Studies concerned with general verbal ability rather than specifically reading have also found an important role for order information in individual differences. Hunt, Frost, and Lunneborg (1973) reported an experiment by Nix that indicated that high verbals were more proficient than low verbals at retaining order information. Schwartz and Wiedel (1978) also found high verbal subjects superior to lows in their ability to retain information about item order.

Taken as a whole, the research literature strongly suggests that there is a relationship between memory for the order of events in short-term memory and reading proficiency. It is possible that poor readers, who engage in less efficient information-processing strategies (rehearsing items less than good readers, for instance), have less efficient memory for order *because* of their failure to rehearse. Poor readers may also have a smaller short-term memory capacity (a structural deficit) than skilled readers, which results in their poor memory for order, although, as already noted, the structural deficit itself may actually be a secondary result of their control-processing deficit.

The control-processing deficit among poor readers (their failure to rehearse and to retain order information) has been shown to be amenable to treatment. Wong (1978) found a marked improvement in recall among reading disabled subjects who were given cues to use certain rehearsal strategies. Thus, the short-term memory deficit among poor readers may indicate a *performance* failure rather than a total inability to use certain cognitive strategies.

One aspect of short-term memory performance that has not yet been touched on is the speed with which memory can be searched. Jackson and McClelland (1979) asked subjects of varying reading ability to decide whether a target letter appeared in a subsequently presented "memory search set" of letters. The search set varied from two to six letters. As expected, larger search sets took longer to scan than small sets, and responses were faster for target-present than target-absent sets. Good readers (defined in their study as fast readers) scanned the search set faster than poor readers, but there were no interactions of reading ability with search set size or response type (present or absent). This means that the rate at which the targets were compared with the items in the search set (the slope of the line relating search set size to reaction time) was the same for both good and poor readers. This finding indicates that whatever the short-term memory problems of poor readers may be, the rate at which items in short-term memory are scanned is not one of them. The overall faster responding of good readers—indexed by the y intercept of the search set size by reaction-time function—is not without interest, as it suggests that good readers may be able to process information faster than poor readers.

Different methods of measuring short-term memory scanning speed have found some relationship between scanning speed and reading ability. Frederiksen (1978) had subjects report "what they had seen" from a brief visual display of two letters and two "masks" (e.g., S H # #). The letters were always adjacent, but they could appear in one of three positions (S H # #, # S H #, # # S H). The difference between the mean reaction time to letters presented in serial positions three and four and the reaction time to letters in positions one and two (divided by two) produced a "scanning speed" measure. This scanning speed measure represented the increment in reaction time for each shift to the right. Frederiksen found his scanning speed measure to be related to reading ability as measured by a standardized reading test.

The difference between Frederiksen's results and those reported by Jackson and McClelland are probably the result of the different scanning tasks used in the two studies. Frederiksen's task permitted subjects to use what they know about the likelihood of letters appearing in different locations in a word and the frequency of letter pairs to help them make a response. This information would not have been helpful in Jackson and McClelland's task. Thus, Frederiksen was measuring prior knowledge as much as he was measuring scanning speed. Indeed, when Frederiksen compared recognition latencies for high- and low-probability letter pairs (as measured by their frequency in the language), he found a greater difference in the ability to recognize low-probability as opposed to high-probability letter pairs among poor readers than among skilled readers. Therefore, Frederiksen's data cannot be taken to refute the findings reported by Jackson and McClelland. It does not appear that poor readers differ from good readers in memory scanning speed *per se*. Instead, they differ in their knowledge of letter frequency, a type of reading knowledge.

Kail and Marshall (1978) used yet a third measure of scanning speed to compare good and poor readers. They had their subjects read several unrelated statements following which they were required to answer questions about them. Skilled readers were found to answer these questions faster than less skilled readers. In this study, like Frederiksen's (1978), language knowledge (and, in this case, comprehension skills) could have exerted a strong effect on the results.

Studies comparing subjects of high and low verbal ability have also found little or no relationship between ability and scanning speed in short-term memory (see Schwartz, 1981, for a review). It seems reasonable to conclude therefore, that short-term memory scanning speed is not an important source of individual differences in reading ability.

To summarize this discussion of short-term memory influences on individual differences in reading ability, five generalizations seem supportable:

1. Poor readers engage in less efficient data-processing strategies in short-term memory than skilled readers.
2. Poor readers appear to have special difficulties in storing and retaining information about the order of events.
3. Poor readers may have a structural short-term memory deficit (smaller capacity), but this deficit may actually be the secondary result of their control-processing deficit.
4. Poor readers show improved short-term memory processing with instruction, suggesting that their deficit is one of performance rather than a structural deficit or total lack of ability.
5. Poor readers are not slower at scanning individual items in short-term memory than good readers, although they may have difficulty in using information about the probability of letters and word sequences to aid scanning.

Besides short-term memory deficits, access to codes stored in long-term memory have also been found to be related to individual differences in reading ability. This source of individual differences is discussed next.

MEMORY ACCESS AND READING ABILITY

Several researchers have used the stimulus-matching task developed by Posner and his colleagues (Posner, Boies, Eichelman, & Taylor, 1969) to examine memory access ability. This task requires subjects to decide rapidly whether two stimuli are the same either physically (*AA*), share the same name (*Aa*), or whether they are different (*Ab*). Hunt and his colleagues (1973, 1975) found no difference between high and low verbal ability subjects in physical match time, but a statistic derived by subtracting physical from name match time did differentiate between subjects of varying levels of verbal aptitude. Goldberg, Schwartz, and Stewart (1977) used words rather than letters in a matching task. In their study, subjects had to determine whether two words were physically identical (*DEER–DEER*), homophonically identical (*DEER–DEAR*), or whether they were taxonomically related (*DEER–ELK*). They found that high verbal subjects were marginally faster than lows at making physical matches but much faster at making taxonomic and fastest of all at making homophonic matches. Keating and Bobbitt (1978) found the relationship between stimulus matching and psychometric ability to be present in children as young as 9.

The matching task is conceived as tapping how long it takes to retrieve overlearned codes from long-term memory. The idea is that physical matches do not require memory access time, as they can be made on the basis of the physical appearance of the stimuli alone. Name matches, on the other hand, cannot be accomplished on the basis of appearance alone, they require access to the letter name (or word name or word sound in the case of Goldberg *et al.*'s experiment). Thus, subtracting physical match time from name match time should provide a relatively pure measure of the time it takes to access information in long-term memory. The studies cited thus far indicate that access time is related to general verbal ability as measured by such tests as the Scholastic Aptitude Test. There is also evidence that access time to long-term memory is related to scores on specific reading tests as well.

Hunt, Davidson, and Lansman (1981) found a relationship between psychometric measures of reading ability and matching tasks using words rather than letters. Similar findings for words as well as letters were reported by Frederiksen (1978) and Jackson and McClelland (1979). Jackson (1980) and Jackson and McClelland (1981) have gone so far as to hypothesize that skilled readers have generally superior visual encoding skills that apply both to normal print and to visually presented shapes. The evidence seems overwhelming—there is a strong relationship between memory access time and reading ability.

A likely explanation for the relationship between memory access time and reading ability is that faster access time leaves more time available for comprehension. That is, for any given unit of time, those with faster access to long-term memory codes have more time available to organize schemas and make inferences about what they are reading.

It should be noted that at least part of the relationship between reading ability and long-term memory-access time could come from their mutual dependence on speed. Most ability tests have a speed component (Carroll, 1981), and it should be no surprise that two tests with speed components correlate (Schwartz, Griffin, and Brown, 1983). Nevertheless, memory access is a good predictor of reading ability as measured by standardized tests. For this reason, it is an important component of the present model and measures.

A special kind of memory access pertinent to reading is access to phonological codes. Numerous studies have shown that unskilled readers are slower and less accurate in pronouncing pseudowords than good readers (Calfee, Venezky, & Chapman, 1969; Perfetti & Hogaboam, 1975a). Pronouncing a pseudoword requires either the application of spelling-to-sound rules (as in the two-pathway model discussed earlier) or using a procedure that seeks analogies between the pseudoword and real words (as claimed by Glushko, 1981). In either case, comparing pseudoword reading time with normal-word reading time allows us to determine whether similar processes are used with each type of stimulus.

Frederiksen (1981), for example, compared pseudoword and normal-word reading in an attempt to determine the "depth" (see Craik, 1973) at which they are processed. He found that the time to read rare words and pseudowords (matched to the rare words for length, vowel type, and so on) was significantly correlated for both good and poor readers. This correlation remained high for poor readers even when common words (and matched pseudowords) were used. Good readers, in contrast, showed a much reduced correlation in the common-word condition. Frederiksen took this finding to illustrate that good readers adjusted their level of word processing in line with text demands, whereas poor readers did not.

Summarizing this section, the evidence strongly suggests that access to long-term memory codes is an important predictor of reading competence. The ability to access phonological codes, in particular, appears to be strongly related to reading skill.

EYE MOVEMENTS AND READING ABILITY

As noted in Chapter 2, many writers have found a relationship between erratic eye movement patterns and reading disability (see Lefton, Nagle, Johnson, & Fisher, 1979; Pavlidis, 1981). The important question for our present purposes is whether erratic eye-movement patterns are responsible for reading disabilities or whether they are the result of these disabilities. Although the relationship between eye movements and reading skill is correlational (making causation difficult to assign), logical analysis suggests that eye movement difficulties are the result rather than the cause of reading problems.

The placement and duration of eye fixations have been shown to be partly predictable from text features. Readers make longer pauses when processing loads are greatest—when reading rare words, integrating information across clauses, and making inferences at the end of sentences (Just & Carpenter, 1980). It also has been shown that eye movements during reading are controlled by the reader's purpose and prior knowledge interacting with text characteristics (Rayner & Pollatsek, 1981). Eye movement patterns that are erratic in all beginning readers have been found to gradually stabilize with age and increasing reading skill (Tinker, 1965). In other words, eye movement patterns are governed by the skill and purpose of the reader and not the other way around. This interpretation is strongly supported by the finding that although training can influence eye movements, it does little to improve reading competence (Tinker, 1958).

The same conclusion can also be applied to the eye–voice span as described by Levin (1979). The eye–voice span is defined as the distance that the eye is ahead of the voice in oral reading. The simplest way to measure the eye–voice span is to have subjects read aloud until reaching some predetermined point in the text when the lights are turned out. The reader reports what she or he has seen beyond the word just read. Levin (1979) reviewed the literature on the eye–voice span and found there is, indeed, a relationship between it and reading disability. Once again, however, the direction of causality is unknown. Because there is no evidence that training aimed at increasing the eye–voice span increases reading competence, it seems likely that like eye movements, the eye–voice span is the result rather than the cause of reading disability. For this reason, eye movement measures have been omitted from the measures presented in the following chapters.

AUTOMATIC VERSUS CONTROLLED PROCESSES

The discussion so far has been concerned with individual differences in the decoding skills necessary for skilled reading. Short-term memory information-processing strategies, memory for order information, the possibility of differences in short-term memory capacity, and the time it takes to access lexical, phonological, and semantic codes in long-term memory have all been shown to be important sources of individual differences in reading ability. Each of these is also an example of how context-free processes at the sentence, word, and subword level exert an important influence on reading competence. A crucial aspect of bottom-up processing that has not yet been touched upon is the tendency for such processes to become "automatic."

When we first learn to perform a task, it takes all of our concentration to get it right. Novice drivers, for example, find themselves totally concentrating on the road and traffic signals. Any distractions (say, listening to the radio) can severely interfere with their driving. With practice, the situation changes. Accomplished drivers have no problem listening to the radio or carrying on a conversation while driving. In fact, should someone dart out into the road, most practiced drivers will hit the brake before they have even had time to consciously think about it. This is one of the characteristics of automatic behavior; it occurs in response to a triggering situation without conscious intent. Automatic responses are also not attention demanding. That is why the skilled driver can seemingly do two things at once. One of those things, driving, is going on automatically outside the conscious confines of short-term ("working") memory. Once a behavior or skill becomes automatic, attentional skill becomes available for other tasks (like carrying on a conversation). Should the driving environment change (when visiting a country where driving is on the opposite side of the road, for instance), attention to driving will once again be required and conversation will become difficult. The characteristics of automatic processing are compared with attention-demanding controlled processing in Table 3.

Many of the decoding processes involved in reading also become automatic with practice (LaBerge & Samuels, 1974). Whereas accessing phonological codes for print requires conscious attention and cognitive capacity from beginning readers, skilled readers can perform these tasks without any conscious effort. In

TABLE 3. Characteristics of Automatic and Attention-Demanding Processing[a]

Automatic processing	Attention-demanding processing
Proceeds without subject control	Under subject control
Does not use attentional capacity	Requires attentional capacity
Not affected by a competing task	Deteriorates with a competing task
Outside awareness	Under conscious control
Stimulus directly accesses long-term memory	Stimulus must first be decoded before long-term memory can be accessed

[a]Adapted from "Controlled and Automatic Human Information Processing: I. Detection, Search, and Attention" by W. Schneider and R. M. Shiffrin, 1977, *Psychological Review, 84*, 1–66. Copyright 1977 by the American Psychological Association.

fact, skilled readers can hardly look at print without reading it, the processes are so inevitable and automatic. An important advantage conveyed by automatizing encoding processes is that more cognitive capacity is thereby made available for higher level processes such as drawing inferences and constructing schematic representations.

If automatic decoding characterizes skilled readers and attention-demanding decoding is the norm among beginning readers, then it is reasonable to hypothesize that poor readers may not have developed sufficient automaticity in decoding tasks. The evidence discussed earlier that suggests that poor readers are slower at accessing overlearned information in long-term memory supports this view. So too does a finding reported by Willows (1978). Willows found that poor readers are more distracted by pictures in the text than good readers. This greater distractibility suggests that poor readers are less able to do two things at once than good readers. That is, they have less cognitive capacity available for other tasks while reading than do good readers.

Evidence that poor readers are less likely to use automatic processes than good readers comes from experiments reported by Frederiksen (1981). He found that poor readers showed a higher correlation between their reading times for high- and low-frequency words than good readers and that a strongly constraining sentence context reduced reading time (as compared with reading time for the word in isolation) for poor readers. The facilitating effect of context was particularly strong for low-frequency words. Frederiksen interpreted these findings as indicating that good readers who decode words automatically are less affected by context than poor readers who use a controlled, serial process to generate words in context and who trade off some low-level decoding processes against higher level ones.

An important point about highly practiced skills is their ability to reflect individual differences. When first learning a new skill (tennis, piano, reading), most people are erratic performers; their exact behavior is unpredictable. This variability in individual performance makes it very difficult to identify stable individual differences between people. With continued practice, however, individual variability declines and differences among people become more apparent. In fact, Schwartz (1981), after reviewing some of the literature on individual differences in information processing, concluded that highly practiced, automatic processes are the best place to look for individual differences.

Accessing phonological and other information in long-term memory has already been seen to be an important part of skilled reading. Frederiksen's (1981) data suggest that skilled readers access a word's meaning and associated codes automatically in long-term memory, whereas poor readers use controlled, attention-demanding processes. This may be one reason why poor readers have been found to be more sensitive to misspelling than good readers.

DECODING SKILLS: SUMMARY

Decoding skills, which are largely bottom-up processes (although not entirely), are an important part of reading competence. This discussion has identified several decoding skills (short-term memory strategies, long-term memory access time, and so on) that appear to be sources of individual differences in reading. Moreover, it was noted that the degree to which these skills have become automatic is an important source of information about reading ability. It has been argued that those who decode rapidly achieve higher scores on standardized comprehension tests than slow decoders (Seifert, 1976). This has been interpreted to mean that automatic decoding frees cognitive capacity for comprehension processes. The nature of these processes is addressed in the next section.

Before proceeding, it is worthwhile noting that the experiments described so far, although suggestive, are hardly the last word on any of the topics discussed. Reading research continues to be an active field, and it is possible that some of the conclusions reported here may be overturned in the future. For example, negative findings (that good and poor readers do not differ in a specific skill) are notoriously difficult to interpret because it is always possible that insensitive experimental methods simply failed to reveal a difference that was actually there. In the future, more sensitive measures may show the difference. In addition, because studies use different criteria for assigning subjects to good and poor reading groups, some discrepancies in their results are to be expected. Finally, it is not always clear (because the data are not reported) whether differences between good and poor readers reflect reading differences or differences in overall intelligence. For these reasons, the model developed in this chapter must be considered tentative and subject to future revision.

SOURCES OF INDIVIDUAL DIFFERENCES: COMPREHENSION SKILLS

One of the main purposes of reading is to "make sense" out of the printed page. *Making sense* has been defined in various ways by test publishers (see Chapter 3 and Rosenshine, 1980). For some, it means being able to extract the main idea from a passage. For others, making sense of a passage means being able to answer simple questions about it; and for still others, drawing inferences from what is read is the hallmark of comprehension. Actually, comprehension includes all of these skills and more. It also includes the ability to integrate already existing knowledge with what is being read. Some of these comprehension skills have been shown to discriminate between good and poor readers, although it has not always been easy to distinguish between the various skills themselves. The evidence for individual differences in comprehension skills is discussed next.

SYNTAX, COMPREHENSION, AND INDIVIDUAL DIFFERENCES

Understanding English requires an appreciation of word order. *John loves Mary* does not mean the same thing as *Mary loves John.* (Many novels, songs, and poems have been based on the difference between these two sentences.) As already noted, memory for order has been found to be a significant skill in text decoding. Perhaps the reason for this is that memory for order is a help in unraveling syntax. This conclusion is supported by Graesser, Hoffman, and Clark's (1980) finding that poor readers are more susceptible to decreases in syntactic predictability than good readers. Cromer (1970) also found that giving poor readers cues to the syntactic structure of a sentence (by grouping words together according to their phrase structure rather than leaving equal spaces between words) improved comprehension.

Syntax processing was also shown to be an important source of individual differences in comprehension in a study by Mackworth (1972). Mackworth had subjects choose one of six words (three nouns, three verbs) to complete sentences that were missing either a noun or a verb. Eye movement recordings showed that poorer readers spent more time examining inappropriate words (nouns when they should have been choosing verbs and vice versa) than good readers.

Several studies (e.g., Guthrie & Taylor, 1976) have failed to find a specific syntactic deficit among poor readers. Instead, poor readers, in their studies, attempt to apply the same syntactic rules as more skilled readers—they just have trouble doing so. This suggests that the syntactic deficit may indeed be secondary to the difficulty poor readers have in maintaining order information in short-term memory.

SEMANTIC CONTEXT AND COMPREHENSION DIFFERENCES

The importance of semantic context to comprehension differences has been the subject of a great deal of research. The typical experimental paradigm involves providing some sort of context (a few words or a few sentences) prior to a target item that is either a word or a pseudoword made up of a pronounceable string of English letters. The subject's task is to decide whether the target item is a word or nonword. Fast presentation of the target item makes this a difficult task. By manipulating the context so that it is either semantically appropriate to the target item or inappropriate to the item, experimenters can tell whether the subject is influenced by semantic context. The literature on such "lexical decision tasks" is large and complicated, but the standard finding is that poor readers are as sensitive to semantic context as good readers (West & Stanovich, 1978).

A rather different task used by Perfetti, Goldman, and Hogaboam (1979) produced comparable results. They found that words were pronounced faster at the end of sentences than at the end of meaningless word strings and that this difference was specially large for poor readers. In another version of the same task, they had subjects guess what word was omitted from a passage (this is known as the cloze procedure). They scored subject's responses as correct; appropriate to the context; incorrect, but appropriate; or totally inappropriate. They also recorded the response latency (the time between being presented the passage and making a response) for each judgment. Perfetti *et al.* found that context helped the poor readers to guess the correct words at least to the same extent as it helped good readers, if not more.

Although poor readers are sensitive to semantic context, they are by no means as good at predicting missing words, using the cloze procedure, as good readers (Doehring, 1977). Carr (1981) and Frederiksen (1981) have suggested that good readers use context automatically but poor readers need to engage in attention-demanding cognitive processing to take advantage of the facilitation provided by having a cognitive context. In any case, there seems to be little reason to believe that good and poor readers differ in their sensitivity to semantic context. Instead, Carr's and Frederiksen's position seems to suggest that poor readers' mediocre performance on cloze tasks results from a deficit in automatic semantic processing.

The importance of semantic decoding is illustrated by a study reported by Merrill, Sperber, and McCauley (1981). Their subjects read sentences followed by target words that were printed in one of four colors. The subjects' job was to name the color of the target word. The semantic relationship between the target word and sentences was arranged so that the targets were either appropriate, inappropriate but related, or unrelated to the sentence. For example, the sentence

"The girl touched the cat" was appropriate to the target word "fur" but inappropriate to the target word "claw." The opposite relationship holds for the sentence "The girl fought the cat." Merrill *et al.* found that good readers were slower to name the target word's color when targets were appropriate to sentence meaning than when targets were totally unrelated to the sentence (e.g., "The man washed the car—fur.") This did not occur for inappropriate targets whose color was recognized as fast as the color of unrelated targets.

For poor readers, both appropriate and inappropriate targets interfered with color naming. It would appear that poor readers rely less than good readers on integrating what they read into a coherent semantic schema; they seem more influenced by individual words. This interpretation of Merrill *et al.*'s findings is given further support by their report that when a single word is used instead of a sentence (e.g., "cat—fur"), both good and poor readers take longer to identify the color of both types of words.

Garner (1980) also found poor readers to be less efficient at creating semantic text interpretations than good readers. Her technique was to alter stories by introducing errors that contradicted a story's main theme. For example, she altered a story about Thomas Jefferson and the beginning of American coinage by replacing a reference to coins with one to "letters." This change, although syntactically and semantically appropriate to the sentence in which it occurred, violated the story's main theme. She asked subjects to consider themselves editors and proofread the text. Poor readers were found to be less sensitive to these thematic errors than good readers. Presumably, the poor readers, who depend on word level semantic interpretations, have difficulty building the overall organizing schema that would help them spot thematic errors. Graesser *et al.* (1980) also found that poor readers had more trouble integrating propositions derived from text than good readers.

An important skill differentiating good from poor readers, then, is their ability to generate semantic interpretations of text. The performance of poor readers seems to stem from their concentration on smaller units of processing (words, letters) than good readers.

STRATEGIES AND COMPREHENSION DIFFERENCES

Reading for pleasure and reading to prepare for an exam require different "strategies" from the reader. Reading for pleasure does not generally require linking what is currently being read with previously learned material so that it can be recalled later, and it does not usually require committing such new information to memory. Studying for an exam requires both.

Psychological studies of reading purpose have either given subjects specific reading goals ("Learn how to calculate the area of cylinder," for example), or purpose has been manipulated by asking direct questions ("How do you calculate the area of a cylinder?"). Both approaches have been shown to influence inferences that are drawn from a text and later memory for these inferences (Anderson & Biddle, 1975; Frase, 1975).

Several researchers have approached reading strategies from a "levels-of-processing" point of view (see Craik, 1973). The idea behind this approach is that text can be analyzed at several levels. Proofreaders and typists, for instance, concentrate on spelling and punctuation, avoiding semantic interpretations. They are often unable to give a summary of the materials that they have been working on. In contrast, reading for meaning can result in missing typographical and grammatical errors. From an interactive viewpoint (Perfetti & Roth, 1981), all levels contribute to skilled reading. Nevertheless, it is possible to focus attention on one or another level by using orienting instructions.

Black (1981), for example, gave subjects one of three types of orienting instructions. Subjects who had been asked to read two essays were instructed to rate the essays for comprehensibility (a relatively "shallow" level of processing), to read them in preparation for a subsequent recall test (a middle-level task), or to abstract the author's main point in preparation for an essay exam on a related topic (a deep-processing level). Black found that fewer inferences were drawn from the text by those given the shallow orienting instructions than by those in the other two instruction conditions.

Schwartz (1980) had subjects read and recall prepared texts. These texts had been altered so as to induce varying processing levels. For example, a shallow level of processing was induced by having some words printed backwards. Deeper processing was induced by having subjects choose which of two words best completed sentences. He found that these manipulations influenced subsequent recall of the passages. Deeper processing led to better recall.

These studies show that both overall recall and the type of inferences readers make can be affected by reading purpose. Readers' ability to adjust their level of processing in line with their goals and text characteristics reflects the use of different reading strategies. There is some evidence that the ability to adopt different strategies is an important aspect of skilled reading. Graesser *et al.* (1980) found that subjects who expected an essay exam on what they read allocated more of their reading time to overall text characteristics (what they called the text *macrostructure*) than subjects led to expect a multiple-choice exam.

Although it seems clear that reading strategies vary with reading purpose (and with text characteristics), the relationship between these various strategies and individual differences in comprehension is less clear.

Graesser *et al.* (1980) found that good and poor readers (defined in their study as fast and slow readers) could not be differentiated on the basis of their respective macrostructure processing times (the times influenced by the strategies under discussion). Instead, it was word and sentence level decoding skills that differentiated among their reading groups. This finding is in agreement with the literature on decoding reviewed in the previous section of this chapter. There is some evidence, however, that reading ability groups may differ in their respective comprehension strategies (Olshavsky, 1976–1977; Royer, Hastings, & Hook, 1979).

Royer *et al.* (1979) used a sentence-verification technique to measure reading comprehension. They asked primary school-aged children to read text passages selected to be below, above, or at their respective reading-grade levels. The children had to decide whether sentences presented after the passages were read were actually in the original passage. These sentences were comprised of original sentences, paraphrases of original sentences, sentences in which the original meaning had been changed, and totally irrelevant sentences that were unrelated to the original passage. As might be expected, children frequently misidentified paraphrased and, to a lesser extent, meaning-changed sentences as original. The crucial finding was that children were more likely to make misidentifications on difficult material (above grade level) than easy material. That is, there was a relationship between recognition accuracy and passage difficulty.

An even more direct relationship between strategy and comprehension was reported by Hunt, Davidson, and Lansman (1981; see also Palmer, MacLeod, Hunt, & Davidson, 1981). Their task involved sentence–picture verification.

Specifically, they required subjects to decide rapidly whether a phrase or a sentence ("Star above plus," for example) accurately described a picture ($^*_+$). Sentences varied ("Star isn't above plus") as did their relationship to the picture (true or false). This task does not require a large vocabulary (only six words are used), nor does it require the construction of elaborate schema. It is instead a measure of how quickly and accurately meaning is derived from a sentence held in short-term memory. Nevertheless, Hunt *et al.* (1981) found that performance on the sentence–picture verification test correlated .46 ($p. < .001$) with a standardized measure of reading comprehension. Even after controlling for memory access time (by removing the variance due to the correlation between sentence–picture verification and matching task performance), the sentence–picture verification performance still correlated .31 ($p. < .02$) with reading comprehension. Thus, it seems that the sentence–picture verification measure is tapping differences in the way sentences are understood rather than merely speed.

COMPREHENSION SKILLS: SUMMARY

The main goal of reading is to make sense out of printed text. *Making sense* can be defined in various ways (drawing inferences, answering questions, abstracting the main idea) but all share one common characteristic—they all imply the ability to reason about what is read. There is at present no general consensus about the subskills underlying reading comprehension (Rosenshine, 1980). Although several studies have found a syntactic deficit, is possible that this deficit may actually be a secondary problem resulting from poor readers' failure to deal adequately with order information in short-term memory. Both good and poor readers have been found to be sensitive to semantic context, but good readers appear to be able to use context automatically, whereas poor readers require attention-demanding controlled processing to take advantage of contextual cues. Poor readers also seem more bound by local influences (words and sentences) than good readers, who take greater advantage of overall text characteristics. Differences in abstracting meaning at the sentence level such as those measured by the sentence–picture verification task seem to be more sensitive indicators of individual differences than studies of macrostructure processing variables such as overall passage meaning.

OUTLINE OF A MODEL OF DECODING AND COMPREHENSION

The research reviewed in this chapter makes up the data base for the information-processing model of reading presented in this section. A schematic representation of the model apears in Figure 5.

According to the model, reading begins with an eye fixation. The first eye fixation for English readers is generally slightly indented from the left end of a line and typically lasts about one-quarter of a second (Rayner, 1977; Tinker, 1958). Subsequent fixations take place about 10 to 12 letters to the right and each eye movement (except, of course, movements to the beginning of a new line) take about 20 milliseconds. Eye movements are related to the nature of what is being read; their placement is under the control of eye movement routines that interact with text characteristics. Thus, eye movements and fixation times are an instance of the interaction of top-down and bottom-up processes.

The result of a fixation is a visual image that is stored in a visual buffer. This sensory image consists of about 15 or 20 letters and spaces, and it persists until it is replaced by the image taken in on the next fixation (Sperling, 1963).

Information in the sensory buffer is not "categorized" as letters, words, or other meaningful items, it is simply a collection of lines, angles, and spaces. Information storage at this stage does not seem to differentiate good from poor readers (Morrison, Giordani, & Nagy, 1977).

Information is removed from the sensory buffer by processes referred to as filtering and categorizing. These routines are another instance of an interaction between top-down and bottom-up processes. Expectancies (sometimes known as "set") can influence categorization by directing attention toward certain features of the sensory stimulus. For example, if the context called for a letter t, then categorization routines could be specially set to expect a t and to give extra

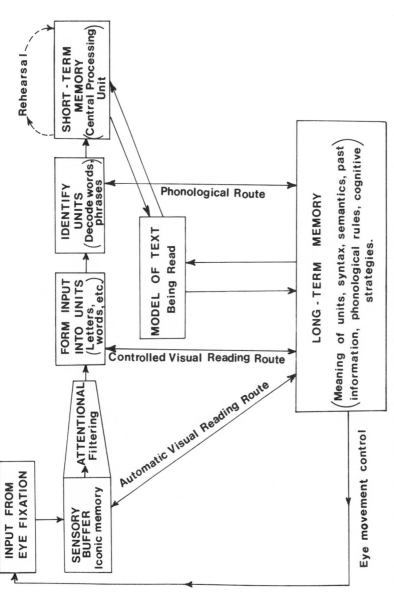

FIGURE 5. Outline of an information-processing model of reading. The arrows indicate the direction of information flow. Visual information is stored briefly in a sensory-specific store. Highly familiar visual units in this sensory store can access meanings in long-term memory directly by the automatic visual reading route. Normally, attentional processes filter extraneous information out of the sensory store while transferring the remainder to short-term memory. This information is used to form reading units that can access meaning in long-term memory via the controlled visual or phonological route. Meaningful units are kept in short-term memory (in their proper order) until a meaningful proposition is found. This proposition is incorporated into a model of the text being read. At every stage in the process, information residing in long-term memory can feed forward to interact with bottom-up decoding processes.

credence to evidence that a *t* is present. At the word level, the same top-down influences operate. If a verb is expected, then the categorizing routine can be set to look for evidence that a verb is present. Filtering, too, can help in the categorizing process by causing the system to ignore irrelevant information like type font or color (see Broadbent, 1971, for a complete discussion of categorizing and filtering). The perceptual filtering and categorizing stage involves more than the mere matching of letter or word templates to the raw sensory information. This is an active recoding stage in which hypotheses generated by top-down processes interact with sensory information to determine what information is abstracted from the sensory buffer store.

The result of perceptual filtering and categorizing is a set of coded or categorized input. This input can be categorized as letters, syllables, other multiletter units (spelling units, for instance), words, or even phrases. These codes can lead directly to the unit's meaning through the so-called visual pathway, or they can be translated into a phonological code (either by "sounding out" or by analogy with known words) that is then used to access the word's meaning. (It should be noted that the unit's meaning can also be used to produce its phonological code.) In either case, the result is "lexical" access—access to all the information stored about a word in long-term memory.

Each time a reading unit's meaning is accessed in long-term memory, this information is stored in short-term memory. As additional units are accessed, they are integrated with information already resident in short-term memory in an attempt to develop a model of the text. Integration takes place as new information becomes available, but capacity limitations make it difficult for short-term memory integration processes to operate over more than a few units at a time. Once propositions or sentences are "understood," they are incorporated into a schematic model that is stored in long-term memory. This schema, which represents the text, is then used to guide further processing by directing eye movements, setting categorization rules, and providing hypotheses that can be tested in short-term memory as new units are integrated with old.

A schematic outline of the interaction between short-term memory integration and the development of a long-term memory schema is presented in Figure 6. Units are decoded and attempts are made to integrate them with concepts already in short-term memory. If this is successful, the process continues until there is a proposition or concept (or sentence, in some cases) that can be incorporated into a schematic model. The model helps to guide the search for additional propositions and constructs.

Decoding at the reading unit level, the integration of concepts in short-term memory, and developing schemas all operate in line with the "logogen" model(s) put forward by Morton (1969; Morton & Patterson, 1980).

A logogen is a hypothetical mental entity that receives information from each processing stage in the reading process. This information concerns the

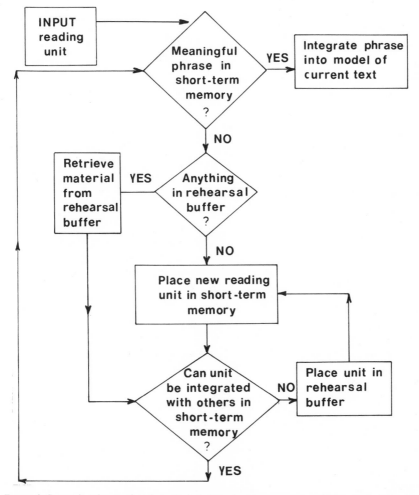

FIGURE 6. Comprehension requires that units be held in short-term memory until they can be integrated into propositions that, in turn, are integrated into schemas. The process begins with a decoded reading unit. If a meaningful proposition or phrase is already in short-term memory, this phrase is output to the schematic text model, otherwise the rehearsal buffer is examined. If empty, the new reading unit is placed in short-term memory. An attempt is made to integrate the new unit with those already in the rehearsal buffer. If unsuccessful, the new unit is also placed in the rehearsal buffer and the process repeats.

visual, phonological, and linguistic characteristics of the text being read. Logogens are also sensitive to the context in which text appears. Thus, expectancies can prime some logogens over others. Logogens all receive input simultaneously. The relevant pieces of information have a cumulative effect on the logogen. When the amount of information is great enough, a logogen becomes "active" and its "response" becomes available. The same sort of mechanism is thought to operate for concepts or propositions. Evidence is collected for several competing propositions until the logogen in favor of one reaches "activation threshold" and that logogen becomes "available." Logogens are thought to reach threshold and respond automatically.

Although the model is presented in terms of a series of stores and feedback loops, it is not assumed that processing at one stage always waits for the completion of processing at an earlier stage. Instead, it is assumed that the model operates in what McClelland (1979) describes as a "cascade." Earlier processes begin to feed information to later processes as the information becomes available and before processing is complete. This information then becomes available to later processes to operate on before earlier processes are complete. To some extent, then, processing at the various stages is simultaneous. A major difference between the present formulation and McClelland's cascade model is that higher levels in the present model do feed back to lower levels.

Within the current model, there is provision for individual differences at practically every stage in the information-processing sequence. Poor readers may differ in their ability to execute perceptual filtering and categorizing processes, in their ability to encode reading units (or in the units they encode), in their tendency to use phonological encoding as oppossed to the direct visual pathway, in their short-term memory integration routines, in their short-term memory for order, in their ability to produce and use schemas, or in the feedback loops by which the schema helps guide the reading process (using routines stored in long-term memory).

On the basis of the literature reviewed in this chapter, poor readers are expected to differ from good readers in one or more of the following ways:

1. Poor readers are expected to have slower access to overlearned codes in long-term memory.
2. Poor readers are expected to have difficulty retaining order information in short-term memory.
3. Poor readers are expected to be less automatic in their responses than good readers.
4. Poor readers should be more dependent on word and letter decoding processes than good readers.
5. Poor readers will have more trouble integrating ideas at the sentence level than good readers.

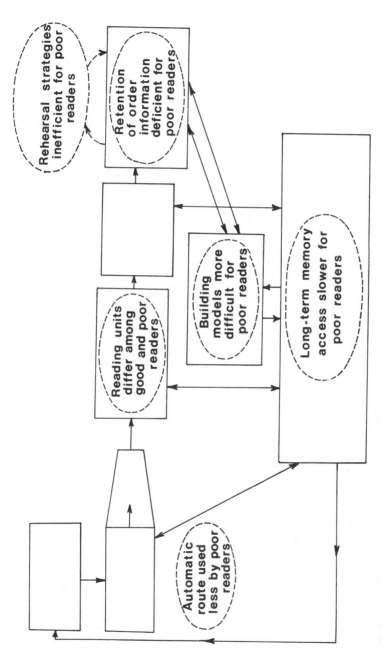

FIGURE 7. Sources of individual differences in reading ability in the information-processing model. The empty boxes refer to processing stages in the model which have not been associated with significant individual differences.

The relationship between these individual difference sources and the general model are depicted in Figure 7.

Measures of these information-processing skills are described in the following chapters. Evidence for the usefulness of these measures is examined and recommendations for their appropriate use are made.

SUMMARY

This chapter was concerned with developing an information-processing model of reading. First, the information-processing approach to important reading questions was described. It was shown that there is no single information-processing unit in reading; readers make use of different units depending on the nature of what they are reading and their skill. Reading was also shown to involve different pathways in that access to a word's meaning does not always require translating print to sound. Language knowledge and the ability to comprehend text were also discussed from an information-processing perspective. The conclusion of this discussion was that information-processing models of reading must involve top-down as well as bottom-up processes that interact to guide the reading process. The middle sections of this chapter discussed sources of individual differences from an information-processing viewpoint. Several sources of individual differences were identified. Interestingly, individual differences were more likely to be found at the decoding level than at higher text-processing levels in the reading process. It was hypothesized that individual differences were most likely to be found at the decoding level because the processes involved become automatic in skilled readers and automatic processes are most likely to reveal stable individual differences. Finally, a model of the reading process from an information-processing point of view was presented and described. Sources of individual differences in the model were identified. The following chapters discuss methods of measuring these individual differences.

PART III

THEORETICALLY BASED READING MEASURES

CHAPTER 5

THEORETICALLY BASED DECODING MEASURES

The information-processing model developed in the last chapter identified several processes thought sensitive to individual differences in reading competence. These processes may be divided into two categories: those primarily involved in decoding and those that exert their influence on comprehension. In this chapter, decoding is broadly defined to include all skills necessary to categorize print into meaningful units as well as those skills necessary to organize these units into interpretable sequences. This last skill involves retaining order information in short-term memory. Memory for the order of events is quite different from the abilities generally believed to underlie comprehension (drawing inferences, abstracting the main idea, imputing cause and effect)—all of which seem to require logical reasoning skills. For this reason, memory for order is considered part of decoding rather than comprehension.

This chapter presents several automated decoding tests as well as evidence for their reliability and validity. The tests include measures of long-term memory access speed, memory for order information, and tests of the automaticity of decoding processes. For each test, the background leading up to its use is discussed first. This is followed by a test description and, finally, the results of validating studies. The validity of the measures taken as a group are discussed at the end of the chapter.

LONG-TERM MEMORY ACCESS SPEED

In the preceding chapter, reference was made to the strong relationship between the time it takes to make same-different matches of briefly presented items (letters, words, or even meaningless shapes) and psychometric measures of verbal ability. The same-different matching task was taken to be a measure of the time required to access "name" codes in long-term memory. Specifically, the difference between match time for physically identical cases (e.g., *AA*) and name identity cases (e.g., *Aa*) provides a relatively straightforward measure of long-term memory access time. On average, the difference between name and physical match times is about 75 msecs, *but* individual differences in memory access time can be quite large (Hunt, 1978).

Hunt, Frost, and Lunneborg (1973) and Hunt, Lunneborg, and Lewis (1975) found that high verbal ability university students (those who scored in the top quarter on a verbal intelligence test) were about 35% faster on the letter matching task than low verbal ability students. Using words rather than letters as stimuli, Goldberg *et al.* (1977) obtained the same result. Goldberg *et al.* used three types of match conditions: a physical match condition (DEER–DEER), a homophonic match condition (DEER–DEAR), and a taxonomic match condition in which subjects had to decide whether two words were members of the same taxonomic category (e.g., DEER–ELK). They found that high verbal ability subjects were faster in accessing both taxonomic and homophonic codes in long-term memory than low verbals. Because both taxonomic and homophonic codes are important in reading, their findings suggest that same-different match time may be an important predictor of reading ability as well as general verbal ability. This conclusion is supported by Keating and Bobbitt (1978), who found that access to linguistic information in long-term memory becomes faster with age and, presumably, with increasing reading skill. Several other studies have confirmed the relationship between memory access speed and verbal ability; these are summarized in Table 4.

Although the strength of the relationship between memory access speed and psychometrically measured verbal ability varies from study to study, the average correlation is about $-.30$ (Carroll, 1981). The negative relationship indicates that psychometric scores increase as memory access time decreases.

Several studies have set out to investigate directly the relationship between same-different match time and reading ability. Jackson and McClelland (1979), using reading speed as their measure of reading ability, found name match time for letters correlated .47 to .49 with reading speed. A problem with this study is that although reading speed is related to reading comprehension, they are not the same thing. At least one explanation for Jackson and McClelland's finding is that both name match time and reading speed are measures of speed. (This is

TABLE 4. Memory Access Speed and Verbal Ability[a]

Group	NI − PI time
High-verbal university students	64
Normal university students	75–80
Low-verbal university students	89
Young adults not in a university	110
Severe epileptic adults	140
Adults past 60	170
10-year-old children	190
Mildly mentally retarded children	310

[a]From "Mechanics of verbal ability" by E. Hunt, 1978, *Psychological Review, 85,* p. 114. Copyright 1978 by the American Psychological Association. Reprinted by permission of the author.

also the reason that their correlation is positive.) However, studies using psychometric tests of reading comprehension as their criterion have also found a relationship between match time and reading ability. Hunt *et al.* (1981), for example, found a correlation of − .34 between semantic word matching (Goldberg *et al.*'s taxonomic category matching task) and reading comprehension. Frederiksen (1978) also found a strong relationship between same-different match time and reading ability. The correlations obtained in these studies are not only statistically significant, given the sample size usually used in these experiments, they also indicate that long-term memory access time is a significant component of reading ability, accounting for approximately 10% of the variance in reading test performance.

The fast reaction times obtained on the same-different match task for skilled readers suggested to Schwartz (1981) that long-term memory access is faster for practiced readers and that the matching task is one way to assess speed of decoding. His idea is that skilled readers respond faster on this task because they can access a word or letter's name (or sound or meaning) faster in long-term memory than unskilled readers. The first measure to be presented in this chapter was designed to measure speed of decoding. The measure is called "long-term memory access speed."

MEASUREMENT PROCEDURE: LONG-TERM MEMORY ACCESS SPEED TEST

This test, and all of the other automated measures described in this book, were programmed into a Cromemco Z-2D microcomputer. This computer was used to drive a visual display unit. It was also fitted with a response box consisting of two colored buttons and a throat microphone (plus amplifier) that could be used to measure vocalization latencies. The computing system contains 64K bytes of random access memory and two floppy disk drives. It also contains a real-time clock, an analog-to-digital converter, and a printer. Although it is possible to implement the measures to be described here on smaller microcomputers, there is a limit to how small a system can be used because of the necessity to store large amounts of data. The specifics of the computing system and the programs that implement the measures are given in more detail in a later chapter.

Subjects* to be tested on the Long-Term Memory Access Speed Test are seated about 35 cm in front of the visual display unit screen. Prior to beginning the task (or any of the other computer-based measures), the subjects engage in a 10 to 20 minute familiarization session in which they become familiar with the computing environment. The nature of this familiarization session depends on the age of the subjects to be tested. For children, the familiarization session consists of several games (tictactoe, mazes) that give them the opportunity to interact with the computer and to become at ease in the situation. For adults, the familiarization session involves using the editor to proofread a letter and also a brief game (Mastermind). This familiarization session is necessary to help subjects to settle down in an unfamiliar environment. It is a sort of computer equivalent of the clinician's establishing rapport. Many people are wary of computers and may not perform optimally without this settling-in procedure.

Following the familiarization task, subjects are told that the first test they will be involved in requires that letters be matched. They are also told that the instructions for the task will appear on the computer screen. These instructions are also read aloud by the experimenter. The specific instructions appear in Table 5.

Subjects' attention is drawn to a two-button response box. They are told to press the black button for a *same* match and the orange button if the two letters they see on the computer's screen are different. Examples of each type of response (name match = *Aa*; physical match = *AA*) are given. The instructions stress that responses should be fast but as accurate as possible. All combinations (upper and lower case) of the stimulus set *A, B, D, E, R* are used.

Once the task is explained, subjects are encouraged to ask questions. In addition, all subjects are asked to give a verbal summary of what they are supposed to do just to ensure that there is no confusion. They are then asked to rest an index finger on each button (the orange is on the left) and to proceed with some practice matches.

A star appears in the center of the video display screen, and the letters to be matched appear soon after the star in the center of the screen disappears. At 35 cm from the subject, the stimuli subtend .8 degrees of visual angle on the

---

*Although the term *subjects* has its drawbacks, it is used here to emphasize the experimental nature of the testing program.

TABLE 5. Long-Term Memory Access Speed Test

Instructions

This is a game to see how well you can tell letters apart. In each trial, you will be shown two letters taken from the set of letters

A, B, D, E, R, a, b, d, e, r.

As soon as you see them, try to decide as quickly but as accurately as possible whether the letters are the same or different.

The letters are the same if they have either the same shape and the same sound, for example, A A, or if they have a different shape but the same sound, for example a A.

If you think the letters are the same, press the black button. If you think the letters are different, press the orange button. For example, if you were shown the letters

R   R

then the correct thing to do would be to press the black button as these two letters have both the same shape and the same sound. If you were shown the letters

B   b

you would also press the black button, as even though these letters have a different shape, they both have the same sound.

But if you were shown the letters

E   d

you would press the orange button because these letters are different. They do not have the same shape, and they do not have the same sound.

You will now be given two sets of practice trials. For the first set of practice trials, the letters will disappear when you answer. In between trials, a star will appear. When you are ready to begin, press the orange button.

(First set of practice trials is presented)

For this next set of practice trials, we will be speeding things up a little. The two letters will stay on for only a very short time, much shorter than they did for the first set of practice trials. You must answer before the star appears.

Remember: The two letters are the same if they have either the same shape and the same sound, for example, A A, or if they have a different shape but the same sound, for example, a A.

If you think the letters are the same, then press the black button. If you think the letters are different, then press the orange button.

(Second set of practice trials is presented)

That is the end of the practice trials. The real trials are next.

(Nonpractice trials are presented)

horizontal axis and 1 degree on the vertical axis. Subjects who wear spectacles are instructed to wear them throughout the test. For the practice matches, the letters remain on the screen until one of the two buttons is pressed. After the examinees have successfully completed the first set of practice matches, they are told that subsequent match trials will only permit a short time for a response before the letters disappear. Therefore, they should try to respond quickly and accurately. The next practice match trial, and all test matches, consists of a fixation star that appears in the middle of the screen for $\frac{1}{10}$ second followed by a pair of letters that remain visible in the center of the screen for $\frac{1}{2}$ second or until a button is pushed, whichever comes first. One-tenth of a second intervenes between matches. The subjects are given feedback about their performance after 50 practice matches. This feedback consists of their mean reaction time for the preceding 50 matches as well as the percentage of their matches that were correct. The purpose of this feedback is to maintain motivation by inducing a set to achieve high speed and accuracy. If accuracy is below 50%, the 50 speeded practice matches are repeated until this criterion is reached.

The actual Long-Term Memory Access Speed Test commences immediately following the practice matches. The test consists of five blocks of 30 matches each. Feedback is provided after each block, and subjects can rest as long as they like between blocks.

Several items of data are accumulated by the computer for this test. First, the reaction time on each match is recorded. Second, the response (same or different) is noted. These data are stored along with the actual match type presented. Thus, after the test is completed, each subject's data file includes match reaction times (RT) for *physically identical* trials (e.g., *AA*), *name identical* trials (e.g., *Aa*) and *different* trials (e.g., *AB*). Also recorded is whether the subject's response was accurate or incorrect. An example of the data file for one subject appears in Table 6.

TABLE 6. Long-Term Memory Access Speed Test: Sample Summary Data File[a]

Block	Mismatch number correct	Physical		Name	
		Number correct	Average RT	Number correct	Average RT
1	5	15	137	15	125
2	15	16	634	15	730
3	10	10	682	8	749
4	9	10	588	8	763
5	8	10	656	9	746
6	9	10	764	6	846
7	10	10	695	9	804

[a]All times in msecs. Blocks 1 and 2 are practice.

RELIABILITY AND VALIDITY STUDY 1

To assess the reliability and validity of the Long-Term Memory Access Speed Test, a reliability and validity study was conducted by Tim Griffin of the University of Queensland.

Subjects. Fifty-one randomly selected female students at an Australian technical school served as subjects. Their ages ranged from 15.5 to 20 years, with a mean of 16. They were enrolled in secretarial studies and remedial courses, and all had been previously tested with a standardized reading test.

Environment. All subjects were tested in a quiet room equipped with a desk and several comfortable chairs. After first engaging in the familiarization exercises described in the last section, each subject proceeded through the Long-Term Memory Access Speed Test. Subjects also participated in other tests that will be described later in this chapter.

Psychometric Test. Every subject in this study was tested with the GAPA-DOL reading test (McLeod & Anderson, 1972). The GAPADOL is a variation of the GAP test developed by McLeod (1965). Whereas the GAP test is used for children under 12 years of age, the GAPADOL is designed for adolescents. Both tests use the cloze technique, which requires subjects to fill in words missing from short passages. The responses are scored with reference to the most appropriate criterion words as supplied by the test publisher. Several GAPADOL examples appear in Table 7. The GAPADOL has not only been standardized on the Australian population, but it also provides a fast, easy to administer, and reliable (the median split-half reliability coefficient is .91 for five different year groups) measure of reading comprehension. Performance on cloze tests like the GAPADOL has been shown to correlate highly with scores obtained on other measures of reading comprehension (Rankin & Culhane, 1969).

The subjects had been tested with the GAPADOL approximately 4 months prior to the present study. The highest possible score on the test is 83. The raw

TABLE 7. Sample GAPADOL Items[a]

Item	Answer
"Ten, nine, eight, seven, six, five, four, three, _____, one, zero. Fire!" . . .	two
Mars is the only planet whose solid surface can be _____ and studied; . . .	seen[b]

[a]From *GAPADOL reading comprehension manual* by J. McLeod and J. Anderson, 1972, Melbourne; Heinemann Educational Australia. Copyright 1972 by Heinemann Educational Australia. Reprinted by permission.
[b]Synonyms of the correct answer are also acceptable.

scores of the sample ranged from a low of 15 to a high of 73. The mean was 44.24, and the standard deviation was 11.60. This is equivalent to an average reading age of about 15.1.

Results

Means. The mean physical match time was 596.73 msecs (standard deviation = 39.98); the mean name match time was 711.67 msecs (standard deviation = 51.49). These reaction times are slightly slower (60 to 70 msecs) than those reported by Hunt *et al.* (1975) and by Jackson and McClelland (1979), who both used university students as subjects but about the same as other studies using nonuniversity populations (see Hunt, 1978).

Reliability. Split-half reliability was calculated by comparing the means on alternate match blocks for correct reaction times corrected using the Spearman–Brown formula. The reaction time reliability was found to be .90, which is statistically significant ($p < .01$). This high reliability has also been reported for matching tasks by Hunt *et al.* (1981), who found reliabilities of .90 and higher for many matching tasks. Thus, it seems safe to conclude that the Long-Term Memory Access Speed Test is at least as reliable as most psychometric tests and perhaps even more reliable than the GAPADOL.

Validity. The typical way to approach the question of validity is to examine how well a measure predicts performance on criterion tests (or behaviors) thought to reflect the ability in question. In the present study, this means examining the relationship between performance on the Long-Term Memory Access Speed Test and performance on the GAPADOL. Before this can be done, however, one problem must be overcome. The Long-Term Memory Access Speed Test is conceived to be a test of how quickly an individual can access information in long-term memory. To measure this, we must assume that long-term memory access has, indeed, occurred. If an error is made in a match (saying "same" instead of "different" or vice versa), we cannot say that long-term memory access has occurred. The individual could have merely been guessing on the basis of visual appearance or the subject may have been responding randomly. In other words, errors on the Long-Term Memory Access Speed Test are uninterpretable. Although subjects in previous experiments have been found to make very few errors (see Goldberg *et al.*, 1977; Hunt *et al.*, 1973, 1975), this was not true in the present experiment. Some subjects made errors on 10% of the match trials. Although error patterns were not found to be related to GAPADOL scores, there were some relationships between errors and speed within the Long-Term Memory Access Speed Test itself. These relationships will be dealt with later in this section. For now, it is important to note that to ensure that long-term memory access time is actually being measured, only reaction times for subjects who made fewer than 10% errors were analyzed in the first instance.

Three different statistics were derived from the Long-Term Memory Access Speed Test. These are physical identity match reaction time (PI), name identity reaction time (NI), and the difference between these two reaction times (NI − PI). The last statistic is thought to be particularly sensitive to long-term memory access time (Hunt, 1978). Each of these statistics was correlated with GAPADOL scores separately for each trial block. The median correlations were: PI time and GAPADOL = −.16; NI time and GAPADOL = −.19; and NI − PI and GAPADOL = −.21. Only the NI − PI correlation reached statistical significance ($p < .05$, one tailed).

The low correlation between PI match time and GAPADOL score was not unexpected, as physical matches do not require access to long-term memory codes; they require only the time necessary to compare two stimuli and carry out a button-pressing response. Because NI matches require long-term memory access as well as the time necessary to organize a button-press, its correlation with the GAPADOL is understandably higher. The difference score (NI − PI) eliminates the time required to compare two stimuli and organize a button-press, leaving just the time it takes to access long-term memory. This pure measure of access time correlated at a statistically significant level with GAPADOL scores. Although the correlation found in this study is slightly lower than the average correlation of −.30 found in studies using general verbal ability tests as their criterion (Carroll, 1981), it is very close to those reported by Hunt *et al.* (1981), who used a reading comprehension test as one of their criterion measures.

An investigation of the error patterns made by subjects in the present validational study did not show any relationship between errors on any of the match types and score on the GAPADOL. The correlations between errors on NI matches, PI matches, and different matches and the GAPADOL were −.08, .03, and −.01 respectively. Thus, there is no indication that matching accuracy, itself, is related to comprehension. There was also no evidence for a speed–accuracy trade-off. That is, if subjects were sacrificing accuracy for speed, then we would expect to find a negative correlation between reaction time and errors (as reaction times get shorter, the number of errors increases). Instead, these correlations were positive; slower subjects made more classification errors. This suggests that it is the subjects with slow access to long-term memory who are also most likely to make errors, probably because they did not have time to access the proper code before the letters disappeared.

The analyses performed so far seem to provide support for the validity of the Long-Term Memory Access Speed Test as measuring an important component of reading comprehension (it accounts for around five percent of the variance in scores on a measure of reading comprehension). However, the relationship between the NI − PI statistic and long-term memory access speed may not be as simple as first thought.

The logic behind the NI − PI measure is that NI match times reflect a process (long-term memory access) that is not part of PI match time. This extra process is thought to add time to NI matches. So, subtracting PI from NI match time should leave the time required for long-term memory access. If this logic is correct, manipulations designed to affect only PI matching should have no effect on NI − PI match times. However, Kirsner, Wells, and Sang (1982) found that manipulating letter similarity does not effect only PI match time but NI − PI times as well. This suggests that the logic assuming two independent processes in PI and NI matches may be incorrect.

Carroll (1981) has also questioned the logic behind subtracting PI from NI reaction time to obtain a pure measure of long-term memory access speed. He argued that this procedure was somewhat arbitrary and lacking in proof. Because the NI − PI formula implicitly weights the NI variable as +1 and the PI variable as −1 when predicting reading scores, Carroll suggested that the standardized regression weights for NI and PI should approximate +1 and −1 when regressed against criterion measures such as the GAPADOL. A regression analysis performed on the present data (for all blocks) produced regression weights of −.31 and +.28 for the NI and PI variables respectively. These regression weights are not only opposite in sign to those predicted by the NI − PI logic, their ratio of 2 to 1 indicates that they are not equally important predictors. It should also be noted that NI and PI reaction times are highly correlated ($r = .67$, $p < .01$). Thus, although it seems that NI − PI is certainly related to memory retrieval speed, it is not possible to say that it is the pure measure of long-term memory access time that we would like it to be.

A rather different problem is the finding that to some extent, the size of the correlation between NI − PI reaction time and reading comprehension depends on the measure of reading comprehension an experimenter decides to use. This point is brought home clearly by the varying validity coefficients reported in the literature. Experimenters who use different measures of reading comprehension observe different correlations between NI − PI and reading scores. By far the highest correlations are produced by reading measures with a substantial speed component. Jackson and McClelland (1979) used reading speed as their measure of reading ability and found a higher correlation between long-term memory access time and reading competence than Hunt et al. (1981), who used a more traditional psychometric measure. The reading comprehension test used in the present study, the GAPADOL, is time limited, but the time permitted is so generous that virtually no one fails to complete all the questions in the time allowed. Thus, the difference between the correlations found in the present study and those reported by Jackson and McClelland could be the result of the low speed component in the GAPADOL measure. Schwartz, Griffin, and Brown (1983) investigated the relationship between the NI − PI statistic and two criterion measures of reading competence. One of these was the GAPADOL test and the other was a reading-speed measure. They found the NI − PI statistic a better predictor of reading speed than reading comprehension. (Their analysis showed NI − PI to be a poorer predictor of GAPADOL performance than the current results because they calculated their correlations on a more restricted population of subjects.)

Schwartz et al. (1983) interpreted their findings to indicate that the Long-Term Memory Access Speed Test is more a measure of cognitive speed than cognitive power. By power, they meant cognitive functioning that is independent of time considerations. Most psychometric verbal-ability tests have a speed component (see Donlon & Angoff, 1971) that may account for as much as nine percent of their score variance. As Carroll (1981) notes, the typical correlation of NI − PI reaction time with psychometric tests is about − .30, which is exactly the square root of .09. It is, therefore, tempting to hypothesize that the correlation between measures of long-term memory access time and psychometric verbal ability tests may actually reflect the speed component of the psychometric tests.

The data reviewed so far suggest that the Long-Term Memory Access Speed Test is a reliable measure that taps the *speed* it takes to access letter names in long-term memory. In the last chapter, it was argued that access to long-term memory codes is faster for skilled readers. It was also asserted that highly practiced skills are more likely to reveal individual differences than less well learned ones. One way to see this is to plot NI − PI reaction time as a function of GAPADOL scores. For this purpose, subjects were divided equally into three reading groups (low, medium, and high) on the basis of their GAPADOL scores. Figure 8 illustrates changes in NI − PI time as a function of reading group. As can be seen, there is not much difference between the two lower reading groups, but there is a marked decrease in NI − PI reaction time for the highest reading group. This sharp decrease appears to occur around 100 msecs. Jackson and McClelland (1979) reported NI − PI times of about 90 msecs for their fast readers. Hunt (1978) reports NI − PI times of 110 for a young, noncollege group. This does not mean that NI − PI match times cannot become any faster than 90 to 110 msecs. Rather, this level appears to be average for skilled readers.

The test described here is concerned with letter names, but there is other information stored in long-term memory with relevance for reading. There are phonemic rules for pronouncing words, taxonomic rules providing semantic information, and so on. Experiments have shown that matching tasks designed to measure memory access time for various types of information other than letter names also produce reaction times that are related to criterion measures of verbal ability and reading competence (Goldberg et al., 1977; Hunt et al., 1981; Jackson & McClelland, 1979). Jackson (1980) found that good readers even match line drawings faster than poor readers. On the basis of these findings, Jackson and McClelland (1981) characterized skilled readers as having generally faster perceptual processing speed than poor readers.

To investigate more closely the notion of general perceptual processing speed as well as to determine whether the Long-Term Memory Access Speed

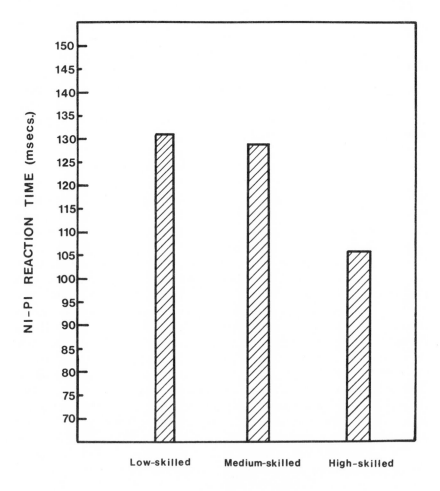

READING GROUP

FIGURE 8. NI − PI reaction time as a function of reading ability.

Test could be improved by using stimuli other than letters as the match targets, a second validity study was undertaken by Timothy Wiedel of the University of Mississippi. This study is described next (see Wiedel & Schwartz, 1982, for a fuller report).

RELIABILITY AND VALIDITY STUDY 2

Subjects. Twenty-six male and 30 female subjects were randomly chosen from a population of university students and the staff of a university hospital. Their mean age was 21.9 years (standard deviation = 2.4). Their education level varied from high school to postdoctoral, with an average of 15 years schooling (standard deviation = 2.0).

Psychometric Test. All subjects were administered the Lorge–Thorndike Intelligence Scale (Lorge, Thorndike, & Hagen, 1964). Although the subjects received all the subtests of the test, the one of special interest here is verbal subtest two, which is a cloze test similar to the GAPADOL. There are 48 items on this test. The mean score of the sample was 12.17 (standard deviation = 3.49).

Long-Term Memory Access Speed Tests. Instead of letters, subjects in this study were asked to match two arrows. In one condition, the subjects were asked to indicate a match if both arrows were pointing down. Otherwise, they were to indicate "different." In a second condition, subjects were required to indicate a match if the two arrows were pointing in the same direction (left, right, up, or down) and to indicate different if the arrows were pointing in different directions. The first arrow-match condition was considered more difficult, as it involved retrieving from long-term memory the meaning of the concept "down." The second arrow-matching task was thought to be similar to a physical identity match. For both conditions, the probability of a match was 50%. Besides the two arrow-matching conditions, subjects were asked to match words that were physically identical (chair–chair) or words that belonged to the same taxonomic category (chair–table). The taxonomic category words were selected from the Battig and Montague (1969) category norms. Half the matches used high-frequency category members and half used moderate-frequency category members. All of the words were between four and six letters long (both match targets were the same length on a particular trial). All subjects completed all tasks but not in the same order. One-third began with arrow matching, one-third with the physical identity task, and one-third with taxonomic matching.

Results

Means. As in Reliability and Validity Study 1, only reaction times from trials in which the correct response was made were analyzed. The mean reaction times for the arrow and word match tasks are given in Table 8. These reaction times are very similar to those reported by Goldberg *et al.* (1977) and by Jackson (1980).

Reliability. Reliability was calculated for the word-matching tasks by correlating one-half of the word match reaction times with the remaining half. These correlations were corrected using the Spearman–Brown formula. The reliability coefficient for the word match tasks was .93. The same procedure was followed to calculate the reliabilities of the two arrow-match tasks, which were .86 and

CHAPTER 5

TABLE 8. Reliability and Validity Study 2 Means and Standard Deviations[a]

Tests	Mean	Standard deviation
Arrows (same direction)	525	117
Arrows (pointing down)	547	91
Physically identical words	636	114
Taxonomic category match	1031	209

[a]From "Verbal Ability and Memory Processing Speed" by T. C. Wiedel and S. Schwartz, 1982, *Current Psychological Research, 2*, p. 252. Copyright 1982 by *Current Psychological Research*. Adapted by permission.

.91 for the *both down* and *same direction* tasks respectively. All of these values are statistically significant ($p < .01$).

Validity. The correlations between the arrow-matching and word-matching tasks and subtest 2 (the cloze test) of the Lorge–Thorndike are given in the first column of Table 9. Only the difficult arrow-matching task ("Are both arrows pointing down?") reached statistical significance as a predictor of subtest 2 scores ($p < .05$, one tailed). When reaction times on the easier arrow-matching task ("Are both arrows pointing in the same direction?") were subtracted from those produced on the more difficult task, the resulting difference score correlated slightly higher with the cloze test than either match task did alone. The increase, however, was not great enough to change the overall conclusion—word- and arrow-matching tasks are no better predictors of cloze-type comprehension scores than letter-match times.

Because the subjects received all subtests of the Lorge–Thorndike, including vocabulary, verbal analogies, and arithmetic tests, the matching tasks were also correlated with total verbal IQ score. These correlations appear in column

TABLE 9. Correlations Between Matching Tests and Cloze Subtest of the Lorge–Thorndike, Verbal IQ, and Education

Tests	Cloze subtest	Verbal IQ	Education
Arrows (same direction)	− .20	− .25[c]	− .17
Arrows (both down)	− .29[b]	− .39[b]	− .07
Physically identical words	− .19	− .18	− .24[b]
Taxonomic Category Match (High frequency category members)	− .20	− .28[b]	− .32[c]

[a]From "Verbal Ability and Memory Processing Speed" by T. C. Wiedel and S. Schwartz, 1982, *Current Psychological Research*, p. 252. Copyright 1982 by *Current Psychological Research*. Adapted by permission.
[b]$p < .05$.
[c]$p < .01$.

two of Table 9. Except for the more difficult matching task, these correlations are not much different from those found in column one. The higher correlation for the difficult arrow-matching task was due to the verbal analogies subtest, which correlated $-.32$ with arrow-match reaction time. It is unclear whether this correlation is the result of a speed component in both measures or whether the difficult arrow-matching task requires more abstract reasoning than is immediately apparent.

Finally, because education level was available for each subject, the tests were correlated with this variable as well. These correlations appear in column three of Table 9. As can be seen, and not surprisingly, education level correlates with word tasks but not with arrow-matching tasks. It seems that while everyone is familiar with arrows, differential familiarity with the words used in the word-matching task could have made a difference to match times. For this reason, match tasks that do not require special knowledge (like the arrow-matching task and presumably the letter-matching task, for just about everyone could be expected to know the alphabet) are better measures of long-term memory access than tasks that require special knowledge. The independence of arrow-matching tasks from education level is illustrated by computing the partial correlation of arrow match time with IQ, thereby removing the effect of education level. This procedure leaves the correlation relatively unchanged at $-.36$.

These results show that the letter match test is as good a predictor as the arrow match or word-match tasks. Although word matches are closer to actual reading than either arrow matches or letter matches, the two latter tests are actually better predictors of reading comprehension scores than the former. This is because they are less dependent on specialized knowledge of words and, therefore, less contaminated by factors other than long-term memory access time. Because it does do not require special knowledge beyond the alphabet, the letter matching test is suitable for young children and relatively culture free.

An analysis of reaction times in the arrow-matching task revealed a pattern similar to that for letter matching. Reaction time differences between the two arrow-match tasks were about the same for low and moderate scorers on the cloze subtest of the Lorge–Thorndike but much faster for high scorers. A regression analysis indicated that the relationship between arrow match times and cloze scores was nonlinear with a marked decrease for the upper third of the cloze test scores. Interestingly, reaction times appeared to be lower for arrow than for letter matching by about 50 msecs.

Finally, in order to evaluate Jackson's (1980) notion that general perceptual-processing speed is faster among good readers, a principle-components analysis and varimax rotation of axes was conducted using all of the matching tasks and all of the Lorge–Thorndike subtest scores as variables. This analysis was designed to determine what underlying regularities exist in the relationships of these measures. This analysis produced a solution in which the first component accounted for 56% of the variance of the entire set of variables. This component not only loaded highly on subtest 2 (the cloze subtest) but also on every match task, particularly the arrow match task. The remaining components were specific to each measurement method producing a component for paper and pencil tasks, a component for reaction time tasks, and so on. Thus, it appears that Jackson's (1980) characterization may be correct; there does seem to be a general perceptual-processing factor measured by matching tasks, and good readers seem to be faster on these tasks than poor readers. Some matching tasks are better reflections of this skill than others because they are less likely to be contaminated by extraneous factors such as word knowledge.

THE LONG-TERM MEMORY ACCESS SPEED TEST: PRELIMINARY CONCLUSIONS

The validational studies presented here support the reliability and validity of the Long-Term Memory Access Speed Test as a measure of one of the component skills (perceptual processing) underlying reading competence. Access to long-term memory codes is crucial for decoding print; and the faster that this can be done, the more time available for the more elaborative processing necessary for reading comprehension. To the extent that long-term memory access is highly practiced, it makes only minimal demands on cognitive capacity. This leaves more capacity devoted to comprehension. On the basis of previous results and the current findings, it appears that long-term memory access for letter names requires about 100 msecs. The usefulness of this observation will be returned to later in this chapter. First, several more tests will be described. Those in the next section are concerned with multi-letter sequences rather than single-letter comparisons.

WORD DECODING

In the preceding chapter, the evidence in favor of two reading pathways (a direct visual route and one that requires phonemic recoding) was reviewed. It was concluded that although there are problems with the two-route model, there was considerable evidence that short, common, regularly spelled English words were pronounced faster than rare words or pronounceable pseudowords. According to the model presented at the end of the last chapter, the advantage of common words lies in their easier access in long-term memory. That is, for these words, processing proceeds directly from the sensory buffer to long-term memory. This occurs without conscious attention and without taxing cognitive capacity. Pseudowords (or rare words), may go through one or more additional decoding stages before their meaning (and associated codes) are accessed in long-term memory. The extra processing takes time; this is why reaction times are longer to pseudowords (there is a longer latency between seeing a pseudoword and reading it aloud) than to real words.

Researchers who have measured pronunciation latencies for rare and common words as well as for pseudowords (regular but meaningless nonwords such as *boppy*) have found that pronunciation latency is related to reading competence as measured by psychometric tests of reading ability. Frederiksen (1981), for example, found vocalization latencies to pseudowords to decrease as a direct function of reading ability. He also found that making words and pseudowords longer had a greater effect on poor readers (it slowed them down more) than good readers.

An interesting aspect of Frederiksen's results was the correlation between real and pseudoword pronunciation latencies. He found this correlation to be higher among poor readers than among good readers, and this difference was particularly large for high frequency words. The implication of this finding is that good readers use different methods to read high- and low-frequency words, whereas the poor readers use the same type of analysis for both. Frederiksen also found that providing a strong context for a word (presenting it in a sentence rather than in isolation) led to a greater decrease in vocalization latency for good readers than for poor readers. Interestingly, poor readers showed hardly any improvement in their vocalization latencies for rare words. It is as if they could not make use of the context in helping them find the word and had to rely instead on the same decoding processes they use for isolated words. This interpretation is supported by Frederiksen's report that for poor readers, word pronunciation time in context was correlated more with pseudoword vocalization latency than for good readers. It seems that poor readers use the same decoding strategies for both real and pseudowords, whereas good readers adjust their strategy to suit the circumstances.

The test described in this section is designed to take advantage of the findings reported by Frederiksen (1981) as well as those reported elsewhere in the literature (Goldberg *et al.*, 1977; Hunt *et al.*, 1981). The test measures "depth-of-processing in reading." It is called the Word-Decoding Test.

MEASUREMENT PROCEDURE: WORD-DECODING TEST

This test is administered by the computer described in the discussion of the Long-Term Memory Access Speed Test. Subjects are seated in the manner described for that test, and they are given a similar familiarization session prior to testing.

The Word-Decoding Test has two parts. The first measures vocalization latencies to a set of real words and matched pseudowords. The second task measures vocalization latencies to a graded list of words standardized for difficulty on the Australian population.

Part 1. Sixteen words and 16 pseudowords serve as the target stimuli for Part 1. These words were chosen from a list compiled by Stewart and Andrews (1979). Words were chosen so that they fell equally into 3, 4, 5, and 6 phoneme* groups. Half of each phoneme group were high-frequency words (words that appear more than 500 times in the Kučera and Francis 1967 list) and half were medium-frequency words (these appear between 190 and 260 times in the Kučera and Francis list). The pseudowords were constructed by changing a vowel in each word for another vowel (*church* was changed to *charch* for example) or by changing one consonant for another (*moment* was changed to *mosent*). Care was taken to ensure that all pseudowords are pronounceable. A high-frequency pseudoword is one derived from a high-frequency word; a medium-frequency pseudoword is one derived from a medium-frequency word. The words and pseudowords used in Part 1 of the Word-Decoding Test appear in Table 10.

Subjects tested with the Word-Decoding Test are told that they will be reading words as well as made-up words as they appear on the computer screen. Each subject is fitted with a sensitive throat microphone just to the left of their Adam's apple. The throat microphone is held in place with a length of surgical tape. This throat microphone is used to signal the computer that a vocalization has begun, thereby permitting the computer to record the latency from the appearance of an item on the screen to the subject's response. The microphone is dead between trials. The instructions to each subject stress accuracy. They are also told not to make any sounds other than pronouncing the words they will see. The complete instructions given to examinees is given in Table 11. These instructions are read aloud by the examiner, who asks each subject to summarize them.

A list of 10 real and 10 pseudowords (repeated twice) serves as practice. These words do not appear in the test list. After completing the practice lists, each examines receives 16 real and 16 pseudowords in blocks of 32. Each block

TABLE 10. Words Used in Part 1 of Word-Decoding Test

name	river	carlet	frog	brick
floder	garden	nist	jumper	biver
flower	nabe	dish	blick	jusper
gardeb	nest	carpet	gish	freg
love	money	mother	person	dress
moment	book	paper	bove	moley
mither	pegson	gress	mosent	vook
pafer	time	home	water	power
world	church	problem	business	tume
hote	wamer	poner	borld	char ch
problet	buriness			

*Phonemes are individual sounds, not syllables.

TABLE 11. Word-Decoding Test: Part 1 Instructions[a]

You will be shown 32 different words, one at a time. Each word will be repeated three times. When you see a word, we want you to try to say it aloud.

Half of these words will be words that you will probably have seen before, for example, "baby." The other half of the words will be made-up words that you will not have seen before, for example, "bapy."

It is important that you try to say each word aloud, but please do not try to say the word until after you have finished reading it to yourself. Don't worry if you think you have said a word incorrectly. All we want you to do is to try to say each word aloud. It is also very important that you say only the word. Please do not say "Um" or "Ah" or anything else before you say the word. When you have said each word, press the orange button and hold it down until the next word appears.

You will now be given some practice words. When you are ready to begin the practice words, press the G button and hold it down until the first word comes on.

(Practice words are presented.)

Very Good!

That is the end of the practice words. The real words are next. Press the G button when you are ready to begin the real words.

(Nonpractice words are presented.)

---

[a]This test has two parts, Part 1 and Part 2.

is equally divided among high and medium frequency and 3-, 4-, 5-, and 6-phoneme pseudowords. The entire block is repeated three times, each time in a different random order. For each word presented, the computer records vocalization latency, and the experimenter notes whether the word is pronounced accurately. The task is completely self-paced. A new item does not appear on the screen until the examinee indicates (by pushing a button) that he or she is ready.

Part 2. Part 2 also requires that the examinee read words (no pseudowords in this part), as they appear on the computer screen. This time, however, the items that appear are the 100 words of the Schonell *New Order Graded Word Reading Test* (1980). These words (see Table 12) are ordered in terms of increasing difficulty for Australian readers. Each subject's latency and accuracy is recorded. If the latency exceeds by more than 2 seconds the subject's mean latency to real words in Part 1, the word is repeated a second time. If the latency still exceeds by more than 2 seconds, the previous mean latency to real words, the test is ended and the last word reached is recorded. The reason for ending the test this way is to avoid the frustration that might result from stumbling over many difficult words. Pilot testing has indicated that once the latency exceeds 2 seconds plus the previous mean, it is unlikely that any further words will be

TABLE 12. Word-Decoding Test: Part 2 Word List

school	tree	little	milk	book
flower	playing	road	train	light
egg	clock	people	bun	summer
picture	think	sit	dream	frog
something	island	sandwich	postage	downstairs
thirsty	crowd	beginning	nephew	biscuit
shepherd	saucer	canary	appeared	angel
ceiling	gradually	imagine	attractive	smoulder
knowledge	diseased	nourished	university	recent
disposal	situated	forfeit	fascinate	audience
intercede	orchestra	gnome	applaud	choir
heroic	colonel	plausible	physics	siege
soloist	systematic	campaign	slovenly	genuine
classification	prophecy	conscience	preliminary	scintillate
sabre	adamant	pivot	miscellaneous	enigma
susceptible	institution	antique	satirical	oblivion
procrastinate	pneumonia	homonym	terrestrial	rescind
belligerent	statistics	tyrannical	somnambulist	judicature
evangelical	fictitious	metamorphosis	beguile	sepulchre
ineradicable	grotesque	preferential	idiosyncrasy	bibliography

correctly pronounced. The instructions for Part 2 of the Word-Decoding Test appear in Table 13.

The data accumulated for this test include vocalization latencies for each type of word and pseudoword (high and low frequency, 3, 4, 5, and 6 phonemes) as well as vocalization latencies for each of the words in Part 2 along with the last word read if the testee could not complete the list. Accuracy is recorded by the examiner. An example of the data file for one subject appears in Table 14.

RELIABILITY AND VALIDITY STUDY 3

To assess the reliability and validity of the Word-Decoding Test, a study was conducted by Tim Griffin. The subjects for this study were the same 51 who participated in the Long-Term Memory Access Test Reliability and Validity

TABLE 13. Word-Decoding Test: Part 2 Instructions

You will now be shown a different list of words. All of these words will be real words, and you will see each word only once. As before, when you see a word, we want you to try to say it aloud.

It is important that you try to say each word aloud, but please do not try to say the word until after you have finished reading it to yourself. Don't worry if you think you have said a word incorrectly. All we want you to do is to try to say each word aloud. It is also very important you say only the word. Please do not say "Um" or "Ah" or anything else before you say the word. When you have said each word, press the orange button and hold it down until the next word appears.

TABLE 14. Word-Decoding Test Sample Data Summary File[a]

Number of phonemes	Medium word latency	Medium pseudoword latency	High word latency	High pseudoword latency
Block 1				
3	760	932	776	967
4	670	937	702	830
5	693	803	692	841
6	849	1100	1292	1402
Block 2				
3	656	766	630	802
4	768	719	663	764
5	1334	1639	1314	1711
6	1510	2114	2002	2272
Block 3				
3	740	789	636	646
4	630	750	671	731
5	1916	2658	1976	2537
6	2229	3102	2805	3209

[a]All times in msecs.

Study 1. The setting as well as familiarization procedures were identical to those described earlier.

Results

Reliabilities (Part 1). Each subject had three opportunities to pronounce each item (once in each block). To calculate reliabilities, only the last two blocks were used. For each type of item, block two latency was correlated with block three latency (two phoneme high-frequency word with two phoneme high-frequency word and so on). The overall correlation (corrected) was found to be .90, which is statistically significant ($p < .01$).

Reliabilities (Part 2). As subjects only completed Part 2 once, no reliabilities were calculated for this study; these reliabilities were calculated for Reliability and Validity Study 4, which is discussed later in this chapter.

Means (Part 1). The mean latency for each condition in Part 1 appears in Table 15. Note that medium-frequency words have longer latencies than high-frequency words, an indication that phonemic processing (reading out loud) does not take place phoneme by phoneme. Instead, subjects appear to examine the whole word first before trying to pronounce it. Shorter words have shorter latencies than longer words, and the same pattern appears for pseudowords.

TABLE 15. Mean Latencies for Words and Pseudowords[a]

Number of phonemes	Medium word latency	Medium pseudoword latency	High word latency	High pseudoword latency
3	655	840	737	910
4	683	819	719	954
5	1461	1970	1348	2110
6	1414	2088	1478	2122

[a]Latencies are rounded off to the nearest millisecond.

Finally, as expected, real words have shorter latencies than pseudowords, indicating that at least some of the processes used to pronounce real words are highly practiced.

Means (Part 2). Means for Part 2 are given later in this chapter, following a discussion of Part 1 validity.

Validity

GAPADOL scores served as the criterion for reading comprehension ability. The first step was to correlate GAPADOL scores with each subject's mean latency to real and pseudowords. These correlations were $-.15$ and $-.32$ for real and pseudowords respectively. The second correlation is statistically significant ($p < .01$, one tailed). The negative correlations indicate that as latencies decrease, GAPADOL scores increase.

The correlations of latencies with GAPADOL scores were calculated on the entire sample of subjects. If, however, we look only at subjects who made 10% or more errors, the correlations are $-.08$ and $-.57$ for real word and pseudoword latencies respectively. These correlations make quite clear the relationship between pseudoword latencies and comprehension particularly for inaccurate readers.

Frederiksen (1981) hypothesized that poor readers use the same strategies for real and pseudowords, whereas skilled readers adopt different strategies for the two tasks. To explore this hypothesis more closely, contrasts were calculated in which the difference between real word and pseudoword latencies were correlated with GAPADOL scores. The object was to determine whether those contrasts with the largest differences had the highest correlations. Such a finding would indicate that GAPADOL scores are related to pseudoword reading strategies and that the less efficient these are, the lower the GAPADOL score.

The hypothesis was confirmed. Three-phoneme real words were pronounced only slightly faster than three-phoneme pseudowords (see Table 15). The difference between their latencies correlated $-.15$ with GAPADOL scores.

In contrast, the difference in latency for the pronunciation of six-phoneme real words and pseudowords correlated $-.28$ with GAPADOL scores. Similarly, the difference in latencies between high-frequency real words and pseudowords correlated $-.33$ with GAPADOL scores, whereas the medium frequency word minus medium frequency pseudoword latency difference correlated $-.41$ with GAPADOL scores. Overall, the difference in latencies between all real words and pseudowords correlated $-.39$ with GAPADOL scores, thereby accounting for 16% of the variance in the reading comprehension test's scores.

These results support the hypothesis that good readers use different strategies to decode real words and pseudowords, whereas poor readers try to apply the same strategy to both types of items. Because their word pronunciation strategies are not efficient for pseudowords, poor readers show a marked slowing down for these items.

To compare the current results more directly with Frederiksen's (1981), subjects were divided into high- and low-ability reading comprehension groups on the basis of their scores on the GAPADOL (they were split into a high-ability group of 26 subjects and a low-ability group of 25 subjects, using the median GAPADOL score as the cutoff). The correlation between GAPADOL scores and the difference between latencies to real words and pseudowords was calculated for each reading group. These correlations were .87 for the low reading-ability group and .63 for the high reading-ability group. A similar difference between reading groups was also reported by Frederiksen. They support his idea that poor readers use similar strategies to pronounce both types of items, whereas skilled readers adapt their strategy to the type of item (real or pseudoword) being presented.

In an attempt to identify strategy differences, Frederiksen (1981) characterized poor readers as dealing with real words and pseudowords at the same "level of processing." Skilled readers, on the other hand, seem to be able to vary their processing level depending on the type of item to be read. One way they could do this is to use the direct reading route from the sensory buffer to the stored phonological code in long-term memory for familiar words and the indirect reading route (in which phonemes are encoded into multiletter units first) for pseudowords. These different routes would produce lower correlations between word and pseudoword reading times for skilled readers compared with poor readers who encode both real words and pseudowords into multiletter units. (They use the same strategy for both types of items.) One way to examine this idea is to look at how much longer it takes to pronounce a word as its length increases. If poor readers encode letters into intermediate units, increasing word length should have a greater effect on them than on the high-ability readers who go directly from a word's appearance in the sensory buffer to its phonological code in long-term memory. This prediction was confirmed in the present study. Low-ability readers produced latencies to six-phoneme words that were about

1400 msecs longer than their latencies to three-phoneme words. For the high-skilled readers, the latency increment was only 450 msecs. Not surprisingly, reaction times for different length words were also more similar for high reading skill subjects ($r = .60$) than for low reading skill subjects ($r = .44$).

Part 1 of the Word-Decoding Test was designed to measure the relative efficiency of the two routes described in the information-processing model developed in the last chapter. It has been shown to be a reliable and valid predictor of comprehension as measured by the GAPADOL. The correlation between pseudoword minus real word latencies and GAPADOL scores is $-.40$ and accounts for 16% of the variance in GAPADOL scores. A multiple regression analysis using the difference between matched real words and pseudowords as predictors (e.g., three-phoneme high-frequency pseudoword latency minus three-phoneme high-frequency real word latency, six-phoneme high-frequency pseudoword latency minus six-phoneme high-frequency real word latency, and so on) and GAPADOL scores as the criterion produced a multiple R of $-.47$, which accounts for 22% of the variance in GAPADOL scores. Clearly, the contrast between the vocalization latency to real words and matched pseudowords is an important predictor of reading comprehension.

Part 2 of the Word-Decoding Test is designed to determine at what stage in reading a graded list of words subjects show encoding difficulty. The rationale behind the test is that latencies will increase markedly when reading is no longer direct from print to meaning, but rather involves intermediate recoding steps. In Chapter 7, it will be shown how this information can be used to develop remedial reading programs.

The mean word reached by the subjects was number 89. Although many subjects were cut off by twice exceeding, by more than 2 seconds, their mean reaction time to real words in Part 1, a large number (16) proceeded through all of the words. This means that variability would have been greater had there been more words in the list. Nevertheless, the number of words read correlated .33 with GAPADOL scores; this correlation accounted for 11% of the variance in reading-comprehension test scores.

Part 2 of the Word-Decoding Test gives us a method for determining the "level" of decoding by examining vocalization latencies. Figure 9 displays a graph of vocalization latencies plotted for the words in Part 2. The graphs represent the latencies of one high-skilled reader (who scored in the upper half of scores on the GAPADOL) and one low-skilled reader (who fell in the lower half of scores on the GAPADOL). As can be seen, the latencies are stable for most words and then go abruptly up, indicating a change in processing strategy. This abrupt change may be taken to indicate that words are no longer being processed "directly." In the present study, the definition of an abrupt change is a latency increase of more than 50% that does not return to the previous base rate within the next two words. Thus, if a subject makes only one or two slower

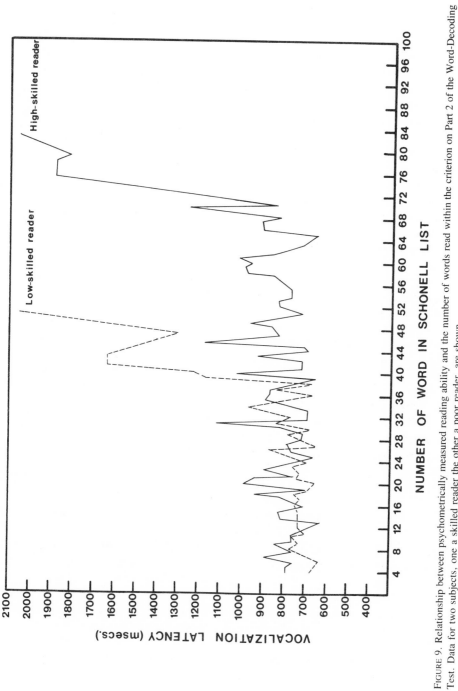

FIGURE 9. Relationship between psychometrically measured reading ability and the number of words read within the criterion on Part 2 of the Word-Decoding Test. Data for two subjects, one a skilled reader the other a poor reader, are shown.

responses, this is not considered a change. If, however, the slower responses last for three words in a row, then the subject is no longer considered to be using the direct route. Using this definition, the difference between the average latency prior to the change and the latencies after the abrupt change was calculated for the entire group and found to be about 1 second. As a tentative working definition, then, the direct access of phonological codes is considered to end when latency increases by more than 1 second from the mean of the previous words.

Using this definition, the number of words each subject could read "directly" (without further recoding) was calculated. The correlation between this score and GAPADOL scores was .47 for the entire group. This finding suggests that "decoding level" is an important predictor of reading-comprehension ability. It should be noted that Perfetti and Hogaboam (1975b) found a similar 1 second difference in latencies to high- and low-frequency words among poor primary school readers.

Because the measures obtained from Part 1 and those from Part 2 are both based on vocalization latencies, it is no surprise that they are correlated. It is, however, interesting to note that the number of words read has a higher correlation with vocalization latencies to pseudowords ($r = -.41$) than with vocalization latencies to real words ($r = -.20$). The explanation for this finding follows directly from the earlier discussion. Vocalization latencies to pseudowords are more sensitive indicators of reading ability than real-word vocalization latencies because most subjects can read real words by going directly from print to sound without the need for additional recoding. This means there is little variability in vocalization latencies for real words and, therefore, low correlations with the GAPADOL.

The difference between real-word and pseudoword latencies correlated with the number of words read in Part 2 produced an r of $-.48$. To determine whether these two measures are actually measuring the same thing (and are, therefore, redundant predictors of GAPADOL scores), two analyses were conducted. The first was a multiple regression analysis using (1) the number of words read and (2) the inverse difference between pseudoword and real word reading latencies as predictors and GAPADOL scores as the criterion. This produced a multiple R of .49, which is greater than the correlation of either variable with GAPADOL alone. Clearly, however, there is a lot of overlap. The last word test adds only .09 to the correlation of pseudoword minus real-word vocalization latency with the GAPADOL alone.

The second analysis was a principle components analysis and varimax rotation of axes undertaken to examine the underlying regularities in the relationships of the various tasks. This analysis included the various contrasts derived from Part 1 as well as the last word read in Part 2 and GAPADOL score. The first component derived from this analysis accounted for 42% of the variance in the matrix. All of the vocalization latency tests loaded on this component as did the number of words read and the GAPADOL. The number of words read in Part 2 also loaded on the second component, as did the GAPADOL. This component accounted for 15% of the variance in the matrix. This analysis indicates that both Part 1 and Part 2 of the Word-Decoding Test are measuring similar things, but there is some additional information coming from the Part 2 measure— the number of words read. It is not unlikely that this extra information consists of word knowledge. That is, subjects more familiar with the words used in Part 2 vocalize faster and also get higher GAPADOL scores than subjects who are unfamiliar with the words. Interestingly, this specialized knowledge is not as important a predictor of reading comprehension as vocalization time to pseudowords.

To test the generality of the findings of Reliability and Validity Study 3, another reliability and validity study was conducted on a different population. This study was conducted by Christine Butler-Smith, a school guidance counselor, and is described next.

RELIABILITY AND VALIDITY STUDY 4

Subjects. Forty-five primary-school children served as subjects in this study. Thirty of the children were boys; 15, girls. All were enrolled in the fourth grade (mean age was 8.5 years, standard deviation = .8 years). All of the children were found to fall in the average IQ range (90–110) as measured by the Wechsler Intelligence Scale for Children—Revised (WISC-R).

Psychometric Test. The children were all tested with the GAP reading-comprehension test (McLeod, 1965). The GAP test is a cloze test in which children must supply the most appropriate missing word. It is, in essence, a children's version of the GAPADOL.

Procedure. The Word-Decoding Test was administered to the children in the same manner described in the previous study. After being familiarized with the computer setup (see the familiarization procedure described earlier) each child proceeded through the test once. A week later, each child repeated Part 2 only.

Results

Reliability. Reliability was calculated for Part 1 latencies in the manner described in the previous reliability and validity study. The reliability coefficient was found to be .92. Test–retest reliability for Part 2 was estimated by correlating the two last word scores obtained by each subject. This reliability was found to be .89.

Means. The mean vocalization latencies for the various conditions were longer than those reported for the previous study, but the relationships remain the same. Long words produce longer latencies than short words, pseudowords produce longer latencies than real words, and common words have shorter latencies than rare words. The overall longer latencies are a reflection of the lower level of reading development in the present sample.

Validity

Part 1. The correlation between GAP score and pseudoword vocalization latency was $-.32$. For real words, the correlation was $-.25$. Once again, the correlation was higher for pseudowords than for real words. Although the pseudoword correlation is almost identical to the one obtained in the earlier study, the real word correlation is higher, probably because many of the medium-frequency words were unknown to some of the subjects in this study (effectively making them pseudowords). The difference between pseudoword and real word latencies correlated $-.38$ with GAP scores, paralleling quite closely the findings of the first study.

Part 2. The correlation between the number of words read in Part 2 and GAP scores was .48. This correlation was considerably higher than the .33 found in the previous study and accounts for 23% of the variability in the comprehension test's scores. This higher correlation is doubtlessly due to the greater restriction in range (ceiling effect) in the previous study. In that study, the mean number of words read was 89, and a large number of subjects read all 100. In the present study, the mean number of words read was 46 (standard deviation = 21), and only two subjects reached the final word.

As in the previous study, the number of words read was found to correlate with the latency data collected in Part 1. Also, as in the previous study, latency to pseudowords was a better predictor of GAPADOL scores than number of words read. A multiple regression analysis found that the last word test improved the predictability of latency data alone by .14. The multiple R including the data from Parts 1 and 2 was .52. A principle components analysis found the same pattern of loadings as those reported for the previous study, indicating that although they share common variance, each Part includes independent information as well.

The latencies for each word in Part 2 were plotted for each subject in order to determine whether there is an abrupt increase similar to that noted in the earlier study. Although there was somewhat more variability among the subjects in the present study, once again, the average difference between latencies on the first part of the list and the latencies after a 50% latency increase also averaged 1 second. The correlation between this measure of reading automaticity (last word read before 1 second latency increase) and GAP scores was .51.

The Word-Decoding Test was conceived as a way to measure the efficiency with which readers could use the direct "visual" and the indirect "phonemic" routes to decode print. The results of two reliability and validity studies indicate that the data derived from the test are reliable and that they do predict reading ability as measured by the GAPADOL. Part 1 of the test provides several contrasts. The most straightforward is the comparison of real-word vocalization latencies and pseudoword vocalization latencies. Poor readers tend to show a bigger difference between these latencies than good readers, and they also show a greater increase in latency as words get longer. The finding that real word and pseudoword latencies are more highly correlated among poor than good readers suggests that the poor readers are using the same decoding strategy for both items, whereas the skilled readers change their decoding strategy, depending on the nature of the material to be read.

Part 2 of the Word-Decoding Test was designed as a measure of "decoding level" that could be used to help plan remedial reading programs. The number of words read in the reading list has been shown to be a good predictor of comprehension scores. For the younger readers, it accounts for more than 23% of the variance in those scores. This finding is not new, of course. But the present procedure goes one step further. Using this test, it is possible to see at what point in the graded list, a subject is no longer using the direct visual route because there is an abrupt increase (of 50% or more) in reading vocalization latencies that do not return to baseline. This information is not only a good predictor of reading comprehension, it may also be used to help tailor remedial programs to specific children by highlighting exactly where instruction should begin. This point will be returned to later in this book.

So far we have discussed tests that are primarily concerned with processes that are highly practiced and very fast. The next section discusses a test that is concerned with an attention-demanding aspect of reading—the memory and manipulation of order information in short-term memory. The test is called the Memory for Order Test.

MEMORY FOR ORDER

In Chapter 4, memory for the order of events was identified as an important short-term memory process with direct implications for reading ability. The information-processing model presented in that chapter requires that reading units be decoded and stored in short-term memory in such a way that the order of units does not violate the rules of English syntax. This is because sentence parsing depends on maintaining proper item order.

Evidence that poor readers are deficient in retaining order information has been reported by Bakker (1967), Koppitz (1973, 1975), and by Schwartz and

Wiedel (1978). Order information is not only necessary for reading, it is also an important component of spoken language. However, a crucial difference between printed and spoken language is that in spoken language, the order of events is temporal (they follow one another in time), whereas in the printed language, items follow one another in space (left to right for English).

In traditional studies of serial learning, temporal and spatial order are usually in one-to-one correspondence. In fact, temporal order is implied whenever memory for order is discussed; spatial order is usually ignored. Consequently, most theoretical discussions assume that temporal order is the main factor in serial learning (Mandler & Dean, 1969).

There have been studies, however, that attempted to vary the congruence of temporal and spatial orders to investigate their relative importance in short-term memory. Mandler and Anderson (1971), for example, reported a study in which the temporal and spatial order of visually presented digits was incongruent. They found that both types of order could be recalled by adult subjects. In the same study, Mandler and Anderson showed that recall of temporal order was better than recall of spatial order when subjects were informed before or after presentation which order they will be required to recall. An important, unanswered question is whether the same relationship between temporal and spatial-order recall holds true for good and poor readers. The Memory-for-Order Test was designed to evaluate memory for spatial and temporal order separately.

MEASUREMENT PROCEDURE: MEMORY FOR ORDER

The Memory-for-Order Test, like the tests described earlier, is administered by the computer system. The test stimuli consist of visually presented letters that appear on the computer screen in such a way that they can be organized sequentially (first to last) or spatially (left to right or right to left). This technique was adapted from one used by O'Connor and Hermelin (1973). There are three testing conditions. In one, subjects are merely asked to recall the "order" of the letters. Temporal or spatial order are not specified. This condition was designed to assess a subject's preference for reporting one or the other order. The second condition requires subjects to report the temporal order, and the third condition requires memory for spatial order. The specific instructions given to subjects appear in Table 16.

The same four letters are used throughout the test (Q, W, S, K). These letters were chosen because they are not visually similar and they are never pronounced alike. The four letters are displayed horizontally across the top of the screen in an unpredictable spatial and temporal order. The way this is done is illustrated in Table 17. Each letter appears for 500 msecs, when it disappears and the next letter appears.

Immediately following the presentation of the letters, three arrangements of the same four letters appear in the middle of the screen. These are numbered

TABLE 16. Memory-for-Order Test: Instructions

Part 1

In this game you will be shown four letters, one at a time. You will then be asked what order the letters were in and given three choices from which to choose your answer.

If you think it's the first choice, then press the *1* button. If you think it's the second choice, then press the *2* button. If you think it's the third choice, then press the *3* button.

You will now be given some practice trials. Watch the top part of the screen closely, and you will be shown four letters. Press the orange button when you are ready to begin.

(Practice trials are now presented.)

That is the end of the practice trials. The real trials are next. Press the orange button when you are ready to go on.

(Nonpractice trials are now presented.)

Part 2

For this next set of trials, you will again be shown four letters, one at a time. You will then be asked what was the order in which the letters were shown to you, that is, which letter were you shown first, which letter were you shown second, which letter were you shown third, and which letter were you shown last? You will then be given three choices from which to choose your answer.

You will now be given some practice trials. Press the orange button when you are ready to begin.

(Practice trials are now presented.)

That is the end of the practice trials. The real trials are next. Press the orange button when you are ready to begin.

(Nonpractice trials are now presented.)

Part 3

For this next set of trials, you will again be shown four letters, one at a time. You will then be asked what was the order of the letters going from the left-hand side of the screen to the right-hand side of the screen. That is:

The letter you see here is the *first* letter	The letter you see here is the *second* letter	The letter you see here is the *third* letter	The letter you see here is the *last* letter

You will now be given some practice trials. Press the orange button when you are ready to begin.

(Practice trials are now presented.)

That is the end of the practice trials. The real trials are next. Press the orange button when you are ready to go on.

(Nonpractice trials are now presented.)

TABLE 17. Schematic Outline of Stimulus Presentations

Spatial:		Q	S	W	K	
Temporal:		4	1	3	2	
	1.	S	K	W Q		(correct temporal response)
Task 1	2.	Q	S	W K		(correct spatial response)
	3.	S	W	K Q		(incorrect error response)
	1.	S	K	W Q		(correct temporal response)
Task 2	2.	Q	S	W K		(incorrect spatial response)
	3.	S	W	K Q		(incorrect error response)
	1.	S	K	W Q		(incorrect temporal response)
Task 3	2.	Q	S	W K		(correct spatial response)
	3.	S	W	K Q		(incorrect error response)

1, 2, and 3. One of these three sets is arranged in the temporal order of the previously presented letters, one is arranged in their spatial order, and one is a completely random order that does not coincide with either the spatial or temporal order of that trial. The subjects indicate their choice of one of the three orders by depressing the corresponding key—1, 2, or 3—on the video display unit's keyboard. The subjects can take as long as they like to respond.

Immediately following each trial, a message appears on the computer screen informing the subject if the choice was correct. This message remains on the screen for $\frac{1}{2}$ second. After a $\frac{1}{10}$ second delay, the next trial begins.

To determine the letter sequences presented, four random lists of the 24 possible combinations were generated. These lists were then edited to be sure that none of the stimulus presentations offered identical spatial, temporal (or random) orders.

The test begins with practice trials. As soon as five correct trials are completed (trials on which the subject does not choose the random order sequence), the practice trials are terminated. Subjects are then given the opportunity to ask any questions they like. Extra practice is permitted for those who do not seem to understand.

The Memory-for-Order Test, itself, consists of three blocks of 30 trials each. The first block requires recall to be in either spatial or temporal order (nonspecific condition). The second block asks for temporal order, and the last block asks for spatial order recall. The order of the second and third tasks may be altered, but the first task must be the nonspecific one.

The data collected for this test consist of the response on each trial of each block under the various conditions. A data file for one subject is given in Table 18.

Table 18. Memory-for-Order Test Sample Data File[a]

Trial	Correct spatial	Correct temporal	Incorrect spatial	Incorrect temporal	Incorrect random
1		1	0	0	0
2		1	0	0	0
3		1	0	0	0
4		1	0	0	0
5		1	0	0	0
6		1	0	0	0
7		1	0	0	0
8		0	1	0	0
9		1	0	0	0
10		1	0	0	0
11		1	0	0	0
12		1	0	0	0
13		1	0	0	0
14		1	0	0	0
15		0	0	0	1
16		1	0	0	0
17		1	0	0	0
18		1	0	0	0
19		0	1	0	0
20		1	0	0	0
21		1	0	0	0
22		0	1	0	0
23		1	0	0	0
24		1	0	0	0
25		1	0	0	0
26		0	0	0	1
27		1	0	0	0
28		1	0	0	0
29		1	0	0	0
30		1	0	0	0

RELIABILITY AND VALIDITY STUDY 5

This reliability and validity study was conducted by Christine Butler-Smith, using the primary school population described in Reliability and Validity Study 4. For data analysis, scores on the GAP test were used to divide the 45 children into three equal-sized reading groups. The high-skilled group had a mean reading age of 10.88 years, the medium-skilled group had a reading age of 9.4 years, and the low group had a mean reading age of 7.9 years. (All of the children had IQ scores within the range 90 to 110 as measured by the WISC-R. The groups were specially constructed to ensure that there were no differences in IQ scores between reading groups.) The children were familiarized with the environment before testing began, and they also received other tests.

Results

Reliabilities. For this test, reliability was calculated by correlating the number of correct choices for the first 15 trials in each block with the number of correct choices in the second 15 trials corrected using the Spearman–Brown formula. For the nonspecific condition, either a temporal or a spatial order choice was considered correct. The reliabilities were .91 for the nonspecific condition, .92 for the temporal-order condition, and .91 for the spatial-order condition. All reliabilities are statistically significant ($p < .01$).

Validity. For each condition, the percentage of correct and incorrect choices was calculated. (For the nonspecific condition, both temporal and spatial order choices were considered correct.) The mean percentages for the three reading groups appear in Table 19. As may be seen, when given nonspecific instructions, most children preferred to recall temporal order, but they could switch to spatial order when the task demanded it.

To determine the relationship between performance on the Memory-for-Order Test and reading comprehension skill, the percentages found in Table 19 were each correlated with GAP scores. Table 20 gives these correlations across the entire group of subjects.

The most striking finding of this correlational analysis is the negative correlation between the percentage of spatial order choices in the nonspecific and temporal order conditions and GAP scores. This suggests that subjects who prefer spatial order choices in the nonspecific condition and who make spatial order errors in the temporal order condition are poorer in reading comprehension than those subjects who choose the temporal order in these conditions. In the spatial condition, this relationship is reversed. Now, choosing the temporal order is negatively related to GAP scores. In every condition, choosing the random score was negatively related to GAP scores.

Taken together, Tables 19 and 20 present a pattern of results that indicate a relationship between the ability to maintain order (spatial or temporal) in short-term memory and reading comprehension.

Although the present test is concerned with memory for order, the results may be interpreted more generally. That is, better readers appear to be more flexible and therefore able to use various short-term memory strategies more effectively than poor readers. This conclusion would agree with the literature on short-term memory rehearsal strategies reviewed in the previous chapter (see also Torgeson, 1977). In other words, the present results support the view that poor readers have poorer short-term memory for order than skilled readers and may also indicate a general lack of flexibility in implementing short-term memory-rehearsal strategies.

TABLE 19. Percentage Choices in Each Condition for Three Reading Groups

	Task 1			Task 2			Task 3		
	Spatial	Temporal	Random error	Temporal	Incorrect spatial	Random error	Spatial	Incorrect temporal	Random error
Above average readers	7.86	83.81	8.33	88.33	5.00	6.19	74.05	15.95	10.00
Average readers	18.33	68.96	12.71	77.50	13.54	8.96	64.38	21.25	14.38
Reading disabled	19.33	62.44	18.22	71.78	17.11	11.11	56.66	24.67	18.67

TABLE 20. Correlation of Choices in Three Conditions

Condition/Choice		Nonspecific			Temporal			Spatial			GAP
		Spatial	Temporal	Random	Temporal	Spatial	Random	Spatial	Temporal	Random	
Nonspecific	Spatial	1.00									
	Temporal	$-.93^b$	1.00								
	Random	$.39^b$	$-.71^b$	1.00							
Temporal	Temporal	$-.61^b$	$.72^b$	$-.63^b$	1.00						
	Spatial	$.54^b$	$-.66^b$	$.59^b$	$-.91^b$	1.00					
	Random	$.54^b$	$-.62^b$	$.51^b$	$-.86^b$	$.56^b$	1.00				
Spatial	Spatial	$-.40^b$	$-.46^b$	$-.40^b$	$.46^b$	$-.43^b$	$-.39^b$	1.00			
	Temporal	$.32^a$	$-.34^a$	$.24$	$-.36^a$	$.37^b$	$.26$	$-.92^b$	1.00		
	Random	$.38^b$	$-.50^b$	$.51^b$	$-.46^b$	$.37^b$	$.45^b$	$-.78^b$	$.48^b$	1.00	
GAP		$-.30^a$	$.44^b$	$-.51^b$	$.40^b$	$-.43^b$	$-.27$	$.32^a$	$-.26$	$-.29^a$	1.00

[a] $p < .05$.
[b] $p < .01$.

To determine how well the Memory-for-Order Test as a whole predicts reading comprehension scores, a multiple regression analysis was performed using the GAP score as the criterion and the temporal and spatial coding scores on each of the three tasks, as predictors. Because the percentage of random error choices is constrained by the number of spatial and temporal choices, they were omitted from the analysis. The results were significant ($p < .01$) and yielded a multiple correlation of .54, indicating that approximately 30% of the variance in reading ability can be accounted for on the basis of performance on the three order tasks. The criterion was best predicted by the percentage of temporal choices in the nonspecific condition.

THE MEMORY-FOR-ORDER TEST: PRELIMINARY CONCLUSIONS

Memory for order in short-term memory as measured by the present test is a reliable and valid predictor of reading comprehension as measured by the GAPADOL. In fact, it accounts for about 30% of the variance in comprehension test scores. Although the test was designed specifically to measure memory for order information, it also indicates flexibility by showing whether a subject can switch strategies when the test demands change. In general, poor readers were less flexible (had more difficulty switching strategies) than skilled readers.

Although the tests described so far have been described in isolation, they are best seen as items in a test battery. The next section explores interrelationships among the tests.

THE DECODING BATTERY

The Long-Term Memory Access Speed Test, the Word-Decoding Test, and the Memory-for-Order Test were administered to the 45 subjects described in Reliability and Validity Study 4. Representative scores from each test were intercorrelated producing a correlation matrix composed of the following variables:

1. Long-Term Memory Access Speed: NI − PI reaction time
2. Word-Decoding Test
   a. Real word versus pseudoword vocalization latency
   b. Number of words read (Part 2)
3. Memory-for-Order Test (Percent Choices)
   a. Temporal (in temporal conditions)
   b. Spatial (in spatial condition)
4. GAP Scores

The resulting correlation matrix appears in Table 21.

TABLE 21. Intercorrelations of Selective Decoding Test Variables

Variable	Variable					
	NI − PI	Real/pseudo	Last word	Temporal	Spatial	GAP
NI − PI	(.92)					
Real vs. pseudo	−.17	(.87)				
Last word	−.27	−.48[b]	(.93)			
Temporal recall	−.03	−.02	.28[a]	(.95)		
Spatial recall	−.05	−.05	.36[a]	.40[b]	(.91)	
GAP	−.29[a]	−.38[a]	.51[b]	.40[b]	.32[a]	(.91)

[a] $p < .05$.
[b] $p < .01$.

Although the tests are not completely independent, the intercorrelation pattern suggests that the various measures are tapping different reading skills. To test this hypothesis statistically, a principle components analysis and varimax rotation of axes were undertaken. The result of this analysis appears in Table 22.

The data found in Table 22 indicate that there are six independent components underlying the correlation matrix depicted in Table 21. The components are about equally important in accounting for variance in the intercorrelation matrix. (The first component accounts for 16% of the variance, the next three for just under 16, and the last two for 14% each.) Taken together, the six components account for 91.50% of the variance. The first component has its heaviest loading on temporal order recall, the second on the real word–pseudoword contrast, the third on NI − PI reaction time, the fourth on spatial order recall, the fifth loads heaviest on the GAP, and the sixth loads most heavily on the last word read.

The principal components analysis illustrates that the various tests, although related, reflect different underlying factors contributing to reading comprehension. To examine the overall predictive accuracy of the decoding battery, a multiple regression analysis was conducted using the variables analyzed in the

TABLE 22. Principal Components Analysis of Decoding Tests

Component	Variable					
	1	2	3	4	5	6
1. NI − PI time	.00	−.11	.93	−.01	−.14	−.13
2. Real vs. pseudoword latency	.02	.87	−.14	.00	−.19	−.23
3. Number of words read	.13	−.31	−.18	.21	.20	.83
4. Temporal order correct	.93	.01	.01	.21	.18	.10
5. Spatial order correct	.18	.00	.00	.92	.13	.14
6. GAP score	.22	−.22	.18	.15	.84	.21

principle components analysis as predictors and GAP scores as the criterion. The multiple R obtained was .79. The decoding tests, therefore, account for 62% of the variance in comprehension test scores.

In some ways, this result is quite extraordinary. Although the Word-Decoding Test does involve pronouncing words in isolation, the Long-Term Memory Access Test and the Memory-for-Order Test do not require that the subject even know how to read. Knowing letter names is sufficient. Nevertheless, these tests predict performance on a comprehension test that not only requires that the examinees know how to read but also that they understand what they are reading.

If we assume that performance on a comprehension test like the cloze-type test used here depends on a combination of knowledge (about words and their meanings as well as about syntax, grammar, and text meaning) and mechanized decoding processes, then the present results indicate that mechanistic decoding processes are a more important source of individual variability than specific knowledge. However, the present multiple regression analysis left 38% of comprehension test score variance unaccounted for. This variance may be due to specific comprehension processes. A test of these processes is described in the next chapter.

SUMMARY

This chapter described three computer-administered tests of decoding. These tests were derived from the information-processing model presented in Chapter 4. Each test was designed to measure a separate aspect of decoding. The Long-Term Memory Access Test measures the time required to access reading-related information in long-term memory. The Word-Decoding Test is concerned with the level at which words are processed. It also indicates a way to determine the point in reading a word series graded for difficulty when visual reading gives way to a less-direct reading route. Finally, the Memory-for-Order Test was designed to measure short-term memory for order information and flexibility in applying cognitive strategies.

Although the Word-Decoding Test requires the ability to read at least a few short words, the other two tests do not require reading ability beyond a knowledge of the alphabet. Thus, they are appropriate for young children.

The tests, taken as a group, account for over 60% of the variance in reading comprehension test scores. Clearly, decoding is an important part of reading. But a fair amount of variability in reading comprehension test scores remains unaccounted for. This variability is doubtlessly due to factors such as comprehension skills and experience. These factors are discussed in the next chapter.

CHAPTER 6

A THEORETICALLY BASED COMPREHENSION MEASURE

As noted several times in previous chapters, comprehension is not easily defined. In some situations, comprehension means nothing more than being able to recall facts presented in a text. In other circumstances, comprehension requires abstracting a text's main theme; and in still others, comprehension involves drawing inferences from what is read.

Typical reading tests (the cloze-type tests are an exception) measure comprehension by having examinees read passages under time pressure and then answer a series of multiple-choice questions. These questions require examinees to abstract the main idea (sometimes by choosing the best title), recall facts, and draw inferences from what they have read. Examples of several such tests were given in Chapter 3.

An important problem for the typical approach is that it leaves totally uncontrolled the influence of individual differences in previous knowledge. That is, the topic of a test passage may be familiar to some examinees and new to others. The research reviewed in Chapter 4 makes it abundantly clear that it is much easier to form text models of familiar than unfamiliar materials. For example, an American reading a passage about the English game cricket will find it more difficult to comprehend—by any measure including factual recall—than someone intimately familiar with the game. The consequence of leaving subject matter uncontrolled is that specialized knowledge plays an important role in determining a test's outcome. When a topic is familiar, the examinee does well; when it is unfamiliar, the same examinee may do poorly. This can make for unreliable and unstable tests.

The decoding tests described in the previous chapter avoid the problem of prior knowledge by minimizing (or in some cases eliminating altogether) any special knowledge needed to perform the test. The ideal comprehension test would also require little or no specialized prior knowledge. Such a test is described in this chapter. The chapter begins by explaining the background and rationale of the test. This is followed by a description of the test itself and the results of a reliability and validity study. Finally, the predictive validity of the entire battery of decoding and comprehension tests is examined.

BACKGROUND AND RATIONALE

The comprehension measure to be described in this chapter is based on the information-processing model developed in Chapter 4. In that model, reading units are decoded and temporarily stored in short-term memory. The information stored in short-term memory is continually checked against the grammatical, syntactical, and other knowledge bases resident in long-term memory. The goal is to obtain a meaningful interpretation of the reading unit (or, more often, units). Once found, this interpretation is incorporated into the schematic model of the text, which is, in effect, a meaningful interpretation of what is being read.

To incorporate meaningful interpretations of reading units into a coherent text model, each reading unit must be properly understood. Errors in interpretation will necessarily lead to models that distort a text's meaning. For example, the statements *All airplanes have wings* and *Some rockets have wings* are not logically equivalent. The first statement ensures that objects called airplanes inevitably have wings. The second statement does not permit rockets to be described with the same degree of certainty. Dawes (1966) found that statements of the first type were easier to recall than those of the second type. In addition, he found that readers often "simplify" the second type of statement (by making it into a certainty), thereby producing a comprehension error.

At the most basic level, comprehension depends upon finding the correct interpretation for a proposition. This usually involves comparing the proposition with some referential event. The proposition *All airplanes have wings* is meaningful to us because it calls forth images and incidents concerning winged aircraft. For someone with no experience of aviation, the statement is as difficult to comprehend as one that says *All glecks have forbats*. However, it is not necessary to use nonsense materials to study the process of interpretation. There is an easier way to study sentence comprehension while still minimizing the influence of prior knowledge. The technique is to use a restricted range of materials that is available to all subjects. This was the approach adopted by Trabasso (1972) and Chase and Clark (1972).

Trabasso asked subjects to read a sentence like "The ball is red" and then compare the sentence with a picture showing either a red or blue ball. The subjects had to decide quickly whether the sentence was an accurate description of the picture. The time required to perform the comparison and make the response was found to vary with the complexity of the sentence. For example, the negative statement "The ball is not red" takes longer to compare with the picture than a simple declarative sentence like "The ball is red."

Chase and Clark asked their subjects to perform a task very similar to Trabasso's except their subjects matched sentences like "Cross is above star" with pictures of a cross and a star ($_+^*$). Again, more complicated statements (e.g., "The cross is not above the star") took longer to verify.

The experimental procedure used by Trabasso and by Chase and Clark has become known as the sentence-verification task. It was extensively studied by Carpenter and Just (1975), who presented a detailed information-processing model of the cognitive operations required to complete the task. They called their model the "Constituent Comparison Model." Their model contains the following important assumptions:

1. Sentences are represented internally by logical propositions that are equivalent to the sentences.
2. Pictures are also represented internally by logical propositions equivalent to the affirmative statement that describes them.
3. After both pictures and sentences have been transformed into propositions, they are compared, component by component. If a mismatch occurs, the two constituents are resolved (one is changed), and the comparison process begins again. This matching process ends only when all constituent comparisons result in either agreement or "resolved" (nonagreed) components.

In simple terms, Carpenter and Just view the sentence verification task as a linguistic problem. Both sentences and pictures are transformed into an abstract propositional code, and it is these abstract codes that are actually compared.

Carpenter and Just examined four types of sentence–picture combinations. True affirmative (TA) combinations were simple declarative sentences that accurately matched the subsequent pictures (e.g., "The star is above the plus": $_+^*$). False affirmatives (FA) were similar except the sentence and picture did not match (e.g., "The star is above the plus": $_*^+$) True negatives (TN) were matched pairs of the type: "The star is not above the plus" ($_*^+$) and false negatives (FN) were the opposite (e.g., "The star is not above the plus": $_+^*$).

If each sequence of comparisons is labelled a *scan*, then the four trial types (TA, FA, TN, FN) each require a different number of scans. This is because complex sentences like TNs have more constituents than simple sentences like TAs. Carpenter and Just further assume that each scan will require a constant amount of time, arbitrarily set to one time unit. Thus, the initial coding of the picture (plus response time) takes K units of time. Carpenter and Just's model, therefore, predicts that the average amount of time required for each trial type will vary from K units for a simple TA trial to K + 5 units for a more complicated TN trial.

MacLeod, Hunt, and Mathews (1978) had university students perform the sentence–picture verification task and found their data did not neatly fit Carpenter and Just's model. Instead, their subjects appeared to fall basically into two groups, one whose performance was described well by the Constituent Comparison Model and one that behaved differently. This led them to propose the existence of two models (or approaches) for sentence verification tasks, a linguistic model and a pictorial model. These two models are outlined in Table 23.

The linguistic model is essentially identical to the one developed by Carpenter and Just. Subjects following a linguistic strategy transform the sentence into a set of abstract propositions, and then they do the same with the pictures. As each constituent comparison requires another unit of time, the more constituents to process, the more time necessary to make a response. For this reason, the graph relating reaction time to the number of constituent comparisons is predicted to be an increasing linear function.

The pictorial strategy is quite different. Subjects adopting this approach transform the sentence into a pictorial image. In other words, they visualize a plus and a star. It is this image rather than a set of abstract propositions that is compared with the subsequent picture. Because all picture–picture comparisons

TABLE 23. Information-Processing Requirements of Linguistic and Pictorial Strategies[a]

Information-processing stage	Model	
	Linguistic	Pictorial
Comprehension	Read sentence	Read sentence
	Represent sentence	Represent sentence
	(Abstract propositions)	Convert sentence to picture image
Verification	Observe picture	Observe picture
	Represent picture	Compare picture with picture image
	(Abstract propositions)	
	Compare 2 sets of abstract propositions	
Response	True or false	True or false

[a]Adapted from "Individual Differences in the Verification of Sentence–Picture Relationships" by C. M. MacLead, E. B. Hunt, and N. N. Mathews, 1978, *Journal of Verbal Learning and Verbal Behavior, 17*, pp. 493–507. Copyright 1978 by *Academic Press* .

take about the same amount of time, subjects using the pictorial strategy do not produce an increasing linear function relating the number of constituent comparisons and reaction time. Instead, they produce a flat sloped graph. That is, all sentence–picture verification take about the same amount of time. The predicted relationship between sentence type and verification reaction time for the two models is displayed in Figure 10.

There is some evidence indicating that strategy choice is partly dependent on experimental procedures. Tversky (1975) suggested that the linguistic strategy is dominant when the sentence and the picture are presented simultaneously, whereas the pictorial strategy requires a separation between sentence and picture. Carpenter and Just exposed their sentences for a fixed 2-second period. MacLeod *et al.* allowed their subjects to examine the sentences for as long as they needed.

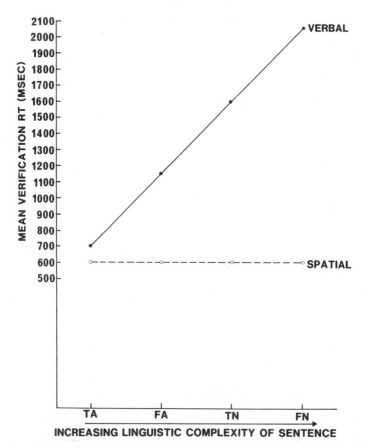

FIGURE 10. Predicted relationship between verification reaction time and number of constituent comparisons (sentence complexity) for the linguistic (verbal) and pictorial (spatial) strategy groups.

If Tversky is correct, then MacLeod *et al.* maximized the probability that their subjects would adopt the pictorial strategy.

Experimental procedure notwithstanding, not all of MacLeod *et al.*'s subjects used the pictorial strategy; many preferred to use the linguistic one. MacLeod *et al.* reported that the strategy a subject chooses can be predicted from psychometric test scores. Specifically, those who score high on tests of spatial ability prefer the pictorial strategy and those who score low on such tests seem to prefer the linguistic strategy (all of the subjects were of about the same level of verbal ability). The same pattern of relationships was reported by Mathews, Hunt, and MacLeod (1980), although the strength of the relationship was not as strong as in the earlier study. Schwartz and Hartley (1984) also found a relationship between psychometric test score and strategy choice. In their studies, it was not spatial or verbal ability that predicted what strategy a subject would choose. Instead, they found that subjects with higher intelligence test scores tended to choose the pictorial strategy. This is not so surprising when one considers that the test instructions require subjects to respond as quickly as possible and the pictorial strategy does lead to significantly faster reaction times.

For the present purpose, the most important finding in regard to the sentence–picture verification tests is that it is related to reading comprehension (Hunt *et al.*, 1981; Lansman, 1978; Palmer *et al.*, 1981; also see Baddeley, 1968). In the version of the task used by Hunt *et al.* (called the sentence–picture comprehension task), subjects were given a fixed period of time to complete a large number of sentence–picture comparisons. They found that the correlation between the number of comparisons correctly completed in the time allowed and reading comprehension as measured by a standardized test was .31. (This correlation was actually a partial correlation, the effects of long-term memory access speed having been partialled out.)

The sentence–picture comprehension paradigm obviously depends on knowing what the words in the sentence mean. However, because there are only six words used—and even these are constantly repeated—the role of prior knowledge in this test is minimal. For this reason, a version of the sentence–picture comprehension test was developed to be used as a test of reading comprehension. It is called the Sentence Comprehension Test.

SENTENCE COMPREHENSION TEST

The Sentence Comprehension Test is designed to provide information about comprehension processes without depending much on a person's prior knowledge. Although anyone who takes the test must be able to read the six words used in the sentences (the same words are repeated throughout the test), no other reading ability is necessary.

MEASUREMENT PROCEDURE: SENTENCE COMPREHENSION TEST

The Sentence Comprehension Test, like the decoding tests described in the previous chapter, is presented entirely by the computing system. Testing sessions begin with the familiarization process discussed in Chapter 5. Usually, the decoding tests are administered first, but this is not necessary; the tests can be administered in any order.

The test stimuli consist of 16 sentence–picture pairs. The pairs were constructed by taking four binary dimensions (star, plus), (is, is not), (above, below), and ($^*_+$, $^+_*$) and putting them together in all possible combinations. The resulting 16 comparison pairs are contained in Table 24.

Examinees are told that they will be seeing a sentence on the computer screen. The sentence remains on the screen until they press a button when it is replaced by a picture. Their task is to determine whether the sentence is an accurate description of the picture. After each sentence–picture comparison, the examinee is told whether the preceding answer is correct as well as how long it took her or him to respond. Examples are given, and the examinees are encouraged to go as quickly but as accurately as possible. The precise directions for the Sentence Comprehension Test appear in Table 25.

Following the instructions, subjects are told there will be two blocks of 16 practice trials, followed by two blocks of 16 test trials.

Within each block of trials, each of the 16 sentence–picture pairs is presented once, in a random order. There is an opportunity for subjects to ask questions following the instructions and each practice block.

On each trial, the stimulus sentence is presented horizontally across the center of the screen. After reading the sentence, the subject presses either a

TABLE 24. The Sentence–Picture Pairs[a]

Sentence	Picture consistent	Picture inconsistent
Star is above plus	$^*_+$	$^+_*$
Plus is below star	$^*_+$	$^+_*$
Plus is above star	$^+_*$	$^*_+$
Star is below plus	$^+_*$	$^*_+$
Plus is not above star	$^*_+$	$^+_*$
Star is not below plus	$^*_+$	$^+_*$
Star is not above plus	$^+_*$	$^*_+$
Plus is not below star	$^+_*$	$^*_+$

[a]Each sentence is paired with both consistent and inconsistent pictures to produce 16 different combinations.

TABLE 25. Sentence Comprehension Test Instructions

This is a game to see how quickly and how well you understand what you read. First of all, you will be shown a sentence, for example, "STAR is above PLUS." Read this sentence as quickly but as carefully as you can. Then, when you are sure you understand what it means, press either the black button or the orange button. The sentence will then disappear and you will be shown a picture like this one:

```
*
+
```

You have to decide whether the sentence is true or false by looking at the picture. If you think the sentence is true, press the black button. If you think the sentence is false, press the orange button.

After you have answered, you will be told whether your answer was right or wrong and how long you took to answer.

In the example just given, you would be correct if you pressed the black button because the sentence says the star is above the plus and in the picture, the star is above the plus.

But if you were shown the sentence "PLUS is not below STAR" and then shown the picture

```
*
+
```

you would be correct if you pressed the orange button because the plus is below the star.

It is important that you go as quickly as you can, but it is also important that you get as many right as possible. So when you see the sentence, read it as quickly but as carefully as you can, when you are sure you understand it, press either the black button or the orange button.

Then when the picture comes on, try to decide as quickly but as accurately as you can, whether the sentence is true or false by looking at the picture. If you think the sentence is true, press the black button. If you think the sentence is false, press the orange button.

You will now be given two sets of practice trials. Press the orange button when you are ready to begin the first set of practice trials.

(First set of practice trials are now presented.)

That is the end of the first set of practice trials. The second set of practice trials is next. Remember it is important that you go as quickly as you can, but it is also important that you get as many right as possible. So when you see the sentence, read it as quickly but as carefully as you can; when you are sure you understand it, press either the black button or the orange button.

Then, when the picture comes on, try to decide as quickly but as accurately as you can whether the sentence is true or false by looking at the picture. If you think the sentence is true, press the black button. If you think the sentence is false, press the orange button. Press the orange button when you're ready to go on.

(The second set of practice trials are now presented.)

That is the end of the practice trials. The real trials are next. Remember, it is important that you go as quickly as you can, but it is also important that you get as many right as possible. So when you see the sentence, read it as quickly but as carefully as you can; when you are sure you understand it, press either the black button or the orange button.

Then, when the picture comes on, try to decide as quickly but as accurately as you can whether the sentence is true or false by looking at the picture. If you think the sentence is true, press the black button. If you think the sentence is false, press the orange button. Press the orange button when you're ready to go on.

(The nonpractice trials are now presented.)

"true" or "false" button, and the stimulus sentence is immediately replaced by the picture. When the subject responds by pressing the true (black) or false (orange) button, the picture is immediately followed by feedback. Subjects are informed if they were correct or incorrect, and the verification reaction time is stated. This is displayed on the screen for 500 msec. There is a 100 msec. interval before the stimulus sentence of the next trial is displayed.

For each sentence–picture pair, three types of information are recorded:

1. Comprehension time (from the onset of a sentence to the subject's first button push)
2. Verification time (from the onset of the picture to the subject's true or false response)
3. The subject's response (true or false) and whether it is correct or incorrect

Besides these data, a multiple-regression analysis is automatically conducted using the sentence types as predictors and comprehension and verification times, respectively, as criteria. The corresponding regression weights and arctangent transformations of these weights are recorded in each subject's file. As will be seen later in this discussion, these transformed regression weights serve as measures of the slope of the function relating comprehension and verification reaction times to sentence type. A sample data file for a single subject appears in Table 26.

RELIABILITY AND VALIDITY STUDY 6

Christine Butler-Smith conducted a reliability and validity study of the Sentence Comprehension Test using 45 primary school children as subjects. The subject population is described in detail in Reliability and Validity Study 4. All of the children had been previously tested with the GAP test of reading comprehension, and all of the children received the decoding tests described in Chapter 5.

Results

Reaction time data were collected from each subject twice for every sentence–picture comparison. The first reaction time was the time required to comprehend the sentence; the second was the time necessary to compare the sentence with the picture and verify whether it was true or false. In addition, the actual response made on each trial was noted as correct or incorrect.

Reliability. According to MacLeod *et al.* (1978), the split-half reliability of comprehension and verification reaction times is .97 and .99 respectively. In the present study, reliability was calculated by correlating reaction times in Block 3 with equivalent reaction times in Block 4. The number of errors in

TABLE 26. Sentence Comprehension Test: Sample Data File[a]

Stimulus code	Number correct	Comp. time	Verification time	Number wrong	Comp. time	Verification time
(Block 3)						
k6	3	5741	2683	1	6185	564
k1	3	6919	2825	1	3236	1970
k4	3	9283	2768	1	14913	3983
k5	2	9263	3573	2	6470	2163

Comp.B Weight = .3387 Comp. Arctan (B) = 18.7131
Verif.B Weight = .0860 Verif. Arctan (B) = 4.9133

(Block 4)						
k6	3	6868	5988	1	5375	2852
k1	2	6272	4283	2	11373	3220
k4	1	12126	5324	3	6206	5186
k5	1	3547	2682	3	8362	3749

Comp. B Weight = .5505 Comp. Arctan (B) = 28.8306
Verif. B Weight = − .3079 Verif. Arctan (B) = − 17.1155

All times in msecs. Blocks 1 and 2 are practice.

Block 3 was also correlated with the number of errors in Block 4. All correlations were corrected using the Spearman–Brown formula. The reliability coefficients were .91 for comprehension reaction time, .90 for verification reaction time, and .92 for errors. All of these correlations are statistically significant ($p < .01$).

Validity. The 45 children participating in this study were divided into three reading groups of 15 children each on the basis of their scores on the GAP reading test. The highest reading group had a mean reading age of 10.8 years, the middle group had a mean reading age of 9.4 years, and the lowest reading group had a mean reading age of 7.9 years. All of the children had IQ scores within the normal range.

Several measures derived from the Sentence Comprehension Test were examined. The first was the number of verification errors (pressing the true button when false was correct or vice versa). The mean number of errors for the total group was 4.60 (standard deviation = 2.91). However, these errors were not evenly distributed across all reading groups. As indicated in Table 27, the lowest reading group made more than twice the number of errors of the highest reading group.

Similar findings were obtained for comprehension and verification reaction times. The mean comprehension reaction time was 4,844.48 msecs (standard

TABLE 27. Mean Error Scores and Reaction Times for Three Reading Groups

	Errors	Comprehension RT	Verification RT
Above average readers	2.75	3763.45	2221.93
Average readers	4.55	4204.88	2232.73
Reading-disabled children	6.50	5210.71	2391.89

deviation = 3,592.35 msecs), and the mean verification reaction time was 2,244.63 msecs (standard deviation = 910.78). Like the number of errors, these reaction times varied across the reading groups. Thus, as indicated in Table 27, reading ability is negatively correlated with reaction time as well as errors. Poorer readers find the task more difficult than good readers. This difficulty is reflected in both a higher number of errors and slower reaction times.

To determine the strength of the relationship between comprehension as measured by the GAP test and the measures derived from the Sentence Comprehension Test, GAP scores were correlated with errors, mean comprehension times, and mean verification times respectively. The resulting correlations were:

- GAP and comprehension reaction time = −.15
- GAP and verification reaction time = −.13
- GAP and number of errors = −.44

As can be seen by the level of these correlations, the relationship between GAP scores and reaction times is quite weak, but the relationship between errors and GAP scores is substantial and statistically significant ($p < .01$).

As there was a fair amount of variability in individual reaction times, verification and comprehension reaction times were also analyzed for the three reading groups. Figures 11 and 12 portray the relationship between sentence type and comprehension and verification reaction times respectively.

As can be seen, there appears to be a relationship between reading skill and comprehension reaction times. The more skilled readers had faster reaction times. But once again, the correlation (−.23) was not statistically significant ($p > .10$). Verification reaction times also did not differentiate reading groups ($r = −.14, p > .10$).

The results reviewed so far indicate that errors on the Sentence Comprehension Test are related to comprehension as measured by the GAP, but mean reaction times are only weakly related to GAP scores. Mean reaction times, however, do not reflect the strategy that subjects are using to accomplish the sentence–picture comparison. According to MacLeod *et al.* (1978), subjects using the linguistic strategy should show an increasing linear relationship between the number of constituent comparisons in a sentence and verification reaction

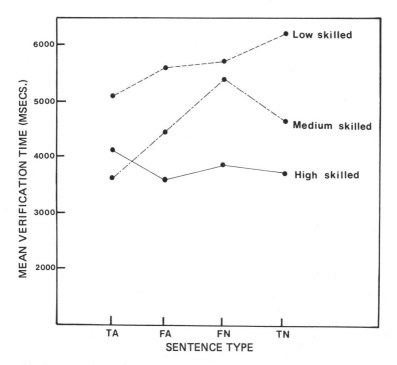

FIGURE 11. Comprehension reaction time as a function of sentence type for three reading groups.

time. In contrast, those using the pictorial strategy should produce a relatively flat function relating these variables because picture–picture comparisons all take about the same amount of time regardless of the number of constituent comparisons in the sentence. By the same reasoning, those using the pictorial strategy should have longer *comprehension* times than those using the linguistic strategy. This difference is due to the extra time required by those using the pictorial strategy to produce a pictorial representation of the sentence.

The multiple regression analyses referred to earlier were used to classify subjects into strategy groups. That is, a multiple regression was conducted using sentence type (number of constituent comparisons) as the predictor and verification reaction time as the criterion. The regression weight obtained in these analyses (for each subject) was transformed into degrees. Thus, for each subject, a measure of the slope of the function relating sentence type to verification reaction time was obtained. This slope measure indicates how much more time is required to verify increasingly complex sentences. A steep slope (high number) indicates that sentences with more constituent comparisons require more time to verify. A flat slope (low number) indicates that increasing the number of constituent comparisons does not increase verification reaction time. In other

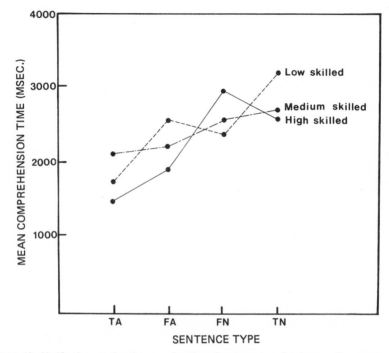

FIGURE 12. Verification reaction time as a function of sentence type for three reading groups.

words, a flat slope reflects the pictorial strategy and a steep slope the linguistic one.

The slopes obtained for each subject were correlated with GAP scores to determine whether there is any relationship between reading comprehension and strategy choice. The correlation obtained between GAP score and slope of the line linking sentence type with verification reaction time was − .15. Although this correlation indicates a tendency for slopes to get smaller as reading comprehension scores get higher, the relationship is too small to conclude that good readers prefer to use the pictorial strategy. The correlation between GAP scores and the slope of the line linking sentence type with comprehension reaction time was even smaller (− .07), indicating that neither slope measure is a good predictor of comprehension. A multiple regression analysis using both verification and comprehension slopes as predictors and GAP scores as the criterion also failed to reach statistical significance ($p < .25$). It is necessary to conclude, therefore, that the strategies identified by MacLeod *et al.* do not predict reading comprehension ability as measured by the GAP. These findings are also supported by the group data depicted in Figures 11 and 12. In both cases, there is little evidence that reading groups differed in their respective slopes.

In contrast, reading comprehension is related to the number of errors made on the Sentence Comprehension Test. The correlation between the number of errors and GAP scores (.44) accounts for 19% of the variance in the comprehension test's scores. This finding is in agreement with the results reported by Hunt *et. al.* (1981), who found that the partial correlation between sentence-comprehension errors and a psychometric measure of reading comprehension (controlling for semantic match time) was .31. As the children in the present study also received the Long-Term Memory Access Speed Test, their NI − PI times were used as a measure of memory access speed in a partial correlation analysis. The partial correlation between GAP scores and errors on the Sentence Comprehension Test (controlling for long-term memory access speed) was .40 ($p < .01$). Obviously, the Sentence Comprehension Test is not simply another measure of information-processing speed. It appears to be tapping the processes involved in holding a series of reading units in memory until their meaning can be derived. Whether this is accomplished using the linguistic or the pictorial strategy, the result is the same—more errors are associated with poorer performance on a measure of reading comprehension. The Sentence Comprehension Test is not only reliable, it is a valid measure of reading competence that accounts for more than 16% of the variance in reading comprehension test scores.

Convergent validity for the present approach to measuring reading comprehension is provided by Daneman (1982). Beginning with the assumption that readers must retain a series of propositions in memory to form a coherent interpretation of what they are reading, Daneman argues that comprehension must be related to the functional capacity of short-term memory. Daneman's measure of functional capacity is the "Reading Span Test." This test involves giving subjects a set of unrelated sentences one at a time to read out loud. After the last sentence, subjects must recall the final word of each sentence in the set. The number of sentences in a set is increased by one and the procedure is repeated until the subject can no longer recall all of the final words. The rationale behind this test is similar to the rationale underlying the Sentence Comprehension Test. Because poor readers devote more of their processing capacity to decoding, they have less capacity available for comprehension. Daneman found her measure related to more traditional methods of measuring comprehension.

Both the Sentence Comprehension Test and the Reading Span Test are based on similar notions of the information-processing requirements of reading comprehension, and future research comparing the two approaches is planned.

VALIDITY OF THE TEST BATTERY

The decoding and comprehension measures taken separately have all been found to be both reliable and valid measures of reading comprehension as measured by cloze-type standardized tests. At the end of the last chapter, it was shown that all the decoding tests taken together account for 62% of the variance in comprehension test scores. In this section, the validity of the entire test battery is considered.

The 45 children described in Reliability and Validity Study 4 received all of the decoding and comprehension tests. Representative scores from each test were intercorrelated in order to form the correlation matrix found in Table 28. These scores were

1. Long-Term Memory Access Speed Test: NI − PI reaction time
2. Word-Decoding Test
    a. Real versus pseudoword vocalization latency (Part 1)
    b. Number of words read (Part 2)
3. Memory-for-Order Test
    a. Number of temporal choices (in temporal conditions)
    b. Number of spatial choices (in spatial conditions)
4. Sentence Comprehension Test: Number of errors
5. GAP scores

Although the tests show some intercorrelations, the overall pattern of results appears to indicate that the tests are tapping different reading skills. Interestingly, the Sentence Comprehension Test measure (number of errors) not only correlates with the GAP but also with memory for spatial order. This finding is not unexpected as the model developed in Chapter 4 requires that reading units be stored in working memory *in their correct order* until a meaningful proposition can be interpreted. The somewhat lower correlation between the number of errors in the Sentence Comprehension Test and temporal order memory suggests that the short-term memory store may be spatially rather than temporally ordered.

TABLE 28. Intercorrelations of Variables Taken from Each Decoding and Comprehension Test

Variables	Variables						
	NI − PI	Real/pseudo	Last word	Temporal	Spatial	GAP	Comp.
NI − PI	(.92)						
Real vs. pseudo	−.17^c	(.87)					
Last word	−.27	.48^b	(.93)				
Temporal recall	−.03	−.02	.28^a	(.95)			
Spatial recall	−.05	−.05	.36^a	.40^b	(.91)		
GAP	−.29^a	−.38^a	.51^b	.40^b	.32^a	(.91)	
Comprehension	−.05	.28^a	−.03	.22	−.45^b	−.44^b	(.92)

[a] $p = < .05$.
[b] $p = < .01$.
[c] This correlation is negative because real words are read faster than pseudowords. Thus, a smaller difference between the two produces a larger number.

To determine the underlying relationship among the various measures, a principle components analysis and varimax rotation of axes was undertaken. The result of this analysis appears in Table 29.

The loadings found in Table 29 indicate there are seven different components underlying the correlation matrix of Table 28. The components are all about equally important in accounting for variability in the correlation matrix. The smallest component accounts for 11.67% of the variance, the largest, 14.26% of the variance. Taken together, the components account for 92% of the variance in the correlation matrix. The first component has its heaviest loading on the number of words read in the second part of the Word-Decoding Test. The second component loads most heavily on the NI − PI variable of the Access to Long-Term Memory Speed Test. The next component represents memory for temporal order on the Memory-for-Order Test. The fourth factor loads most strongly on the error score of the Sentence Comprehension Test. The fifth component represents a spatial order factor, the sixth loads most heavily on the GAP test, and the last represents the real-pseudoword contrast derived from the first part of the Word-Decoding Test. In each case, the other loadings are much smaller than the relevant ones.

The principle components analysis illustrates that although the various tests are clearly related, different underlying factors are being tapped by each of the measures. Put another way, each measure appears to be making an independent contribution toward predicting reading ability. Nevertheless, there is some overlap. Both the number of words read in Part 2 of the Word-Decoding Test and the real-pseudoword contrast derived from Part 1 of the same test load on component 7. There are also loadings of about .2 or so on some of the other components. The possibility exists, therefore, that another factor solution, perhaps

TABLE 29. Principle Components Analysis of Decoding and Comprehension Tests

Variables	Components						
	1	2	3	4	5	6	7
NI − PI	−.11	−.94	.01	−.02	.00	−.13	−.10
Real vs. pseudoword latency	−.24	.14	.03	.16	.03	−.18	.85
Number of words read	.81	.20	.14	.08	.21	.22	−.34
Temporal order correct	.11	.00	.94	−.09	.17	.16	.02
Spatial order correct	.17	.02	.21	−.23	.88	.10	.02
GAP	.21	.20	.22	−.21	.12	.82	−.21
Comprehension errors	.06	.03	−.08	.90	.25	−.17	.14

based on a different number of factors, would better explain the interrelationships among the tests. For this reason, a second analysis was conducted. The technique employed a principal factors solution using squared multiple correlations as estimates of factor commonalities. Three roots were extracted by this method producing the factors loadings depicted in Table 30. As can be seen, the first factor appears to be a general one with high loadings for all of the variables except the first three. This factor appears to represent the memory skills required in the Memory-for-Order Test as well as similar skills underlying the Sentence Comprehension Test. The second factor appears to represent the real-word–pseudoword contrast and can probably be characterized as a decoding factor. The third factor represents the time required to access long-term memory codes for letters and for words. The GAP loads on all three factors. Although this principle factors solution is interpretable, the solution accounts for only 56% of the variance in the correlation matrix. This contrasts with the 92% of the variance accounted for by the former solution. Clearly, the data suggest that the first solution is better. The seven measures are best considered as measuring independent skills.

To examine the overall predictive accuracy of the Decoding and Comprehension Test Battery, a multiple regression analysis was conducted using the variables analyzed in the principle components analysis as predictors with the exception of GAP scores which served as the criterion. The multiple R obtained was .87. The entire test battery, therefore, accounts for 76% of the variance in comprehension test scores.

As noted earlier, the test battery makes little use of prior knowledge. In fact, it hardly requires reading ability at all. Nevertheless, the tests account for most of the variability in comprehension test scores. As seen in the last chapter, 62% of the variance in GAP scores is accounted for by the decoding tests alone. The Sentence Comprehension Test brings this figure up to 76%. As even the GAP test requires some degree of prior knowledge of the topic of its passages,

TABLE 30. Principal Factors Analysis of Decoding and Comprehension Tests

Variables	Factors		
	1	2	3
NI − PI	− .05	− .11	− .44
Real vs. pseudoword latency	− .11	.99	.05
Number of words read	.21	− .47	.73
Temporal order correct	.47	− .01	.26
Spatial order correct	.64	− .01	.19
GAP	.52	− .32	.41
Comprehension Errors	− .74	.18	.25

it is not unreasonable to assume that the remaining unexplained 24% of variance is due to differences among testees in background experiences and exposure to test topics. Although it would have been preferable (but somewhat unbelieveable) if the present test battery had accounted for 100% of the variability in comprehension test scores, the present multiple correlation of .87 is high enough to be convincing that the tests are tapping most of the important factors determining reading comprehension ability.

IMPLICATIONS FOR THE READING MODEL

The tests presented in this chapter and in Chapter 5 were derived from the information-processing model of reading developed in Chapter 4. In that model, reading was viewed as a complex information-processing sequence in which visual stimuli are transformed into meaningful units. These units are temporarily stored in short-term memory until interpretable propositions are formed. These propositions are then integrated into a schema that serves as a model of the text being read. At every stage in this process, information residing in long-term memory (syntactical rules, grammatical rules, and so on) interacts in a top-down fashion with the output from bottom-up decoding processes to produce comprehension.

The decoding tests described in Chapter 5 were designed to measure different aspects of the decoding process. The Long-Term Memory Access Speed Test measures how long it takes to retrieve highly overlearned codes stored in long-term memory. As the test is currently designed, it reflects the efficiency of the direct visual route as pictured in the reading model. The Word-Decoding Test, while also concerned with decoding, reflects the efficiency of the controlled visual reading route and the phonological route depicted in Figure 5. The contrast between real-word and pseudoword latencies not only permits us to determine the relative efficiency of these routes, their correlation also indicates how flexible a subject's reading strategies are. Good readers appear to be able to switch routes and strategies depending on the material to be read, whereas poor readers tend to use the same strategies for all materials. The second part of the Word-Decoding Test allows us to isolate the precise stage in a graded series of words when reading is no longer by the direct route.

The Memory-for-Order Test is a measure of how well spatial and temporal order information can be maintained in short-term memory. Because the model requires that reading units be maintained in short-term memory in their proper order until they are formed into meaningful propositions, memory for order is an important determiner of comprehension.

The Sentence Comprehension Test is a measure of how accurately units are formed into propositions. That is, errors on this test indicate that units are either not held in short-term memory long enough or their order is somehow confused. An incorrect propositional interpretation (or a lost one) will lead to inaccurate schemas and poor performance on comprehension measures.

Although each of the tests is related to comprehension as measured by the GAP or GAPADOL, they are also related to one another. Thus, the correlation between NI − PI reaction time as measured by the Access to Long-Term Memory Test correlates .27 with the number of words read in Part 2 of the Word-Decoding Test. Similarly, the real-word versus pseudoword contrast of Part 1 of the Word-Decoding Test correlates − .48 with the number of words read in Part 2. The various intercorrelations can be examined to determine whether a hierarchical relationship exists among the various subskills involved in reading.

The method used to evaluate the relationship among the various reading subskills is a form of causal modeling in which structural equations are tested to see how well they fit the correlation matrix constructed by intercorrelating all of the scores from the population who received all four automated reading tests plus the GAP test. In simple terms, the present approach involved a series of multiple regression analyses in which tests not only were examined as predictors of GAP scores but also as predictors of one another. This procedure decomposes each test into two factors. One mirrors the test's direct effect on the GAP score, the other its indirect effect through other tests. Figure 13 presents the outcome of this analysis in the form of a hierarchical model.

As can be seen, the tests not only predict GAP scores but they also predict one another. Interestingly, many of the tests appear to be predicting the number of words read in Part 2 of the Word-Decoding Test. For example, the Access to Long-Term Memory Test predicts the number of words read in Part 2 and so does Part 1 of the Word-Decoding Test. Those with faster access times to long-term memory codes read more words directly than those with slower long-term

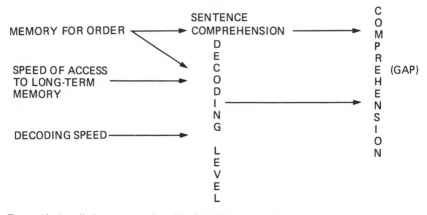

FIGURE 13. A preliminary structural model of the hierarchical relationships among the reading tests.

memory access times. Memory for spatial and temporal order also predicts how many words will be read on Part 2 of the Word-Decoding Test. Thus, all of the decoding tests predict the number of words read which, in turn, predicts GAP scores. The Sentence Comprehension Test, which is also a predictor of GAP scores, is itself predicted only by the Memory-for-Order Test. This reinforces the conclusion that the Sentence Comprehension Test is not merely another decoding measure. The Sentence Comprehension Test is an independent predictor of GAP scores. As expected, sentence comprehension is affected by memory for spatial and temporal order because these skills make it possible to keep reading units in short-term memory until a proposition is abstracted.

The structural model depicted in Figure 13 is only tentative, of course. It will need to be verified through further empirical research. However, even in its present form, the model is well in accord with the information-processing model developed in Chapter 4. The decoding skills that operate at the reading unit level appear to be good predictors of word reading as measured by Part 2 of the Word Decoding Test. Word reading, in turn, predicts the accuracy of comprehension as measured by the GAP test. Comprehension, as measured by the Sentence Comprehension Test, makes its own contribution to predicting GAP scores, and both word reading and sentence comprehension depend on memory for order.

Because 23% of the variance in GAP scores remains unexplained (probably the contribution of specialized prior knowledge), it may be necessary to introduce an additional test or tests to achieve a complete hierarchical model. As it stands, however, the model is plausible, and the information-processing analysis underlying the tests' development appears to be accurate.

SUMMARY

This chapter was concerned with measuring reading comprehension. Typical reading tests depend on prior knowledge that varies from person to person and can seriously bias the results. The Sentence Comprehension Test developed here uses only six words that should be familiar to even beginning readers. Instead of examining the ability to abstract themes from passages or to make complex inferences, the Sentence Comprehension Test is concerned only with verifying the truth or falsity of a single sentence. Nevertheless, the test is a good predictor of reading comprehension as measured by cloze-type tests like the GAP. A reliability and validity study found the number of errors on the Sentence Comprehension Test correlates .44 with scores on the GAP.

The entire test battery comprising all four tests accounted for 76% of the variance in GAP comprehension scores. A principle components analysis and a factor analysis were performed on the correlation matrix made up of the inter-correlations of all tests given to a single population. These showed that the various measures are best considered as reflecting independent skills.

The tests developed here are not only useful predictors of reading comprehension scores, they also serve to validate the reading model developed in Chapter 4. That is, although each test measures an independent skill, a structural analysis of the causal relationships among the tests shows that they interrelate in the manner predicted by the reading model. Tests of decoding speed and level predict the number of words that can be read using the visual route. This test, in turn, predicts reading comprehension scores. Performance on the Sentence Comprehension Test independently predicts comprehension as measured by the GAP. Both sentence comprehension and the number of words read directly are predicted by memory for order.

Chapters 5 and 6 described four automated reading measures and presented data supporting their reliability and validity. The next chapter is concerned with using the tests in practical situations.

PART IV

TESTING AND INSTRUCTION

CHAPTER 7

APPLICATIONS OF TESTS IN READING INSTRUCTION

As noted in Chapter 2, reading instruction has always been an area of intense controversy. Writers (Flesch, 1955, for example) have argued strenuously that reading problems are largely the result of using improper teaching methods. But just what constitutes "proper teaching methods" is a matter of some dispute. Goodman and Goodman (1979) argue for "language-based" methods; Flesch is a champion of decoding and "phonics" instruction. Most experts imply that it is nothing short of a miracle that anyone taught using techniques different from those they advocate ever learns to read. Yet most children manage quite well in any type of reading course. There is, of course, a great deal of overlap among teaching methods, so that rarely is a child exposed to a "pure" language or phonics curriculum. Nevertheless, it seems fair to say that for the average child,* reading instruction by any method is equally likely to be successful.

Problems arise, however, when children do not learn to read. Remediation is in order, but it is not clear what form this should take. Most teachers (and researchers) feel that remediation should be tailored to the needs of the particular child (Spache, 1976), but there is no clear consensus about how this should be done. Remediation requires the careful description of a child's reading problem, usually using diagnostic tests. But, as noted earlier, tests rarely provide the information necessary to develop specific teaching interventions. To serve this purpose, tests must be based on a theory of how reading is accomplished. Few tests are.

---

*Although this chapter, and indeed this book, refer to the problems encountered by children in learning to read, similar problems are encountered by illiterate adults.

This chapter is concerned with reading instruction. It begins with a brief review of teaching methods both past and present. This is followed by a discussion of remedial reading techniques and their relation to testing. The final section of this chapter describes the ways in which tests like those developed in the previous chapters can be used in reading instruction and remediation.

TEACHING READING

D. E. P. Smith (1976), in a "task analysis" of reading, describes a teaching "technology" based largely on Skinnerian operant-conditioning principles. Children are required to learn a "hierarchy of skills" beginning with perceptual ones such as letter identification and working their way up to comprehension. A different Smith (F. Smith, 1973) argues that such skill hierarchies should be inverted and that reading instruction should begin with sentence (or at least word) comprehension and letter identification should come later, if at all. This disagreement between experts is by no means unusual. A visitor to any university library can easily discover shelves full of books on reading instruction, each with a rather different view on the correct way to go about teaching children to read. One thing they all seem to agree on (well, almost all) is that the teaching methods used in the past were hopelessly inefficient compared with modern techniques. But children did learn to read, even in the past. Either the old-time teaching methods were not so bad or children learned to read in spite of them. This section consists of a critical look at reading instruction both past and present with particular emphasis on the role of theory in curriculum development. First, various philosophies of reading instruction will be described and then specific teaching techniques will be examined.

READING INSTRUCTION: WHAT COMES FIRST?

There are as many approaches to reading instruction as there are writers on the subject—actually, there are more. Reid and Hresko (1981) alone cite nine different methods of reading instruction without mentioning one or two described by Spache (1976). In the present section, teaching approaches are organized according to the type of instruction they place first. As the reason for starting reading instruction with one or another type of material is more philosophical than practical, the following approaches are best considered philosophies of reading instruction.

Alphabet First

Several early instructional programs were reviewed in Chapter 2. What they all had in common was their starting point. The first task faced by the child was learning the names of the letters of the alphabet. According to Crowder

(1982), wealthy Greeks hired 24 slaves, each one named for a different letter of the Greek alphabet. Presumably daily interaction and play with the slaves was a way of teaching the child letter names. Pretzels, cookies, and various other items baked in the shape of letters was a favored approach to teaching the alphabet in early America. Besides letter names, children were also required to learn their sounds. This was usually accomplished by having them spell and pronounce simple words and syllables. As education was largely religious, most of the content of early reading programs was religious as well. As printing technology developed, primers such as those described in Chapter 2 were published. In addition to simple words and phrases, these reading books also contained pictures.

Words First

Reading instruction beginning with the alphabet and moving to simple syllables and words was popular for hundreds (perhaps thousands) of years. It is still the approach favored by many teachers and appears to be the basis for the endless repetition of letter names on the "Sesame Street" television show. Moreover, knowledge of letter names prior to entering school has been shown to be a good predictor of reading success (Jansky & de Hirsch, 1972). There seems little doubt that most children taught the names of letters first eventually learn to read. Some children do have difficulty, however, and alternative approaches to reading instruction have been suggested. Three hundred years ago, in the *Visible Word,* the Moravian bishop John Comenius advocated teaching whole words as units without first teaching the alphabet. His technique was to use pictures to indicate word meanings and simple sentences to show how the words could be used in a meaningful context. Developing a "sight" vocabulary is a major goal of all modern reading programs (Johnson & Pearson, 1978); the main difference among them is whether vocabulary development should follow or precede learning the names and sounds of the various letters.

Teaching whole words first, prior to their individual letters, was defended in the early part of this century by appeals to Gestalt theory and its well-known dictum that in perception, the whole is more than the sum of its parts. This was taken to mean that whole words are unique and not easily reducible to their constituent letters. Of course, taken literally, Gestalt theory also implies that because the meaning of a sentence is not reducible to its constituent words, whole sentences should be taught instead of words or letters. Crowder (1982) reports that just such an approach was used in Binghamton, New York, in the latter part of the 19th century. Children viewed sentences while they were read aloud by the instructor. Presumably, the children were ultimately meant to break down sentences into their constituent words.

Even when curriculum designers agree that whole words should come first, they may not agree on exactly which words. One school of thought argues that the words should be the common ones that children have in their spoken vocabulary (Goodman & Goodman, 1979; Smith, 1973), whereas others (Bloomfield, 1942, for instance) have advocated that the words be chosen for their "regularity" of pronunciation. According to the latter view, choosing "regular" words will help children learn phonic principles by exposing them to examples of regular pronunciations.

Sounds First

An emphasis on *phonics* or "sounding out" words in early reading instruction can be found in European educational writings as long ago as the early 1700s. Exactly when such skills should be taught (if ever) remains the subject of much controversy (Chall, 1967, 1979). Perhaps the most frequently advanced argument against phonics is that English letters are not consistently associated with specific sounds. There have been attempts to solve this problem by introducing simplified alphabets in which letters are always associated with a single sound (Downing, 1965). These alphabets have never really caught on with teachers, perhaps because of the difficulty involved in transferring children from the special alphabet to the regular one (Henderson, 1982).

Because a knowledge of letter sounds is usually thought necessary for the reading of "new" words (but see Glushko, 1981, for another viewpoint), practically all modern reading programs require children to learn both whole words and letter sounds. If letter sounds are learned first and then gradually formed into higher-order units such as syllables and words, children are said to be learning "synthetic" word identification skills. If, on the other hand, words are learned first followed by smaller units, the child is said to be learning "analytic" word identification skills. Reading programs today use a combination of both analytic and synthetic methods.

Although the research evidence appears to suggest that early phonics training is more efficient than other approaches (Chall, 1967, 1979), most children learn to read no matter which approach is used. Perhaps this is because the instructional techniques used by different reading programs are actually quite similar. The various instructional techniques are the subject of the next section.

INSTRUCTIONAL TECHNIQUES

Each approach to reading has its preferred instructional tasks. Phonics programs emphasize pairing letters and sounds, language-based programs prefer tasks that emphasize the meaning of words. Nevertheless, there is a great deal of overlap in the methods used by different reading programs. Just as different reading tests use the same task to measure different things, different instructional programs use the same technique to teach supposedly "different" skills. Also, just as reading tests use different tasks to measure the same skill, instructional programs use different teaching techniques to teach what is supposed to be the same skill. The tasks used in reading instruction can be divided into two main classes, those concerned with "decoding" or identifying words and those concerned with reading comprehension.

Decoding Tasks

Sight Words. The goal of decoding instruction is to teach children to identify words. To read fluently, the child must be able to identify at least some words directly on sight. Sight words are commonly used words with familiar meanings. Reading from a series of graded "basal" readers was once the most common method of teaching sight words. Today, basal readers have lost some of their appeal and sight words are taught by showing them to the child on flash cards, by writing them on the blackboard, reading the words aloud, discussing their meanings, using them in a sentence, and writing them in meaningful contexts. To make learning words more interesting, reading programs often include games that require that words be correctly identified to score points. Additional instructional tasks such as requiring children to find the missing letters in words or to search pages full of letters, circling those sequences that spell a word, are also thought to help children learn sight words.

Phonics. Phonic skills are thought to enable children to read words not already in their sight vocabulary. The idea is to enable the child to associate a sound (or sounds) with a letter or group of letters. Workbooks in which children must circle the letter that sounds like the last letter in *drum* or find rhymes or otherwise show they can relate a letter to a sound are the most common way of teaching phonic relationships. Phonics training is sometimes alleged to be best for children with poor short-term memory, although whether this is actually true is controversial (Reid & Hresko, 1981).

Word Analysis. Word analysis skills are also taught as part of decoding. These skills include recognizing and understanding prefixes, suffixes, contractions, compound words, and so on. Often these skills are taught by actually having the child place a prefix in front of a word and note how its meaning changes.

Contextual Analysis. Recognizing a word used in a meaningful context is also part of decoding. Contextual analysis is frequently taught using the cloze procedure in which children are required to fill in words missing from sentences.

Additional Skills. Besides the decoding skills already described, many reading programs also include instruction on one or more of the following skills (adapted from Schank, 1982):

1. How to use a dictionary and a thesaurus
2. Punctuation
3. Expressive reading
4. Using a table of contents and index
5. Reading charts
6. Finding synonyms and antonyms
7. Spelling
8. Dividing words into syllables
9. Grammar
10. Capitalization rules

Although many of these additional tasks are important things for children to know, their relationship to reading is tenuous at best. Consider syllabication, for instance. Many reading programs include exercises in which children are required to draw lines between the syllables of a word. This task is supposed to help children learn to decode new words, but it is often useless for this purpose. This is because the syllables cannot be identified unless the child can first pronounce the word. The problem is illustrated by Johnson and Pearson (1978) with the following example: "One syllabication rule says 'divide before the consonant if the vowel is long (ra/di/o) and after the consonant if the vowel is short (rap/id).' Of what use is such a rule? One must know the pronunciation in order to divide correctly" (p. 6). Clearly, syllabication is not a useful way to teach reading.

Similarly, spelling and reading are not necessarily related skills. The task in spelling is to recall a correct spelling rule (or exception) from memory. The task in reading is to recognize a string of printed letters present in front of the reader. Recognition and recall are two entirely different memory processes, and there is no obvious reason why they should go together (Schank, 1982).

Even some of the most common tasks found in reading programs are of dubious significance in teaching children to read. For instance, virtually all programs use the following type of item in their workbooks:

Write "dis" or "re" in the blank space:

The library sign said, "Please do not _____turb other readers."

If the child does not know the word "disturb," then a guess is the best that can be expected. On the other hand, if the child already knows the word, it is difficult to see what this type of task accomplishes.

There are, of course, many other tasks used in teaching decoding. In fact, the ingenuity of curriculum designers, textbook publishers, and teachers has lead to the development of dozens of different decoding tasks. Although it is not clear whether any one task is more effective than any other, each has its adherents. Moreover, despite ample evidence that some tasks are not teaching any useful reading skill (syllabication, for instance), they continue to make their appearance in each new reading program. Interestingly, the philosophy behind a reading program does not always determine the decoding tasks the program will use. "Phonics first" and "words first" programs both use very similar teaching tasks. Decoding, however, is only part of reading instruction; the ultimate goal is comprehension, which requires the rather different skills discussed next.

Comprehension Tasks

Not all reading programs offer explicit methodological advice about how to teach comprehension skills. Some curriculum designers even deny that comprehension is teachable, arguing that once word identification skills are learned, comprehension is simply a matter of intelligence or common sense. Of those programs that do include specific instruction in comprehension, few concentrate on "comprehending" (the process by which comprehension takes place), preferring instead to concentrate on the products of comprehension such as the ability to give a title to a passage or identify the "main thought" of a paragraph.

As mentioned in Chapter 3, comprehension was at one time measured simply by determining how much of a passage a reader could remember. Over the years, however, an emphasis on meaning has become predominant. Today, readers are said to have demonstrated comprehension when they can somehow use the information in a passage to answer questions or show that they can follow written instructions. The comprehension tasks included in reading programs are intended to help readers display their comprehension; they are not generally designed to improve the process of comprehending.

Word-Level Comprehension. One type of comprehension task described by Johnson and Pearson (1978) is concerned with word meanings in isolation. Examples of such instructional tasks are requiring children to find a word's synonym or its antonym. Differentiating between homophones (*deer* and *dear*, for example) is also a way of permitting children to demonstrate their knowledge of word meanings. In each of these tasks, children are required to demonstrate their word comprehension skills rather than their ability to simply read words as in decoding. These tasks, however, are not concerned with teaching comprehending. That is, they focus on the products of comprehension rather than on the comprehension process itself. There are word-level tasks that are useful in teaching comprehending. For example, word analogies (*up* is to *down* as *right* is to _____) are problems that require the reader to predict the proper word to complete the analogy. By reasoning through such problems, teachers can demonstrate for beginning readers the procedure by which such analogies are solved. This type of instruction focuses on the comprehension process rather than solely on the product. Teaching novice readers to predict what comes next is a technique that is also useful in higher-level comprehension instruction.

Higher-Level Comprehension Tasks. Comprehension at the word level is really only remotely related to actual reading, where phrases, sentences, and longer passages convey meanings that are rarely merely the sum of their constituent words. For this reason, most instruction in comprehension is concerned with sentences and longer passages. Readers are asked to give titles to passages, to answer questions about the content of passages, and to make inferences based on what they have read. Sometimes readers are asked to demonstrate their knowledge by paraphrasing what they have read. Again, as in the word level tasks, many of these higher level tasks focus on the outcome of comprehension rather than the comprehension process itself. A possible exception is the cloze method introduced in previous chapters as a way of measuring reading competence. Having children predict what will come next in a passage can be a useful method for teaching comprehension skills particularly when the teacher models the reasoning process by which a decision is made. Schank (1982) gives many examples of how cloze-type tasks may be used to teach the *process* of comprehension.

Schank also stresses the importance of helping the child acquire general "scripts," which are nothing more than schematic representations of common situations. A script organizes all the information in memory about a common occurrence. For example, a going-to-the-barber script incorporates the events likely to occur on a visit to the barber as well as the behaviors expected from each of the participants (where to wait, when to pay, and so on). Scripts permit us to understand what we read by organizing the information we gain into familiar "knowledge structures." Scripts also permit the reader to predict what will come next and to fill in missing information. Scripts can be taught before passages are read to help organize the new material; they can also be used to design stories for beginning readers. However, the main use of scripts in reading instruction is to permit the beginning readers to discover how knowledge they already have can be applied to comprehension.

As in decoding, there are many techniques used to aid comprehension instruction. Most are concerned with demonstrating comprehension rather than teaching comprehending as a skill. Also, as in decoding, most children learn to comprehend regardless of the instructional technique employed.

TEACHING READING: SUMMARY

Through the years, educators, writers, and scientists have periodically suggested that reading instruction would be more efficient or effective if it were done in some way other than the currently popular one. Virtually every approach has been tried at one time or another. Techniques that are considered modern—the whole-word approach, for instance—were already in use hundreds of years ago. Because most children learn to read regardless of the teaching method used, it seems reasonable to conclude that all techniques are equally effective for the average student. Teachers and teaching techniques may merely be ways of making reading materials available—the student does the rest. Certainly, research seems to indicate that individual differences (in intelligence, family background, and so on) are more important determiners of learning to read than teaching techniques (Newman, 1972).

Although just about all reading programs are effective for most children, there are those who have difficulty learning and for whom extra help becomes necessary. Programs for remediating children's reading problems are discussed in the next section.

REMEDIAL READING INSTRUCTION

Children who have difficulty learning to read are at a great disadvantage in our increasingly complicated society. For this reason, educational authorities have made major efforts to help all children who, for whatever reason, fall behind in the normal classroom. Needless to say, there is no single, generally agreed upon method for helping backward readers. However, Jorm (1983b) has identified three broad approaches to reading remediation that appear to include most programs. Jorm calls the first method *direct instruction*. This approach assumes that all children require similar instruction but some learn best at a slower pace. Remediation by direct instruction involves mainly the same training as normal teaching but at a pace suited to the slower learning student. The second type of remedial program discussed by Jorm is called the *cognitive deficits* approach. From the cognitive deficits point of view, reading problems are not produced by improper (or too hurried) teaching. Instead, a reading problem is assumed to result from a child's inability to perform one or more of the cognitive tasks involved in reading. Remediation, therefore, involves ameliorating these underlying cognitive deficits before turning to reading instruction. The final approach identified by Jorm is a mixed one in which reading instruction is given but this instruction is geared to a specific child's abilities. Remediation, in the mixed approach, is a matter of *compensatory education*—providing special training where a child needs it most. In this section, Jorm's scheme will be used to compare and contrast several approaches to remedial reading instruction.

DIRECT INSTRUCTION

Few books dealing with reading advocate direct instruction as a remedial method. Virtually all recommend that a remedial reading program be specially tailored to the needs of the individual child. But this is rather difficult to do, and many remedial reading programs (despite protestations to the contrary) are merely copies of normal reading instruction programs conducted at a slower pace. There are, however, some remedial programs that explicitly set out to use a direct instructional approach. These programs share a belief that the reading retarded do not need to learn unique skills nor do they have to be taught in special ways. Most direct approaches are based on logical task analyses of the skills involved in reading, and many rely on conditioning models of learning.

A good example of the direct instructional approach that can be applied to either normal or remedial reading teaching is the *DISTAR* program (Engelmann and Bruner, 1974). The *DISTAR* program has three levels beginning with simple decoding skills and moving up to comprehension. At the lowest level, children are taught to identify letters and their sounds, read letters in sequence, blend letter sounds together to make words, and rhyming. Each skill is introduced at a different point in the program, and training continues until the child meets a criterion of mastery. Children who pick up the skills quickly can move ahead, whereas slower children receive extra practice. In this way, the program is tailored to the child, even though no individual diagnosis of a child's reading problem is undertaken. The *DISTAR* approach has been found successful in helping disadvantaged and other "high-risk" children reach higher levels of reading ability than would otherwise be expected (Abt Associates, 1976).

Today, there are many instructional programs based on task analyses and behavioral principles being used in the schools (see Bateman, 1979, for a description of several). Although none of these programs involves a diagnostic assessment of the child's abilities, many seem to be effective methods for helping problems readers improve their decoding skills. A problem reported with some direct instruction programs is that the gains made by children are sometimes short-lived (Carroll, 1972), but this is not always the case. It appears that longer programs lead to more lasting gains than short, intensive ones (Guthrie, Siefert, & Kline, 1978).

Although the positive findings reported above have increased confidence in the direct instructional approach to remediation, it is still a minority position. The cognitive deficits approach to be discussed next has far more adherents.

COGNITIVE DEFICITS

Blaming reading failure on external forces has a long history in the field of reading remediation. At one time or another, brain injury, malnutrition, unstimulating home environments, abnormal cerebral lateralization, speech defects, visual defects, left-handedness, unresolved Oedipal conflicts, and even undescended testicles have been put forward as causes of reading disability. As pointed out by Bateman (1979), from whom this list of causes was adapted, at least some children suffering from each of these maladies have learned to read. Moreover, few of these supposed causes have any specific teaching implications. How many teachers would argue that all boys should be psychoanalyzed (to make sure their Oedipal conflicts are straightened out) before they are taught to read?

Blaming the child for reading failure also has a long history in remedial reading. The notion that a child's cognitive deficits have prevented learning to read has been particularly popular. The philosophy behind the cognitive deficit approach to reading remediation is that when a child fails to learn to read, it is not the instructional technique that is at fault but rather the child's inability to make use of reading instruction. The idea is that no amount of teaching will help the child learn to read until cognitive deficits are overcome. Implicit in this view is that educators know what cognitive skills are necessary to learn to read and how to teach these skills. As noted in Chapter 4, from an information-processing viewpoint, quite a few cognitive processes are involved in reading. Relatively few of these processes are addressed by cognitive deficits programs. In fact, virtually all efforts have been directed toward visual and auditory perceptual skills, sensory integration, linguistic awareness, and—more recently—attention. Each of these will be discussed in turn.

Visual Perception

We need to see in order to read. If for some reason, a child has an uncorrected visual problem that prevents her or him from clearly seeing print, than it is entirely likely that such a child will have difficulty learning to read. It has already been noted in Chapter 2 that some writers have turned this logic around arguing that because some children with visual defects have trouble learning to read, children with reading problems must have visual defects. Not only is this faulty reasoning, but it was also shown to be contrary to a great deal of research evidence indicating that vast majority of poor readers have perfectly normal vision. Perhaps for this reason, the emphasis in remediation has not been on visual problems (although see Spache, 1976), but on perceptual ones. That is, cognitive deficits programs do not assume that reading disabled children cannot see properly but that they fail to "perceive" properly. Perception is a higher-order cognitive skill. It involves not only seeing but also interpreting what has been seen.

The reason for focusing on visual perception is the often-noted finding that children with reading problems frequently have difficulty learning letter names and sounds. Indeed, knowing the letter names before reading instruction begins is often found to be the single best predictor of reading achievement (Jansky & de Hirsch, 1972). However, it is not at all clear that a failure to learn letter names is the result of poor visual perception. Children who have not learned letter names can usually discriminate between letters (Vellutino, 1978) and can even learn to tell apart several dozen Chinese characters after a short training session (Harrigan, 1976). As Chinese characters are no easier to differentiate than English letters, it seems difficult to argue that just because children do not know the names of alphabetic letters, they must have a problem in visual perception. The results of some of the validity studies reported in Chapter 5 also argue against poor readers having a special problem in visual perception. Validity studies of the Long-Term Memory Access Speed Test, found that poor readers could make physical identity matches (B—B, for instance) as accurately and as quickly as good readers. Poor readers were slower and less accurate only when name identity (B—b) was involved. Clearly, the poor readers' problem was not in visual perception but in retrieving letter names from memory.

In Chapter 2, perceptual training programs designed to ameliorate cognitive deficits (such as the one developed by Frostig, 1963) were described. Although these programs were designed to improve school performance, Hammill, Goodman, and Wiederholt (1974), after reviewing over 70 studies of the Frostig and other training programs, concluded that they have little or no effect on helping children learn to read.

Auditory Perception

Although at first glance, it may appear that reading, being a visual task, should not be related to auditory perception, there is a fair amount of correlational evidence for just such a relationship. The interpretation of these studies is presently a matter of some controversy (Bateman, 1979). As in the case of visual perception, poor readers do not appear to have a problem in auditory acuity or in telling one sound from another (Hammill & Larsen, 1974). Instead, the difficulty appears to be in knowing how letters, syllables, and words are pronounced. Calfee, Chapman, and Venezky (1972), for example, found that prereaders who could provide rhymes for words made the best progress when they began reading instruction. More recently, Bradley and Bryant (1983) found that poor readers were not only deficient in finding rhymes and identifying word sounds, but instruction in these skills improved reading performance. Additional evidence for the relationship between knowledge about how words are pronounced and reading ability is reviewed by Crowder (1982). These studies show a clear relationship between knowledge of letter–sound correspondences and reading achievement. Thus, auditory perception, like visual perception, is not an important contributor to reading ability, whereas identifying letter and word sounds probably is.

Sensory Intergration

Some writers (Birch & Belmont, 1964, for example) have suggested that a cognitive deficit responsible for at least some reading problems is a difficulty integrating across sensory systems. What is usually meant by this is that children with reading disabilities display a difficulty translating stimuli presented in one sensory modality to a response in another modality. For example, a sensory integration task might require a child to listen to a pattern of tones (auditory modality) and tap out the pattern on a tabletop (tactile modality). The rationale for including sensory integration in the list of prereading skills is that in the initial stages, learning to read involves coordinating the way a word looks with the way it sounds. Now, in one sense, it is self-evident that a child who cannot read a word out loud lacks sensory integration because this is one way sensory integration is measured. But an inability to read words aloud does not mean the child has a problem at the sensory-motor level. It may merely mean that the child has not learned the proper pronunciations for certain letters and words. Clearly, such children need training in attaching sounds to print, but any other training in sensory integration particularly in other sense modalities has not proven to be a useful aid in reading remediation (see Bateman, 1979, and Spache, 1976).

Linguistic Training

As reading comprehension is certainly related to language understanding, several writers have emphasized the need for children to overcome their "language deficits" before they can hope to profit from reading instruction. These recommendations frequently involve the use of the *Illinois Test of Psycholinguistic Abilities* (ITPA, Kirk *et al.*, 1968) as the proper diagnostic instrument to help plan teaching programs. To a large degree, the use of this test appears to result from its title which includes the word "psycholinguistic." Carroll (1972) found the test to be just another intelligence test with no particular claim to be a test of linguistic abilities. When the ITPA has been administered to both good and poor readers, about the only consistent difference between them has been on the subtests called "Auditory and Visual Sequential Memory" (digit-span tests). Although these results are in agreement with those reported in Chapter 5 for the Memory-for-Order Test, there seems little else of linguistic significance has been identified as deficient in poor readers.

Attention

Ross (1976), in a book dealing with "learning disabilities," concludes that learning-disabled children have difficulty maintaining selective attention. Although the term "selective attention" has attracted many meanings in experimental psychology, it is generally used to describe a situation in which an individual must attend to one class of stimuli in the face of irrelevant, distracting stimuli. According to Ross, the ability to selectively attend develops as a child grows up, and many learning-disabled children have been delayed in its development. Ross recommends that the reading disabled be taught with materials that make discriminations easier. For example, the color, size, and even type styles of letters can be changed while their shape remains constant. This will help the child to concentrate on important stimulus dimensions. Ross also advocates the use of systematic, operant-style reinforcements to motivate and teach children to read. Indeed, Ross conceptualizes the entire reading process in operant conditioning terms:

> When a child looks at a printed word on a page and says the word aloud, it is easy to view this sequence as the presentation of a stimulus and the emission of a verbal response. If, following the correct response, the teacher said "good" . . . the next time the child is presented with that word, the child will again emit the correct reading response. (p. 159)

Working within this framework, Ryback and Staats (1970) showed that behavior modification techniques can be useful in improving reading performance among the disabled. Other writers have also testified to the value of reinforcement in teaching decoding skills (Bateman, 1979) if not to the theory of reading that it implies (Schwartz & Johnson, 1981).

Cognitive Deficits: Summary

Overall, the cognitive deficits approach to reading remediation has not been very effective (with the possible exception of Ross's attentional training). The main problem, of course, is that the cognitive deficits approach concentrates on teaching skills like visual and auditory perception—skills that are largely unrelated to reading performance. The result is an improvement on measures of the particular cognitive task (training with the Frostig perceptual program increases scores on the Frostig test) with no effect on reading performance. On the other hand, when skills that are related to reading such as rhyming and letter-sound correspondences are taught, reading improvement follows. Despite its disappointing history, the cognitive deficits approach remains popular among teachers. However, the compensatory education approach that is discussed next is quickly gaining adherents.

COMPENSATORY EDUCATION

The compensatory education approach to reading remediation represents a mixture of the preceding approaches. It involves direct reading instruction matched to a particular child. As already noted, virtually all books on reading remediation recommend compensatory education, but fews teachers actually manage to tailor remedial programs to the needs of specific children. This is because to vary instructional methods to suit a child's abilities, teachers must first know what a child's abilities are and how to design teaching programs to fit them. In both areas, our knowledge is currently deficient. Most reading tests are not adequate to define precisely what a child's reading problems are, and even those tests that are diagnostic are not tied closely to any reading program. Nevertheless, compensatory education remains an excellent idea that seems to include what is best about each of the other approaches.

Compensatory education depends on what are known as "aptitude by treatment interactions." Aptitudes are cognitive skills and treatments are teaching methods. Their interaction is thought to determine a child's reading level. To take a simple example, a child who knows only a few letter sounds may be better off beginning reading instruction using the whole-word approach, whereas a child who knows many sounds may benefit more from early phonics instruction. In many ways, the entire compensatory education approach depends upon the existence of aptitude by treatment interactions. Several attempts to discover and use such interactions in remedial reading will be discussed next.

Aptitude by Treatment Interactions

In a study of teachers of the learning disabled conducted in Illinois, the vast majority were found to believe that children should be taught in the "modality" that best fits their particular pattern of strengths (Arter & Jenkins, cited by Bateman, 1979). To the teachers, this meant "auditory learners" should be given phonics training, whereas "visual learners" do best in a sight-word program. Seventy-eight percent of teachers reported that they "frequently" or "always" assigned children to reading programs based on their relative strengths. Unfortunately, the faith demonstrated by the teachers has not been confirmed by research. Few studies have found that children progress more rapidly when teaching programs are designed to fit specific auditory or visual learning skills (Arter & Jenkins, cited by Bateman, 1979; Derevensky, 1978; Ysseldyke, 1973). Either the hypothesis of a treatment by aptitude interaction is wrong, or the diagnostic and teaching techniques studied so far have been inappropriate.

Because children can be divided into two groups on the basis of any number of dichotomies, many other treatment by aptitude interactions have been looked at. Introversion versus extroversion (Whitehill & Jipson, 1970), brain injured versus non-brain injured (Reed, Rabe & Mankinen, 1970), and a host of other dichotomies have been investigated (Berliner & Cohen, 1973). Thus far, none have fared more favorably than modality. This does not mean that the compensatory approach to remedial reading is wrong. It may be that the proper dimension on which to divide children and most effective teaching techniques for helping them improve have still not been discovered. This subject will be returned to later in this chapter. For the present, it is fair to say that compensatory teaching remains an unfulfilled promise.

Although the various remedial approaches vary in the emphasis they put on diagnosing a child's specific reading problem, all methods must decide which children require remediation. This in itself is a kind of diagnosis and requires some discussion. In a way, this entire book is concerned with diagnosis, but the specific issue was discussed most directly in Chapter 3 when various reading tests were described. Some of the problems with both formal and informal reading tests were pointed out in that chapter as well as elsewhere in this book. To the extent that remedial reading programs rely on typical tests to diagnose children's reading problems, they, too, will suffer from the same serious problems of reliability and validity. Unfortunately (and not surprisingly, because there is little else to choose from), most remedial reading programs do rely on traditional tests as well as a variety of informal methods to diagnose readers's strengths and weaknesses. Thus, the reliability and validity of their diagnoses are suspect.

Besides their reliance on dubious diagnostic methods, some remedial reading programs advocate calculating threshold and "expected reading" levels against which a child's progress may be judged. In doing this, program designers often display a cavalier disregard for test theory and statistics in their recommendations. Gilliland (1974), for instance, recommends that every child whose reading level is not three-quarters of the average requires remediation. As already noted, however, a specified proportion of children will always be above and below average because of the way standardized tests are constructed. Following Gilliland's rule would mean that successful teaching will just raise the average score on the test; someone would still score less than three-quarters of average.

Perhaps even worse than this definition of who needs remediation is Gilliland's definition of reading potential. The formula for reading potential is given as:

$$\frac{IQ + (IQ - 100)}{100} \times \text{grade in school}$$

A child with a 120 IQ who is presently in the fourth grade would have a reading potential of 5.6 (fifth grade, 6th month). This formula is based on the assumption that IQ is a measure of reading ability that correlates perfectly with reading test scores and that reading competence progresses smoothly through the grades. Thus, a child with an average IQ of 100 is expected to read at grade level, a child with an above average IQ is expected to read above grade level, and a child with an IQ below 100 is expected to read below grade level. Gilliland explains the formula by stating that an IQ score "represents a percentage of normal intelligence . . . 80 IQ means 80 percent . . . of average intelligence, while 120 IQ means 1.20 or 120 percent" (p. 43).

Now, it is not clear where Gilliland got this idea, but it is completely wrong. Putting aside just what "80 percent of normal intelligence" means, it should be obvious that in the terminology of Chapter 3, IQ tests are norm-referenced, standardized tests. That is, there is no particular relationship between the raw scores achieved by testees and their IQ score. The mean raw score (whatever it is) is fixed at an IQ score of 100, and the raw score standard deviation is usually set equal to 15 IQ points. Thus, the relationship between IQ scores and percentiles is not the one that Gilliland implies. Instead, the relationship is determined by the percentage of testees falling in various parts of the normal curve as described in Chapter 3. That is, seven percent of test takers can be expected to score below 80 or above 120 on an IQ test. The same holds true for standardized reading tests. They, too, conform to the normal curve. Thus, seven percent of testees will also score lower than 1.3 standard deviations below the mean on the reading test. But will these people be the same ones who scored 1.3 standard deviations below the mean on the IQ test as Gilliland's formula requires? The answer is no. Some students will fall into the same part of the distribution on both tests and some will not. For all students to fall into the same parts of the distribution on both the IQ and reading tests, the correlation between IQ and reading tests must be perfect. In reality, correlations around .60 to .70 are usually obtained.

Given the obvious usefulness of knowing a child's reading potential, it should be expected that measures of potential will continue to be developed. Unfortunately, the ones presently available are all similar to Gilliland's, and none do the job they were meant to do.

REMEDIAL READING INSTRUCTION: SUMMARY

The importance of reading in today's society has brought special concern for those who have difficulty learning in the normal classroom. Several approaches to reading remediation were reviewed in this section. The direct instructional method involves providing extra reading instruction for slow readers. This approach does not assume that slow readers require unique skills, nor does it involve special assessments of a child's cognitive strengths and weaknesses. Most direct instructional approaches to remediation do, however, permit children to proceed at their own pace. In contrast to direct instruction, cognitive deficit programs are based on the notion that a child who has trouble learning to read suffers from cognitive deficits that must be ameliorated before reading instruction can take place. This approach assumes that the cognitive deficits underlying reading disability can be identified, measured, and ameliorated. Thus far, none of these assumptions has been substantiated. Although training on some basic cognitive tasks (visual perception, for instance) has been shown to improve performance on tests of those tasks, such training has not been shown to improve reading. The third approach to reading remediation reviewed in this section was based on compensatory education. Compensatory education programs diagnose children's strengths and weaknesses and try to supply a teaching program tailored to the individual child. Thus far, specific treatment by aptitude interactions have not been found.

On the whole, research comparing various remedial techniques has failed to provide strong evidence indicating that complicated remedial approaches are more effective than direct instruction. In fact, Bradley and Bryant's (1983) demonstration that teaching prereaders to pronounce letter sequences improves their reading performance when instruction begins is an excellent illustration of the power of direct reading instruction and the importance of phonics in learning to read.

Although the promise of the compensatory education approach has yet to be fulfilled, extra direct instruction can be targeted to those who need it most. This is exactly what Bradley and Bryant did. Indeed, one might even call their approach (as well as the one represented by *DISTAR*), a modified form of compensatory education in the sense that only children who require extra instruction receive it. This approach to remediation involves neither elaborate diagnoses of reading skills nor aptitude by treatment interactions; nevertheless, it has been found to be effective for many backward readers. The next section describes how the tests developed in this book can be used in a modified form of compensatory education to help remediate reading problems.

TEST-GUIDED INSTRUCTION

The tests presented in Chapters 5 and 6 covered several aspects of decoding and comprehension. These tests are certainly not the last word in measuring reading competence, but they do provide a convenient means of diagnosing deficiencies and providing extra practice. Although diagnosis is involved, the type of practice offered will be the same for all those found deficient in a skill. Hence, the approach followed here is similar to the modified version of the compensatory education technique described above.

INCREASING READING SPEED

Even poor readers can get through most texts if given enough time. Their oral reading may be halting and slow and their comprehension minimal, but they eventually get most of the words out. Because even the poorest reader can learn to grind out some words, reading problems have often been attributed to higher-order comprehension deficits rather than decoding problems. This view is derived from a simple model of reading in which the various stages (decoding, comprehension, and so on) operate independently. In contrast, the model of information processing in reading presented in Chapter 4 assumes that comprehension and decoding affect one another. That is, because comprehension and decoding overlap in time and because both depend on the limited capacity short-term memory store, poor performance in one area is likely to affect the other. For example, slow decoding has a deleterious effect on comprehension because devoting more effort and attention to decoding leaves less cognitive capacity available for comprehension. Poor comprehension, of course, has a similar negative effect on decoding (Glaser, 1982), but because comprehension is virtually impossible without decoding, most writers believe that decoding is primary (Perfetti and Lesgold, 1979).

If one important determinant of reading ability is the speed and efficacy of decoding, then it seems reasonable to devote remedial efforts to decoding practice. For those who need it, practice in speedy decoding should improve decoding skill and thereby decrease the demand on short-term memory. The ultimate effect of increased decoding efficiency, therefore, is to free up cognitive capacity that can be devoted to comprehension. By the same reasoning, comprehension practice, if it leads to more efficient comprehension skills, should release spare capacity that can be devoted to decoding. There is some evidence that comprehension practice has precisely this effect (Curtis, 1980). Two of the present tests are particularly useful aids for increasing decoding efficiency—the Long-Term Memory Access Speed Test and the Word-Decoding Test. Each will be discussed in this section.

LONG-TERM MEMORY ACCESS SPEED

The Long-Term Memory Access Speed Test produces data directly relevant to decoding speed, namely the amount of time it takes to access a letter name in long-term memory. The test also measures accuracy, which makes it useful in teaching as well as testing.

Consider a primary school-age child who does poorly on the Long-Term Memory Access Speed Test. If the child knows capital and lowercase letter names but takes a long time to retrieve them from memory, slow but accurate performance can result. Continued practice should lead to faster reaction times and, therefore, faster decoding. Indeed, the validity studies reported in Chapter 5 did find reaction times to increase with practice on the task. Thus, for the accurate but slow child, this test can serve not only as an evaluation instrument but also as a means of teaching.

Using the test to provide routine practice relieves the teacher for other duties. It is also perceived by children as an enjoyable game (unlike other forms of drill). Virtually all children tested in the studies reported in this book enjoyed interacting with the computer, particularly when feedback was provided. Letting children know how accurate and how fast they are performing provides motivation for them to continue playing the game and trying to beat their own score. Similar positive reactions to computer-assisted drill have been reported by researchers in the field of computer-assisted instruction (Fletcher, 1979).

Although using the test to provide practice in this way makes sense for those who already know the letter names, the child who does not know them will still be in the dark no matter how much practice the test provides. However, the test program may be easily modified to provide the necessary instruction. For example, a proper match (A–a, for instance) can be demonstrated for the student first and then matching trials using this combination can be interspersed with physical matches (A–A) and nonmatches (A–B). This can be repeated for the various capital and lower-case combinations until the child learns to match the proper letter pairs.

Following Ross (1976), color, size, and other cues can be used to help the student learn matches; these extra cues can be faded out as accuracy improves. Learning, in this situation, is monitored by noting match accuracy. Until virtually perfect accuracy is achieved, speed is neglected. Once the accuracy criterion is met, continued practice can be provided to increase speed. If the computing system being used does not have voice capability, the letter names will have to be said aloud by a teacher. However, adding a voice synthesizer is a relatively inexpensive option. It should be possible, for a relatively small amount, to have the computer say the letter name aloud as a pair is presented. Voice synthesizers will be discussed further in the next chapter.

By pairing the oral presentation of a letter name with the letter pair (e.g., A–a), followed by extensive practice in matching pairs, it should be possible to improve both the speed and accuracy of long-term memory access of most readers. The value of the test in reading instruction does not end there, however. The matching task can also be used to help speed access to other relevant codes in long-term memory. For instance, instead of letters, Goldberg *et. al* (1977) had subjects match whole words. The words were either identical (deer–deer), homophones (deer–dear), or members of the same semantic category (deer–elk). In their study, subjects with high verbal ability were found to make these matches faster than low verbal ability subjects. As in the letter-matching task, practice in matching words increases matching speed. However, accuracy depends on knowing word sounds or meanings in the first place. For this reason, practice in matching words must be preceded by instruction if it is to be of any practical use. For example, children taught particular word "sounds" can then be given opportunities to match these sounds using the computer-driven task. As demonstrated by Bradley and Bryant (1983), the ability to identify word sounds is an important predictor of reading performance. Synonyms, antonyms, semantic category, and other matches can also be used to increase memory retrieval efficiency. In each case, of course, the particular relationship being matched must be taught first. Accuracy can then be monitored by the test. Once the child has mastered the relationship being taught, further practice may be given to increase speed. The rationale for this approach is the same one given earlier. Faster access time leaves cognitive capacity available for comprehension and other reading tasks.

To summarize, the Long-Term Memory Access Speed Test is not only a measure of the speed and accuracy with which linguistic codes can be retrieved from long-term memory, it is also a useful way to give students practice in speeded retrieval. As noted, the test must be paired with instruction if the children are expected to learn new relationships. Once such relationships are learned (and the process of learning can be monitored by recording test accuracy), further practice increases the efficiency of reaction time and, presumably, decoding. The steps involved in using the test are:

1. Identify children who perform slower than average on the test. Although slowness is relative, those children more than one standard deviation below the mean can probably benefit from practice.

2. If accuracy is high, further practice on the test should improve reaction time.

3. If accuracy is low, the matching dimension (letter names, letter sounds, word sounds, word meanings, and so on) must be taught. For some dimensions, this may be accomplished by the computer itself, particularly if it is fitted with a voice synthesizer. For other dimensions, teachers will have to demonstrate the relationship. The test can be used to monitor accuracy and provide the necessary practice.

Long-term memory access speed is only one determinant of decoding efficiency; the actual time taken to read words as measured by the Word-Decoding Test is another. The use of the Word-Decoding Test in remediation is described next.

WORD-DECODING

The Word-Decoding Test provides several valuable types of information for teaching reading. Perhaps the most important information provided by this test is the speed with which words can be read from the graded word reading list (Part 2 of the test). In the validity studies described in Chapter 6, it was noted that reaction times tended to remain steady from the beginning of the test until they suddenly and dramatically increased. This increase was thought to represent a transition from highly practiced words that most children could read by sight to relatively new words that have to be read by slower methods (pre-sumably by sounding them out). The point at which reaction times suddenly increase differs from person to person. Thus, the abrupt change is a good indicator of vocabulary level.

It is important to note that after reaction times increase, there are still some words the individual can read. Reading latencies to these words are slow because they are not familiar enough to the subject to be read purely by sight as the preceding words were. Practice reading these "slow" words results in faster decoding and an increase in sight-reading vocabulary. If the words used in the test are chosen from those encountered in everyday reading, practice results in increased decoding speed and more fluent reading. Practice should also make available more cognitive capacity that can be devoted to comprehension.

Part 1 of the Word-Decoding Test is also useful for decoding practice. Pronouncing pseudowords, for instance, provides practice in learning letter–sound correspondences. If the computer is fitted with a speech synthesizer, each item in Part 1 of the test can be pronounced for the child, who then must model what she or he hears. As the child learns the appropriate pronunciations, emphasis can shift from accuracy to speed. The correlation between reading latencies for real and pseudowords can serve as an index of progress. As noted in Chapter 5, this correlation should decrease with practice because the child is learning to read the real words by sight while continuing to use a "sounding out" strategy for reading pseudowords.

Increasing Reading Speed: Summary

Two of the tests described in Chapter 5 are useful in helping increase reading speed. The Long-Term Memory Access Test permits the reader to practice retrieving information from memory, and the Word-Decoding Test provides a means of increasing sight vocabulary. Practice of the sort recommended here has been found to increase reading speed (Perfetti & Hogaboam, 1975b). Practice on both tests also increases decoding efficiency, thereby releasing cognitive capacity for comprehension. But this is not where their usefulness ends. Not only can these tests be used to provide practice on skills already learned, they can also be used to teach new skills. The use of a voice synthesizer, for example, permits the Word-Decoding Test not only to determine the subject's decoding speed and vocabulary level but also to indicate to the subject how various words and pseudowords are pronounced. The child can use the computer as a dedicated teacher who never gets impatient or distracted.

As is evident from the discussion so far, much emphasis has been placed on practice and drill. Computer-directed practice is a particularly efficient way of providing drill for children. The computer keeps accurate records of responses (including reaction times), it does not get bored or impatient, and it demands accuracy. Children enjoy interacting with computers, and it is relatively easy to turn computer drill into a game (the next chapter contains more discussion on this topic). Although most researchers agree that practice and drill are necessary to remedial teaching (Bateman, 1979; Perfetti & Lesgold, 1979), not all teachers agree. Williams (1979) suggests that part of this resistance is the belief among many teachers that education should be "meaningful" and that rote drill is not really teaching. As Bateman (1979) points out, this attitude may be appropriate "for the majority of children who do seem to learn to read by osmosis and without intensive, systematic, or structured instruction" (p. 248). For those children who have problems learning to read, however, there seems no substitute for practice and drill. Rather than avoiding it, we should try to make practice and drill as palatable and effective as possible.

The two tests described in this section lend themselves to both diagnosis and remediation. The remaining two tests, Memory-for-Order and Sentence Comprehension are not themselves useful teaching devices. But they are still valuable in planning remediation programs as described next.

MEMORY-FOR-ORDER TEST

In the last section, methods to increase decoding speed were described. As noted in Chapter 4, however, some poor readers are not only slow decoders but have other reading problems as well. For example, the information-processing model described in Chapter 4 requires that reading units be decoded and stored in short-term memory in such a way that the order of units does not violate the rules of English syntax. This is because understanding a sentence requires maintaining words in their proper order. At a different level, order information is also required if words are to be read successfully. Readers must realize that letter order determines meaning and that *tap*, for instance, is not the same as *pat*. Evidence that poor readers are deficient in maintaining order information in short-term memory was reviewed in Chapter 4. The results of the validity study reported in Chapter 5 were in accord with the findings of that literature review— poor readers are deficient in memory for order. In addition, poor readers are less able to switch from temporal to spatial order recall strategies in response to test demands.

The Memory-for-Order Test does not lend itself to teaching in the same way that the Long-Term Memory Access and Word-Decoding tests do. Although poor memory for order and an inability to switch from a temporal to a spatial order strategy can be diagnosed by this test, it is not clear that practice on the Memory-for-Order Test will necessarily generalize to reading. That is, practice (combined with feedback and reinforcement) may improve performance on the test, but this improvement will not necessarily carry over to reading where meaningful materials are used. For this reason, children who perform poorly on this test should be given practice in ordering meaningful reading materials.

At the letter level, perhaps the simplest method of increasing sensitivity to order is an adaptation of a method for teaching sight words described by Schank (1982).

Training begins with simple three-letter words such as *pat, pot, ten, mad, pit* and *lap*. These words were chosen because switching their first and last letters produces real words. Instruction begins by teaching children to pronounce the first word. The teacher illustrates the correct pronunciation by first saying "at" and then adding the *p* sound. Children are also required to say the words out loud. Once children have learned the words, they can be shown what happens when letter order is manipulated. For example, children can learn to shift the first and last letters in *pat* to produce *tap*. Similarly, *pot* can be transformed to *top*, *ten* to *net*, and so forth. As the child progresses, other tasks that emphasize order (solving simple anagrams, for instance) can be introduced.

Although it is important for beginning readers to be sensitive to letter order, as sight vocabulary develops, word order becomes more important. Children must learn to maintain words and phrases in their proper order in short-term memory; otherwise sentence meanings will be lost. Generalizing from the method described for letters, sensitivity to word order can be increased by exercises that require children to manipulate the order of words. For instance, the meaning of *The boy saw the cat* can be shown to change by shifting only two words: *The cat saw the boy*. Experimentation with similar sentences (*The boy hit the ball, The girl frightened the bird*) will sensitize the child to ways in which word order determines meaning. Naturally, as the child becomes a more proficient reader, sentences can be made more difficult, but the rationale behind the task remains unchanged. Finally, children can be taught to unscramble "sentence anagrams" constructed by mixing up the word order of meaningful sentences. Weaver (cited by Perfetti & Lesgold, 1979) found that practice solving sentence anagrams increased reading comprehension as measured by a cloze test.

In essence, what is being recommended here is instruction in language syntax. Not syntax in some abstract, linguistic sense, but a knowledge of how word order affects meaning. Such knowledge permits children to predict what will come next in a sentence (the skill measured in cloze tasks). Although some writers have claimed that an ability to predict what comes next is the very essence of reading (Schank, 1982), few reading programs devote much explicit attention to word order (a "syntax" entry does not even appear in the index of most modern books on reading instruction). This is a peculiar omission because a sensitivity to word order is one of the most basic language skills.

The Memory-for-Order Test is a useful method for diagnosing those children who have difficulty maintaining items in their proper order in short-term memory, but it is not sensitive to all the short-term memory problems that may interfere with reading. Some of these other problems are measured by the Sentence Comprehension Test, discussed next.

SENTENCE COMPREHENSION TEST

The Sentence Comprehension Test described in Chapter 6 was designed to measure the cognitive processes involved in comprehension without relying on an individual's specific knowledge of people, places, and events. In this regard, the test measures the process of comprehending rather than the comprehension products measured by most reading tests. A validity study of the test found that poor readers made many more errors than proficient readers when comparing sentences to subsequently shown pictures. Because the test demands speedy responding, some of the poor readers' difficulty is doubtless the result of slow decoding and memory access speed. However, even when these factors are taken into account, performance on the Sentence Comprehension Test is still a good predictor of comprehension as measured by a cloze test. This finding was interpreted as indicating that the ability to manipulate and store meaningful units in short-term memory is an important aspect of reading comprehension.

Although it is possible that poor readers have smaller short-term memory stores than good readers, a more likely explanation for their poor performance on the Sentence Comprehension Test is their failure to use efficient short-term memory coding strategies. In the words of Wong et al. (1977), poor readers tend to be "inactive learners" who rely on rote memory rather than active rehearsal or recoding to aid recall. This view is reinforced by Wong's (1978) findings that recall among poor readers is improved by giving them instructions concerning how to use more efficient rehearsal strategies.

Suggested ways to improve short-term memory coding strategies can be found in books and articles by Bakker (1967, 1970), Koppitz (1970, 1973, 1975), and, as already mentioned, Wong (1978). Although the methods suggested by these and other writers do appear to improve recall, their relevance to reading is unclear. Most techniques for improving short-term memory involve grouping related items together and other ways of organizing disparate material. For example, word lists are easier to recall if semantically related words are grouped together and mnemonic techniques are also useful in recalling lists of items. Rarely, however, does reading involve verbatim recall. Instead, it is the sense of what is being read that must be remembered. As noted in Chapter 4, concentrating on the precise words may even be inimical to reading, as it distracts readers from examining the meaning of what they have read. Indeed, it is highly likely that poor readers on the Sentence Comprehension Test are making many errors on the task precisely because they are concentrating on retaining the precise words of the sentences rather than their meanings. When subjects are instructed to "form a mental image of the sentence" or to visualize the picture that the sentence represents, performance improves (Schwartz & Hartley, 1984). Findings such as these suggest that poor performance on the Sentence Comprehension Test reflects the failure to develop an appropriate representational strategy. That is, poor performers fail to realize that it is the picture the sentence evokes and not its precise wording that is important. For this reason, subjects who perform poorly on the Sentence Comprehension Test require training in how to derive meaning from sentences and longer texts.

Instruction in how to gain meaning from sentences is not part of typical reading curricula. As already discussed, most reading programs concentrate on the products of comprehension rather than the comprehension process itself. There are some exceptions, however. Collins and Smith (1982) and Schank (1982) have both offered similar suggestions for how reading comprehension may be taught.

These authors emphasize the role of cognitive schemas in understanding texts and the importance of prediction or hypothesis formation as a teaching tool. For Schank, prediction can occur at many levels. The child who tries to guess the missing letters in the sentence *H__W M__NY R__ADS M__ST A M__N W__LK D__WN* is predicting at the letter level. If words are missing rather than letters, the child is predicting at the word level. Higher order prediction is also possible. In every case, the child must learn to use the context to help guide prediction. That few people have trouble filling in the letters in the sentence above is testimony to how familiarity and context aid comprehension.

Besides prediction, Schank's teaching method makes use of scripts, plans, and goals. Scripts were defined in a previous section of this chapter and refer to organized knowledge the reader has gained from experience. Scripts are arranged hierarchically in long-term memory. To take the example used earlier, a going-to-the-barber script includes everything the child knows about a visit to the barbershop (who pays, where one sits, and so on). Embedded within this script are subscripts relating to specific barbers (for example, hairstylists, corner barbers, and so on). Within these subscripts are even narrower ones concerning particular aspects of getting a haircut (how to hold one's head, etc.). At any particular point in reading about a trip to the barber, the child can use knowledge of the various scripts to determine what is happening. Besides scripts, children must also learn to understand characters' goals and plans and to use this under-standing to guide reading comprehension.

It is not really possible to do justice to the richness of Schank's or Collins and Smith's approach in a book concerned with measuring reading competence. The topic deserves a book to itself. Schank particularly makes many specific suggestions for teaching reading comprehension that are worthwhile reading for any reading teacher. For our present purposes, suffice to say that it is the training offered by programs like Schank's that is needed by students who perform poorly on the Sentence Comprehension Test. Although simple in structure, the Sentence Comprehension Test demands that the student devise a strategy if performance is to be successful. The task cannot be done simply by reading and retaining the words. Unfortunately, the comprehension tasks used in typical reading programs (find the main thought, give a title to a paragraph, and so on) do not teach children how to formulate such strategies.

In this section, the tests presented in Chapters 5 and 6 were shown to be useful aids in remediating reading disorders. Two of the tests, Long-Term Memory Access and Word-Decoding, were found not only to be useful in diagnosing reading problems but also in providing the type and amount of practice necessary to overcome them. The Memory-for-Order and Sentence Comprehension Tests are not suitable for providing practice as their task requirements are not directly generalizable to reading. However, poor performance on these tests does have direct implications for the type of remediation students require and these implications were discussed.

Needless to say, the suggested teaching techniques described in this section are not the only types of remedial exercises that might help children improve their reading performance. They are meant to be illustrative only. The number of teaching techniques that fit the requirements stated above is limited only by the imagination of teachers and curriculum designers.

SUMMARY

This chapter was concerned with reading instruction. It began with a brief overview of teaching philosophies and commonly used instructional techniques. Although strong arguments have been made for the superiority of one or another technique, most children eventually learn to read no matter how reading is taught. When children do have difficulty learning to read, however, remedial help is called for. In this field, too, there are strongly held opinions about how to proceed. Although many of the arguments in favor of one or another approach seem quite logical (ameliorate a child's cognitive deficits, look for treatment by aptitude interactions), no approach to remediating reading disorders has been found more effective than direct reading instruction, particularly instruction in phonics. Several of the tests presented in the preceding chapters can be used not only to identify children who are deficient in some cognitive skill involved in reading but also to provide the practice necessary to overcome these deficiencies. Methods for using the tests to guide instruction were described.

Although the tests developed in this book can be used to guide instruction, it must be emphasized that they are only a beginning. Their development has been presented in great detail so that other teachers and researchers can follow the same steps while profiting from my errors. Clearly, much work remains to be done. The next chapter explores some of the directions in which this work may proceed.

CHAPTER 8

WHAT THE FUTURE HOLDS

It is dangerous to make predictions about the future. Unforseen events and new discoveries often have a way of rendering even the most carefully thought out predictions no better than mere guesses. This does not mean that making such predictions is a waste of time. On the contrary, pointing out areas where more work needs to be done and indicating the possible forms this work can take are valuable exercises for developing fields such as reading research. Indeed, a set of predictions can serve as a blueprint for guiding future research and development.

This chapter represents an attempt to extrapolate from present trends to possible future directions. The approach adopted here is a conservative one. No new inventions or biomedical discoveries (genetic engineering for reading, for example) are postulated. Instead, the present chapter examines how the field is likely to develop with the tools presently available. The chapter is divided into three parts. The first deals with theory, the second with testing, and the third with likely new developments in teaching.

THEORY

The information-processing theory of reading presented in Chapter 4 is based on an interpretation of the reading research reviewed in that chapter and throughout the book. Although the theory is a fair representation of the field as it now stands, reading research is continuing at an explosive rate. Dozens of research papers dealing with one or another aspect of reading are published each month. Add to these the hundreds of books, films, technical reports, and conference papers dealing with reading that appear each year, and it seems obvious that the theory presented in this book is hardly likely to be the final one.

Although much reading research merely serves to reinforce the findings reported in this book, some researchers have truly broken new ground. Among these researchers, the ones most likely to influence future work are those that provide new theoretical or research tools. For example, when psychologists first began to study reading in the latter part of the last century, most studies were concerned with measuring the time required to perform various reading tasks. The introduction of techniques to monitor eye movements during reading lead to a whole new type of research and theory based on this new source of information. Besides inferring the processing demands of various reading skills from the time they took, researchers could observe how long readers spent looking at different parts of text. Scanning habits also became open to direct study. The power of this research technique turned out to be such that it is still being used today (see Chapter 4). In this section, a new approach to developing cognitive theories, componential analysis, will be described. This will be followed by an overview of other directions in which research appears to be going.

COMPONENTIAL ANALYSIS

A relatively new approach to studying cognitive skills, *componential analysis* (a term first used by Sternberg, 1977) attempts to identify the specific information-processing components involved in accomplishing complex tasks. Components operate in specific cognitive situations and involve specifiable actions (data transformations). A componential theory of reading, therefore, specifies the various cognitive components involved in getting meaning from print.

According to Frederiksen (1982), reading skill is largely a matter of "automating" the components. That is, through practice, skilled readers learn to execute components automatically, with little conscious effort (cf. Shiffrin & Schneider, 1977). Automatic components can be performed simultaneously with other components without affecting their efficiency. Unskilled readers have few automatic components. When they try to execute more than one component at a time, performance on both is degraded. Although unskilled readers are characterized by nonautomatic components, the specific components that require greater practice can differ from person to person. The notion that different problem readers may actually have different deficits fits in well with the viewpoint taken in the present book.

Frederiksen (1982), building on his previous reseach (some of which is reported in earlier chapters of the present book) identifies a set of components that appear to account for much of the variability among individuals in reading ability. Frederiksen's components can be grouped into three major processing areas in reading: word analysis processes, discourse analysis processes, and integrative processes.

Word analysis processes are those cognitive components concerned with what has been referred to as decoding. In this category are such components as "grapheme encoding" (recognizing letters), "translating graphemic units to phonemic units," and other components concerned with processing information about single words. *Discourse analysis processes* are concerned with reading at the text level and include such components as "parsing sentence constituents," "establishing cohesive relations among propositions," and other aspects of what this book has called comprehension. The third group, *integrative processes*, are those concerned with combining perceptual information (decoding) with conceptual information (comprehension). Integrative processes make it possible for readers to use their knowledge of the language to guide reading. It is through them that expectancies about the language can be used to determine how perceptual information is interpreted and even what sources of perceptual information are processed.

Frederiksen developed a test battery to measure the various components. At the word analysis level, these tests included an anagram identification task in which subjects are required to report the letters they see in a brief display. The tests also included a letter-matching task, pseudoword pronunciation, word pronunciation, and a test requiring subjects to identify two letters from various parts of a four-letter array. (It is no accident, of course, that three of these tasks also appear among the tests presented in Chapter 5. After all, much of the rationale for the present tests comes from Frederiksen's earlier work.) Frederiksen's test for discourse analysis requires subjects to supply referents for pronouns in texts that vary in the way in which the pronoun is introduced. The tests of integrative processes involve word recognition in context and measures of visual span.

The multiple correlation between the various component measures and a conventional reading test was found to be quite high. As in his earlier research (and in accord with the present findings), decoding components were the best predictors of conventional reading test performance. This does not mean that the discourse analysis and integrative components are not tapping important aspects of reading ability. Indeed, the opposite explanation is more likely—most standard reading tests are poor measures of comprehension processes.

Componential analyses are likely to be an important tool in the future development of many reading related tests. For example, there is an extensive literature on text comprehension (see Kintsch & Van Dijk, 1978, for the flavor of this work) that could be used as a basis for developing componential tests of the story understanding process. Similarly, models of how children use words (cf. Gentner, 1975) can serve as the basis of componential tests of vocabulary. Although the approach used to develop the tests presented in this book is not unlike the componential method, the componential approach differs in the insistence that each measure be based on a single reading component. In fact, Frederiksen identifies components in the first place by showing how manipulating reading stimuli in specified ways has an effect on reading performance that can only be understood by invoking independent components. The componential approach also permits interactions among the various components to be specified. Such interactions are obviously important to a complex skill like reading, but they have been largely neglected up to now. Further development of component-specific reading measures is to be expected as is more precise specification of how the components interact.

Although componential analysis is an effective tool for cognitive theory building and test development, it deals, as do the tests developed in the present book, with only one aspect of reading performance. Future developments in theory will probably embrace more than merely information-processing skills. They will most likely be enlarged to include the many other factors affecting test performance. Some of these are described next.

BROADENING THE THEORETICAL BASE

Although standardized tests are intended to measure cognitve skills (reading ability, mathematical aptitude) it is no secret that performance on these tests is determined by factors other than just the ability in question. Motivation, test-taking attitudes, test anxiety, prior knowledge, minority group membership, health, learning history, and many other factors influence test performance. Although all of these factors interact (for example, poor health can lead to poor motivation), they can be conceptualized as operating hierarchically.

Figure 14 depicts such a hierarchy. As illustrated, experience, and a child's biological endowment, are basic determiners of how well the child will perform on standard reading tests. Experience refers not only to the child's home life but also to the type and amount of instruction received. Children can differ in

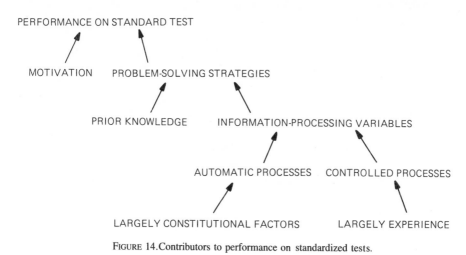

FIGURE 14.Contributors to performance on standardized tests.

whether they come from homes that are intellectually stimulating and in which reading is reinforced, and they can also differ in whether their school reading program relies on phonics or some other form of instruction. Bilingualism, minority group status, growing up on a farm or a city, receiving books as gifts, and many other experiential factors will effect reading performance. A child's biological endowment, the other basic determiner of intellectual performance, is no less important than experiential factors. Poor health, recessive genetic traits, sensory–motor problems, brain damage, even to some extent, intellectual capacity, are biological traits that affect performance on reading tests. Although constitutional factors are biologically determined, they are still amenable to change. Medical care, prostheses, compensatory training, and various other interventions can help children overcome their constitutional limitations.

Experience will determine whether the child learns to use the cognitive processes required by reading tests. In other words, a child must be taught to read. The cognitive skills learned are called controlled processes because (at least initially) they are under the control of the child. Automatic processes (retrieving items from memory, perceiving the environment) are largely inborn. This does not mean, of course, that cognitive processes cannot become automatic with practice. But the ultimate speed with which these cognitive processes can be executed will still vary among individuals as a function of largely constitutional factors.

The automatic and controlled processes together determine the efficiency of information processing. Thus, whether a child knows how to pronounce certain words and how efficiently the child does so is determined by whether the child has learned the pronunciation and how practiced the child is at retrieving such information from long-term memory. The same relationship between automatic and controlled processes determines the effectiveness of all the information-processing variables described in this book.

These information-processing variables combine with a child's prior knowledge to affect problem-solving strategies. Prior knowledge, of course, is also a function of experience but of a different kind than that already described. Prior knowledge refers here to having learned specific facts rather than general familiarity with print and books. The child who has visited a restaurant, for example, has a distinct advantage when reading about a restaurant visit over a child who has no such experience. This is because the experienced child has a cognitive "script" that can be used to help organize the new material.

Problem-solving strategies are general approaches to handling a difficult task. They include budgeting one's time so that the test is completed, judging how to answer questions, and so on. How many times have students complained about being unable to "take" multiple-choice (or essay) exams. Assuming they know the material, what the students mean by this is that they lack the proper problem-solving strategies. There is substantial evidence that many test-taking-problems stem not from a lack of knowledge but from a failure to use knowledge effectively. As long ago as 1950, Bloom and Broder observed that poor students give up on questions they cannot immediately answer, whereas good students reorganize their knowledge in a form appropriate to the question. This same observation has been made many times since.

Finally, problem-solving strategies and motivation combine to produce test performance. Motivation, like prior knowledge, obviously derives from experience, but again this is a rather different type of experience from the ones discussed. Children who develop in cultures where competition is discouraged or who resent the power structure, or who are depressed, uninterested, uncooperative, and so forth are obviously responding to their experiences but they are the type of experiences that affect personality rather than cognition.

Clearly, Figure 14 is oversimplified. Information-processing strategies and even automatic processes affect performance on standard tests directly as well as through their influence on problem-solving strategies. It is also true that motivational factors and prior knowledge are at least partially determined by cognitive variables (frequent failure lowers motivation), and vice versa. To be totally accurate, therefore, the diagram should have arrows connecting every factor to every other factor. Unfortunately, such a diagram would be unreadable. In any event, the important point to make about Figure 14 is that very few of the factors depicted are included in reading theories. The effect of prior knowledge, motivation, constitutional factors, and so forth have been neglected despite research evidence indicating that they are probably more important than factors such as teaching method in determining reading test performance (Newman, 1972).

Although most of today's theorists pay lip service to the importance of noncognitve factors, future theorists can be expected to go much further, including them directly in their theories. Ultimately, these factors will be included in tests as well. This will mean that we will be using different reading tests from the ones currently available. Some possible directions for test development are described in the next section.

TESTING

A recurring theme throughout this book is that reading tests should be based on psychological theories of the reading process. Pleas for the development of theoretically based tests have also been made by Hunt *et al.* (1973) for mental tests in general and by Glaser (1981) for educational tests in particular. The tests developed in the present book are an attempt to heed these pleas, but more work remains to be done. In the present section, some of the directions this additional work may take are described. Five specific areas for future development are addressed: new concepts of competence, measuring reading potential, metacognitive strategies, interactive testing, and hardware development.

NEW CONCEPTS OF COMPETENCE

Measuring reading competence from a theoretical perspective involves not only specifying a theory of reading but also a definition of competence. Standardized reading tests either ignore the issue of competence altogether or simply take it to be the average score achieved by the members of the standardization sample. This definition of competence is completely inadequate, however, because it changes with the population tested. Using this definition, the mean of a population of illiterates and the mean of a population of university graduates would both be considered equally valid measures of reading competence. Criterion-referenced tests provide a more reasonable definition of competence; namely, performance at, or above, a specified criterion level. But this definition also has an important drawback—it is concerned with minimal competence only. No attention is given to highly skilled readers. It is just assumed that experts read in the same manner as average readers, only better. However, research in other areas of cognitive psychology brings this assumption into question.

Studies of chess players, for example, have found dramatic differences between the way grand masters and average players approach the game (de Groot, 1965). Contrary to intuition, grand masters (the most-expert players) consider *fewer* moves on each turn than less-skillful players. The experts, it seems, build up a large mental repertoire of games and board patterns that they can retrieve quickly. This permits them to plan their moves on the basis of strategies appropriate to the particular game and relieves them of having to tediously consider and reject a series of inappropriate moves as less skillful players do. Although grand masters are able to recall many chessboard arrangements, their memory for other types of information is not extraordinary. It seems their memory skill is limited to chess. These findings indicate that chess experts do not necessarily use the same cognitive strategies as average players. Similar results have been reported by studies of expert physicists, who have been found to possess a kind of scientific "intuition" that permits them to eliminate incorrect solutions to physics problems without consciously considering them (Larkin, McDermott, Simon, & Simon, 1980). Studies of experts in areas more closely related to school performance have confirmed the experiments on chess masters and physicists—being an expert means avoiding unproductive lines of thought (see Chase & Chi, 1981, for a review).

Because avoiding "blind alleys" requires the ability to retrieve familiar patterns directly from long-term memory, one possible way that experts differ from less-skillful performers is the way in which they organize information in memory. Efficient memory organization permits the expert to go directly to the appropriate information without necessitating a tedious memory search. The result is that experts have greater accuracy and lower cognitive processing loads than beginners.

The importance of memory organization in reading was illustrated in the results of the validity studies of the Word-Decoding Test reported in Chapter 5. In these studies, the correlation between real-word and pseudoword reading latency was lower for good than for poor readers. This result was explained by assuming that good readers are able to access word pronunciations directly in long-term memory, whereas poor readers use the same inefficient "sounding out" strategy for both words and pseudowords. No doubt future experiments will reveal other ways in which skilled readers differ from the less skilled in knowledge organization. Comparisons of experts with average and poor readers should also lead to the development of tests sensitive to knowledge organization differences. Using these tests, it will be possible to determine a subject's "competence level." Instead of simply setting minimal competence criteria, as now, test designers will be able to establish criteria for levels from beginner to expert. Finally, once we know how to assess an individual's competence level (and the qualitative differences between levels), it should be possible to begin teaching less-skillful readers the information-processing techniques used by the experts.

MEASURING POTENTIAL

Although it would be wonderful if every child could read like an expert, there will always be some children who never reach that level. From a practical point of view it would be useful if our tests indicated not only a child's current performance level but also what some writers (Vygotsky, 1978, for one) call their "zone of potential development." Simpleminded approaches to measuring reading potential based on dubious manipulations of IQ scores were discussed in the last chapter. These reading-potential indicators were shown to be indefensible both statistically and theoretically. But this does not mean that measuring reading potential is a waste of time, just that it is not easy. One approach to measuring reading potential that may lead to valuable tests is described by Vygotsky (1978).

Vygotsky's technique is to measure how well a child performs an intellectual task alone and then to observe what the same child can accomplish when working with a teacher or a more advanced classmate. The difference between what a child can do alone and the same child's performance under a teacher's guidance represents that child's "learning potential." Although there are a number of problems that must be ironed out before Vygotsky's technique can become a practical test (what form "guidance" should take, for example), the technique could prove very valuable in tailoring teaching to the needs of specific children. For example, a child who cannot guess a missing word in a sentence when working alone may be able to do so when a teacher demonstrates the reasoning involved in solving such tasks (first look for the subject, then the verb, and so on). Not only has the teacher who adopts Vygotsky's approach discovered that the child has the potential to improve performance but also the type of training most likely to lead to improvement.

One type of training that may improve performance for almost all poor readers involves learning "metacognitive" skills. These are discussed next.

METACOGNITIVE STRATEGIES

In Figure 14, information-processing strategies (themselves determined by many factors) were depicted as combining with motivation to determine test performance. Although most of these information-processing strategies are specific to the reading process, some are more general. "Metacognitive" strategies include monitoring one's performance, apportioning time and cognitive capacity to various cognitive tasks, checking one's answers, learning from mistakes, and all the other strategies involved in orchestrating an intellectual performance. Metacognitive strategies are also responsible for "generalizing" skills learned in one situation to another cognitive task.

Metacognition in children, particularly as it relates to language, has been shown to affect reading competence (Tunmer & Herriman, 1983). Even simple metacognitive strategies ("Always consider all of the offered alternatives in a multiple-choice vocabulary test") can have an important influence on reading test performance. Measures of metacognitive strategies in memory tasks have already been developed (Brown, 1978). Metacognition tests appropriate to reading are not yet available, but given the importance of these strategies to reading competence, their future development seems assured.

INTERACTIVE TESTING AND HARDWARE DEVELOPMENT

The present book does not represent the first attempt to devise theoretically based reading measures. Calfee (1977; Calfee & Drum, 1979) describes several reading tests that fit this description. An important difference between his measures and the ones described in this book is the present reliance on computer administration.

Computers have been involved in psychological testing for over 20 years. For most of this time, the computer's role has been limited to scorekeeper. Students are examined with traditional paper and pencil instruments; but instead of indicating their answers in the test booklet, their responses are recorded on answer sheets scorable by computers. Sometimes, for personality tests, the computer also provides a report interpreting the scores. With the advent of minicomputers followed by low-cost microcomputers, it became feasible for computers not only to score tests but to adminster them as well. "Automated" psychological testing has now become quite common (Elithorn, Powell, Telford, & Cooper, 1980). Indeed, computer workstations designed for adminstering a variety of psychological tests are commercially available from several suppliers.

Although computerized test administration and scoring is a time saver for psychometricians, it is really not much of a theoretical advance over paper-and-pencil tests. In fact, most of the tests computers adminster today are merely the old paper-and-pencil ones presented on a cathode ray screen rather than in a test booklet. Like traditional tests, computerized tests provide all testees with virtually identical test situations; little effort has been made to adapt tests to the individual. But this is beginning to change as interactive (also known as adaptive) testing becomes more popular.

In interactive testing, the choice of test items and sequence is under the computer's control. Test items are chosen on the basis of a subject's response to previous items. For example, an error may cause the computer to backtrack to easier items; a series of correct answers may cause the computer to skip ahead. Interactive testing makes it possible to measure competence much more quickly and flexibly than with traditional tests, where all items are chosen prior to the testing session. The reading tests presented in this book are not fully adaptive although they have some interactive components. The next stage in their development will include making them even more interactive. Starting and stopping points on the Word-Decoding Test, for instance, will be determined interactively by probing at various levels in the graded word list, and all of the tests will be given cutoff criteria that will be used to make sure that no child is continually tested on any task he cannot perform. These improvements should make the tests more efficient measuring instruments as well as less frustrating for children.

The ever decreasing cost of computers and related devices will also play a role in the future development of automated reading testing. As already noted, a voice synthesizer could be added to the computer to give students more effective practice on several decoding tasks. The voice synthesizer could also be used to give test directions and performance feedback to children with only minimal reading skills and to produce oral versions of the reading measures. These oral measures could be used to compare each child's auding and reading performance as suggested by Sticht (1979). Eye movement recording apparatus could also be added to the computing system making it possible to design tests based on visual fixations and scanning patterns in reading. Electrophysiological recording both of brain activity and autonomic functions can also be added to the test apparatus. The result of adding this extra hardware will be the freedom to design even more sophisticated tests and to collect additional information in the testing situation. We are currently testing out all of these suggestions in our own laboratory.

Although the decreasing cost of microcomputers will soon mean that every school will have them, the cost of the various "peripheral" devices and the complicated programming required to analyze the various types of data probably means that some resource sharing will always be necessary. For this reason, an important future development will be organized computer testing networks linking testing stations in each school to a central computer that stores tests, performs statistical analsyses, prepares reports, and (someday) provides remedial practice (see Hunt, 1982, for more discussion on this and the other forecasts made in this section).

THE FUTURE OF READING TESTING

Refinements in theory combined with technical advances such as componential analysis have arrived on the scene at a time when computing costs have fallen dramatically. This makes the time particularly right for linking computer-based testing with psychological analyses of the reading process. Besides a continuation of the work described in the present book, the future should bring the development of reading measures based on the behavior of reading experts, usable measures of reading potential, tests of metacognition, and completely interactive computerized tests. These developments are not just around the corner, but they are not matters for the distant future either. It would not be surprising to see all of the developments forecast in this section come to fruition in the next 10 years.

Although improved reading tests are a desirable goal in themselves, the reason for developing theoretical tests is that they aid teaching. The next section takes a look at what the future holds for test-guided instruction.

TEACHING

Although there is no necessary connection between computer-administered tests and computer-assisted instruction, it should be obvious from the teaching examples given in the preceding chapter that the two techniques complement one another. Up to now, however, tests and teaching programs have been designed independently. Pairing them requires a fair amount of ingenuity and more than a few compromises. In the future, computerized tests and instructional programs will be designed together from the start. This will ensure that every reading skill measured by the tests has a corresponding set of programs specifically designed to teach the test-measured skills. The present section focuses on developments in computer-aided reading instruction. As will be shown, computer instruction holds great promise for the future, but it is no panacea for all reading problems. The section begins with a brief discussion of the computer's place in education. This is followed by a specific description of how computers are used in reading teaching and how they may be used in the future.

COMPUTER TEACHERS

Since the beginning of the Industrial Revolution, advances in technology and automation have been resisted by those who fear the loss of their jobs and those who see technology as dehumanizing and threatening. The same technology that strikes fear in the hearts of some is often welcomed by others—sometimes in extravagant terms. Although this type of polarization occurs whenever new technology is introduced, no new development has been more controversial than computers. Depending on whom one listens to, computers either represent the "third industrial revolution" or a form of dehumanization greater than any yet introduced. Needless to say, there is little evidence to justify either of these extreme views. Computers, like any other technology, bring with them both costs and benefits. Using them, in any particular setting, depends on whether the benefits outweigh the costs.

Ever since computers were invented 40 or so years ago, some educators have been predicting that they will revolutionize teaching. Needless to say, such predictions have yet to come true. For many years, computers were just too expensive for general use. Most schools could not afford a computer, even one that permitted many children to use it simultaneously. But costs were not the only reason computer-assisted instruction failed to revolutionize education. Another was teacher resistance. Because the computer's place in the education process was not clearly defined, teachers (most of whom had little familiarity with computers) felt they were being put in competition with machines. Many decided to reduce the threat by ignoring computers altogether.

As everyone knows, the cost of computing equipment has dropped dramatically with the coming of the microcomputer. It is now possible to buy powerful computers at a price nearly every school can afford—and schools are buying them. In 1983, 200 million dollars worth of computers were bought by schools in America alone. Although this is only a small fraction of the amount spent on computers by business and personal users, it represents an enormous increase in the number of computers available in schools. In fact, more computers were placed in classrooms in 1983 than in the total of the preceding 10 years. As prices continue to fall, it is reasonable to suppose that every school will have one or more computers before very long.

But what about teachers? Do not they still feel threatened? Perhaps some do, but they are now a minority. Younger teachers, many of whom became familiar with computers in college, and the increasing "friendliness" of computers (not to mention clever advertising), have changed educators' attitudes toward computers. Today, they are welcome in most classrooms. Unfortunately, much of the new-found enthusiasm for computers is nothing more than the familiar "bandwagon" effect that has always plagued education (Harris, 1976). Every new theoretical or technological development is extravagantly praised and viewed as definitive only to be dropped when the next fad comes along. Television, when it was first introduced, was described in much the same terms that computers are today. Television was also going to revolutionize education and make for a more intelligent, enlightened, and cultured citizenry. What we got instead was "The Gong Show," "Laverne and Shirley," and "Let's Make a Deal." This does not mean that television has no place in education. It does and it has found it; but we can hardly call television's effect on education revolutionary. Much the same outcome can be expected for computers.

Although computers have a definite place in education, it is too soon to say what that place will be. At present, computers are being used in schools, but only rarely are they used to do things that could not be done before they arrived. Most often, educational computers merely mechanically mimic what teachers were doing all along. In *Microcomputers in the Schools* (Thomas, 1981), a book extolling the educational virtues of low-cost computers, several dozen authors give their views on how computers can be used to improve teaching. Except for learning about computers themselves, practically every other application suggested in the book is simply a computer adaptation of a typical teaching method. The real power of computers has yet to be exploited by educators. There are things computers can do that can not be accomplished without them. Only when their unique capabilities are incorporated into teaching, can we really be justified in calling computers a revolutionary force in education. The next section deals with computer instruction and reading. Some areas in which the unique characteristics of computers may be exploited are discussed.

COMPUTERS AND READING

A recent annotated bibliography on computer applications in reading (Mason, Blanchard, & Daniel, 1983) includes 910 references. Because some of the articles they cite are themselves bibliographies, it is easy to see that the literature on computers and reading is very large. Rather than try to summarize the field here (a vain hope anyway), the present discussion focuses on trends, particularly those most relevant to the present interest—using computers to teach in novel ways.

The most well-known attempt to teach reading by computer was initiated 20 years ago by Richard Atkinson and his associates at Stanford (see Fletcher, 1979, for a review). Two programs (designed to run on different computers) were developed and used as adjuncts to whatever reading instruction the child received in the traditional classroom. The focus of both programs was primarily on decoding, particularly learning "pronunciation rules."

The first computer-assisted program developed by the Stanford group was designed to run on an IBM 1500 computer. Besides the central computer, there were two teacher stations and 16 student terminals. Although the system was established in the 1960s, it was quite advanced for its time. In addition to a keyboard, each student terminal also included rear-projection filmstrips, a light pen, and audiotape facilities that could deliver stimuli and messages through headphones. Despite its cleverness, the system had distinct shortcomings (Fletcher, 1979). Audio and photographic access was slow, it was difficult to organize visual displays, and, most importantly, there was no direct method of determining whether students were pronouncing stimuli correctly, even though this was the main goal of the program. On the other hand, the teaching program was adaptive, skipping ahead when the child demonstrated knowledge and giving extra practice if the child needed it. Although the emphasis in this program was on decoding, some comprehension training (mostly at the word level) was also included. Games and other motivating materials (stories, for instance) were provided as part of the teaching package.

Although the initial program was judged successful, it was too expensive for general use. So the Stanford group set out to design a low-cost computer-assisted supplement to traditional reading teaching. This second project (which was based on Digital Equipment Corportion's PDP 10 computer) lasted 6 years and included hundreds of school children. The terminals were simpler than those of the first program. All each student had to work on was a teletype that printed uppercase characters only and an audio output device. (Audio output, however, was superior to that of the first project in that it allowed fast, random access to messages.) The curriculum of the second project was essentially a matter of "drill and practice" (a redundant but vivid educational expression). The skills to be practiced were organized into six "strands": (1) learning to use the terminal and follow instructions; (2) letter recognition; (3) sight-word vocabulary; (4) discriminating spelling patterns; (5) phonics; and (6) word and sentence comprehension. Each strand contained many items of increasing difficulty through which the children progressed at their own speed. The length of each daily lesson was adjusted to the requirements of each child; the average session lasted 10 minutes, during which the child spent 2 minutes working on each strand. The children enjoyed the time they spent with the computer even when the use of motivational games and stories was reduced.

A comparison of the reading test scores of children in the program with those of control children found the former group to score more than 1 year higher, about the same level of improvement produced by the more expensive program (Fletcher, 1979). Interestingly, the superior performance of those who participated in the computer curriculum was evident on measures of paragraph comprehension, a skill not even taught in the program (Fletcher & Atkinson, 1972).

The Stanford experiment ended in the mid 1970s, but is has influenced virtually all subsequent efforts to develop computer-assisted reading programs. Mason *et al.* (1983) provide a list of more than 60 commercial software publishers offering computer-assisted instruction programs similar to those used in the

Stanford projects. Some of these instructional programs offer more comprehension practice than the older programs, but the emphasis is still on decoding.

The Stanford programs and their many successors provide evidence that reinforces three of the conclusions reached in the preceding chapter. Specifically:

1. Children like working with computers.
2. Drill and practice improve reading test performance.
3. Improving decoding also benefits comprehension.

Despite their apparent success, it should be clear that from an instructional viewpoint, there is nothing really new about these programs. That is, they do not involve teaching procedures unique to computers. Virtually every teaching technique used in computer-assisted reading programs has also been used in traditional classroom settings. Participating in one of these computer-assisted programs is like having an infinitely patient and entertaining teacher—worthwhile but hardly revolutionary. We have already seen that computers are capable of much more. For example, the tests described in Chapter 5 show that the computer can measure the speed of mental processes as well as their outcome. Validity studies of these tests indicated that poor readers are slow in accessing information in long-term memory and in other aspects of decoding. Few computer-assisted reading programs are concerned with measuring reaction times. Fewer still involve physiological or eye-movement recordings, even though these tasks are easily handled by computers.

Chapter 7 contained several suggestions for how slow readers can be given practice designed to help improve their reading speed. These suggestions, however, were the tip of the iceberg. Games that use a computer's timing, graphics, and sound capabilities could be used to provide enjoyable practice for a variety of reading skills. For example, Lesgold (1982) describes "beat-the-clock" format games in which children compete with their own prior reaction times (and accuracy) in tasks such as word reading or deciding on word meanings. Using color graphics, a scoreboard, and a clock, an arcade game can easily be designed. Such a game might look like fun (and it would be fun), but its purpose is serious. It is designed to make entertaining what would otherwise be boring drill. Once lower-level decoding skills reach adequate levels, comprehension games can be introduced. Games that facilitate learning to comprehend have been described by Beck (1977). Nearly all these games can be implemented today on a moderately priced computer. Even skilled readers can be accommodated by computer-assisted instruction. For example, Lesgold (1982) suggests the development of computer-presented stories in conjunction with on-line dictionaries so that a child who gets confused by a word or phrase can indicate this and receive an immediate explanation.

Lesgold (1982), notes the importance of adequate equipment for effective computer-assisted instruction. The cheapest computers are inadequate for instruction, as they often have only capital letters (although this did not seem to interfere with progress in the Stanford experiment). Moreover, because many children read poorly and type even worse, touch-sensitive screens, joysticks, and other nonlanguage response devices are also valuable. Voice synthesizers have already been touched on. Although they may sound less realistic than tapes or other stored language communication devices, they permit maximum programing flexibility. As hardware costs decrease even further, it may also be possible to introduce "intelligent" programs that go beyond drill and practice to teach problem solving strategies (Carbonell, 1970).

Implementing the kind of programs described here would mark a new era in computer-assisted instruction. Instructional programs would no longer be mere adaptations of traditional classroom practice. Instead, the full powers of computers would be used. In addition, this approach opens the way for the integration of testing and teaching. Theoretically based tests like the ones described in this book are concerned with measuring the information-processing skills involved in reading. Deficiencies in any of these cognitive skills can best be remediated by instruction directly related to these skills. It is just such instruction that the games suggested here are designed to provide. The presence of computers in the classroom means that tests may be used from the beginning of a child's school career. Problems can be identified and remediated early; perhaps some reading disabilities can even be prevented from occurring.

SUMMARY

Although predicting the future is always a risky enterprise, extrapolations from present practice provide some basis for determining what directions the field is likely to take. Advances in theory will likely come from further application of componential analysis. Future theories are also likely to be broader based including the influence of noncognitive factors on reading. Tests will become more interactive and adaptable to individuals. Moreover, as computing equipment becomes less expensive, skills not measured previously (scanning habits and so on) will become testable. In future tests, various competence levels will be specified going from beginner to expert, and qualitative differences in the way information is stored will be assessed. Finally, computer-assisted instruction will continue to flourish, but new programs will make greater use of the computer's unique abilities. Teaching will involve more eductional computer games and will be more closely allied to testing.

Naturally, all this is not going to happen overnight. It is going to take a lot of work. In the hope of getting at least some readers involved in this effort, the next chapter contains a description of the specific equipment and programs necessary to implement the tests described in this book.

PART V

TECHNICAL SPECIFICATIONS

CHAPTER 9

SPECIFICATIONS FOR IMPLEMENTING THE TESTS

As anyone who has ever tried knows, translating programs from one computer to another is no easy task. For this reason, the easiest way to try out the tests described in this book is to buy an identical computing system. However, adapting the programs to run on another computing system is not impossible. In fact, the programs were purposely written in BASIC so that they could be run by most microcomputers. Unfortunately, BASIC comes in many different dialects, so some rewriting cannot be avoided. The present chapter is intended to make the job of adapting the programs to different computers as easy as possible. First, the necessary hardware requirements are discussed and then the programs themselves are presented.

HARDWARE

The Cromemco Z-2D computer used to develop and administer the tests described in this book is a microcomputer based on the Z-80A computer chip. The system has two double-sided, double-density disk drives and 64 kilobytes of random access memory. A Televideo (model 912) terminal is fitted to the computer along with an NEC Spinwriter printer. The computer also has an analog-to-digital converter, connections that permit it to communicate with other computers, a real-time clock (Mountain Computer's 100,000 Day Clock), a locally made response box consisting of two colored buttons that can be used to record subjects' responses, and a voice-activated microphone and amplifier.

Although the user's system should approximate the one described above as closely as possible, not all of the features described are necessary for running the test programs. The printer, for example, is used only to produce hard copy of a subject's data. As these data are also stored on disk, they may be displayed

221

on the screen without the need for printed output. The analog-to-digital converter and the inter-computer communication devices are also not essential to implementing the tests. Even the response box can be dispensed with; keyboard input can be used instead. The minimum requirements a computing system must possess in order to run the tests are

1. Sixty-four kilobytes of random access memory
2. At least one, and preferably two, disk drives capable of storing 170 kilobytes of information
3. A real-time clock accurate to one millisecond
4. A computer-driven screen capable of displaying 20 lines of information simultaneously (that is, a screen that can be switched on and off under computer control)
5. A BASIC compiler or interpreter that includes "peek" and "poke" instructions
6. A voice-activated throat microphone and amplifier
7. A two-button response box or large keys on a standard keyboard that can be isolated from the other keys.

Except for the throat microphone and amplifier, which are relatively inexpensive and readily available from electronics suppliers, these capabilities can be found in most average-priced microcomputers available today. Moderate priced, at the time this book was written, meant about $2,500 to $4,500. The programs cannot be implemented on the cheap (under $1000) computers sold for home use. Needless to say, computer prices will continue to fall, making the tests accessible to users with limited budgets.

Although most of the required equipment is standard and easily connected, a word should be said about the response box and microphone. Ideally, these should be connected to the computer through "interrupt" lines, but for some computers (and some users) this may be technologically impossible. Therefore, to simplify matters, the programs presented here merely assume that the buttons and microphone are soldered to the computer keyboard, so that the computer "reads" their input as either an "ESCAPE" or "RETURN" ("ENTER" on some keyboards). In other words, whenever an impulse is received by the computer from the microphone amplifier, it is interpreted in the same way as if the ESCAPE key had been pressed. Similarly, the response buttons are interpreted as either an ESCAPE key press or a RETURN key press. This convention means that users who wish to use the keyboard for subject responses can do so merely by specifying the ESCAPE and RETURN keys as the response "buttons" without the need to modify the programs. Throughout the programs, it is assumed that the orange button is attached to the RETURN key, and the black button as well as the microphone are connected to the ESCAPE key.

SOFTWARE

The programs presented here were designed to be used as a package. They include an initialization program that establishes data acquisition files and serves as an executive for the other programs, two games to familiarize children with the computer, programs that run each of the four reading tests, and a program that concatenates each subject's data files. (With slight revisions, each program can be run individually as well as part of the whole package.) The various programs are described in this section. Besides the BASIC code, each program's purpose is explained. Programer's notes are included to aid those who wish to adapt the programs for new machines.

INIT: INITIALIZATION PROGRAM

As already mentioned, the first program, called INIT, was designed to establish data files and serve as an executive routine for the other programs. The INIT program permits the user to administer as few or as many of the tests and games as desired. Testing may even extend over more than one session.

Two categories of information are obtained from the user by the INIT program. The first category includes subject details (initials, date of birth, and so on). This information is stored in a file using the subject's initials as the file name. It is also used to create data file names. The program also determines which programs the user wishes to run and any other information necessary to run the programs.

The program is interactive, prompting the user for the required information (e.g., "Subject Initials?").

Although most of the questions asked by INIT are self-explanatory, it is worthwhile mentioning the responses expected by the program. Note that in the examples given below, the computer's end of the conversation is in italics and everything typed by the user must be followed by hitting RETURN.

- *Subject's Initials?* ABCD (Up to four letters may be entered).
- *Subject's Code?* ABC111 (Up to 10 character codes are permitted).
- *Date of Birth?* 3/3/70
- *Do you wish to run all the programs?* Y ("Y" or "N" are the only possible answers. If the answer is N, the computer will list each program and ask the user if it is to be run. For the Memory-for-Order-Test, the computer will also ask which sequence of the temporal, spatial, and order tasks the user prefers).

When testing is complete, the subject's data from the various tests will be concatenated into a single file. The format of the data output files was illustrated in Chapters 5 and 6.

INIT LISTING

```
70040 DIM A9$(10),B9$(10),C9$(10),E9$(0)

70060 DIM F$(11),F1$(9),I9$(3),S8$(1),S9$(79),T9$(6)

70065 REM THE NEXT 6 STATEMENTS ARE A MACRO ROUTINE FOR
      CLEARING THE SCREEN

70070 DATA%00D1%,%00C1%,%00CD%,%0005%,%0000%

70080 DATA%0016%,%0000%,%005F%,%00C9%

70090 FOR I=%0103%TO%010B%

70100 READ K9

70110 POKE I,K9

70120 NEXT I

70130 DIM E$(0)

70140 PRINT : PRINT" Subject's initials (enter up to 3 letters)";

70150 INPUT I9$(0,2)

70160 PRINT : PRINT" The subject's initials are ";I9$(0,2);".
      Are they correct?  (Type Y or N).  ";

70170 INPUT E$

70180 IF E$="Y"THEN 70210

70190 IF E$="N"THEN I9$(0,2)=" " :  GOTO 70140

70200 GOTO 70160

70210 F$="B:  " :  F$(2,4)=I9$ :  I=0

70220 IF ASC(I9$(I,I))=0 THEN 70240

70230 I=I+1 :  GOTO 70220

70240 F$(I+2,-3)=".ID"

70250 ON ERROR GOTO 70300

70260 CREATE F$

70270 ON ERROR STOP

70280 OPEN1,79,2F$

70290 GOTO 70460
```

```
70300 F1$=F$(2,11)
70310 PRINT :  PRINT" ";F1$;" already exists.
      If this is the same subject, press S and INIT"
70320 PRINT" will continue.  If this is a different subject,
      press D and you will be"
70330 PRINT" asked for the initials again.";
70340 INPUT S8$
70350 IF S8$<>"D"THEN 70410
70360 I=0
70370 IF(ASC(I9$(I,I))=0)THEN 70130
70380 I9$(I,I)=CHR$(0)
70390 I=I+1
70400 GOTO 70370
70410 IF S8$<>"S"THEN 70310
70420 ERASE F$
70430 ON ERROR STOP
70440 CREATE F$
70450 OPEN\1,79,2\F$
70460 PRINT :  PRINT Subject's code (enter up to 10
      alphanumerics)";
70470 INPUT C9$
70480 PRINT :  PRINT" Subject's date of birth (day/month/
      year)";
70490 INPUT B9$
70500 PRINT :  PRINT" Do you want to run all of the programs?
      (Type Y or N)";
70510 INPUT A9$
70520 IF A9$="Y"THEN 70730
70530 IF A9$<>"N"THEN 70500
```

```
70540 PRINT :  PRINT" Which program/s do you want to play?
   (Type Y or N)"
70550 PRINT :  PRINT" Maze";
70560 INPUT T9$(1,1)
70570 IF NOT(T9$(1,1)="Y"OR T9$(1,1)="N")THEN 70550
70580 PRINT :  PRINT" Tictactoe";
70590 INPUT T9$(2,2)
70600 IF NOT(T9$(2,2)="Y"OR T9$(2,2)="N")THEN 70580
70610 PRINT :  PRINT" Long-Term Memory Access Speed";
70620 INPUT T9$(3,3)
70630 IF NOT(T9$(3,3)="Y"OR T9$(3,3)="N")THEN 70610
70640 PRINT :  PRINT" Sentence Comprehension";
70650 INPUT T9$(4,4)
70660 IF NOT(T9$(4,4)="Y"OR T9$(4,4)="N")THEN 70640
70670 PRINT :  PRINT" Memory for Order";
70680 INPUT T9$(5,5)
70690 IF NOT(T9$(5,5)="Y"OR T9$(5,5)="N")THEN 70670
70700 PRINT :  PRINT" Word Decoding";
70710 INPUT T9$(6,6)
70720 IF NOT(T9$(6,6)="Y"OR T9$(6,6)="N")THEN 70700
70730 IF A9$="N"THEN 70790
70740 PRINT :  PRINT" You want to run all programs.
   Is that correct?  (Type Y or N).";
70750 INPUT E$
70760 IF E$="Y"THEN 70930
70770 IF E$="N"THEN 70540
70780 PRINT :  PRINT" Please type Y or N.";  :  GOTO 70750
70790 G1$=""
70800 G2$=G1$ :  G3$=G1$ :  G4$=G1$ :  G5$=G1$ :  G6$=G1$
```

```
70810 IF T9$(1,1)="Y"THEN G1$=" Maze"

70820 IF T9$(2,2)="Y"THEN G2$=" Tictactoe"

70830 IF T9$(3,3)="Y"THEN G3$=" Long-Term Memory Access
      Speed"

70840 IF T9$(4,4)="Y"THEN G4$=" Sentence Comprehension"

70850 IF T9$(5,5)="Y"THEN G5$=" Memory for Order"

70860 IF T9$(6,6)="Y"THEN G6$=" Word Decoding"

70870 IF T9$(1,6)="NNNNNN"THEN G1$=" NO Programs"

70880 PRINT : PRINT" You want to
      play";G1$;G2$;G3$;G4$;G5$;G6$;"
      Is that correct?  (Type Y or N).";

70890 INPUT E$

70900 IF E$="Y"THEN 70930

70910 IF E$="N"THEN T9$="" :  GOTO 70540

70920 PRINT : PRINT" Please type Y or N."; :  GOTO 70890

70930 IF NOT(A9$="Y"OR T9$(5,5)="Y")THEN 71030

70940 ON ERROR GOTO 70950

70950 PRINT : PRINT" Which order block sequence do you want?
      (Type 1 or 2)"

70960 PRINT

70970 PRINT" 1.  Both, temporal,spatial"

70980 PRINT" or"

70990 PRINT" 2.  Both, spatial, temporal"

71000 PRINT" "; :  INPUT O

71010 IF NOT(O=1 OR O=2)THEN 70950

71020 ON ERROR STOP

71030 PRINT\1\"SUBJECT'S INITIALS:";I9$

71040 PRINT\1\ :  PRINT\1\"SUBJECT'S CODE:";C9$

71050 PRINT\1\ :  PRINT\1\"SUBJECT'S DATE OF BIRTH:";B9$
```

```
71060 PRINT\1\ :  PRINT\1\"BLOCK SEQUENCE ORDER:   ";O
71070 CLOSE\1\
71080 ON ERROR GOTO 71130
71090 F$="B:SBJID"
71100 CREATE F$
71110 ON ERROR STOP
71120 GOTO 71150
71130 ERASE F$
71140 GOTO 71100
71150 OPEN\1,79,2\F$
71160 PRINT\1\I9$
71170 PRINT\1\C9$
71180 PRINT\1\A9$
71190 PRINT\1\T9$(1,6)
71200 PRINT\1\O
71210 CLOSE\1\
71220 DELETE 70020,71210
71230 IF NOT(A9$="Y"OR T9$(1,1)="Y")THEN 71250
71240 RUN"MAZE1"
71250 IF NOT(T9$(2,2)="Y")THEN 71270
71260 RUN"TICTAC1"
71270 IF NOT(T9$(3,3)="Y")THEN 71290
71280 RUN"MATCH1"
71290 IF NOT(T9$(4,4)="Y")THEN 71310
71300 RUN"STARPLS1"
71310 IF NOT(T9$(5,5)="Y")THEN 71330
71320 RUN"ORDER1"
71330 IF NOT(T9$(6,6)="Y")THEN 71350
71340 RUN"WORDS1"
```

```
71350 CLOSE :   ERASE"B:SBJID" :   END
```

MAZE GAME

This game is included in the package mainly as a motivator for young children. It permits them to interact with the computer in a simple, nonverbal way. The program asks children to provide two numbers that are used to generate mazes on the computer screen. The child can then use the cursor to trace a path through the maze. Although the game is very simple, the examiner should be actively involved helping the child where necessary and putting her or him at ease in the situation.

Maze Listing

```
60010 INTEGER W(20,78),V(20,78)

60020 INTEGER C,H,I,J,K9,Q,R,S,X,Z

60030 DIM A$(1),T9$(6)

60040 RANDOMIZE

60045 REM THE NEXT 6 STATEMENTS BLANK THE SCREEN

60050 DATA%00D1%,%00C1%,%00CD%,%0005%,%0000%

60060 DATA%0016%,%0000%,%005F%,%00C9%

60070 FOR I=%0103%TO%010B%

60080 READ K9

60090 POKE I,K9

60100 NEXT I

60110 GOSUB 62540

60120 PRINT :  PRINT :  PRINT :  PRINT :  PRINT :  PRINT
      PRINT :  PRINT :  PRINT :  PRINT :  PRINT

60130 NOESC

60135 PRINT SPC(13);" Press the orange button when
      you're ready to play 'Maze'."

60150 IF BINAND(INP(0),%0040%)=0 THEN 60150

60170 H9=INP(1) :   H9=BINAND(H9,%007F%)

60175 ESC
```

```
60180 IF H9=%000D%THEN 60210

60190 IF H9=%0003%THEN 62530

60200 GOTO 60130

60210 GOSUB 62540

60220 PRINT SPC(32);"Instructions"

60230 PRINT SPC(32);"============"

60240 PRINT : PRINT" This game will print out a maze for you.
      All you have to do is input"

60250 PRINT" the dimensions.  You may have a maze of up to 20
      by 10 units, but nothing"

60260 PRINT" beyond that."

60270 PRINT

60280 PRINT" Each maze is different and has only one path
      through it.  Trace the"

60290 PRINT" path through the maze by pushing the arrow keys."

60300 PRINT

60310 MAT W=0

60320 MAT V=0

60330 ON ERROR GOTO 60335

60335 PRINT : PRINT" What are your dimensions (<=20,<=10)";

60340 INPUT H,V

60345 ON ERROR STOP

60350 IF(H<=20 AND H=INT(H))THEN IF(V<=10 AND V=INT(V))
      THEN 60390

60360 PRINT : PRINT" Sorry, your dimensions may not
      be bigger than 20 by 10.  Try again."

60370 GOTO 60340

60380 PRINT

60390 IF(H<>1 AND V<>1)THEN 60420
```

```
60400 PRINT" Meaningless dimensions, try again."

60410 GOTO 60340

60420 GOSUB 62540

60430 PRINT

60440 Q=0 :   Z=0

60450 X=INT(RND(0)*H+1)

60460 PRINT" ";

60470 FOR I=1 TO H

60480 IF I=X THEN 60510

60490 PRINT":--";

60500 GOTO 60520

60510 PRINT":   ";

60520 NEXT I

60530 PRINT":"

60540 C=1

60550 W(X,1)=C

60560 C=C+1

60570 R=X

60580 S=1

60590 GOTO 60690

60600 IF R<>H THEN 60670

60610 IF S<>V THEN 60640

60620 R=1 :   S=1

60630 GOTO 60680

60640 R=1

60650 S=S+1

60660 GOTO 60680

60670 R=R+1

60680 IF W(R,S)=0 THEN 60600
```

```
60690 IF R-1=0 THEN 61140

60700 IF W(R-1,S)THEN 61140

60710 IF S-1=0 THEN 60910

60720 IF W(R,S-1)<>0 THEN 60910

60730 IF R=H THEN 60790

60740 IF W(R+1,S)THEN 60790

60750 X=INT(RND(0)*3+1)

60760 IF X=1 THEN 61570

60770 IF X=2 THEN 61640

60780 IF X=3 THEN 61710

60790 IF S<>V THEN 60830

60800 IF Z=1 THEN 60880

60810 Q=1

60820 GOTO 60840

60830 IF W(R,S+1)THEN 60880

60840 X=INT(RND(0)*3+1)

60850 IF X=1 THEN 61570

60860 IF X=2 THEN 61640

60870 IF X=3 THEN 61810

60880 X=INT(RND(0)*2+1)

60890 IF X=1 THEN 61570

60900 IF X=2 THEN 61640

60910 IF R=H THEN 61050

60920 IF W(R+1,S)THEN 61050

60930 IF S<>V THEN 60970

60940 IF Z=1 THEN 61020

60950 Q=1

60960 GOTO 60980

60970 IF W(R,S+1)THEN 61020
```

```
60980 X=INT(RND(0)*3+1)

60990 IF X=1 THEN 61570

61000 IF X=2 THEN 61710

61010 IF X=3 THEN 61810

61020 X=INT(RND(0)*2+1)

61030 IF X=1 THEN 61570

61040 IF X=2 THEN 61710

61050 IF S<>V THEN 61090

61060 IF Z=1 THEN 61130

61070 Q=1

61080 GOTO 61100

61090 IF W(R,S+1)THEN 61130

61100 X=INT(RND(0)*2+1)

61110 IF X=1 THEN 61570

61120 IF X=2 THEN 61810

61130 GOTO 61570

61140 IF S-1=0 THEN 61390

61150 IF W(R,S-1)THEN 61390

61160 IF R=H THEN 61300

61170 IF W(R+1,S)THEN 61300

61180 IF S<>V THEN 61220

61190 IF Z=1 THEN 61270

61200 Q=1

61210 GOTO 61230

61220 IF W(R,S+1)THEN 61270

61230 X=INT(RND(0)*3+1)

61240 IF X=1 THEN 61640

61250 IF X=2 THEN 61710

61260 IF X=3 THEN 61810
```

```
61270 X=INT(RND(0)*2+1)

61280 IF X=1 THEN 61640

61290 IF X=2 THEN 61710

61300 IF S<>V THEN 61340

61310 IF Z=1 THEN 61380

61320 Q=1

61330 GOTO 61350

61340 IF W(R,S+1)THEN 61380

61350 X=INT(RND(0)*2+1)

61360 IF X=1 THEN 61640

61370 IF X=2 THEN 61810

61380 GOTO 61640

61390 IF R=H THEN 61500

61400 IF W(R+1,S)THEN 61500

61410 IF S<>V THEN 61450

61420 IF Z=1 THEN 61490

61430 Q=1

61440 GOTO 61460

61450 IF W(R,S+1)THEN 61490

61460 X=INT(RND(0)*2+1)

61470 IF X=1 THEN 61710

61480 IF X=2 THEN 61810

61490 GOTO 61710

61500 IF S<>V THEN 61540

61510 IF Z=1 THEN 61560

61520 Q=1

61530 GOTO 61550

61540 IF W(R,S+1)THEN 61560

61550 GOTO 61810
```

```
61560 GOTO 62000
61570 W(R-1,S)=C
61580 C=C+1
61590 V(R-1,S)=2
61600 R=R-1
61610 IF C=H*V+1 THEN 62010
61620 Q=0
61630 GOTO 60690
61640 W(R,S-1)=C
61650 C=C+1
61660 V(R,S-1)=1
61670 S=S-1
61680 IF C=H*V+1 THEN 62010
61690 Q=0
61700 GOTO 60690
61710 W(R+1,S)=C
61720 C=C+1
61730 IF V(R,S)=0 THEN 61760
61740 V(R,S)=3
61750 GOTO 61770
61760 V(R,S)=2
61770 R=R+1
61780 IF C=H*V+1 THEN 62010
61790 Q=0
61800 GOTO 61140
61810 IF Q=1 THEN 61910
61820 W(R,S+1)=C
61830 C=C+1
61840 IF V(R,S)=0 THEN 61870
```

```
61850 V(R,S)=3
61860 GOTO 61880
61870 V(R,S)=1
61880 S=S+1
61890 IF C=H*V+1 THEN 62010
61900 GOTO 60690
61910 Z=1
61920 IF V(R,S)=0 THEN 61960
61930 V(R,S)=3
61940 Q=0
61950 GOTO 62000
61960 V(R,S)=1
61970 Q=0
61980 R=1 :  S=1
61990 GOTO 60680
62000 GOTO 60600
62010 FOR J=1 TO V
62020 PRINT" I";
62030 FOR I=1 TO H
62040 IF V(I,J)<2 THEN 62070
62050 PRINT" ";
62060 GOTO 62080
62070 PRINT" I";
62080 NEXT I
62090 PRINT :  PRINT" ";
62100 FOR I=1 TO H
62110 IF V(I,J)=0 THEN 62150
62120 IF V(I,J)=2 THEN 62150
62130 PRINT": ";
```

```
62140 GOTO 62160

62150 PRINT":--";

62160 NEXT I

62170 PRINT":"

62180 NEXT J

62190 PRINT : PRINT" Do you want another maze?
      (Type Y or N)";

62200 INPUT A$(1,1)

62210 IF A$(1,1)="Y"THEN 60310

62220 IF A$(1,1)="N"THEN 62250

62230 PRINT" Please type Y or N"

62240 GOTO 62190

62250 GOSUB 62540

62260 PRINT : PRINT : PRINT : PRINT : PRINT
      PRINT : PRINT : PRINT : PRINT : PRINT
      PRINT SPC(21);"The End.  Thank you for playing 'Maze'.

62270 F$="B:SBJID"

62280 OPEN\1,79,1\F$

62290 INPUT\1\I9$

62300 INPUT\1\C9$

62310 INPUT\1\A9$

62320 INPUT\1\T9$(1,6)

62330 CLOSE\1\

62340 DELETE 60000,62330

62350 IF NOT(A9$="Y"OR T9$(2,2)="Y")THEN 62380

62360 RUN"TICTAC1"

62380 IF NOT(T9$(3,3)="Y")THEN 62410

62390 RUN"MATCH1"

62410 IF NOT(T9$(4,4)="Y")THEN 62440
```

```
62420 RUN"STARPLS1"

62440 IF NOT(T9$(5,5)="Y")THEN 62470

62450 RUN"ORDER1"

62470 IF NOT(T9$(6,6)="Y")THEN 62530

62480 RUN"WORDS1"

62530 CLOSE : ERASE"B:SBJID" :  END

62540 REM THE NEXT STATEMENT BLANKS THE SCREEN

62550 A=USR(%0103%,27,2) :  A=USR(%0103%,42,2)

62560 RETURN
```

TICTACTOE GAME

The Tictactoe game is included to help motivate subjects and to put them at ease in the testing situation. It is a more demanding game than the maze game and requires a higher level of interaction with the computer. Most children enjoy playing this game even though the computer almost always wins. Once again, most children will require the examiner's help with the directions.

Tictactoe Listing

```
50010 INTEGER B(10),C,C0,C1,C2,E,F,G,H,H9,I,K9(9),N,O,R,X

50015 DIM T9$(6)

50020 RANDOMIZE

50025 REM THE FOLLOWING MACRO CLEARS THE SCREEN

50030 K9(1)=%00D1% :  K9(2)=%00C1% :  K9(3)=%00CD% :
      K9(4)=%0005%

50040 K9(5)=%0000% :  K9(6)=%0016% :  K9(7)=%0000% :
      K9(8)=%005F% :
      K9(9)=%00C9%

50050 J=1

50060 FOR I=%0103%TO%010B%

50070 POKE I,K9(J)

50080 J=J+1
```

```
50090 NEXT I

50100 GOSUB 52210

50110 PRINT : PRINT : PRINT : PRINT : PRINT : PRINT
      PRINT : PRINT : PRINT : PRINT : PRINT

50120 PRINT SPC(11);"Press the orange button when you're ready
      to play 'Tictactoe.'"

50130 NOESC

50140 IF BINAND(INP(0),%0040%)=0 THEN 50140

50150 ESC

50160 H9=INT(1) :  H9=BINAND(H9,%007F%)

50180 IF H9=%000D%THEN 50210

50190 IF H9=%0003%THEN 51490

50200 GOTO 50100

50210 GOSUB 52210

50220 N=48

50230 FOR I=1 TO 9

50240 B(I)=N+I

50250 NEXT I

50260 PRINT SPC(32);"Instructions"

50270 PRINT SPC(32);"============"

50280 PRINT : PRINT" This machine plays expert tictactoe.
      Make just one error"

50290 PRINT" and the machine will win.  Play a perfect game
      and the machine will draw."

50300 GOSUB 51890

50310 PRINT : PRINT" Study the board.  When you are ready to
      continue, press the C button"

50320 NOESC

50330 IF BINAND(INP(0),%0040%)=0 THEN 50330
```

```
50340 ESC
50350 PRINT :  PRINT" To make your move, type the digit from one
      to nine that corresponds"
50360 PRINT" with the board cell that you wish to occupy.
      The computer will then decide"
50370 PRINT" on its response and update the playing board.
      To start, the computer"
50380 PRINT" will select a cell."
50390 PRINT
50400 PRINT SPC(23);"Computer moves are X"
50410 PRINT SPC(23);"Your moves are O"
50420 PRINT :  PRINT
50430 F=RND(-1)
50440 RESTORE 50450
50450 DATA 4,6,8,2,3,7,0,9,0,0,7,3,1,4,9,3,7,6,9,4
50460 DATA 2,8,6,4,1,9,0,7,0,0,1,9,3,7,2,7,3,8,9,2
50470 DATA 9,1,8,2,7,3,7,1,2,9,8,2,1,9,6,4,0,3,0,0
50480 DATA 9,1,6,3,4,1,9,7,4,3,6,4,2,8,7,3,0,1,0,0
50490 DATA 5,8,7,3,6,4,0,9,0,0,5,8,6,4,1,9,0,7,0,0
50500 DATA 1,3,5,9,8,5,8,3,1,7,1,3,7,4,6,0,9,0,8,0
50510 DATA 3,1,5,7,8,5,8,3,1,7,1,3,5,8,9,0,0,0,0,0
50520 DATA 1,5,7,4,6,3,6,5,7,4,3,1,5,8,7,0,0,0,0,0
50530 DATA 4,7,5,6,9,5,9,7,4,3,9,5,7,8,4,7,4,9,5,8
50540 DATA 5,9,2,8,3,3,2,9,5,6,5,9,3,2,7,2,3,5,8,9
50550 DATA 2,3,5,8,9,9,5,3,2,6,3,2,5,9,7,7,4,5,3,9
50560 DATA 7,4,3,5,2,3,2,7,4,5
50570 E=O
50580 F=INT(RND(1)*2)
50590 G=1 :  H=0 :  C1=10 :  C2=10 :  N=0
```

```
50600 FOR I=1 TO 9
50610 B(I)=32
50620 NEXT I
50630 C=INT(RND(1)*3)
50640 IF C=0 THEN C=5
50650 U=10-C
50660 GOSUB 52160
50670 IF C=5 THEN GOTO 51850
50680 IF C=2 THEN GOTO 51560
50690 IF U=5 THEN GOTO 50940
50700 R=10*U+140
50710 IF U>5 THEN LET R=R-10
50720 E=1
50730 IF F=1 THEN LET R=R+5
50740 F=1
50750 IF R=0 THEN GOTO 50790
50760 FOR I=1 TO R
50770 READ C
50780 NEXT I
50790 F=F-1
50800 F=F*F
50810 READ C
50820 C2=C1
50830 C1=C
50840 N=N+1
50850 IF C=0 OR C=U THEN 50790
50860 B(C)=88
50870 IF C2=0 OR C=H THEN 51130
50880 IF F=1 THEN 52130
```

```
50890 IF E=0 THEN 50910

50900 IF N=5 THEN 52130

50910 GOSUB 51890

50920 GOSUB 51970

50930 GOTO 50790

50940 U=1

50950 GOSUB 52160

50960 IF U=3 OR U=7 THEN 51500

50970 IF U=4 OR U=8 THEN G=0

50980 GOSUB 52160

50990 C=7

51000 IF G=0 THEN C=3

51010 IF C<>U THEN 52120

51020 GOSUB 52160

51030 IF G=0 THEN 51080

51040 C=2

51050 IF B(2)<>32 THEN LET C=6

51060 IF B(C)=32 THEN 52120

51070 GOTO 51110

51080 C=4

51090 IF B(4)<>32 THEN LET C=8

51100 IF B(C)=32 THEN 52120

51110 C=10-U

51120 B(C)=88

51130 GOSUB 51890

51140 PRINT

51150 PRINT :  PRINT SPC(22);"Very Good!  You have won a draw!"

51160 PRINT SPC(18);"Do you want to play again?  (Type Y or N)"

51170 NOESC
```

```
51180 IF BINAND(INP(0),%0040%)=0 THEN 51180

51190 ESC

51200 H9=INP(1)

51210 H9=BINAND(H9,%007F%)

51220 IF NOT(H9=%0059%)THEN 51250

51230 GOSUB 52210

51240 GOTO 50440

51250 IF H9<>%004E%THEN 51180

51260 GOSUB 52210

51270 PRINT : PRINT : PRINT : PRINT : PRINT : PRINT
      PRINT : PRINT : PRINT : PRINT : PRINT : PRINT
      SPC(12);"The End.  Thank you for playing
      Tictactoe."

51280 OPEN\1,79,1\"B:SBJID"

51290 INPUT\1\A9$

51300 INPUT\1\A9$

51310 INPUT\1\A9$

51320 INPUT\1\T9$(1,6)

51330 CLOSE\1\

51340 IF NOT(A9$="Y"OR T9$(3,3)="Y")THEN 51370

51350 RUN"MATCH1"

51370 IF NOT(T9$(4,4)="Y")THEN 51400

51380 RUN"STARPLS1"

51400 IF NOT(T9$(5,5)="Y")THEN 51430

51410 RUN"ORDER1"

51430 IF NOT(T9$(6,6)="Y")THEN 51460

51440 RUN"WORDS1"

51460 CLOSE : ERASE"B:SBJID" : END

51500 C0=2
```

```
51510 IF U=3 THEN LET C0=4
51520 GOSUB 52160
51530 C=C0
51540 IF U=C THEN LET C=C+4
51550 GOTO 52120
51560 IF U=8 THEN 51620
51570 R=10*U+60
51580 IF U=1 THEN LET R=80
51590 IF INT(U/2)=U/2 THEN 50720
51600 IF U>6 THEN LET E=1
51610 GOTO 50740
51620 B(9)=88
51630 GOSUB 51890
51640 GOSUB 51970
51650 IF U<4 THEN 51730
51660 IF U>5 THEN 51790
51670 B(3)=88
51680 GOSUB 51890
51690 GOSUB 51970
51700 C=1
51710 IF U=1 THEN LET C=6
51720 GOTO 52120
51730 F=0
51740 H=6
51750 IF U<>1 THEN 51770
51760 H=4
51770 R=140
51780 GOTO 50720
51790 B(1)=88
```

```
51800 GOSUB 51890
51810 GOSUB 51970
51820 C=3
51830 IF U=3 THEN LET C=5
51840 GOTO 52120
51850 R=U*10-10
51860 IF U>5 THEN LET R=R-10
51870 IF INT(U/2)=U/2 THEN 50720
51880 GOTO 50740
51890 PRINT :  PRINT TAB(35);"I I"
51900 PRINT TAB(33);CHR$(B(1));" I ";CHR$(B(2));" I ";CHR$(B(3))
51910 PRINT SPC(31);"----+---+----"
51920 PRINT TAB(33);CHR$(B(4));" I ";CHR$(B(5));" I ";CHR$(B(6))
51930 PRINT SPC(31);"----+---+----"
51940 PRINT SPC(33);CHR$(B(7));" I ";CHR$(B(8));" I ";CHR$(B(9))
51950 PRINT TAB(35);"I I"
51960 RETURN
51970 PRINT :  PRINT SPC(29);"What is your move?  ";
51980 NOESC
51990 IF BINAND(INP(0),%0040%)=0 THEN 51990
52000 ESC
52010 U=INP(1)
52020 U=BINAND(U,%007F%)
52030 U=U-48
52040 PRINT U
52050 IF U<1 OR U>9 THEN 52100
52060 IF INT(U)<>U THEN 52100
52070 IF B(U)<>32 THEN 52100
52080 B(U)=79
```

```
52090 RETURN

52100 PRINT :   PRINT SPC(13);"Sorry, that is an illegal move number
      Try again."

52110 GOTO 51970

52170 B(C)=88

52180 GOSUB 51890

52190 GOSUB 51970

52200 RETURN

52210 K9=USR(%0103%,27,2)

52220 K9=USR(%0103%,42,2)

52230 RETURN
```

THE TESTS

The following sections contain the program code for the various tests. As noted earlier, the tests are a package, and they use similar variables. The following list of variables are common to all tests:

Name	Meaning/Purpose
C9$	Subject's code
H9	Input character from keyboard
J9	Lowest number clock port (see below for more on clocks)
K9	Used in clear-screen macro routine
R9	Array used to store random numbers
X9	The number of random numbers to be generated
Q9,V9,Y9	All used to generate random numbers.
Z1–Z9	Used to input and manipulate clock values
Z$–Z9$	Used to input and print instructions.

Word-Decoding Test

The rationale and procedures of the Word Decoding Test were presented in Chapter 5. The test has two parts. In the first, words and matched pseudowords are presented on the computer screen, and the child must read them aloud. In the second part, a graded list of words is presented, and the child is once again required to read them aloud. For both parts, the child's reading latency is recorded by a throat microphone that is activated as soon as the child begins to read. The throat microphone should be adjusted to have the highest possible sensitivity without picking up extraneous sounds (footsteps outside the room, traffic sounds, and so on). The test is self-paced. That is, each new trial is initiated by the child, who presses the RETURN key on the keyboard to indicate she or he is ready for the next word. Rest is given after every block of 32 trials. The next block is initiated by pressing the G key on the keyboard. For younger children, it may be necessary for the examiner to help by pressing the various keys when the child indicates she or he is ready.

A flowchart illustrating how the program works appears in Figure 15. This flowchart should help programers to follow the program code. As can be seen, Part 1 consists of four blocks of trials. Each trial involves a random sequence of 32 items (16 words and 16 pseudowords). The time from the presentation of each word to the subject's vocalization is recorded. Once all four blocks are completed, the mean reaction time for words is calculated. This time plus 1 second serves as the criterion for terminating Part 2. That is, when the subject's reaction time exceeds this amount two trials in a row, the test is over.

The program can be divided into 10 separate stages as follows:

1. A macro routine used to clear the screen is placed in memory.
2. Subject data and stimulus files are opened. Instructions are stored in a file called Instruct.Wrd.
3. The subject's initials and code are sent to a data file along with headings to be used to organize the data.
4. All words and pseudowords are contained in stimulus file Stim.Wrd. Different words are accessed by specifying the file records to be read.
5. Random numbers are generated and stored in an array. These numbers are used to access and present the stimuli.
6. Instructions are presented.
7. A flag is set to indicate whether trials are practice or real.
8. On each trial, a stimulus is presented, the clock is started, a loop is set to sense a vocalization (ESCAPE), and reaction time is recorded.
9. The program waits for the subject to indicate that she or he is ready to continue.
10. In Part 2, the reading latency is compared with the criterion; if it is longer, a flag is set. If it is longer a second time, the task is terminated.

A portion of the code in this and the remaining programs that may look strange to some programers involves a series of instructions labelled In and Out. These are concerned with setting and reading the real-time clock. The clock input and output ports are located at memory locations F0 to FF (240 to 264 decimal). The program must be told where the lowest numbered port is. The clock sends interrupts to these ports ranging from one every 100 microseconds to the port at location 240 to one every 10,000 days to the port at location 264. A port is initialized by outputting a 0 to it (e.g., OUT 240, 0). The clock is

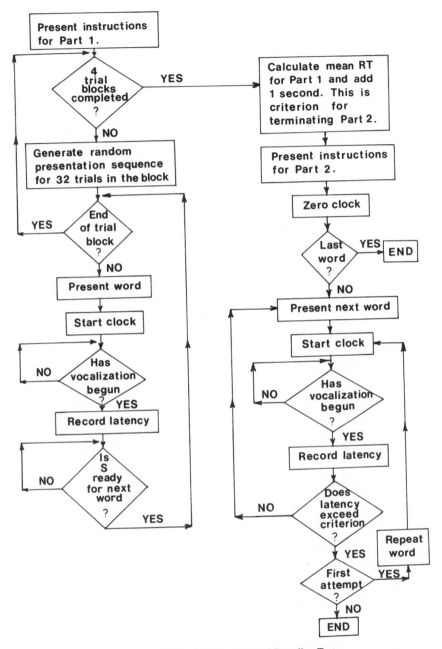

FIGURE 15. Flow chart for the Word-Decoding Test.

restarted by assigning a variable to the port (e.g., X = INP(240)). The clock can be read without any effect on its timing by simply inputting from a port (e.g., W = INP(240)). The number of microseconds since the clock was started will be stored in variable W. Of course, if this number is greater than 9, the millisecond port will be incremented by 1, and it too will have to be read and so on. For the purposes of the present test, timing was done only to the millisecond level. Data obtained from the various clock ports must be transformed to calculate reaction time in milliseconds.

   Note that many of the instructions are for the examiner, not the subject. Throughout the test battery, the tests are referred to as "games" in the instructions to the children.

Listing: Word-Decoding Test

```
3000 REM   NAME     MEANING

3010 REM   B        BLOCK NUMBER

3020 REM   B1       NUMBER OF BLOCKS

3030 REM   C        TERMINATION CRITERION

3040 REM   D        ARRAY FOR STORING RTS

3050 REM   D1,D2    DUMMY VARIABLES

3060 REM   F1       ESCAPE FLAG

3070 REM   F2       PRACTICE TRIALS FLAG

3080 REM   F3       TASK 2 FLAG

3090 REM   F4       TASK 2 NO.  OF TRYS FLAG

3000 REM   F1$      SUBJECT'S DATA FILE NAME

4010 REM   F2$      STIMULUS FILE NAME

4020 REM   F3$      INSTRUCTIONS FILE NAME

4030 REM   G        GROUP NUMBER

4040 REM   G1       NUMBER OF GROUPS

4050 REM   N        NUMBER IN EACH STIMULUS TYPE

4060 REM   P        NUMBER OF PHONEMES

4070 REM   P1       LOWEST NO.  OF PHONEMES

4080 REM   P2       HIGHEST NUMBER OF PHONEMES
```

```
4090 REM   R          LOWEST STIMULUS RECORD FOR INPUT

5020 NOESC

5030 ON ESC GOTO 6940

5040 F1=0 :   F3=0

5050 DELETE 7510,7520

5060 RANDOMIZE

5070 DIM C9$(10),F1$(12),F2$(12),F3$(12),F5$(12),F6$(12),
     F7$(12)

5080 DIM W$(14),Z$(79),Z1$(79),Z2$(79),Z3$(79),Z4$(79)

5090 DIM Z5$(79),Z6$(79),Z7$(79),Z8$(79),Z9$(79)

5100 INTEGER A9,B,B1,D(6,4),F1,F2,G,G1,H9,I,J,J9,K9

5110 INTEGER N,P,P1,P2,Q9,R,R9(100),T1(100),W9,X9,Y9(60)

5120 SHORT T1(101)

5130 INTEGER Z1,Z2,Z3,Z4,Z6,Z7

5140 SHORT D(6,4)

5150 DATA%00D1%,%00C1%,%00CD%,%0005%,%0000%

5160 DATA%0016%,%0000%,%005F%,%00C9%

5170 FOR I=%0103%TO%010B%

5180 READ K9

5190 POKE I,K9

5200 NEXT I

5210 GOSUB 7240

5220 PRINT : PRINT : PRINT : PRINT : PRINT : PRINT
     PRINT : PRINT : PRINT : PRINT : PRINT

5230 PRINT SPC(8);"Press the orange button when you're
     ready to play the 'Words' game."

5240 IF BINAND(INP(0),%0040%)=0 THEN 5240

5250 H9=INP(1) :   H9=BINAND(H9,%007F%)

5260 IF H9=%000D%THEN 5290
```

```
5270 IF H9=%0003%THEN 6680

5280 GOTO 5230

5290 GOSUB 7240

5300 F5$="B:SBJID"

5310 OPEN\1,79,1\F5$

5320 F1$="B:WRD "

5330 INPUT\1\F1$(5,7)

5340 IF F1$(6,6)=" "THEN F1$(6,9)=".DAT" :  GOTO 5370

5350 IF F1$(7,7)=" "THEN F1$(7,10)=".DAT" :  GOTO 5370

5360 IF F1$(8,8)=" "THEN F1$(8,11)=".DAT"

5370 F2$="STIM.WRD"

5380 F3$="INSTRUCT.WRD"

5390 INPUT\1\C9$

5400 CLOSE\1\

5410 ON ERROR GOTO 5460

5420 CREATE F1$

5430 ON ERROR STOP

5440 GOTO 5620

5450 F7$=F1$(2,11)

5460 GOSUB 7240

5470 PRINT" ";F7$;" already exists.  Do you want to keep
     it or do you want to write over"

5480 PRINT" it?  Press K if you want to keep it, and you
     will be asked to input a new"

5490 PRINT" name for it.  Press W if you want to write
     over ";F7$;

5500 INPUT E9$

5510 IF E9$<>"K"THEN 5590

5520 PRINT :  PRINT" New file name";
```

```
5530 INPUT F6$(2,11) :  F6$(0,1)="B:"

5540 ON ERROR GOTO 5570

5550 F1$=F6$

5560 GOTO 5420

5570 PRINT :  PRINT" ";F6$;" already exists.

     Please input another name";

5580 GOTO 5530

5590 IF E9$<>"W"THEN 5460

5600 ERASE F1$

5610 GOTO 5420

5620 OPEN\1,20,2\F1$

5630 OPEN\2,20,1\F2$

5640 OPEN\3,79,1\F3$

5650 PRINT\1\"FILE NAME:  ";F1$;" SBJ CODE:  ";C9$ :  PRINT\1\

5660 PRINT\1\"ALL TIMES IN MSECS."  :  PRINT\1\

5670 PRINT\1\" NUM MED MED

     HIGH HIGH"

5680 PRINT\1\"PHONEMES WORD PSEUDO

     WORD PSEUDO"

5690 PRINT\1\" RT RT

     RT RT"

5700 J9=240 :  B1=3 :  G1=4 :  N=2

5710 P1=4 :  P2=6 :  X9=20 :  R=0 :  R$=""

5715 REM SET INPUT RECORD ARRAY = TO ONE

5720 FOR I=1 TO X9

5730 R9(I)=I

5740 NEXT I

5745 REM CLEAR SCREEN

5750 GOSUB 7240
```

```
5760 INPUT\3\Z$,Z1$,Z2$,Z3$,Z4$,Z5$,Z6$,Z7$,Z8$,Z9$
5770 PRINT Z$,Z1$ :  PRINT :  PRINT Z2$ :  PRINT :  PRINT Z3$ :
     PRINT Z4$;Z5$;Z6$;Z7$;Z8$;Z9$;
5780 INPUT\3\Z$,Z1$,Z2$,Z3$,Z4$,Z5$,Z6$,Z7$,Z8$,Z9$
5790 PRINT Z$;Z1$;Z2$;Z3$;Z4$;Z5$;Z6$;Z7$;Z8$;Z9$
5795 REM SENSE A "G" FLAG
5800 A9=199
5810 GOSUB 7450
5820 GOSUB 7240
5825 REM SET PRACTICE TRIAL FLAG ON
5830 F2=1
5835 REM GO BLOCK OF TRIAL SUBROUTINE
5840 GOSUB 6820
5845 REM SET PRACTICE TRIAL FLAG OFF
5850 F2=0
5860 INPUT\3\Z$,Z1$,Z2$
5870 PRINT Z$ :  PRINT :  PRINT Z1$;Z2$
5875 REM SENSE A "G"
5880 A9=199
5890 GOSUB 7450
5900 INPUT\3\Z1$,Z2$
5910 GOSUB 7240
5915 REM FOR EACH BLOCK..
5920 C=0
5930 FOR B=1 TO B1
5940 IF B=1 THEN 5960
5950 GOSUB 7370
5955 REM INITIALIZE D(P,G)
5960 PRINT :  PRINT :  PRINT :  PRINT :  PRINT :  PRINT
```

```
     PRINT :  PRINT SPC(37);"Ready"

5970 FOR I=1 TO P1

5980 FOR J=1 TO G1

5990 D(I,J)=0

6000 NEXT J

6010 NEXT I

6020 X9=32

6030 R=20

6035 REM GO RANDOM NUMBER GENERATOR

6040 GOSUB 7270

6050 GOSUB 6820

6055 REM OUTPUT DATA TO FILE

6060 PRINT\1\ :  PRINT\1\" BLOCK ";B

6070 FOR P=P1-1 TO P2

6080 PRINT\1\ :  PRINT\1\USING"
     ",P,D(P,1)/N,D(P,2)/N;

6090 PRINT\1\USING" ",
     D(P,3)/N,D(P,4)/N

6100 NEXT P

6110 C=C+D(3,1)+D(4,1)+D(5,1)+D(6,1)

6120 NEXT B

6130 C=C/24+2000

6140 GOSUB 7240

6150 PRINT :  PRINT :  PRINT :  PRINT :  PRINT :  PRINT
     PRINT :  PRINT :  PRINT :  PRINT Z$ :  PRINT

6160 PRINT SPC(25);"That is the end of Part A."

6170 PRINT

6180 PRINT Z1$;Z2$

6190 A9=199
```

```
6200 GOSUB 7450

6210 GOSUB 7240

6220 INPUT\3\Z3$,Z4$,Z5$,Z6$,Z7$,Z8$,Z9$

6230 PRINT Z3$ :  PRINT Z4$ :  PRINT :  PRINT Z5$;Z6$;Z7$;Z8$;Z9$;

6240 INPUT\3\Z3$,Z4$,Z5$,Z6$

6250 PRINT Z3$;Z4$;Z5$;Z6$;Z1$;Z2$

6260 A9=199

6270 GOSUB 7450

6280 GOSUB 7240

6290 R=52

6300 X9=100

6310 F3=1

6320 FOR I=1 TO X9

6330 R9(I)=I

6340 NEXT I

6345 REM GO BLOCK OF TRIAL SUBROUTINE

6350 GOSUB 6820

6360 PRINT\1\ :   PRINT\1\ :  PRINT\1\"TASK  2  RTS" :
     PRINT\1\

6370 J=0

6380 FOR I=1 TO E

6390 J=J+1

6400 PRINT\1\USING"####### ",T1(I);

6410 IF J=5 THEN PRINT\1\ :  PRINT\1\ :  J=0

6420 NEXT I

6430 PRINT\1\ :  PRINT\1\"LAST WORD:  ";W$

6440 GOSUB 7240

6450 PRINT : PRINT : PRINT : PRINT : PRINT : PRINT
     PRINT : PRINT : PRINT : PRINT : PRINT
```

```
      PRINT SPC(35);"Very Good!"  :  PRINT
6460 PRINT SPC(23);"That is the end of this game."
6470 PRINT SPC(29);"Thank you for playing."
6480 OUT J9+1,0 :  OUT J9+2,0 :  OUT J9+3,0 :
     OUT J9+4,0 :  W9=INP(J9)
6490 Z4=INP(J9+4)
6500 IF Z4<>117 THEN 6490
6510 PRINT\1\"EOF"
6520 CLOSE
6530 GOSUB 7240
6540 PRINT :  PRINT :  PRINT :  PRINT :  PRINT :  PRINT
     PRINT :  PRINT :  PRINT :  PRINT :  PRINT
     PRINT SPC(22);"That is the end of all the games."
6550 PRINT SPC(29);"Thank you for playing."
6560 OUT J9+1,0 :  OUT J9+2,0 :  OUT J9+3,0 :
     OUT J9+4,0 :  W9=INP(J9)
6570 Z4=INP(J9+4)
6580 IF Z4<>117 THEN 6570
6590 GOSUB 7240
6600 F$="B:SBJID"
6610 OPEN\1,79,2\F$
6620 PRINT\1\I9$
6630 PRINT\1\C9$
6640 PRINT\1\A9$
6650 PRINT\1\T9$(1,6)
6660 PRINT\1\0
6670 CLOSE\1\
6680 CLOSE :  ERASE"B:SBJID"
6690 GOSUB 7240
```

```
6700 PRINT :  PRINT :  PRINT :  PRINT :  PRINT :  PRINT
     PRINT :  PRINT :  PRINT :  PRINT :  PRINT
6710 PRINT" Press the orange button if you want to run
     Init; otherwise press  C."
6720 IF BINAND(INP(0),%0040%)=0 THEN 6720
6730 H9=INP(1) :  H9=BINAND(H9,%007F%)
6740 IF H9=%000D%THEN 6770
6750 IF H9=%0003%THEN 6810
6760 GOTO 6690
6770 GOSUB 7240
6780 DELETE 5000,6770
6790 DELETE 6810,7500
6800 RUN"INIT"
6810 END
6815 REM BLOCK OF TRIALS SUBROUTINE
6820 FOR I=1 TO X9
6830 INPUT\2,R9(I)-1+R\G,P,W$
6840 IF F3=1 THEN F4=1
6845 REM INITIALIZE CLOCK PORTS
6850 OUT J9+7,0 :  OUT J9+6,0 :  OUT J9+5,0
6860 OUT J9+4,0 :   OUT J9+3,0 :   OUT J9+2,0 :   OUT
     J9+1,0
6870 GOSUB 7240
6880 ESC
6890 F1=1
6895 REM CENTER AND PRINT WORD
6900 PRINT :  PRINT :  PRINT :  PRINT :  PRINT :  PRINT
     PRINT :  PRINT :  PRINT :  PRINT
     PRINT :   PRINT SPC(30);W$
```

```
6910 W9=INP(J9)
6915 REM LOOP FOR WAITING UNTIL S RESPONDS
6920 J=1
6930 IF J=1 THEN 6930
6935 REM JUMP HERE ON ESCAPE
6940 NOESC
6945 REM GET CLOCK PORT VALUES
6950 Z1=INP(J9+1) :  Z2=INP(J9+2) :  Z3=INP(J9+3)
     :  Z4=INP(J9+4)
6960 Z5=INP(J9+5) :  Z6=INP(J9+6) :  Z7=INP(J9+7)
6970 IF F1=0 THEN 6880
6980 F1=0
6985 REM IF PRACTICE TRIALS FORGET RT
6990 IF F2=1 THEN 7070
7000 Z1=Z1-112 :  Z2=Z2-112 :  Z3=Z3-112 :  Z4=Z4-112
7010 Z5=Z5-112 :  Z6=Z6-112 :  Z7=Z7-112
7020 IF Z6<>0 THEN Z5=Z5+Z6*60
7030 IF Z7<>0 THEN Z5=Z5+Z7*600
7040 T=Z5*10000.0+Z4*1000+Z3*100+Z2*10+Z1
7050 IF F3=1 THEN 7070
7060 D(P,G)=D(P,G)+T
7065 REM SENSE A RETURN BEFORE PROCEEDING
7070 A9=13
7080 GOSUB 7450
7090 GOSUB 7240
7100 IF F3=0 THEN 7220
7110 T1(I)=T
7120 IF T<=C THEN 7220
7130 IF F4=2 THEN 7230
```

```
7140 F4=F4+1
7150 PRINT :  PRINT :  PRINT :  PRINT :  PRINT :  PRINT
     PRINT :  PRINT :  PRINT :  PRINT :  PRINT
7160 PRINT SPC(26);"Please try that word again."
7170 OUT  J9+4,0  :   OUT  J9+3,0  :   OUT  J9+2,0  :   OUT
     J9+1,0
     :  W9=INP(J9)
7180 Z4=INP(J9+4)
7190 IF Z4<>115 THEN 7180
7200 GOSUB 7240
7210 GOTO 6850
7220 NEXT I
7230 E=I :  RETURN
7235 REM CLEAR SCREEN SUBROUTINE
7240 K9=USR(%0103%,27,2)
7250 K9=USR(%0103%,42,2)
7260 RETURN
7265 REM RANDOM NUMBER GENERATOR
7270 FOR Q9=1 TO X9
7280 Y9(Q9)=0
7290 NEXT Q9
7300 FOR Q9=1 TO X9
7310 V9=INT(RND(2)*X9)+1
7320 IF Y9(V9)=V9 THEN 7310
7330 Y9(V9)=V9
7340 R9(Q9)=V9
7350 NEXT Q9
7360 RETURN
7365 READY TO GO ON SUBROUTINE
```

```
7370 GOSUB 7240

7380 PRINT Z$

7390 PRINT

7400 PRINT Z1$;Z2$

7410 A9=199

7420 GOSUB 7450

7430 GOSUB 7240

7440 RETURN

7445 REM SENSE A CHARACTER SUBROUTINE

7450 IF BINAND(INP(0),%0040%)=0 THEN 7450

7460 H9=INP(1)

7470 IF H9=131 THEN 6680

7480 IF H9<>A9 THEN 7450

7490 RETURN
```

Listing: Stimulus file Stim.Wrd

```
0,0,          name
0,0,          river
0,0,          carlet
0,0,          frog
0,0,          brick
0,0,          floder
0,0,          garden
0,0,          nist
0,0,          jumper
0,0,          biver
0,0,          flower
0,0,          nabe
0,0,          dish
0,0,          blick
0,0,          jusper
0,0,          gardeb
0,0,          nest
0,0,          carpet
0,0,          gish
0,0,          freg
1,3,          love
1,4,          money
1,5,          mother
1,6,          person
1,4,          dress
```

```
1,6,            moment
1,3,              book
1,5,             paper
2,3,              bove
2,4,             moley
2,5,            mither
2,6,            pegson
2,4,             gress
2,6,            mosent
2,3,              vook
2,5,             pafer
3,3,              time
3,3,              home
3,5,           ·  water
3,4,             power
3,5,             world
3,4,            church
3,6,           problem
3,6,          business
4,3,              tume
4,3,              hote
4,5,             wamer
4,4,             poner
4,5,             borld
4,4,            charch
4,6,           problet
4,6,          buriness
0,0,            school
0,0,              tree
0,0,            little
0,0,              milk
0,0,              book
0,0,            flower
0,0,           playing
0,0,              road
0,0,             train
0,0,             light
0,0,               egg
0,0,             clock
0,0,            people
0,0,               bun
0,0,            summer
0,0,           picture
0,0,             think
0,0,               sit
0,0,             dream
0,0,              frog
0,0,         something
0,0,            island
0,0,          sandwich
0,0,           postage
0,0,        downstairs
0,0,           thirsty
0,0,             crowd
0,0,         beginning
0,0,            nephew
0,0,           biscuit
```

```
0,0,           shepherd
0,0,             saucer
0,0,             canary
0,0,           appeared
0,0,              angel
0,0,            ceiling
0,0,           gradually
0,0,            imagine
0,0,          attractive
0,0,             smolder
0,0,           knowledge
0,0,            diseased
0,0,           nourished
0,0,          university
0,0,             recent
0,0,            disposal
0,0,            situated
0,0,             forfeit
0,0,           fascinate
0,0,            audience
0,0,           intercede
0,0,           orchestra
0,0,              gnome
0,0,            applaud
0,0,              choir
0,0,             heroic
0,0,            colonel
0,0,           plausible
0,0,            physics
0,0,              siege
0,0,            soloist
0,0,          systematic
0,0,           campaign
0,0,            slovenly
0,0,            genuine
0,0,classification
0,0,           prophecy
0,0,          conscience
0,0,          preliminary
0,0,          scintillate
0,0,              saber
0,0,            adamant
0,0,              pivot
0,0, miscellaneous
0,0,             enigma
0,0,          susceptible
0,0,          institution
0,0,            antique
0,0,           satirical
0,0,            oblivion
0,0, procrastinate
0,0,           pneumonia
0,0,            homonym
0,0,          terrestrial
0,0,            rescind
0,0,          belligerent
0,0,           statistics
0,0,           tyrannical
```

```
0,0,   somnambulist
0,0,      judicature
0,0,      evangelical
0,0,       fictitious
0,0,    metamorphosis
0,0,          beguile
0,0,         sepulcher
0,0,     ineradicable
0,0,        grotesque
0,0,      preferential
0,0,      idiosyncrasy
0,0,      bibliography
```

SENTENCE COMPREHENSION TEST

The Sentence Comprehension Test was described in Chapter 6. The procedure is to first present a sentence followed, when the subject indicates she or he is ready, by a picture. The subject must press a button indicating whether the picture is or is not a true representation of the sentence. A flowchart indicating the structure of the computer program appears in Figure 16.

As can be seen, the program presents the 16 sentence–picture combinations in a random sequence. The sentence–picture combinations are stored in a file called Stim.Sta. There are four repetitions. The time from the presentation of the sentence to the subject's button press is recorded and so is the time from picture presentation to the second button press. The subject's accuracy is also recorded. After each attempt, the subject is given feedback on performance.

The program requires two input files and the name of one output file. The first input file, called Spec.Sta, contains the following specifications in the stated order: number of practice blocks (e.g., 2); number of nonpractice blocks (e.g., 2); and how long, in milliseconds, the practice blocks should leave the sentence on the screen (e.g., 500). The second file contains the sentence–picture combinations and the correct response for each one (T or F). Each line also contains the number of spaces required to center the sentence on the screen. The stimulus file, Stim.Sta, appears following the program listing. The output file is the subject's data file.

To run the program, the user supplies the file names one per line followed by the subject's code. Instructions will appear on the screen. These remain there until the subject types a G. The program permits blocks to be repeated and prompts the user to indicate when the program should be aborted. Typing CONTROL C will end the test at the *end* of the next block of trials. The instructions for this test are stored in a file called Inst.Sta.

Listing: Sentence Comprehension Test

```
19800 REM     NAME     DEFINITION

19810 REM     B$       NUMBER OF SPACES INSERTED BEFORE SENTENCE
```

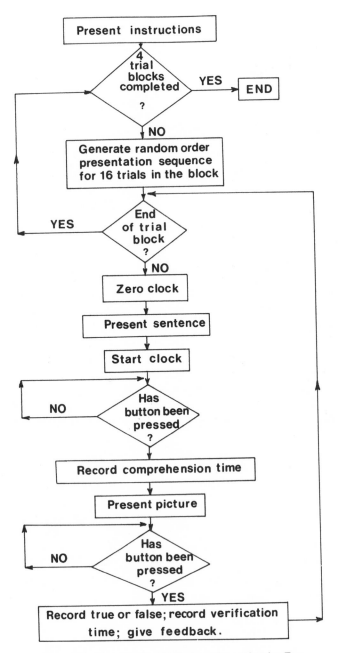

FIGURE 16. Flow chart for the Sentence Comprehension Test.

```
19820 REM      C       CORRECT RESPONSE ARRAY

19830 REM      F1      REPEAT FLAG

19840 REM      F1$     SPECIFICATION FILE NAME

19850 REM      F2$     STIMULUS FILE NAME

19860 REM      F3$     DATA FILE NAME

19870 REM      N1      NUMBER OF PRACTICE BLOCKS

19880 REM      N2      NUMBER OF NONPRACTICE BLOCKS

19890 REM      P1$     DISPLAYED ABOVE

19900 REM      P2$     DISPLAYED BELOW

19910 REM      R1$     CORRECT RESPONSE FOR CURRENT TRIAL

19920 REM      S       INTEGER EQUIVALENT OF B$

19930 REM      T5      CORRECT COMPREHENSION TIME

19940 REM      T6      CORRECT VERIFICATION TIME

19950 REM      T7      INCORRECT COMPREHENSION TIME

19960 REM      T8      INCORRECT VERIFICATION TIME

19970 REM      W       INCORRECT RESPONSE ARRAY

20020 NOESC

20030 F1=0

20040 DELETE 22850,22860

20050 RANDOMIZE

20060 INTEGER B,F1,H9,I,J9,K,K9,N1,N2,Q9,S,T1,V9,W9,X9

20070 INTEGER Z1,Z2,Z3,Z4,Z5,Z6,Z7,C(16),R9(16),Y9(16),
      W(16)

20080 DIM A9$(0),B$(1),C9$(10),F1$(12),F2$(12),F6$(12),
      F7$(12)

20090 DIM F3$(12),F4$(12),P1$(0),P2$(0),R$(0),R1$(0),
      S$(22),T9$(6),X$(27)

20100 DIM Z$(79),Z1$(79),Z2$(79),Z3$(79),Z4$(79),Z5$(79),
      Z6$(79),Z7$(79)

20110 DIM Z8$(79),Z9$(79)
```

```
20120 SHORT T5(16),T6(16),T7(16),T8(16)
20130 DATA%00D1%,%00C1%,%00CD%,%0005%,%0000%,%0016%,%0000%,
      %005F%,%00C9%
20140 FOR I=%0103%TO%010B%
20150 READ K9
20160 POKE I,K9
20170 NEXT I
20180 GOSUB 22330
20190 PRINT : PRINT : PRINT : PRINT : PRINT : PRINT
      PRINT : PRINT : PRINT : PRINT : PRINT
20200 PRINT SPC(8);"Press the orange button when you're ready to
      play the 'Starplus' game."
20210 IF BINAND(INP(0),%0040%)=0 THEN 20210
20220 H9=INP(1) :  H9=BINAND(H9,%007F%)
20230 IF H9=%000D%THEN 20260
20240 IF H9=%0003%THEN 22200
20250 GOTO 20200
20260 GOSUB 22330
20270 F5$="B:SBJID"
20280 OPEN\1,79,1\F5$
20290 F3$="B:STA "
20300 INPUT\1\F3$(5,7)
20310 IF F3$(6,6)=" "THEN F3$(6,9)=".DAT" :  GOTO 20340
20320 IF F3$(7,7)=" "THEN F3$(7,10)=".DAT" :  GOTO 20340
20330 IF F3$(8,8)=" "THEN F3$(8,11)=".DAT"
20340 INPUT\1\C9$
20350 INPUT\1\A9$
20360 INPUT\1\T9$(1,6)
20370 CLOSE\1\
```

```
20380 F1$="SPEC.STA"

20390 F2$="STIM.STA"

20400 F4$="INSTRUCT.STA"

20410 OPEN\1,10,1\F1$

20420 INPUT\1\N1,N2,T1

20430 CLOSE\1\

20440 OPEN\1,79,1\F4$

20450 OPEN\2,29,1\F2$

20460 ON ERROR GOTO 20500

20470 CREATE F3$

20480 ON ERROR STOP

20490 GOTO 20670

20500 F7$=F3$(2,11)

20510 GOSUB 22330

20520 PRINT" ";F7$;" already exists.  Do you want to keep
      it or do you want write over"

20530 PRINT" it?  Press K if you want to keep it, and you
      will be asked to input a new"

20540 PRINT" name for it.  Press W if you want to write over
      ";F7$;

20550 INPUT E9$

20560 IF E9$<>"K"THEN 20640

20570 PRINT :  PRINT" New file name";

20580 INPUT F6$(2,11) :  F6$(0,1)="B:"

20590 ON ERROR GOTO 20620

20600 F3$=F6$

20610 GOTO 20470

20620 PRINT :  PRINT" ";F6$;" already exists.  Please input
      another name";
```

```
20630 GOTO 20580
20640 IF E9$<>"W"THEN 20510
20650 ERASE F3$
20660 GOTO 20470
20670 OPEN\3,25,2\F3$
20680 PRINT\3\"FILE NAME:  ";F3$;" SBJ CODE:  ";C9$
20690 PRINT\3\
20700 PRINT\3\"ALL TIMES IN MSECS.  BLOCKS 1 AND 2 ARE
      PRACTICE."
20710 PRINT\3\
20720 PRINT\3\"STIM CORRECT COMPREHENSION REACTION
      WRONG COMPREHENSION REACTION"
20730 PRINT\3\"CODE RESP TIME TIME
      RESP TIME TIME"
20740 J9=240
20745 REM DO FOR EACH BLOCK.  .  .  .
20750 R$=""
20760 FOR B=1 TO N1+N2
20765 REM CLEAR SCREEN
20770 GOSUB 22330
20780 IF B>3 THEN 21150
20790 IF B<>1 THEN 20950
20800 IF F1=1 THEN F1=0
20810 INPUT\1\Z$,Z1$,Z2$,Z3$,Z4$,Z5$,Z6$,Z7$,Z8$,Z9$
20820 PRINT Z$;Z1$;Z2$;Z3$;Z4$;Z5$;Z6$;Z7$
20830 PRINT R$,R$,Z8$,R$,Z9$,R$
20840 INPUT\1\Z$,Z1$,Z2$,Z3$,Z4$,Z5$,Z6$,Z7$,Z8$
20850 PRINT R$,Z$;Z1$;Z2$;Z3$;Z4$;Z5$;Z6$;Z7$;Z8$;
20860 GOSUB 22700
```

```
20870 INPUT\1\Z$,Z1$,Z2$,Z3$,Z4$,Z5$,Z6$,Z7$,Z8$,Z9$

20880 PRINT Z2$,R$,Z3$

20890 PRINT R$,Z4$;Z5$;Z6$;Z7$;Z8$;Z9$;

20900 INPUT\1\Z$,Z1$,Z2$,Z3$,Z4$,Z5$

20910 PRINT Z$;Z1$;Z2$;Z3$;Z4$;Z5$

20920 GOSUB 22700

20930 CLOSE\1\ :  OPEN\1,79,1\F4$

20940 GOTO 21160

20950 IF B<>2 THEN 21050

20960 IF F1=0 THEN 20970

20970 FOR I=1 TO 35

20980 INPUT\1\Z4$

20990 NEXT I

21000 F1=0

21010 INPUT\1\Z4$,Z5$

21020 PRINT Z4$;Z5$

21030 PRINT :  PRINT SPC(36);"Remember"

21040 PRINT :  PRINT Z6$;Z7$;Z8$;Z9$;Z$;Z1$;Z2$;Z3$

21050 GOTO 21150

21060 IF F1=0 THEN 21110

21070 FOR I=1 TO 37

21080 INPUT\1\Z4$

21090 NEXT I

21100 F1=0

21110 INPUT\1\Z4$

21120 PRINT Z4$

21130 PRINT :  PRINT SPC(36);"Remember"

21140 PRINT :  PRINT Z6$;Z7$;Z8$;Z9$;Z$;Z1$;Z2$;Z3$

21150 GOSUB 22690
```

```
21160 PRINT : PRINT : PRINT : PRINT : PRINT : PRINT
      PRINT : PRINT : PRINT : PRINT : PRINT
21170 PRINT SPC(37);"Ready"
21180 X9=16
21190 FOR K=1 TO X9
21200 C(K)=0 :  T5(K)=0 :  T6(K)=0
21210 W(K)=0 :  T7(K)=0 :  T8(K)=0
21220 NEXT K
21225 REM GENERATE RANDOM NUMBER SEQUENCE
21230 GOSUB 22370
21240 FOR I=1 TO X9
21245 REM FOR EACH SENTENCE-PICTURE COMBINATION
21250 GOSUB 22330
21255 REM INITALIZE CLOCK PORTS
21260 OUT J9+7,0 :  OUT J9+6,0 :  OUT J9+5,0 :  OUT J9+4,0
21270 OUT J9+3,0 :  OUT J9+2,0 :  OUT J9+1,0 :  W9=INP(J9)
21275 REM READ CLOCK PORT
21280 Z3=INP(J9+3)
21290 IF Z3<>113 THEN 21280
21300 T2=0
21305 REM RANDOMLY READ STIMULUS FILE RECORD
21310 INPUT\2,R9(I)-1\X$
21320 R1$=X$(0,0)
21330 B$=X$(1,2)
21340 S$=X$(3,24)
21350 P1$=X$(25,25)
21360 P2$=X$(26,26)
21370 S=VAL(B$)
21380 OUT J9+7,0 :  OUT J9+6,0 :  OUT J9+5,0 :  OUT J9+4,0
```

```
21390 OUT J9+3,0 : OUT J9+2,0 : OUT J9+1,0
21400 PRINT : PRINT : PRINT : PRINT : PRINT : PRINT
      PRINT : PRINT : PRINT : PRINT : PRINT
21405 REM DISPLAY SENTENCE
21410 PRINT SPC(S);S$
21420 W9=INP(J9): REM START CLOCK
21430 PRINT : PRINT : PRINT : PRINT : PRINT : PRINT
      PRINT : PRINT : PRINT : PRINT : PRINT
21435 REM CLEAR SCREEN WHEN S RESPONDS
21440 IF BINAND(INP(0),%0040%)=0 THEN 21440
21450 H9=INP(1): REM CONVERT CLOCK PORT TO REAL TIME
21460 Z1=INP(J9+1) : Z2=INP(J9+2) : Z3=INP(J9+3)
21470 Z4=INP(J9+4) : Z5=INP(J9+5) : Z6=INP(J9+6) :
      Z7=INP(J9+7)
21480 H9=BINAND(H9,%007F%)
21490 IF H9=%0003%THEN 22200
21500 GOSUB 22330
21510 Z1=Z1-112 : Z2=Z2-112 : Z3=Z3-112
21520 Z4=Z4-112 : Z5=Z5-112 : Z6=Z6-112 : Z7=Z7-112
21530 IF Z6<>0 THEN Z5=Z5+Z6*60
21540 IF Z7<>0 THEN Z5=Z5+Z7*600
21550 T2=Z5*10000.0+Z4*1000+Z3*100+Z2*10+Z1
21560 OUT J9+7,0 : OUT J9+6,0 : OUT J9+5,0 :
      OUT J9+4,0
21570 OUT J9+3,0 : OUT J9+2,0 : OUT J9+1,0
21580 PRINT : PRINT : PRINT : PRINT : PRINT
      PRINT : PRINT : PRINT : PRINT : PRINT
21585 REM DISPLAY PICTURES CENTERED
21590 PRINT SPC(39);P1$ : PRINT : PRINT SPC(39);P2$
```

```
21600 W9=INP(J9):   START CLOCK
21610 PRINT :  PRINT :  PRINT :  PRINT :  PRINT :  PRINT
      PRINT :  PRINT :  PRINT
21615 REM WAIT UNTIL SUBJECT RESPONDS AND READ CLOCK
21620 IF BINAND(INP(0),%0040%)=0 THEN 21620
21630 H9=INP(1)
21640 Z1=INP(J9+1) :   Z2=INP(J9+2) :   Z3=INP(J9+3)
21650 Z4=INP(J9+4) :   Z5=INP(J9+5) :   Z6=INP(J9+6) :
      Z7=INP(J9+7)
21660 H9=BINAND(H9,%007F%)
21665 REM IF S GIVES CORRECT TRUE RESPONSE.
21670 IF H9=%0003%THEN 22200
21680 GOSUB 22330
21690 Z7=Z7-112 :   Z6=Z6-112 :   Z5=Z5-112 :   Z4=Z4-112
21700 Z3=Z3-112 :   Z2=Z2-112 :   Z1=Z1-112
21710 IF Z6<>0 THEN Z5=Z5+Z6*60
21720 IF Z7<>0 THEN Z5=Z5+Z7*600
21730 T4=Z5*10000.0+Z4*1000+Z3*100+Z2*10+Z1
21740 H9=BINAND(H9,%007F%)
21750 IF H9=%0003%THEN 22200
21755 REM IF S GIVES CORRECT FALSE RESPONSE
21760 IF NOT(H9=%001B%AND R1$="T")THEN 21790
21770 GOSUB 22470
21780 GOTO 21870:REM IF INCORRECT RESPONSE . . .
21790 IF NOT(H9=%000D%AND R1$="F")THEN 21820
21800 GOSUB 22470
21810 GOTO 21870
21820 IF NOT(H9=%001B%AND R1$="F")THEN 21850
21830 GOSUB 22580
```

```
21840 GOTO 21870

21850 IF NOT(H9=%000D%AND R1$="T")THEN 21870

21860 GOSUB 22580

21870 Z4=INP(J9+4)

21880 IF Z4<>117 THEN 21870

21890 NEXT I

21895 REM WRITE DATA TO FILE

21900 IF B<=N1 THEN 21970

21910 PRINT\3\

21920 PRINT\3\"BLOCK ";B

21930 FOR K=1 TO X9

21940 PRINT\3\USING"## # #######
      ########",K,C(K),T5(K),T6(K);

21950 PRINT\3\USING" # #######
      #######",W(K),T7(K),T8(K)

21960 NEXT K

21970 NEXT B

21980 GOSUB 22330

21990 PRINT : PRINT : PRINT : PRINT : PRINT : PRINT
      PRINT : PRINT : PRINT : PRINT : PRINT

22000 PRINT SPC(23);"That is the end of the Starplus game."

22010 PRINT SPC(29);"Thank you for playing."

22020 OUT J9+1,0 : OUT J9+2,0 : OUT J9+3,0 : OUT J9+4,0 :
      W9=INP(J9)

22030 Z4=INP(J9+4)

22040 IF Z4<>117 THEN 22030

22050 GOSUB 22330

22060 PRINT\3\"EOF"

22070 CLOSE
```

```
22080 DELETE 20010,22070
22090 DELETE 22360,22830
22100 IF NOT(A9$="Y"OR T9$(5,5)="Y")THEN 22120
22110 RUN"ORDER1"
22120 IF NOT(T9$(6,6)="Y")THEN 22140
22130 RUN"WORDS1"
22140 PRINT : PRINT : PRINT : PRINT : PRINT : PRINT
PRINT : PRINT : PRINT : PRINT : PRINT
    PRINT SPC(23);"That is the end of all the games."
22150 PRINT SPC(29);"Thank you for playing."
22160 OUT J9+1,0 : OUT J9+2,0 : OUT J9+3,0 : OUT J9+4,0 :
    W9=INP(J9)
22170 Z4=INP(J9+4)
22180 IF Z4<>117 THEN 22170
22190 GOSUB 22330
22200 CLOSE : ERASE"B:SBJID"
22210 GOSUB 22330
22220 PRINT : PRINT : PRINT : PRINT : PRINT : PRINT
PRINT : PRINT : PRINT : PRINT : PRINT : PRINT
    ;"Press the orange button if you want to run Init;
    otherwise press  C."
22230 IF BINAND(INP(0),%0040%)=0 THEN 22230
22240 H9=INP(1) :  H9=BINAND(H9,%007F%)
22250 IF H9=%000D%THEN 22280
22260 IF H9=%0003%THEN 22320
22270 GOTO 22210
22280 GOSUB 22330
22290 DELETE 20000,22280
22300 DELETE 22320,22840
```

```
22310 RUN"INIT"

22320 END

22325 REM CLEAR SCREEN SUBROUTINE

22330 K9=USR(%0103%,27,2)

22340 K9=USR(%0103%,42,2)

22350 RETURN:REM RANDOM NUMBER GENERATOR

22370 FOR Q9=1 TO X9

22380 Y9(Q9)=0

22390 NEXT Q9

22400 FOR Q9=1 TO X9

22410 V9=INT(RND(2)*X9)+1

22420 IF Y9(V9)=V9 THEN 22410

22430 Y9(V9)=V9

22440 R9(Q9)=V9

22450 NEXT Q9

22460 RETURN

22465 REM CORRECT RESPONSE SUBROUTINE

22470 PRINT : PRINT : PRINT : PRINT : PRINT : PRINT
      PRINT : PRINT : PRINT : PRINT

22480 PRINT SPC(26);"Very good!  That was right!"  :  PRINT

22490 PRINT SPC(21);"Your time to answer was";

22500 PRINT USING"####.###",T4/1000;

22510 PRINT" seconds."

22520 OUT J9+4,0 :  OUT J9+3,0 :  OUT J9+2,0 :  OUT J9+1,0 :
      W9=INP(J9)

22530 IF B<=N1 THEN 22570

22540 C(R9(I))=1

22550 T5(R9(I))=T2

22560 T6(R9(I))=T4
```

```
22570 RETURN

22575 REM INCORRECT RESPONSE SUBROUTINE

22580 PRINT : PRINT : PRINT : PRINT : PRINT : PRINT
      PRINT : PRINT : PRINT : PRINT

22590 PRINT SPC(21);"Sorry, that was wrong.  Try the next
      one."
      : PRINT

22600 PRINT SPC(21);"Your time to answer was";

22610 PRINT USING"###.###",T4/1000;

22620 PRINT" seconds."

22630 OUT J9+4,0 : OUT J9+3,0 : OUT J9+2,0 : OUT J9+1,0
      : W9=INP(J9)

22640 IF B<=N1 THEN 22680

22650 W(R9(I))=1

22660 T7(R9(I))=T2

22670 T8(R9(I))=T4

22680 RETURN

22690 PRINT SPC(17);"Press the orange button when you're
      ready
      to go on."

22700 IF BINAND(INP(0),%0040%)=0 THEN 22700

22710 H9=INP(1)

22720 H9=BINAND(H9,%007F%)

22730 IF H9=%000D%THEN 22820

22740 IF H9=%0003%THEN 22200

22750 IF NOT(H9=%0012%)THEN 22690

22760 PRINT"Enter block number to be repeated."

22770 INPUT B

22780 IF B<1 OR B>N1+N2 THEN PRINT"Invalid block number"
```

```
     :   GOTO 22760

22790 PRINT\3\"BLOCK ";B;"REPEATED"

22800 F1=1

22810 GOTO 20770

22820 GOSUB 22330

22830 RETURN
```

Listing of Stimulus file Stim.Sta

```
T30STAR is above PLUS     *+
T30PLUS is below STAR     *+
F30PLUS is above STAR     *+
F30STAR is below PLUS     *+
T28PLUS is not above STAR*+
T28STAR is not below PLUS*+
F28STAR is not above PLUS*+
F28PLUS is not below STAR*+
F30STAR is above PLUS     +*
F30PLUS is below STAR     +*
T30PLUS is above STAR     +*
T30STAR is below PLUS     +*
F28PLUS is not above STAR+*
F28STAR is not below PLUS+*
T28STAR is not above PLUS+*
T28PLUS is not below STAR+*
```

Long-Term Memory Access Speed Test

This test was described in Chapter 5. The instructions given to the subjects were included in the earlier description; they are stored in file Instruct.Mat. The program displays a pair of letters in the center of the computer screen, separated by two spaces. The subject must press one of two buttons depending on whether she or he thinks the two letters are the same or different. Letters can be the same physically or share the same name (B and b, for example). Only the letters A, B, D, E, R and the corresponding lowercase letters are used. For each trial, the subject's accuracy and reaction time are recorded. In practice trials, the letters stay on the screen indefinitely. For the remaining blocks, the subject must respond within 500 milliseconds.

The specifications for the program reside in a file called Spec.Mat. These specifications include in the first line the size of the Stim.Mat data file (file containing the various matches), the size of the Stim.Mis file (which contains the mismatches), and the number of trial blocks. The following lines in the specifications indicate the number of matches, mismatches, and presentation

time for each block plus two dummy variables. The Spec.Mat file used in the
validity experiments described in Chapter 5 looked like this:

```
20,80,7
35,15,5,0,0
35,15,5,0,0
20,10,5,0,0
20,10,5,0,0
20,10,5,0,0
20,10,5,0,0
20,10,5,0,0
20,10,5,0,0
20,10,5,0,0
20,10,5,0,0
20,10,5,0,0
20,10,5,0,0
```

The Stim.Mat file and the Stim.Mis files are given following the program listing.

For the practice blocks, the subject can take as long as needed to respond;
during the remainder of the task, the subject has only 500 milliseconds to respond.
Between trials, an asterisk appears in the center of the screen.

Listing: Long-Term Memory Access Speed Test

```
29000   NAME      DEFINITION

29010   A1$       CHARACTER ARRAY

29020   B         BLOCK NUMBER

29030   C         NUMBER OF CORRECT RESPONSES

29040   C1        CORRECT PHYSICAL RESPONSES

29050   C2        CORRECT NAME RESPONSES

29060   F1$       MATCH FILE NAME

29070   F2$       MISMATCH FILE NAME

29080   F3$       DATA FILE NAME

29090   F1        TRIAL-ON FLAG

29100   F2        RESPONSE-ON FLAG

29110   L$(0,0)   TRIAL STIMULUS CODE

29120   L$(1,1)   TRIAL STIMULUS LETTER 1

29130   L$(2,2)   TRIAL STIMULUS LETTER 2
```

```
29140  N        MEAN NAME RESPONSE TIME

29150  N1       NUMBER OF BLOCKS

29160  N2       NUMBER OF MATCHES IN BLOCK

29170  N3       NUMBER OF MISMATCHES IN BLOCK

29180  P        MEAN PHYSICAL MATCH TIME

29190  S1       NUMBER OF MATCHES IN MATCH FILE

29200  S2       NUMBER OF MISMATCHES IN MISMATCH FILE

29210  T1       TOTAL PI RESPONSE TIME

29220  T2       TOTAL NAME TRIAL RESPONSE TIME

29230  T3       CLOCK TIME

29240  T4       TOTAL TRIAL RESPONSE TIME

29250  T5       STIMULUS PRESENTATION TIME

29260  T6       TRIAL RESPONSE TIME

30020 NOESC

30030 RANDOMIZE

30040 F1=0

30050 ON ESC GOTO 31960

30060 DELETE 33140,33150

30070 INTEGER B,C,C1,C2,C4,D,F1,F2,H9,I

30080 INTEGER J2,J3,J9,K,K9,N,N1,P,Q9,S1

30090 INTEGER S1,S2,T,T1,T2,T4,T6,V9,W9,X9

30100 INTEGER N2(30),N3(30),R9(80),Y9(80),T5(30,3)

30110 DIM A1$(120),A9$(0),C9$(10),F1$(12),F2$(12)

30120 DIM F3$(12),F4$(12),F5$(12),F6$(12),F7$(12),L$(3)

30130 DIM R$(0),T9$(6),Z$(79),Z1$(79),Z2$(79)

30140 DIM Z3$(79),Z4$(79),Z5$(79),Z6$(79)

30150 DIM Z7$(79),Z8$(79),Z9$(79)

30155 REM READ MACRO TO CLEAR SCREEN

30160 DATA%00D1%,%00C1%,%00CD%,%0005%,%0000%
```

```
30170 DATA%0016%,%0000%,%005F%,%00C9%

30180 FOR I=%0103%TO%010B%

30190 READ K9

30200 POKE I,K9

30210 NEXT I

30220 GOSUB 32910

30230 PRINT : PRINT : PRINT : PRINT : PRINT : PRINT
      PRINT : PRINT : PRINT : PRINT : PRINT

30240 PRINT SPC(8);"Press the orange button when you're ready to
      play the 'Match' game."

30250 IF BINAND(INP(0),%0040%)=0 THEN 30250

30260 H9=INP(1)

30270 H9=BINAND(H9,%007F%)

30280 IF H9=%000D%THEN 30310

30290 IF H9=%0003%THEN 32750

30300 GOTO 30240

30310 GOSUB 32910

30320 F5$="B:SBJID"

30330 OPEN\1,79,1\F5$

30340 F4$="B:MAT "

30350 INPUT\1\F4$(5,7)

30360 IF F4$(6,6)=" "THEN F4$(6,9)=".DAT" :  GOTO 30390

30370 IF F4$(7,7)=" "THEN F4$(7,10)=".DAT" :  GOTO 30390

30380 IF F4$(8,8)=" "THEN F4$(8,11)=".DAT"

30390 INPUT\1\C9$

30400 INPUT\1\A9$,T9$(1,6)

30410 CLOSE\1\

30420 F1$="SPEC.MAT"

30430 F2$="STIM.MAT"
```

```
30440 F3$="STIM.MIS"
30450 F5$="INSTRUCT.MAT"
30460 OPEN\1,10,1\F1$
30470 INPUT\1\S1,S2,N1
30475 REM OBTAIN SPECIFICATIONS
30480 FOR I=1 TO N1
30490 INPUT\1\N2(I),N3(I),T5(I,1),T5(I,2),T5(I,3)
30500 NEXT I
30510 CLOSE\1\
30520 OPEN\2,5,1\F2$
30530 OPEN\3,5,1\F3$
30540 ON ERROR GOTO 30580
30550 CREATE F4$
30560 ON ERROR STOP
30570 GOTO 30750
30580 F7$=F4$(2,11)
30590 GOSUB 32910
30600 PRINT" ";F7$;" already exists.  Do you want to keep it
      or do you want write over"
30610 PRINT" it?  Press K if you want to keep it and you will
      be asked to input a new"
30620 PRINT" name for it.  Press W if you want to write over "
      ;F7$;
30630 INPUT E9$
30640 IF E9$<>"K"THEN 30720
30650 PRINT :  PRINT" New file name";
30660 INPUT F6$(2,11) :  F6$(0,1)="B:"
30670 ON ERROR GOTO 30700
30680 F4$=F6$
```

```
30690 GOTO 30550

30700 PRINT :  PRINT" ";F6$;" already exists.  Please input anothe
      name";

30710 GOTO 30660

30720 IF E9$<>"W"THEN 30590

30730 ERASE F4$

30740 GOTO 30550

30750 OPEN\4,20,2\F4$

30760 ON ERROR GOTO 30780

30770 CREATE"SCRATCH"

30780 PRINT\4\"FILE NAME:  ";F4$;" SBJ CODE:  ";C9$

30790 PRINT\4\

30800 PRINT\4\"ALL TIMES IN MSECS.  BLOCKS 1 AND 2 ARE PRACTICE"

30810 PRINT\4\

30820 PRINT\4\" MISMATCH PHYSICAL
      NAME"

30830 PRINT\4\" NUMBER NUMBER AVERAGE
      NUMBER AVERAGE"

30840 PRINT\4\"BLOCK CORRECT CORRECT RT
      CORRECT RT"

30845 REM CLEAR SCREEN

30855 GOSUB 32910

30850 REM FOR EACH BLOCK . . .

30860 R$=""

30870 FOR B=1 TO N1

30880 IF B>3 THEN 31240

30890 OPEN\1,79,1\F5$

30900 IF B<>1 THEN 31070

30910 INPUT\1\Z$,Z1$,Z2$,Z3$,Z4$,Z5$,Z6$,Z7$,Z8$,Z9$
```

```
30920 PRINT Z$;Z1$;Z2$;Z3$;Z4$;Z5$;Z6$;Z7$;Z8$;Z9$;
30930 INPUT\1\Z$,Z1$,Z2$,Z3$,Z4$,Z5$,Z6$,Z7$,Z8$,Z9$
30940 PRINT Z$;Z1$;Z2$
30950 PRINT R$,R$,Z3$,R$,Z4$;Z5$;Z6$
30960 PRINT Z7$,R$,Z8$;Z9$;
30970 INPUT\1\Z$
30980 PRINT Z$;
30990 GOSUB 33050
31000 INPUT\1\Z$,Z1$,Z2$,Z3$,Z4$,Z5$,Z6$,Z7$
31010 GOSUB 32910
31020 PRINT Z$
31030 PRINT R$,R$,Z1$,R$,Z2$;Z3$;Z4$;Z5$;Z6$;Z7$
31040 GOSUB 33050
31050 GOSUB 32910
31060 GOTO 31230
31070 IF B<>2 THEN 31160
31080 FOR I=1 TO 29
31090 INPUT\1\Z$
31100 NEXT I
31110 INPUT\1\Z$,Z1$,Z2$,Z3$,Z4$,Z5$,Z6$,Z7$,Z8$
31120 PRINT Z$;Z1$;Z2$;Z3$;Z4$;Z5$;Z6$
31130 PRINT R$,Z7$;Z8$
31140 PRINT : PRINT : PRINT : PRINT
31150 GOTO 31230
31160 IF B<>3 THEN 31230
31170 FOR I=1 TO 38
31180 INPUT\1\Z$
31190 NEXT I
31200 INPUT\1\Z$
```

```
31210 PRINT Z$,Z4$;Z5$;Z6$

31220 PRINT R$,Z7$;Z8$

31230 CLOSE\1\ :  IF B=1 THEN 31260

31240 PRINT :  PRINT :  PRINT :  PRINT

31245 REM GO WHEN READY GO ON SUB

31250 GOSUB 33040

31260 PRINT :  PRINT :  PRINT :  PRINT :  PRINT
      PRINT :  PRINT :  PRINT :  PRINT :  PRINT

31270 PRINT SPC(37);"Ready"

31280 OPEN\1,5,3\"SCRATCH"

31290 X9=1

31300 K=3*S1

31305 REM LOOP TO READ EACH TRIAL CODE AND LETTERS

31310 FOR I=1 TO K STEP 3

31320 INPUT\2\A1$(I,I+2)

31330 NEXT I

31335 REM LOOP TO WRITE EACH CODE TO SCRATCH FILE

31340 FOR I=1 TO K STEP 3

31350 PRINT\1\A1$(I,I+2)

31360 NEXT I

31365 REM IF NUMBER OF MATCH TRIALS REQUIRED EQUALS

31366 REM NUMBER OF RECORDS IN MATCH FILE GO TO ?

31370 IF(N2(B)=S1)THEN 31500

31375 REM X9=NO. OF EXTRA MATCHES REQUIRED

31380 X9=S1:REM GO RANDOM NUMBER GENERATOR

31390 GOSUB 32940

31400 X9=N2(B)-S1

31410 K=3*X9:  REM LOOP TO RANDOM X9 RECORDS

31420 D=1
```

```
31430 FOR I=1 TO K STEP 3

31440 INPUT\2,R9(D)-1\A1$(I,I+2)

31450 D=D+1

31460 NEXT I:REM WRITE X9 RECORDS TO SCRATCH FILE

31470 FOR I=1 TO K STEP 3

31480 PRINT\1\A1$(I,I+2)

31490 NEXT I

31500 X9=S2

31510 GOSUB 31940

31520 K=3*N3(B):REM GET MISMATCH TRIALS

31530 D=1

31540 FOR I=1 TO K STEP 3

31550 INPUT\3,R9(D)-1\A1$(I,I+2)

31560 D=D+1

31570 NEXT I

31580 FOR I=1 TO K STEP 3

31590 PRINT\1\A1$(I,I+2)

31600 NEXT I

31610 K=3*(N2(B)+N3(B))

31620 X9=N2(B)+N3(B)

31630 GOSUB 32940

31640 C=0 :  C1=0 :  C2=0 :  C4=0

31650 T=0 :  T1=0 :  T2=0 :  T4=0

31660 D=1 :  J9=240

31670 IF B=1 THEN 31690

31680 J3=T5(B,1)+112 :  J2=T5(B,2)+112

31685 REM DO FOR EACH TRIAL IN BLOCK

31690 FOR I=1 TO K STEP 3

31695 REM RANDOMLY READ STIMULUS TRIAL FROM SCRATCH FILE
```

```
31700 INPUT\1,R9(D)-1\L$(0,2)

31710 D=D+1

31720 Z4=INP(J9+4)

31730 IF Z4<>114 THEN 31720

31740 GOSUB 32910:REM INITIALIZE CLOCK PORTS

31750 OUT J9+3,0 :  OUT J9+2,0 :  OUT J9+1,0 :  W9=INP(J9)

31760 Z3=INP(J9+3)

31770 IF Z3<>113 THEN 31760

31780 OUT J9+4,0 :  OUT J9+3,0 :  OUT J9+2,0 :  OUT J9+1,0

31790 IF B<>1 THEN ESC

31800 F1=1 :  F2=1

31805 REM PRINT LETTERS IN CENTER OF SCREEN

31810 PRINT :  PRINT :  PRINT :  PRINT :  PRINT :  PRINT
      PRINT :  PRINT :  PRINT :  PRINT

31820 PRINT SPC(36);L$(1,1);SPC(4);L$(2,2)

31830 W9=INP(J9)

31835 REM IF NOT PRACTICE TRIALS

31840 IF B<>1 THEN 31920

31850 IF BINAND(INP(0),%0040%)=0 THEN 31850

31855 REM SET FLAG OFF IF MISMATCH; OTHERWISE SET ON

31860 H9=INP(1)

31870 IF H9=13 THEN F2=0 :  GOTO 31970

31880 H9=BINAND(H9,%007F%)

31890 IF H9=%0003%THEN 32750

31900 F2=1

31910 GOTO 31970

31920 Z4=INP(J9+4)

31930 IF Z4<>113 THEN 31920

31940 NOESC :  F1=0 :  F2=0
```

```
31950 GOTO 32050

31955 REM PROGRAM JUMPS HERE WHEN ESC BUTTON PRESSED

31960 NOESC

31970 Z1=INP(J9+1) :   Z2=INP(J9+2) :   Z3=INP(J9+3) :
      Z4=INP(J9+4)

31980 GOSUB 32910

31990 IF B=1 THEN 32030

32000 IF F1=0 THEN 31790

32010 F1=0

32020 F2=1

32030 Z1=Z1-112 :   Z2=Z2-112 :   Z3=Z3-112 :   Z4=Z4-112

32040 T6=Z4*1000+Z3*100+Z2*10+Z1

32050 GOSUB 32910

32060 OUT J9+3,0 :   OUT J9+2,0 :   OUT J9+1,0 :   W9=INP(J9)

32070 Z3=INP(J9+3)

32080 IF Z3<>113 THEN 32070

32090 PRINT :   PRINT :   PRINT :   PRINT :   PRINT :   PRINT
      PRINT :   PRINT :   PRINT :   PRINT

32100 PRINT SPC(39);"*"

32110 OUT J9+4,0 :   OUT J9+3,0 :   OUT J9+2,0 :   OUT J9+1,0 :
      W9=INP(J9)

32115 REM IF NO RESPONSE MADE ON MISMATCH TRIAL INCREMENT
      NO.   CORRECT COUNTER

32120 IF NOT F2=0 THEN 32150

32130 IF L$(0,0)="3"THEN C=C+1 :   C4=C4+1

32140 GOTO 32190

32145 REM IF RESPONSE MADE, AND MATCH TRIAL INCORRECT, NUMBER
      CORRECT AND RESPONSE TIME COUNTERS ALSO INCREMENT
      PHYSICAL OR NAME COUNTERS AS APPROPRIATE.
```

```
32150 IF L$(0,0)<>"3"THEN C=C+1 :   T4=T4+T6

32160 IF L$(0,0)="1"THEN C1=C1+1 :   T1=T1+T6

32170 IF L$(0,0)="2"THEN C2=C2+1 :   T2=T2+T6

32180 F2=0

32190 T=T+1

32200 NEXT I

32210 C3=C1+C2

32220 GOSUB 32910

32230 PRINT : PRINT : PRINT : PRINT : PRINT : PRINT
      PRINT : PRINT : PRINT : PRINT

32240 PRINT SPC(35);"Very Good!"   :   PRINT

32250 PRINT SPC(25);"You answered ";

32260 PRINT USING"###.##",C*100/T;

32270 PRINT"% correctly."   :   PRINT

32280 IF T4=0 THEN 32320

32290 PRINT SPC(16);"Your average time to answer was ";

32300 PRINT USING"###.###",T4/C3/1000;

32310 PRINT" seconds."

32320 OUT J9+5,0 :   OUT J9+4,0 :   OUT J9+3,0 :   OUT J9+2,0 :
      OUT J9+1,0

32330 W9=INP(J9)

32340 Z5=INP(J9+5)

32350 IF Z5<>113 THEN 32340

32360 GOSUB 32910

32365 REM WRITE TO DATA FILE

32370 IF C1>0 THEN P=T1/C1 :   GOTO 32390

32380 P=0

32390 IF C2>0 THEN N=T2/C2 :   GOTO 32410

32400 N=0
```

```
32410 PRINT\4\
32420 PRINT\4\USING"### ### ###
      ###.###",B,C4,C1,P;
32430 PRINT\4\USING" ### ###.###",C2,N
32440 CLOSE\1\ :  CLOSE\2\ :  CLOSE\3\
32450 OPEN\2,5,1\F2$
32460 OPEN\3,5,1\F3$
32470 NEXT B
32480 GOSUB 32910
32490 PRINT : PRINT : PRINT : PRINT : PRINT : PRINT
      PRINT : PRINT : PRINT : PRINT : PRINT
32500 PRINT SPC(23);"That is the end of the Match game."
32510 PRINT SPC(29);"Thank you for playing."
32520 OUT J9+1,0 :  OUT J9+2,0 :  OUT J9+3,0 :  OUT J9+4,0 :
      W9=INP(J9)
32530 Z4=INP(J9+4)
32540 IF Z4<>117 THEN 32530
32550 GOSUB 32910
32560 PRINT\4\"EOF"
32570 CLOSE
32580 ERASE"SCRATCH"
32590 DELETE 30010,32580
32600 IF NOT(A9$="Y"OR T9$(4,4)="Y")THEN 32630
32610 ENTER"STARPLS1.BAS"
32620 RUN
32630 IF NOT(T9$(5,5)="Y")THEN 32660
32640 ENTER"ORDER1.BAS"
32650 RUN
32660 IF NOT(T9$(6,6)="Y")THEN 32690
```

```
32670 ENTER"WORDS1.BAS"

32680 RUN

32690 PRINT : PRINT : PRINT : PRINT : PRINT : PRINT
      PRINT : PRINT : PRINT : PRINT : PRINT : PRINT
      "That is the end of all the games."

32700 PRINT SPC(29);"Thank you for playing."

32710 OUT J9+1,0 : OUT J9+2,0 : OUT J9+3,0 : OUT J9+4,0 :
      W9=INP(J9)

32720 Z4=INP(J9+4)

32730 IF Z4<>117 THEN 32720

32740 GOSUB 32910

32750 CLOSE

32760 ON ERROR GOTO 32780

32770 ERASE"SCRATCH"

32780 ERASE"B:SBJID"

32790 GOSUB 32910

32800 PRINT : PRINT : PRINT : PRINT : PRINT : PRINT
      PRINT : PRINT : PRINT : PRINT : PRINT : PRINT"
      Press the orange button if you want to run Init; otherwise
      press  C."

32810 IF BINAND(INP(0),%0040%)=0 THEN 32910

32820 H9=INP(1) : H9=BINAND(H9,%007F%)

32830 IF H9=%000D%THEN 32960

32840 IF H9=%0003%THEN 32900

32850 GOTO 32900

32860 GOSUB 32910

32870 DELETE 30000,32860

32880 RUN"INIT"
```

```
32890 DELETE 32900,33130

32900 END

32905 REM CLEAR SCREEN SUBROUTINE

32910 A=USR(%0103%,27,2)

32920 A=USR(%0103%,42,2)

32930 RETURN

32935 REM RANDOM NUMBER GENERATOR

32940 FOR Q9=1 TO X9

32950 Y9(Q9)=0

32960 NEXT Q9

32970 FOR Q9=1 TO X9

32980 V9=INT(RND(2)*X9)+1

32990 IF Y9(V9)=V9 THEN 32980

33000 Y9(V9)=V9

33010 R9(Q9)=V9

33020 NEXT Q9

33030 RETURN

33035 REM READY TO GO ON SUBROUTINE

33040 PRINT SPC(16);"Press the orange button when you're
      ready to go on."

33050 IF BINAND(INP(0),%0040%)=0 THEN 33050

33060 H9=INP(1)

33070 H9=BINAND(H9,%007F%)

33080 IF H9=%000D%THEN 33110

33090 IF H9=%0003%THEN 32750

33100 GOTO 33040

33110 GOTO 32910

33120 RETURN
```

Listing: File Stim. Mat

```
1AA
1BB
1DD
1EE
1RR
1aa
1bb
1dd
1ee
1rr
2Aa
2Bb
2Dd
2Ee
2Rr
2aA
2bB
2dD
2eE
2rR
```

Listing: File Stim.Mis

```
3AB
3AD
3AE
3AR
3BD
3BE
3BR
3DE
3DR
3ER
3ab
3ad
3ae
3ar
3bd
3be
3br
3de
3dr
3er
3Ab
3Ad
3Ae
3Ar
3Bd
3Be
3Br
3De
3Dr
3Er
3aB
```

```
3aD
3aE
3aR
3bD
3bE
3bR
3dE
3dR
3eR
3BA
3DA
3EA
3RA
3DB
3EB
3RB
3ED
3RD
3RE
3ba
3da
3ea
3ra
3db
3eb
3rb
3de
3rd
3re
3bA
3dA
3eA
3rA
3dB
3eB
3rB
3eD
3rD
3rE
3Ba
3Da
3Ea
3Ra
3Db
3Eb
3Rb
3Ed
3Rd
3Re
```

Memory-For-Order Test

As described in Chapter 5, the Memory-For-Order Test involves presenting four letters one at a time in each of four positions across the computer screen. Presentations are randomly varied for each trial in a block of trials. Three response

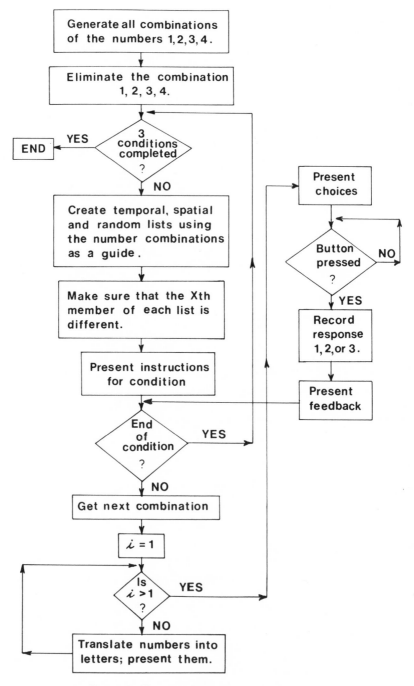

FIGURE 17. Flow chart for the Memory-for-Order Test.

alternatives are provided for each trial: the temporal order, the spatial order, and a random order. These alternatives are also chosen randomly. A flowchart depicting the program appears in Figure 17.

As indicated in the flowchart, the program calculates all possible combinations of the numbers 1 through 4 which are stored in an array. All orders except 1, 2, 3, 4 are used. (This sequence was eliminated because its spatial order could, under certain conditions, be equal to its temporal order.) Each sequence is assigned to a variable in another array; e.g., 1,2,4,3 = N(1). The elements of this array are randomly chosen for use on each trial. Spatial, temporal, and random order combinations are generated by assigning a letter to each number. For each trial, the subject is required to indicate which of the three orders was the same as the one shown by the computer. The subject indicates a choice by a key press, which is then recorded and stored according to the condition.

The instructions for the test were described in Chapter 5. They are stored in a file called Instruct.Ord. Data are output to the subject's data file.

Listing: Memory-for-Order Test

```
9700 REM   NAME    DEFINITION

9710 REM   A1,4..  STORES INTEGER ORDERS

9715 REM   C1      BLOCK NO.  CORRECT

9720 REM   C2      TEMPORAL FLAG

9730 REM   C$      POSITIVE FEEDBACK MESSAGE

9740 REM   D1,2..  SHORTHAND EQUIVALENT OF ORDERS

9750 REM   D1$     CURRENT TRIAL'S LETTERS

9760 REM   I1      INCORRECT SPATIAL

9770 REM   I2      INCORRECT TEMPORAL

9780 REM   I3      INCORRECT RANDOM

9790 REM   L$      LETTER CURRENTLY PRESENTED

9800 REM   L1$     ARRAY CONTAINING STIMULUS SET

9810 REM   M1-M3$  FEEDBACK MESSAGE

9820 REM   N1      NUMBER OF TRIALS IN BLOCK

9830 REM   N2      TOTAL NUMBER OF COMBINATIONS

9840 REM   N3      NUMBER OF STIMULUS LETTERS
```

```
9850 REM   N5      NUMBER OF TRIALS IN CURRENT BLOCK

9860 REM   O       ORDER OF BLOCK PRESENTATION

9870 REM   Q$      QUESTION FOR CURRENT BLOCK

9880 REM   S       NUMBER OF SPACES TO BE INDENTED

9890 REM   T       TRIAL NUMBER

9900 REM   T1$     TEMPORAL RESPONSE ALTERNATIVE

9910 REM   X       BLOCK NUMBER

9920 REM   X1      TOTAL CORRECT SPATIAL

9930 REM   X2      TOTAL CORRECT TEMPORAL

9940 REM   X3      TOTAL INCORRECT SPATIAL

9950 REM   X4      TOTAL INCORRECT TEMPORAL

9960 REM   C5      TOTAL INCORRECT RANDOM

9970 REM   W$-W3$  NEGATIVE FEEDDBACK MESSAGE

10020 NOESC

10030 RANDOMIZE

10040 INTEGER A1(4321),A4(30,4),I,J9,N,N2,N3,Q9,R9(30),V9,
      X9,Y9(30)

10050 N2=23 :  N3=4 :  X9=4 :  J9=240

10060 FOR I=1 TO 4321

10070 A1(I)=0

10080 NEXT I

10090 FOR I=1 TO N2

10100 GOSUB 13550

10110 N=1000*R9(1)+100*R9(2)+10*R9(3)+R9(4)

10120 IF A1(N)=N THEN 10100

10130 IF N=1234 THEN 10100

10140 A1(N)=N

10150 A4(I,1)=R9(1) :  A4(I,2)=R9(2) :  A4(I,3)=R9(3) :
      A4(I,4)=R9(4)
```

```
10160 NEXT I
10170 INTEGER A,A1(1),B,C,C1,C2,D,D1,E,F,F1,H,H9,I1,I2,I3,
      J,J4,K,K9
10180 INTEGER N5,O,P1,R,S,S1,T,T1,W9,X,X1,X2,X3,X4,X5,Z3,
      A5(30),A6(30),A7(30)
10190 DIM A9$(0),C$(79),C9$(10),F1$(12),F5$(12),F6$(12),
      D1$(10),L$(0),L1$(4)
10200 DIM M$(79),M1$(79),M2$(79),M3$(79),Q$(79),R$(0),
      S$(0),S1$(10),T$(0)
10210 DIM Z$(79),Z1$(79),Z2$(79),Z3$(79),Z4$(79),Z5$(79),
      Z6$(79),Z7$(79)
10220 DIM Z8$(79),Z9$(79),F3$(12),F7$(12)
10230 DIM T1$(10),T9$(7),W$(79),W1$(79),W2$(79),W3$(79)
10235 REM INPUT CLEAR SCREEN MACRO
10240 DATA%00D1%,%00C1%,%00CD%,%0005%,%0000%,%0016%,%0000%,
      %005F%,%00C9%
10250 FOR I=%0103%TO%010B%
10260 READ K9 :  POKE I,K9
10270 NEXT I
10280 L1$(1,1)="W"
10290 L1$(2,2)="Q"
10300 L1$(3,3)="S"
10310 L1$(4,4)="K"
10320 GOSUB 13530
10330 PRINT : PRINT : PRINT : PRINT : PRINT : PRINT
      PRINT : PRINT : PRINT
10340 PRINT SPC(8);"Press the orange button when you're ready
      to play the 'Order' game."
10350 IF BINAND(INP(0),%0040%)=0 THEN 10350
```

```
10360 H9=INP(1) :  H9=BINAND(H9,%007F%)

10370 IF H9=%000D%THEN 10400

10380 IF H9=%0003%THEN 11760

10390 GOTO 10340

10400 GOSUB 13530

10410 F5$="B:SBJID"

10420 OPEN\1,79,1\F5$

10430 F1$="B:ORD "

10440 INPUT\1\F1$(5,7)

10450 IF F1$(6,6)=" "THEN F1$(6,9)=".DAT" :  GOTO 10480

10460 IF F1$(7,7)=" "THEN F1$(7,10)=".DAT" :  GOTO 10480

10470 IF F1$(8,8)=" "THEN F1$(8,11)=".DAT"

10480 F3$="INSTRUCT.ORD"

10490 INPUT\1\C9$

10500 INPUT\1\A9$,T9$

10510 INPUT\1\O

10520 CLOSE\1\

10530 OPEN\3,79,1\F3$

10540 ON ERROR GOTO 10580

10550 CREATE F1$

10560 ON ERROR STOP

10570 GOTO 10760

10580 F7$=F1$(2,11)

10590 GOSUB 13530

10600 PRINT" ";F7$;" already exists.  Do you want to keep it
      or do you want to write over"

10610 PRINT" it?  Press K if you want to keep it and you
      will be asked to input a new"

10620 PRINT" name for it.  Press W if you want to write over
```

```
                ";F7$;
10630 INPUT E9$
10640 IF E9$<>"K"THEN 10730
10650 PRINT :   PRINT" New file name";
10660 F6$=" "
10670 INPUT F6$(2,11) :   F6$(0,1)="B:"
10680 ON ERROR GOTO 10710
10690 F1$=F6$
10700 GOTO 10550
10710 PRINT :   PRINT" ";F6$;" already exists.  Please input
      another name";
10720 GOTO 10660
10730 IF E9$<>"W"THEN 10590
10740 ERASE F1$
10750 GOTO 10550
10760 OPEN\1,45,2\F1$
10770 PRINT\1\"FILE NAME:   ";F1$;" SBJ'S CODE:   ";C9$ :
      PRINT\1\
10780 PRINT\1\"BLOCK 1:  ANY ORDER BLOCK 2:  TEMP ORDER
      BLOCK 3:  SPA ORDER" :  PRINT\1\
10790 PRINT\1\"TRIAL CORRECT CORRECT INCORRECT
      INCORRECT INCORRECT"
10800 PRINT\1\" NUM SPA TEMP SPA
      TEMP RANDOM"
10810 X=1
10820 R$=""
10830 Q$=" What was the order of
      the letters?"
10840 C$=" Very Good!  That was
```

```
        right!"
10850 W$=" Sorry, that was wrong.  Try
        the next one."
10855 REM CLEAR SCREEN
10860 GOSUB 13530
10870 INPUT\3\Z$,Z1$,Z2$,Z3$,Z4$,Z5$,Z6$,Z7$,Z8$,Z9$
10880 PRINT Z$;Z1$;Z2$;Z3$;Z4$;Z5$;Z6$;Z7$;Z8$;Z9$;
10890 INPUT\3\Z$ :  PRINT Z$;
10900 IF BINAND(INP(0),%0040%)=0 THEN 10900
10910 H9=INP(1)
10920 H9=BINAND(H9,%007F%)
10930 IF H9=%000D%THEN 10960
10940 IF H9=%0003%THEN 11760
10950 GOTO 10900
10960 GOSUB 13530
10970 PRINT\1\ :  PRINT\1\"BLOCK 1"
10980 GOSUB 11890
10990 IF O=2 THEN 11280
11000 X=2
11010 IF O=1 THEN 11070
11020 CLOSE\3\
11030 OPEN\3,79,1\F3$
11040 FOR I=1 TO 11
11050 INPUT\3\Z$
11060 NEXT I
11070 Q$=" What was the order in which the
        letters were shown?"
11080 W$=" Sorry, that was
        wrong."
```

```
11090 W1$=" You picked the order of the letters
      going from left to right"
11100 W2$=" instead of the order in which
      the letters were shown."
11110 W3$=" Try the next one."
11120 GOSUB 13530
11130 PRINT" "
11140 PRINT" "
11150 PRINT" "
11160 INPUT\3\Z$,Z1$,Z2$,Z3$,Z4$,Z5$,Z6$,Z7$,Z8$,Z9$
11170 PRINT Z$;Z1$;Z2$;Z3$;Z4$;Z5$;Z6$;Z7$;Z8$;Z9$
11180 IF BINAND(INP(0),%0040%)=0 THEN 11180
11190 H9=INP(1)
11200 H9=BINAND(H9,%007F%)
11210 IF H9=%000D%THEN 11240
11220 IF H9=%0003%THEN 11760
11230 GOTO 11180
11240 GOSUB 13530
11250 PRINT\1\ :  PRINT\1\"BLOCK 2"
11260 GOSUB 11890
11270 IF O=2 THEN 11560
11280 X=3
11290 Q$=" What was the order of the letters
      going from left to right?"
11300 W$=" Sorry, that was
      wrong."
11310 W1$=" You picked the order in which the
      letters were shown instead"
11320 W2$=" of the order of the letters
```

```
      going from left to right."
11330 W3$=" Try the next one."
11340 GOSUB 13530
11350 PRINT" "
11360 PRINT" "
11370 PRINT" "
11380 IF O=1 THEN 11430
11390 FOR I=1 TO 8
11400 INPUT\3\Z$
11410 NEXT I
11420 INPUT\3\Z8$,Z9$
11430 INPUT\3\Z$,Z1$,Z2$,Z3$,Z4$,Z5$,Z6$,Z7$
11440 PRINT Z$;Z1$;Z2$;Z3$;Z4$;Z5$;Z6$;Z7$;
11450 INPUT\3\Z$,Z1$,Z2$ :  PRINT R$;Z$;Z1$;Z2$;Z8$;Z9$
11460 IF BINAND(INP(0),%0040%)=0 THEN 11460
11470 H9=INP(1)
11480 H9=BINAND(H9,%007F%)
11490 IF H9=%000D%THEN 11520
11500 IF H9=%0003%THEN 11760
11510 GOTO 11460
11520 GOSUB 13530
11530 PRINT\1\ :  PRINT\1\"BLOCK 3"
11540 GOSUB 11890
11550 IF O=2 THEN 11000
11560 PRINT\1\"EOF"
11570 GOSUB 13530
11580 PRINT : PRINT : PRINT : PRINT : PRINT : PRINT
      PRINT : PRINT : PRINT : PRINT : PRINT
11590 PRINT SPC(23);"That is the end of the Order game."
```

```
11600 PRINT SPC(29);"Thank you for playing."

11610 OUT J9+1,0 :  OUT J9+2,0 :  OUT J9+3,0 :  OUT J9+4,0 :
      W9=INP(J9)

11620 Z4=INP(J9+4)

11630 IF Z4<>117 THEN 11620

11640 GOSUB 13530

11650 CLOSE

11670 DELETE 10010,11660

11680 IF NOT(A9$="Y"OR T9$(6,6)="Y")THEN 11700

11690 RUN"WORDS1"

11700 PRINT :  PRINT :  PRINT :  PRINT :  PRINT :  PRINT
      PRINT :  PRINT :  PRINT :  PRINT :  PRINT :  PRINT
      SPC(23);"That is the end of all the games."

11710 PRINT SPC(29);"Thank you for playing."

11720 OUT J9+1,0 :  OUT J9+2,0 :  OUT J9+3,0 :  OUT J9+4,0 :
      W9=INP(J9)

11730 Z4=INP(J9+4)

11740 IF Z4<>117 THEN 11730

11750 GOSUB 13530

11760 CLOSE :  ERASE"B:SBJID"

11770 GOSUB 13530

11780 PRINT :  PRINT :  PRINT :  PRINT :  PRINT :  PRINT
      PRINT :  PRINT :  PRINT :  PRINT :  PRINT :  PRINT"
      Press the orange button if you want to run Init, otherwise
      press  C."

11790 IF BINAND(INP(0),%0040%)=0 THEN 11790

11800 H9=INP(1) :  H9=BINAND(H9,%007F%)

11810 IF H9=%000D%THEN 11840

11820 IF H9=%0003%THEN 11880
```

```
11830 GOTO 11770

11840 GOSUB 13530

11850 DELETE 10000,11840

11860 DELETE 11880,13700

11870 RUN"INIT"

11880 END

11890 PRINT :  PRINT :  PRINT :  PRINT SPC(37);"Ready"

11895 REM GENERATE THREE LISTS OF SEQUENCES

11900 GOSUB 12190

11910 C=0 :  N5=10

11920 R=A5(N5+1) :  H=A6(N5+1) :  F=A7(N5+1)

11930 GOSUB 13530:  REM PRESENT STIMULI

11940 GOSUB 12780

11950 PRINT :  PRINT:REM RECORD REPONSES

11960 GOSUB 13020

11970 F1=1

11980 GOSUB 12590

11990 PRINT :  PRINT :  PRINT :  PRINT :  PRINT :  PRINT :  PRINT

12000 PRINT SPC(8);"That is the end of the practice trials.
      The real trials are next."

12010 PRINT :  PRINT :  PRINT SPC(35);"Remember:"

12020 PRINT :  PRINT" If you think its the first choice,
      then press the 1 button.  If you"

12030 PRINT :  PRINT" think its the second choice, then press the
      2 button.  If you think its"

12040 PRINT :  PRINT" the third choice, then press the 3 button."
      :  PRINT :  PRINT

12050 GOSUB 12500

12060 PRINT :  PRINT :  PRINT :  PRINT SPC(37);"Ready"
```

```
12070 F1=0 :  N5=30

12075 REM GENERATE 3 LISTS OF SEQUENCES

12080 GOSUB 12190

12090 GOSUB 13530

12100 C=0

12110 GOSUB 12590

12120 PRINT :  PRINT :  PRINT :  PRINT :  PRINT :  PRINT
      PRINT :  PRINT :  PRINT :  PRINT SPC(35);"
      Very Good!"

12130 PRINT :  PRINT SPC(26);"You answered ";C*100/N5;" % correctly."

12140 OUT J9+4,0 :  OUT J9+3,0 :  OUT J9+2,0 :  OUT J9+1,0 :
      W9=INP(J9)

12150 Z4=INP(J9+4)

12160 IF Z4<>117 THEN 12150

12170 GOSUB 13530

12180 RETURN

12185 REM GENERATE 3 ARRAYS EACH WITH A DIFFERENT
      SEQUENCE OF ALL COMBINATIONS OF 1,2,3,4

12190 X9=N2 :  N1=30

12200 GOSUB 13550

12210 FOR K=1 TO N2

12220 A5(K)=R9(K)

12230 NEXT K

12240 GOSUB 13550

12250 FOR K=1 TO N2

12260 A6(K)=R9(K)

12270 NEXT K

12280 GOSUB 13550

12290 FOR K=1 TO N2
```

```
12300 A7(K)=R9(K)

12310 NEXT K

12320 FOR K=1 TO N2

12330 FOR K=1 TO N2

12340 P1=1

12350 IF NOT(A5(K)=A6(K))THEN 12370

12360 D=A6(K) :  A6(K)=A6(K+P1) :  A6(K+P1)=D :  P1=P1+1

12370 P1=1

12380 IF NOT(A6(K)=A7(K))THEN 12400

12390 D=A7(K) :  A7(K)=A7(K+P1) :  A7(K+P1)=D :  P1=P1+1

12400 IF NOT(A5(K)=A7(K))THEN 12430

12410 D=A7(K) :  A7(K)=A7(K+P1) :  A7(K+P1)=D :  P1=P1+1

12420 GOTO 12380

12430 NEXT K

12440 GOSUB 13550

12450 FOR I=1 TO N1-N2

12460 J=I+N1-N2 :  K=I+2*(N1-N2)

12470 A5(I+N2)=R9(I) :  A6(I+N2)=R9(J) :  A7(I+N2)=R9(K)

12480 NEXT I

12490 RETURN

12500 PRINT SPC(16);"Press the orange button when you're
      ready to go on."

12510 IF BINAND(INP(0),%0040%)=0 THEN 12510

12520 H9=INP(1) :  H9=BINAND(H9,%007F%)

12530 IF H9=%000D%THEN 12560

12540 IF H9=%0003%THEN 11750

12550 GOTO 12500

12560 GOSUB 13530

12570 RETURN
```

```
12580 N3=4:BLOCK OF TRIAL SUBROUTINE

12590 X1=0 :  X2=0 :  X3=0 :  X4=0 :  X5=0

12600 FOR T=1 TO N5

12610 C1=0 :  C2=0 :  I1=0 :  I2=0 :  I3=0

12620 R=A5(T) :  H=A6(T) :  F=A7(T)

12630 GOSUB 12780

12640 GOSUB 13020

12650 IF F1=0 THEN 12680

12660 IF C=5 THEN RETURN

12670 GOTO 12700

12680 PRINT\1\USING"### ### ### ###
      ",T,C1,C2,I1;

12690 PRINT\1\USING"### ### ",I2,I3

12700 NEXT T

12710 IF F1<>0 THEN RETURN

12720 PRINT\1\" =====================================
      ===================="

12730 PRINT\1\USING" ### ### ###
      ",X1,X2,X3;

12740 PRINT\1\USING"### ### ",X4,X5;

12750 PRINT\1\"TOTALS"

12760 PRINT\1\" ==================================
      ====================="

12770 RETURN:REM PRESENT STIMULUS SUBROUTINE

12780 E=2

12790 FOR K=1 TO N3

12800 B=E+1 :  S1=A4(R,K) :  S=16*S1 :  T1=A4(H,K) :
      L$=L1$(T1,T1) :  T1$(E,E)=L$

12810 T1$(B,B)=" " :  S1$(2*S1,2*S1)=L$ :
```

```
      S1$(2*S1+1,2*S1+1)=" "
12820 E=E+2
12830 OUT J9+3,0 :  OUT J9+2,0 :  OUT J9+1,0
12840 PRINT :  PRINT :  PRINT :  PRINT SPC(S);L$
12850 W9=INP(J9)
12860 Z3=INP(J9+3)
12870 IF Z3<>117 THEN 12960
12880 GOSUB 13530
12890 NEXT K
12900 A=2
12910 FOR I=1 TO N3
12920 B=A+1 :  D1=A4(F,I) :  D1$(A,A)=L1$(D1,D1) :
      D1$(B,B)=" " :  A=A+2
12930 NEXT I
12940 FOR I=2 TO 8 STEP 2
12950 IF D1$(I,I)<>S1$(I,I)THEN RETURN
12960 NEXT I
12970 A=0
12980 FOR I=2 TO 8 STEP 2
12990 A=A+1 :  D1=A4(R,A) :  D1$(I,I)=L1$(D1,D1)
13000 NEXT I
13010 RETURN:  REM RECORD RESPONSE SUBROUTINE
13020 X9=3
13030 GOSUB 13550
13040 PRINT :  PRINT :  PRINT :  PRINT :  PRINT :  PRINT
      PRINT :  PRINT :  PRINT Q$
13050 PRINT :  PRINT SPC(35);"1.  ";
13060 IF R9(1)=1 THEN PRINT S1$ :  S$="1" :  GOTO 13090
13070 IF R9(1)=2 THEN PRINT T1$ :  T$="1" :  GOTO 13090
```

```
13080 PRINT D1$
13090 PRINT SPC(35);"2.  ";
13100 IF R9(2)=1 THEN PRINT S1$ :  S$="2" :  GOTO 13130
13110 IF R9(2)=2 THEN PRINT T1$ :  T$="2" :  GOTO 13130
13120 PRINT D1$
13130 PRINT SPC(35);"3.  ";
13140 IF R9(3)=1 THEN PRINT S1$ :  S$="3" :  GOTO 13170
13150 IF R9(3)=2 THEN PRINT T1$ :  T$="3" :  GOTO 13170
13160 PRINT D1$
13170 IF BINAND(INP(0),%0040%)=0 THEN 13170
13180 H9=INP(1) :  H9=BINAND(H9,%007F%) :
      IF H9=%0003%THEN 11750
13190 IF CHR$(H9)="1"THEN 13240
13200 IF CHR$(H9)="2"THEN 13240
13210 IF CHR$(H9)="3"THEN 13240
13215 REM GO TO INVALID BUTTON SUB
13220 GOSUB 13640
13230 GOTO 13040
13240 PRINT :  PRINT :  PRINT
13250 M1$=" " :  M2$=" " :  M3$=" "
13260 J4=117
13270 IF NOT(X=1)THEN 13330
13280 IF CHR$(H9)=S$THEN C=C+1 :  C1=1 :  X1=X1+C1 :
      M$=C$ :  GOTO 13470
13290 IF CHR$(H9)=T$THEN C=C+1 :  C2=1 :  X2=X2+C2 :  M$=C$ :
      GOTO 13470
13300 I3=1 :  X5=X5+I3
13310 M$=W$
13320 GOTO 13470
```

```
13330 IF NOT(X=2)THEN 13400
13340 IF CHR$(H9)=T$THEN C=C+1 :  C2=1 :  X2=X2+C2 :  M$=C$ :
      GOTO 13470
13350 IF CHR$(H9)=S$THEN I1=1 :  X3=X3+I1 :  GOTO 13460
13360 I3=1 :  X5=X5+I3
13370 M$=W$
13380 M3$=W3$
13390 GOTO 13470
13400 IF CHR$(H9)=S$THEN C=C+1 :  C1=1 :  X1=X1+C1 :  M$=C$ :
      GOTO 13470
13410 IF CHR$(H9)=T$THEN I2=1 :  X4=X4+I2 :  GOTO 13460
13420 I3=1 :  X5=X5+I3
13430 M$=W$
13440 M3$=W3$
13450 GOTO 13470
13460 M$=W$ :  M1$=W1$ :  M2$=W2$ :  M3$=W3$
13470 PRINT M$ :  PRINT M1$ :  PRINT M2$ :  PRINT M3$
13480 OUT J9+4,0 :  OUT J9+3,0 :  OUT J9+2,0 :  OUT J9+1,0 :
13490 Z4=INP(J9+4)
13500 IF Z4<>J4 THEN 13490
13510 GOSUB 13530
13520 RETURN:REM CLEAR SCREEN SUBROUTINE
13530 K9=USR(%0103%,27,2) :  K9=USR(%0103%,42,2)
13540 RETURN:REM RANDOM NUMBER GENERATOR
13550 FOR Q9=1 TO X9
13560 Y9(Q9)=0
13570 NEXT Q9
13580 FOR Q9=1 TO X9
13590 V9=INT(RND(2)*X9)+1
```

```
13600 IF Y9(V9)=V9 THEN 13590

13610 Y9(V9)=V9 :  R9(Q9)=V9

13620 NEXT Q9

13630 RETURN:REM INVALID BUTTON SUBROUTINE

13640 GOSUB 13530

13650 PRINT : PRINT : PRINT : PRINT : PRINT : PRINT :
      PRINT : PRINT : PRINT SPC(23);"PLEASE
      ANSWER BY PRESSING EITHER"

13660 PRINT SPC(32);"THE 1 BUTTON" :  PRINT SPC(37);"OR" :
      PRINT SPC(32);
      "THE 2 BUTTON"

13670 PRINT SPC(37);"OR" :  PRINT SPC(32);"THE 3 BUTTON" :
      PRINT : PRINT

13680 RETURN
```

ORGANIZING SUBJECTS' DATA

A program called CAT was written for use with the preceding programs. Its purpose is to concatenate the data files for each test into one data file. The new data file name is the subject's initials followed by the extension .Dat. (For example, the author's data file name would be SS.Dat.) The program requires that all of the tests be run. If any have been omitted, the individual data files will have to be used.

Listing: Cat

```
30 DIM E9$(0),F$(11), S9$(79)

60 PRINT " IS TESTING COMPLETE?  (TYPE Y OR N)"

70 INPUT E9$

80 IF NOT (E9$="Y" OR E9$="N") THEN 60

90 IF E9$="N" THEN 330

100 F$="SBJID"

110 OPEN\1,79,1\F$
```

```
120 INPUT\1\I9$
130 CLOSE\1\
140 F$=" "
150 F$(3,6)=I9$
160 F$(0,2)="DAT"
170 GOSUB 420
180 CREATE F$
190 OPEN\2,79,2\F$
200 F$(0,2)="MAT"
210 GOSUB 420
220 GOSUB 340
230 F$(0,2)="STA"
240 GOSUB 420
250 GOSUB 340
260 F$(O,2)="ORD"
270 GOSUB 420
280 GOSUB 340
290 F$(O,2)="WRD"
300 GOSUB 420
310 GOSUB 340
320 CLOSE
330 END
340 OPEN\1,79,1\F$
350 INPUT\1\S9$
360 IF S9$="EOF" THEN 390
370 PRINT\2\S)$
380 GO TO 350
390 PRINT\2\:PRINT\2\:PRINT\2\:PRINT\2\
400 CLOSE\1\
```

```
405 ERASE "SBJID"

410 RETURN

420 IF F$(4,4)=" "THEN F$(4,7)=".DAT" :  RETURN

430 IF F$(5,5)=" "THEN F$(5,8)=".DAT" :  RETURN

440 IF F$(6,6)=" "THEN F$(6,9)=".DAT" :  RETURN

450 IF F$(7,7)=" "THEN F$(7,10)=".DAT"

460 RETURN
```

REFERENCES

Aaron, P. G., Baxter, C. F., & Lucenti, J. (1980). Developmental and acquired alexia: Two sides of the same coin? *Brain and Language, 11*, 1–11.

Abt Associates (1976). *Education as experimentation: A planned variation model* (Vol. 3). Boston: Author.

Adams, M. J., & Collins, A. (1979). A schema-theoretic view of reading. In R. O. Freedle (Ed.), *New directions in discourse processing* (Vol. 2). Norwood, NJ: Ablex Publishing.

American Psychological Association (1974). *Standards for educational and psychological tests.* Washington, DC: Author.

Anderson, R. C., & Biddle, W. B. (1975). On asking people questions about what they are reading. In G. H. Bower (Ed.), *The psychology of learning and motivation* (Vol. 9). New York: Academic Press.

Annett, M. (1975). Hand preference and the laterality of cerebral speech. *Cortex, 11*, 305–328.

Antos, S. J. (1979). Processing facilitation in a lexical decision task. *Journal of Experimental Psychology: Human Perception and Performance, 5*, 527–545.

Australian Optometrical Association (1976). *Vision and specific learning disability. (Submission to the House of Representatives Select Committee on Specific Learning Disabilities.)* Melbourne: Author.

Ausubel, D. B. (1968). *Educational psychology: A cognitive view.* New York: Holt, Rinehart, & Winston.

Badcock, D., & Lovegrove, W. (1981). The effects of contrast, stimulus duration, and spatial frequency on visible persistence in normal and specifically disabled readers. *Journal of Experimental Psychology: Human Perception and Performance, 7*, 495–505.

Baddeley, A. D. (1968). A 3-minute reasoning test based on grammatical transformation. *Psychonomic Science, 10*, 341–342.

Baddeley, A. D., Ellis, N. C., Miles, T. R., & Lewis, V. J. (1982). Developmental and acquired dyslexia: A comparison. *Cognition, 11*, 185–199.

Baddeley, A. D., & Hitch, G. (1974). Working memory. In G. H. Bower (Ed.), *The psychology of learning and motivation* (Vol. 8). New York: Academic Press.

Baddeley, A. D., & Lewis, V. J. (1981). Inner active processes in reading: The inner voice, the inner ear and the inner eye. In A. M. Lesgold & C. A. Perfetti (Eds.), *Interactive processes in reading.* Hillsdale, NJ: Erlbaum.

Bakker, D. J. (1967). Temporal order, meaningfulness and reading ability. *Perceptual and Motor Skills, 24*, 1027–1030.

Bakker, D. J. (1970). Temporal order perception and reading retardation. In D. J. Bakker & P. Satz (Eds.), *Specific reading disability.* Rotterdam: Rotterdam University Press.

Barron, R. W. (1981a). Reading skills and reading strategies: Use of visual and phonological information. In A. M. Lesgold & C. A. Perfetti (Eds.), *Interactive processes in reading.* Hillsdale, NJ: Erlbaum.

Barron, R. W. (1981b). Some aspects of the development of visual word recognition. In T. G. Waller & G. E. MacKinnon (Eds.), *Reading research: Advances in theory and practice* (Vol. 1). New York: Academic Press.

Bateman, B. (1979). Teaching reading to learning disabled and other hard-to-teach children. In L. B. Resnick & P. A. Weaver (Eds.), *Theory and practice of early reading* (Vol. 1). Hillsdale, NJ: Erlbaum.

Battig, W. F., & Montague, W. E. (1969). Category norms for verbal items in 56 categories: A replication and extension of the Connecticut category norms. *Journal of Experimental Psychology Monograph, 80,* (3, Pt. 2), 1–45.

Bauer, R. H. (1977). Memory processes in children with learning disabilities: Evidence for deficient rehearsal. *Journal of Experimental Child Psychology, 24,* 415–430.

Beck, D. L. (1981). Reading problems and instructional practices. In G. E. Mackinnon & T. G. Waller (Eds.), *Reading research: Advances in theory and practice* (Vol. 1). New York: Academic Press.

Beck, I. (1977). Comprehension during the acquisition of coding skills. In J. Guthrie (Ed.), *Cognition, comprehension and curriculum.* Newark, DE: International Reading Association.

Becker, C. A., & Killion, T. H. (1977). Interaction of visual and cognitive effects in word recognition. *Journal of Experimental Psychology: Human Perception and Performance, 3,* 389–401.

Bender, L. (1946). *Visual motor gestalt test.* New York: American Orthopsychiatric Association.

Benenson, T. F. (1974). Prediction of first-grade reading achievement: Criterion validation of a measure of visual recognition memory. *Educational and Psychological Measurement, 34,* 423–427.

Benton, A. R. (1975). Developmental dyslexia: Neurological aspects. In W. J. Friedlander (Ed.), *Advances in neurology* (Vol. 7). New York: Raven Press.

Berk, R. A. (1980). *Criterion-referenced measurement: The state of the art.* Baltimore: Johns Hopkins University Press.

Berlin, C. I. (1977). Hemispheric asymmetry in auditory tasks. In S. R. Harnard, R. W. Doty, L. Goldstein, J. Jaynes, and G. Krauthamer (Eds.), *Lateralization in the nervous system.* New York: Academic Press.

Berlin, C. I., & McNeil, M. R. (1976). Dichotic listening. In N. J. Lass (Ed.), *Contemporary issues in experimental phonetics.* New York: Academic Press.

Berliner, D. C., & Cohen, L. S. (1973). Trait-treatment interaction and learning. In F. N. Kerlinger (Ed.), *Review of research in education* (Vol. 1). Itasco, IL: Peacock Publishing.

Besner, D. (1981). Deep dyslexia and the right hemisphere hypothesis: What's left? *Bulletin of Psychonomic Society, 18,* 176–178.

Birch, H., & Belmont, L. (1964). Auditory-visual integration in normal and retarded readers. *American Journal of Orthopsychiatry, 34,* 852–861.

Black, J. B. (1981). The effects of reading purpose on memory for text. In J. Long and A. D. Baddeley (Eds.), *Attention and performance IX.* Hillsdale, NJ: Erlbaum.

Blanchard, P. (1946). Psychoanalytic contributions to the problems of reading disabilities. *The psychoanalytic study of the child* (Vol. 2). New York: International Universities Press.

Blank, M., Weider, S., & Bridger, W. H. (1968). Verbal deficiencies in abstract thinking in early reading retardation. *American Journal of Orthopsychiatry, 38,* 3823–3834.

Bloom, B., & Broder, L. (1950). *The problem-solving processes of college students.* Chicago: University of Chicago Press.

Bloomfield, L. L. (1942). Linguistics and reading. *Elementary English Review, 19,* 125–130.

Blumstein, S., Goodglass, H., & Tratter, V. (1975). The reliability of ear advantage in dichotic listening. *Brain and Language, 2,* 226–236.

Botel, M. (1978). *Botel reading inventory.* Chicago: Follett.

Bradley, L., & Bryant, P. E. (1983). Categorising sounds and learning to read—a causal connection. *Nature, 301,* 419–421.

Bradshaw, J. L. (1975). Three interrelated problems in reading: A review. *Memory and Cognition, 3*, 123–134.

Brain, R. (1961). The neurology of language. *Brain, 84*, 145–166.

Broadbent, D. E. (1971). *Decision and stress*. New York: Academic Press.

Broadbent, D. E. (1973). *In defense of empirical psychology*. London: Methuen.

Broca, P. (1861). Perte de la parole: Ramollissement chronique et destruction partielle du lobe antérieur gauche du cerveau. *Bulletin de la Société d'Anthropologie, 2*, 235–238.

Brod, N., & Hamilton, D. (1973). Binocularity and reading. *Journal of Learning Disabilities, 6*, 574–576.

Broman, S. H., Nichols, P. L., & Kennedy, W. A. (1975). *Pre-school IQ: Pre-natal and early developmental correlates*. Hillsdale, NJ: Erlbaum.

Brown, A. (1978). Knowing when, where and how to remember: A problem of metacognition. In R. Glaser (Ed.), *Advances in instructional psychology*. Hillsdale, NJ: Erlbaum.

Burgett, R. E., & Glaser, N. A. (1973). Appraising the revised standardized reading test. *Elementary English, 50*, 71–74.

Buros, O. K. (1975). *Reading tests and reviews*. Highland Park, NJ: Gryphon Press.

Buswell, G. T. (1920). An experimental study of the eye–voice span in reading. *Supplementary Educational Monographs*, No. 7.

Byrne, B. (1981). Reading disability, linguistic access and short-term memory: Comments prompted by Jorm's review of developmental dyslexia. *Australian Journal of Psychology, 33*, 83–86.

Calfee, R. C. (1977). Assessment of independent reading skills: Basic research and practical applications. In A. S. Reber & D. L. Scarborough (Eds.), *Toward a psychology of reading*. Hillsdale, NJ: Erlbaum.

Calfee, R. C., Chapman, R. S., & Venezky, R. L. (1972). How a child needs to think in order to learn to read. In L. W. Gregg (Ed.), *Cognition in learning and memory*. New York: Wiley.

Calfee, R. C., & Drum, P. A. (1979). How the researcher can help the reading teacher with classroom assessment. In L. B. Resnick & P. A. Weaver (Eds.), *Theory and practice of early reading* (Vol. 2). Hillsdale, NJ: Erlbaum.

Calfee, R. C., Venezky, R. L., & Chapman, R. S. (1969). *Pronunciation of synthetic words with predictable and unpredictable letter–sound correspondence* (Technical Report 71). Madison, WI: Wisconsin Research and Development Center for Cognitive Learning.

Carbonell, J. R. (1970). AI in CAI: An artificial intelligence approach to computer-aided instruction. *IEEE Transactions on Man-Machine Systems, 11*, 190–202.

Carpenter, P. A., & Daneman, M. (1981). Lexical retrieval and error recovery in reading: A model based on eye fixations. *Journal of Verbal Learning and Verbal Behavior, 20*, 137–160.

Carpenter, P. A., & Just, M. A. (1975). Sentence comprehension: A psycholinguistic processing model of verification. *Psychological Review, 82*, 45–73.

Carpenter, T. W., Gray, G. W., & Galloway, E. W. (1974). A comparison of individual reading gain. *Reading Teacher, 27*, 368–369.

Carr, T. H. (1981). Building theories of reading disability: On the relations between individual differences in cognitive skills and reading comprehension. *Cognition, 9*, 73–114.

Carroll, H. C. M. (1972). The remedial teaching of reading: An evaluation. *Remedial Education, 7*, 10–15.

Carroll, J. B. (1972). Review of the "Illinois Test of Psycholinguistic Abilities." In O. K. Buros (Ed.), *Mental measurements yearbook*. Highland Park, NJ: Gryphon Press.

Carroll, J. B. (1981). Ability and task difficulty in cognitive psychology. *Educational Researcher, 10*, 11–21.

Cattell, J. M. (1886). The time it takes to see and name objects. *Mind, 11*, 63–65.

Chall, J. (1967). *Learning to read: The great debate*. New York: McGraw-Hill.

Chall, J. (1979). The great debate: Ten years later, with a modest proposal for reading stages. In L. B. Resnick & P. A. Weaver (Eds.), *Theory and practice of early reading* (Vol. 1). Hillsdale, NJ: Erlbaum.

Chambers, S. M., & Forster, K. L. (1975). Evidence of lexical access in a simultaneous matching task. *Memory and cognition, 3,* 549–559.

Chapman, L. J., & Chapman, M. F. (1973). *Disordered thought in schizophrenia.* New York: Appleton-Century-Crofts.

Chase, W. G., & Chi, M. T. H. (1981). Cognitive skill: Implications for spatial skill in large-scale environments. In J. Harvey (Ed.), *Cognition, social behavior and the environment.* Hillsdale, NJ: Erlbaum.

Chase, W. G., & Clark, H. H. (1972). Mental operations in the comparison of sentences and pictures. In L. W. Gregg (Ed.), *Cognition in learning and memory.* New York: Wiley.

Clay, M. M. (1979). *The early detection of reading difficulties* (2nd ed.). London: Heinemann.

Clymer, T., & Barrett, T. C. (1967). *Clymer–Barrett pre-reading battery.* Princeton: Personnel Press.

Collins, A., & Smith, E. E. (1982). Teaching the process of reading comprehension. In D. K. Detterman & R. J. Sternberg (Eds.), *How and how much can intelligence be increased?* Norwood, NJ: Ablex.

Coltheart, M. (1980). Deep dyslexia: A review of the syndrome. In M. Coltheart, K. Patterson, & J. C. Marshall (Eds.), *Deep Dyslexia.* London: Routledge & Kegan Paul.

Coltheart, M., Patterson, K., & Marshall, J. C. (Eds.)., (1980). *Deep Dyslexia.* London: Routledge & Kegan Paul.

Committee on Diagnostic Reading Tests (1966). *Diagnostic reading tests.* Mountain Home, NC: Author.

Craik, F. I. M. (1973). A "levels of analysis" view of memory. In P. Pliner, L. Krames, & T. Alloway (Eds.), *Communication and affect: Language and thought.* New York: Academic Press.

Critchley, M. (1970). *The dyslexic child* (2nd ed.). London: Heinemann.

Critchley, M., & Critchley, E. A. (1978). *Dyslexia defined.* Springfield, IL: Charles Thomas.

Cromer, W. (1970). The difference model: A new explanation for some reading difficulties. *Journal of Educational Psychology, 61,* 471–483.

Cronbach, L. J. (1957). The two disciplines of scientific psychology. *American Psychologist, 12,* 671–684.

Cronbach, L. J. (1970). *Essentials of psychological testing* (3rd ed.). New York: Harper & Row.

Crowder, R. G. (1979). Similarity and order in memory. In G. Bower (Ed.), *The psychology of learning and motivation* (Vol. 3). New York: Academic Press.

Crowder, R. G. (1982). *The psychology of reading.* New York: Oxford University Press.

CTB/McGraw-Hill (1974). *Prescriptive reading inventory.* New York: Author.

Curtis, M. E. (1980). Development of competence in reading skill. *Journal of Educational Psychology, 72,* 656–669.

Daneman, M. (1982). The measurement of reading comprehension: How not to trade construct validity for predictive power. *Intelligence, 6,* 331–345.

Daneman, M., & Carpenter, P. A. (1980). Individual differences in working memory and reading. *Journal of Verbal Learning and Verbal Behavior, 19,* 450–466.

Davidoff, J. B., Done, J., & Scully, J. (1981). What does the lateral ear advantage relate to? *Brain and Language, 12,* 332–346.

Davis, E. E., & Ekwall, E. (1976). Mode of perception and frustration in reading. *Journal of Learning Disabilities, 9,* 53–59.

Dawes, R. M. (1966). Memory and distortion of meaningful written material. *British Journal of Psychology, 57,* 72–86.

Dean, J., & Nichols, R. (1974). *Framework for reading.* London: Evans.

Dean, R. S., Schwartz, N. H., & Smith, L. S. (1981). Lateral preference patterns as a discriminator of learning disabilities. *Journal of Consulting and Clinical Psychology, 49,* 227–231.

Dearborn, W. F. (1906). The psychology of reading. *Archives of Philosophy, Psychology and Scientific Methods, 1*, 7–132.

de Groot, A. (1965). *Thought and choice in chess.* The Hague: Mouton.

de Hirsch, K., Jansky, J. J., & Langford, W. S. (1966). *Predicting reading failure.* New York: Harper International.

Déjerine, J. (1892, Feb. 27). Des différentes variétés de cécité verbale. *Mémoires de la Société de Biologie*, pp. 1–30.

Derevensky, J. L. (1978). Modal preferences and strengths: Implications for reading research. *Journal of Reading Behavior, 10*, 7–23.

Dewey, J. (1898). The primary education fetish. *Forum, 25*, 314–328.

Dewey, J. (1900). Psychology and social practice. *Psychological Review, 7*, 105–124.

Diederich, P. B. (1973). *Research 1960–1970 on methods and materials in reading* (TM Report 22). Princeton, NJ: Educational Testing Service.

Dodge, R. (1900). Visual perception during eye movement. *Psychological Review, 7*, 454–465.

Doehring, D. G. (1977). Comprehension of printed sentences by children with reading disability. *Bulletin of the Psychonomic Society, 10*, 350–352.

Dolch, E. W. (1942). *The Basic Sight Word Test.* Champaign, IL: Garrard Press.

Donlon, T. I., & Angoff, W. H. (1971). The scholastic aptitude test. In W. H. Angoff (Ed.), *The college board admissions testing program: A technical report on research and development activities relating to the scholastic aptitude test and achievement tests.* New York: College Entrance Examinations Board.

Dooling, D. J., & Christiaansen, R. E. (1977). Episodic and semantic aspects of memory for prose. *Journal of Experimental Psychology: Human Learning and Memory, 3*, 428–436.

Doren, M. (1964). *Doren diagnostic reading test of word recognition skills.* Circle Pines, MN: American Guidance Service.

Downing, J. A. (1965). *The initial teaching alphabet.* New York: Scott, Foresman.

Downing, J., & Thackray, D. (1971). *Reading readiness.* London: University of London Press.

Drewnowski, A., & Healy, A. F. (1980). Missing *-ing* in reading: Letter detection errors in word endings. *Journal of Verbal Learning and Verbal Behavior, 19*, 247–262.

Dunlop, D. B., & Dunlop, P. (1981). Orthoptic assessment of children with learning difficulties. *Australian Journal of Ophthalmology, 9*, 113–116.

Durrell, D. D. (1955). *Durrell analysis of reading difficulty.* New York: Harcourt, Brace, World.

Dwyer, C. A. (1973). Sex differences in reading: An evaluation and a critique of current theories. *Review of Educational Research, 43*, 455–467.

Dykstra, R., & Tinney, R. (1969). Sex differences in reading readiness—first-grade achievement and second-grade achievement. In J. A. Figurel (Ed.), *Reading and realism.* Newark, DE: International Reading Association.

Education Commission of the States. (1977). Functional literacy study: Basic reading skills improve, but . . . *NAEP Newsletter, 10*, 1–26.

Educational Development Corporation. (1976). *Individualized criterion-referenced tests.* Huntington, NY: Author.

Ehrlichman, H., & Weinberger, A. (1978). Lateral eye movements and hemispheric asymmetry: A critical review. *Psychological Bulletin, 81*, 1080–1101.

Ekwall, E. E. (1974). Should repetitions be counted as errors? *Reading Teacher, 27*, 365–367.

Ekwall, E. E., Solis, J. K. E., & Solis, E. (1973). Investigating informal reading inventory scoring criteria. *Elementary English, 50*, 271–274.

Elithorn, A., Powell, J., Telford, A., & Cooper, R. (1980). An intelligent terminal for automated psychological testing and remedial practice. In R. L. Grimsdale & M. C. A. Hankin (Eds.), *Human factors and interactive displays.* Buckingham, U.K.: Network.

Englemann, S. E., & Bruner, E. C. (1974). *DISTAR reading level I.* Chicago: Science Research Associates.

Erdmann, B., & Dodge, R. (1898). *Psychologische Untersuchungen über das Lesen auf experimentellen Grundlage.* Halle, Germany: Niemeyer.

Estes, W. K. (1975). The locus of inferential and perceptual processes in letter identification. *Journal of Experimental Psychology: General, 104,* 122–145.

Ewert, H. P. (1930). A study of the effect of inverted retinal stimulation upon spatially coordinated behavior. *Genetic Psychology Monographs, 7,* 177–363.

Farr, R. (1969). *Reading: What can be measured?* Newark, DE: International Reading Association.

Farr, R. (1970a, December). Measuring reading comprehension: An historical perspective. Paper presented at the National Reading Conference, St. Petersburg, FL.

Farr, R. (1970b). *Measurement and evaluation of reading.* New York: Harcourt, Brace, Jovanovich.

Farr, R., & Roser, N. L. (1974). Reading assessment: A look at problems and issues. *Journal of Reading, 17,* 592–599.

Feshbach, S., Adelman, H., & Fuller, W. (1977). Prediction of reading and related academic problems. *Journal of Educational Psychology, 69,* 299–308.

Feurstein, M., Ward, M. M., & Le Baron, S. W. (1979). Neuropsychological and neurophysiological assessment of children with learning and behavior problems. In B. Lahey & A. Kazdin (Eds.), *Advances in clinical child psychology* (Vol. 2). New York: Plenum.

Flesch, R. (1955). *Why Johnny can't read: And what you can do about it.* New York: Harper.

Fletcher, J. D. (1979). Computer-assisted instruction in beginning reading: The Stanford projects. In L. B. Resnick & P. A. Weaver (Eds.), *Theory and practice of early reading* (Vol. 2). Hillsdale, NJ: Erlbaum.

Fletcher, J. D., & Atkinson, R. C. (1972). Evaluation of the Stanford CAI program in initial reading. *Journal of Educational Psychology, 63,* 597–602.

Fletcher, J. M., & Satz, P. (1979). Unitary deficit hypotheses of reading disabilities: Has Vellutino led us astray? *Journal of Learning Disabilities, 12,* 22–26.

Frase, L. T. (1975). Prose processing. In G. H. Bower (Ed.), *The psychology of learning and motivation* (Vol. 9). New York: Academic Press.

Frederiksen, J. R. (1978). *A chronometric study of component skills in reading* (Report No. 3757 [2]). Boston: Bolt, Baranek, & Newman.

Frederiksen, J. R. (1981). Sources of process interactions in reading. In A. M. Lesgold & C. A. Perfetti (Eds.), *Interactive processes in reading.* Hillsdale, NJ: Erlbaum.

Frederiksen, J. R. (1982). A componential theory of reading skills and their interactions. In R. J. Sternberg (Ed.), *Advances in the psychology of human intelligence* (Vol. 1). Hillsdale, NJ: Erlbaum.

Froebel, F. (1903). *The education of man.* New York: Appleton.

Frostig, M. (1963). *Frostig developmental test of visual perception.* Palo Alto, CA: Consulting Psychologists Press.

Frostig, M. (1972). Visual perception, integrative functions and academic learning. *Journal of Learning Disabilities, 5,* 1–15.

Fry, D. (1976). Teachers on reading III: Against the testing of reading. *Urban Review, 9,* 105–113.

Fry, E. (1965). Review of the "Developmental Reading Tests." In O. K. Buros (Ed.), *Sixth Mental Measurements Yearbook.* New Brunswick, NJ: Rutgers University Press.

Galton, F. (1962). *Hereditary genius: An inquiry into its laws and consequences.* New York: Macmillan. (Originally published in 1862).

Garner, R. (1980). Monitoring of understanding: An investigation of good and poor readers' awareness of induced miscomprehension of texts. *Journal of Reading Behavior, 12,* 55–63.

Gates, A. I., & MacGinitie, W. H. (1965). *Gates–MacGinitie Reading Test.* New York: Teachers College Press.

Gates, A. I., & MacGinitie, W. H. (1968). *Gates–MacGinitie Reading Tests: Readiness Skills*. New York: Teachers College Press.

Gazzaniga, M. S., Bogen, J. E., & Sperry, R. W. (1965). Some functional effects of sectioning the cerebral commissures in man. *Proceedings of the National Academy of Sciences, 1962, 48* (Prt.1).

Gazzaniga, M. S., & Le Doux, J. E. (1978). *The integrated mind*. New York: Plenum.

Geffen, G., Bradshaw, J. L., & Wallace, G. (1971). Interhemispheric effects on reaction time to verbal and nonverbal visual stimuli. *Journal of Experimental Psychology, 87,* 415–422.

Gentner, D. (1975). Evidence for the psychological reality of semantic components: The verbs of possession. In D. A. Norman & D. E. Rummelhart (Eds.), *Explorations in cognition*. San Francisco: Freeman.

Gibson, E. (1965). Learning to read. *Science, 148,* 1066–1077.

Gibson, E. J., & Levin, H. (1975). *The psychology of reading*. Cambridge, MA: M.I.T. Press.

Gilliland, H. (1974). *A practical guide to remedial reading*. Columbus, Ohio: Charles E. Merrill.

Glaser, R. (1963). Instructional technology and the measurement of learning outcomes: Some questions. *American Psychologist, 18,* 519–521.

Glaser, R. (1981). The future of testing: A research agenda for cognitive psychology and psychometrics. *American Psychologist, 36,* 923–936.

Glaser, R. (1982). Instructional psychology: Past, present and future. *American Psychologist, 37,* 292–305.

Glazzard, P. (1979). Kindergarten predictors of school achievement. *Journal of Learning Disabilities, 12,* 689–694.

Glushko, R. J. (1981). Principles for pronouncing print: The psychology of phonography. In A. M. Lesgold & C. A. Perfetti (Eds.), *Interactive processes in reading*. Hillsdale, NJ: Erlbaum.

Goldberg, R. A., Schwartz, S., & Stewart, M. (1977). Individual differences in cognitive processes. *Journal of Educational Psychology, 69,* 9–14.

Goodman, K. S. (1973). Analysis of oral reading miscues. In F. Smith (Ed.), *Psycholinguistics and reading*. New York: Holt, Rinehart, & Winston.

Goodman, K. S., & Goodman, Y. M. (1979). Learning to read is natural. In L. B. Resnick & P. A. Weaver (Eds.), *Theory and practice of early reading* (Vol. 1). Hillsdale, NJ: Erlbaum.

Goodman, L., & Wiederholt, J. L. (1973). Predicting reading achievement in disadvantaged children. *Psychology in the Schools, 10,* 181–185.

Gough, P. B. (1972). One second of reading. In J. F. Kavanaugh & I. A. Mattingly (Eds.), *Language by ear and eye*. Cambridge, MA: M.I.T. Press.

Graesser, A. C., Hoffman, N. L., & Clark, L. F. (1980). Structural components of reading time. *Journal of Verbal Learning and Verbal Behavior, 19,* 135–151.

Guilford, J. P. (1967). *The nature of human intelligence*. New York: McGraw-Hill.

Gurney, R. (1978, Oct. 6). Why trust the tests? *Times Educational Supplement,* p. 21.

Guthrie, J. T., Samuels, S. J., Martuza, V., Seifert, M., Tyler, S. J., & Edwall, G. A. (1976). *Study of the locus and nature of reading problems in the elementary school*. Washington, DC: National Institute of Education.

Guthrie, J. T., Siefert, M., & Kline, L. W. (1978). Clues from research on programs for poor readers. In S. J. Samuels (Ed.), *What research has to say about reading instruction*. Newark, DE: International Reading Association.

Guthrie, J. T., & Tyler, S. J. (1976). Psycholinguistic processing in reading and listening among good and poor readers. *Journal of Reading Behavior, 8,* 415–426.

Guyer, B. L., & Friedman, M. P. (1975). Hemispheric processing and cognitive styles in learning-disabled and normal children. *Child Development, 46,* 658–668.

Hammill, D. D., Goodman, L., & Wiederholt, J. L. (1974). Visual-motor processes: Can we train them? *The Reading Teacher, 27,* 469–478.

Hammill, D. D., & Larsen, S. C. (1974). The relationship of selected auditory perceptual skills and reading ability. *Journal of Learning Disabilities, 27*, 429–435.

Haney, W., & Madaus, G. (1978). Making sense of the competency testing movement. *Harvard Educational Review, 78*, 462–484.

Harrigan, J. E. (1976). Initial reading instruction: Phonemes, syllables or ideographs? *Journal of Learning Disabilities, 9*, 74–80.

Harris, A. J. (1976). Practical applications of reading research. *Reading Teacher, 29*, 559–565.

Harris, A. J., & Sipay, E. R. (1980). *How to increase reading ability* (7th ed). New York: Longman.

Healy, A. F. (1974). Separating item from order information in short-term memory. *Journal of Verbal Learning and Verbal Behavior, 13*, 644–655.

Healy, A. F. (1981). Cognitive processes in reading. *Cognition, 10*, 119–126.

Hécaen, H. (1978). Right hemisphere contributions to language function. In P. A. Buser & A. Rougeul-Buser (Eds.), *Cerebral correlates of conscious experience*. Amsterdam: North Holland.

Henderson, L. (1981). Information processing approaches to acquired dyslexia. *Quarterly Journal of Experimental Psychology, 33a*, 502–522.

Henderson, L. (1982). *Orthography and word recognition in reading*. London: Academic Press.

Hildreth, G. H., Griffiths, N. L., & McGauvran, M. E. (1966). *Metropolitan reading tests*. New York: Harcourt, Brace, World.

Hines, D., & Satz, P. (1974). Cross-modal asymmetries in perception related to asymmetry in cerebral function. *Neuropsychologica, 12*, 239–247.

Hinshelwood, J. (1917). *Congenital word blindness*. London: Lewis.

House, E. R., Glass, G. V., McLean, L. D., & Walker, D. F. (1978). No simple answer: Critique of the "Follow Through" evaluation. *Harvard Educational Review, 48*, 128–160.

Hubel, D. H., & Wiesel, T. N. (1968). Receptive fields and functional architecture of the monkey striate cortex. *Journal of Physiology, 195*, 215–243.

Huey, E. B. (1968). *The psychology and pedagogy of reading*. Cambridge, MA: M.I.T. Press (reprint).

Humphreys, L. G. (1962). The organization of human abilities. *American Psychologist, 17*, 475–483.

Hunt, E. (1978). Mechanics of verbal ability. *Psychological Review, 85*, 109–130.

Hunt, E. (1982). Towards new ways of assessing intelligence. *Intelligence, 6*, 231–240.

Hunt, E., Davidson, J., & Lansman, M. (1981). Individual differences in long-term memory access. *Memory and Cognition, 9*, 599–608.

Hunt, E., Frost, N., & Lunneborg, C. L. (1973). Individual differences in cognition: A new approach to intelligence. In G. Bower (Ed.), *Advances in learning and motivation* (Vol. 1). New York: Academic Press.

Hunt, E., Lunneborg, C. L., & Lewis, J. (1975). What does it mean to be high verbal? *Cognitive Psychology, 7*, 194–227.

Jackson, M. D. (1980). Further evidence for a relationship between memory access and reading ability. *Journal of Verbal Learning and Verbal Behavior, 19*, 683–694.

Jackson, M. D., & McClelland, J. L. (1979). Processing determinants of reading speed. *Journal of Experimental Psychology: General, 108*, 151–181.

Jackson, M. D., & McClelland, J. L. (1981). Exploring the nature of a basic visual processing component of reading ability. In O. J. L. Tzeng & H. Singer (Eds.), *Perception of Print*. Hillsdale, NJ: Erlbaum.

Jansky, J., & de Hirsch, K. (1972). *Preventing reading failure*. New York: Harper & Row.

Johns, J. L., Garton, S., Schoenfelder, P., & Skriba, P. (1977). *Assessing reading behavior: Informal reading inventories*. Newark, DE: International Reading Association.

Johnson, D. D., & Pearson, P. D. (1978). *Teaching reading vocabulary*. New York: Holt, Rinehart, & Winston.

Johnson, J. C. (1981). Effects of advance pre-cueing of alternative on the perception of letters alone and in words. *Journal of Experimental Psychology: Human Perception and Performance, 7,* 560–572.

Johnson, W. F. (1975). On the function of letters in word identification: Some data and a preliminary model. *Journal of Verbal Learning and Verbal Behavior, 14,* 17–29.

Jonides, J. (1979). Left and right visual field superiority for letter classification. *Quarterly Journal of Experimental Psychology, 31,* 423–439.

Jorm, A. F. (1979). The cognitive and neurological basis of developmental dyslexia: A theoretical framework and review. *Cognition, 7,* 19–32.

Jorm, A. F. (1983a). Specific reading retardation and working memory: A review. *British Journal of Psychology, 74,* 311–342.

Jorm, A. F. (1983b). *The psychology of reading and spelling disabilities.* London: Routledge & Kegan Paul.

Just, M. A., & Carpenter, P. A. (1980). A theory of reading from eye fixations to comprehension. *Psychological Review, 87,* 329–354.

Kail, R. V., & Marshall, C. V. (1978). Reading skill and memory scanning. *Journal of Educational Psychology, 70,* 808–814.

Kamin, L. (1974). *The science and politics of IQ.* Potomac, MD: LEA.

Kapelis, L. (1975). Early identification of reading failure: A comparison of two screening tests and teacher forecasts. *Journal of Learning Disabilities, 8,* 638–641.

Karlsen, B., Madden, R., & Gardner, R. F. (1966). *Stanford diagnostic reading test.* New York: Harcourt, Brace, & World.

Kazdin, W. E. (1975). *Behavior modification in applied settings.* Homewood, IL: Dorsey Press.

Keating, D. P., & Bobbitt, B. L. (1978). Individual and developmental differences in cognitive processing components of mental ability. *Child Development, 49,* 155–167.

Kelley, T. L. (1965). Interpretation of educational measurements. In G. S. Adams (Ed.), *Measurement and evaluation in educational psychology and guidance.* New York: Holt, Rinehart, & Winston.

Kelley, T. L., & Krey, A. C. (1934). *Tests and measurements in the social sciences.* New York: Scribner's.

Keogh, B. K. (1974). Optometric vision training programs for children with language disabilities: Review of issues and research. *Journal of Learning Disabilities, 7,* 219–231.

Kershner, J. R. (1978). Lateralization in normal 6-yr-olds as related to later reading disability. *Developmental Psychobiology, 11,* 309–319.

Kieras, D. E. (1979). *Modelling reading times in different reading tasks with a simulation model of comprehension* (Technical Report No. 2), Tuscon, AZ: University of Arizona.

Kingston, A. J. (Ed.), (1977). *Toward a psychology of reading and language.* Athens, GA: University of Georgia Press.

Kintsch, W. (1974). *The representation of meaning in memory.* Hillsdale, NJ: Erlbaum.

Kintsch, W., & Van Dijk, T. A. (1978). Towards a model of text comprehension. *Psychological Review, 85,* 363–394.

Kirk, S. A., McCarthy, J. J., & Kirk, W. D. (1968). *Illinois test of psycholinguistic abilities* (revised). Urbana, IL: University of Illinois Press.

Kirsner, K., Wells, J. E., & Sang, D. L. (1982). Physical and name match processes in same-different judgements for letters. *Acta Psychologica, 52,* 73–85.

Klasen, E. (1976). Learning disabilities: The German perspective. In L. Tarnopol & M. Tarnopol (Eds.), *Reading disability: An international perspective.* Baltimore: University Park Press.

Kolers, P. A. (1975). Memorial consequences of automatized encoding. *Journal of Experimental Psychology: Human Learning and Memory, 1,* 689–701.

Kolers, P. A. (1976). Reading a year later. *Journal of Experimental Psychology: Human Learning and Memory, 2,* 554–565.

Koppitz, E. M. (1970). The Visual-Oral Digit Span Test with elementary school children. *Journal of Clinical Psychology, 26,* 349–353.

Koppitz, E. M. (1973). Aural Digit Span Test performed by boys with emotional and learning problems. *Journal of Clinical Psychology, 29,* 462–466.

Koppitz, E. M. (1975). Bender Gestalt Test, Visual-Aural Digit Span Test and reading achievement. *Journal of Learning Disabilities, 8,* 154–157.

Kroll, N. E. A., & Madden, D. J. (1978). Verbal and pictorial processing by hemisphere as a function of the subject's verbal Scholastic Aptitude Test score. In J. Requin (Ed.), *Attention and Performance VII.* Hillsdale, NJ: Erlbaum.

Kučera, H., & Francis, W. N. (1967). *Computational analysis of present-day American English.* Providence, RI: Brown University Press.

LaBerge, D. (1981). Unitization and automaticity in perception. In H. E. Howe, Jr. & J. H. Flowers (Eds.), *Nebraska symposium on motivation, 1980.* Lincoln, NE: University of Nebraska Press.

LaBerge, D., & Samuels, S. J. (1974). Toward a theory of automatic information processing in reading. *Cognitive Psychology, 6,* 293–323.

Lake, D. A., & Bryden, M. P. (1976). Handedness and sex differences in hemispheric asymmetry. *Brain and Language, 3,* 266–282.

Lansman, M. (1978). *An attentional approach to individual differences in immediate memory* (Technical Report N. 2). Seattle: University of Washington.

Larkin, J., McDermott, J., Simon, D. P., & Simon, H. A. (1980). Expert and novice performance in solving physics problems. *Science, 208,* 1335–1342.

Larsen, V. S., Mastropier, P. L., Harris, J. A., & Wainwright, G. E. (1966). *Science research associates checklist.* Chicago: Science Research Associates.

Lawson, L. (1968). Ophthalmological factors in learning disabilities. In H. R. Mykelburst (Ed.), *Progress in learning disabilities* (Vol. 1). New York: Grune & Stratton.

Lefton, L. A., Nagle, R. J., Johnson, G., & Fisher, D. F. (1979). Eye movement dynamics of good and poor readers: Then and now. *Journal of Reading Behavior, 11,* 319–328.

Lennon, R. T. (1962). What can be measured? *Reading Teacher, 15,* 326–327.

Lerner, J. W. (1971). A thorn by any other name: Dyslexia or reading disability. *Elementary English, 48,* 75–80.

Lesgold, A. M. (1982). Computer games for the teaching of reading. *Behavior Research Methods and Instrumentation, 14,* 224–226.

Lesgold, A. M., & Perfetti, C. A. (1981). *Interactive processes in reading.* Hillsdale, NJ: Erlbaum.

Lesgold, A. M., & Roth, S. (1981). Some of the interactive processes in reading and their role in reading skill. In A. M. Lesgold & C. A. Perfetti (Eds.), *Interactive processes in reading.* Hillsdale, NJ: Erlbaum.

Lesiak, J. (1977). The *Gates–MacGinitie Readiness Skills Test* and *Illinois Test of Psycholinguistic Abilities* as predictors of first grade reading. *Psychology in the Schools, 14,* 4–10.

Lester, L. A., Benjamin, B. L., & Stagg, D. I. (1978). Eye movements in reading disabled and normal children: A study of systems and strategies. *Journal of Learning Disabilities, 11,* 549–558.

Levin, H. (1979). *The eye–voice span.* Cambridge, MA: M.I.T. Press.

Levine, M. (1976). The academic achievement test: Its historical context and social functions. *American Psychologist, 31,* 228–238.

Lindgren, S. D. (1978). Finger localization and the prediction of reading disability. *Cortex, 14,* 87–101.

Lorge, I., Thorndike, R. L., & Hagen, E. (1964). *The Lorge–Thorndike intelligence tests (multilevel edition)*. New York: Houghton Mifflin.

Lowell, R. E. (1970). Problems in identifying reading levels with informal reading inventories. In W. K. Durr (Ed.), *Reading difficulties: diagnosis, correction and remediation*. Newark, DE: International Reading Association.

Lundburg, J., Olaffson, A., & Woll, S. (1980). Reading and spelling skills in the first school years predicted from phonemic awareness. *Scandinavian Journal of Psychology, 21*, 159–173.

Lunzer, E. A. (1978). Short-term memory and reading, Stage 1. In M. Gruneberg, P. E. Morris, & R. N. Sykes (Eds.), *Practical aspects of memory*. London: Academic Press.

Lyman, E. R. (1976). *PLATO curricular materials*. Urbana, IL: Computer-Based Educational Research Laboratory, University of Illinois.

Mackworth, J. F. (1972). Some models of the reading process: Learners and skilled readers. *Reading Research Quarterly, 7*, 701–733.

MacLeod, C. M., Hunt, E. B., & Mathews, N. N. (1978). Individual differences in the verification of sentence–picture relationships. *Journal of Verbal Learning and Verbal Behavior, 17*, 493–507.

Mandler, G., & Anderson, R. E. (1971). Temporal and spatial cues in seriation. *Journal of Experimental Psychology, 90*, 128–135.

Mandler, G., & Dean, P. J. (1969). Seriation: Development of serial order in free recall. *Journal of Experimental Psychology, 51*, 207–215.

Marshall, J. C., & Newcombe, F. (1973). Patterns of paralexia: A psycholinguistic approach. *Journal of Psycholinguistic Research, 2*, 175–199.

Mason, G. E., Blanchard, J. S., & Daniel, D. B. (1983). *Computer applications in reading* (2nd ed.). Newark, DE: International Reading Association.

Mason, M., Pilkington, C., & Brandau, R. (1981). From print to sound: Reading ability and order information. *Journal of Experimental Psychology: Human Perception and Performance, 7*, 580–591.

Mathews, N. N., Hunt, E. B., & MacLeod, C. M. (1980). Strategy choice and strategy training in sentence–picture verification. *Journal of Verbal Learning and Verbal Behavior, 19*, 531–548.

McClelland, J. L. (1979). On the time relations of mental processes: An examination of systems of processes in a cascade. *Psychological Review, 86*, 287–330.

McCracken, R. A. (1962). Standardized reading tests and informal reading inventories. *Education, 82*, 366–369.

McCusker, L. X., Gough, P. B., & Bias, R. G. (1981). Word recognition inside and out. *Journal of Experimental Psychology: Human Perception and Performance, 7*, 538–551.

McGuffey's eclectic primer (rev. ed.) (1965). Johnsburg, NY: Buck Hill. (Original work published 1881).

McLeod, J. (1965). *GAP manual*. Melbourne: Heinemann Educational Australia.

McLeod, J., & Anderson, J. (1972). *GAPADOL reading comprehension manual*. Melbourne: Heinemann Educational Australia.

McNally, J., & Murray, W. (1962). *Key words to literacy*. London: Schoolmaster Publishing.

Merrill, E. C., Sperber, R. D., & McCauley, C. (1981). Differences in semantic encoding as a function of reading comprehension skill. *Memory and Cognition, 9*, 618–624.

Meyer, D. E., Schvaneveldt, R. W., & Ruddy, M. G. (1974). Function of graphemic and phonemic codes in visual word recognition. *Memory and Cognition, 2*, 309–323.

Miles, J., Forman, P. J., & Anderson, J. (1973). The long and short term predictive efficiency of two tests of reading potential. *Slow Learning Child, 20*, 131–141.

Money, J. (1962). *Reading disability: Progress and research needs in dyslexia*. Baltimore: Johns Hopkins University Press.

Monroe, M. (1932). *Children who cannot read.* Chicago: University of Chicago Press.

Monroe, W. S. (1919). *Monroe's standardized silent reading test.* Indianapolis: Bobbs-Merrill.

Morgan, W. P. (1896). A case of congenital word blindness. *British Medical Journal, 2,* 1378.

Morphett, M. V., & Washburne, C. (1931). When should children learn to read? *Elementary School Journal, 31,* 496–503.

Morrison, F. J., Giordani, B., & Nagy, J. (1977). Reading disability: An information processing analysis. *Science, 196,* 77–79.

Morton, J. (1969). Interaction of information in word recognition. *Psychological Review, 76,* 165–178.

Morton, J., & Patterson, K. (1980). A new attempt at an interpretation, or, an attempt at a new interpretation. In M. Coltheart, K. Patterson,& J. C. Marshall (Eds.), *Deep dyslexia.* London: Routledge & Kegan Paul.

Myers, P. I., & Hammill, D. D. (1976). *Methods for learning disorders* (2nd ed.) New York: Wiley.

National Foundation for Educational Research (1977). *Catalogue of tests for educational guidance and assessment.* Windsor, U.K.: NFER.

Naylor, H. (1980). Reading disability and lateral asymmetry: An information-processing analysis. *Psychological Bulletin, 87,* 531–545.

Neale, M. D. (1958). *Neale analysis of reading ability.* London: Macmillan.

Neisser, U. (1967). *Cognitive psychology.* New York: Appleton-Century-Crofts.

Nelson, M. J., Denny, E. C., & Brown, J. I. (1960). *Nelson–Denny reading test* (rev. ed.). Boston: Houghton-Mifflin.

The New England Primer (1967 reprint). New York: Columbia University Press.

Newcomer, P. L., & Magee, P. (1977). Predictive indices of reading failure in learning disabled children. *Educational Research Quarterly, 2,* 17–23.

Newkirk, T. (1975). The limitations of the standardized reading test. *English Journal, 64,* 50–52.

Newman, A. (1972). Later achievement of pupils underachieving in first grade. *Reading Research Quarterly, 7,* 477–508.

Nyman, G., & Laurinen, P. (1982). Topographic instability of spatial vision as a cause of dyslectic disorder: A case study. *Neuropsychologica, 18,* 181–186.

O'Connor, N., & Hermelin, B. M. (1973). The spatial or temporal organization of short-term memory. *Quarterly Journal of Experimental Psychology, 25,* 335–343.

Olsen, T. (1975). High school reading tests. *Journal of Reading, 18,* 348–351.

Olshavsky, J. E. (1976–1977). Reading as problem solving: An investigation of strategies. *Reading Research Quarterly, 12,* 654–674.

Ornstein, R., Herron, J., Johnston, J., Sueencionis, C. (1979). Differential right hemisphere involvement in two reading tasks. *Psychophysiology, 16,* 398–401.

Orton, T. S. (1966). *"Word-blindness" in school children and other papers on strephosymbolia (specific language disability-dyslexia)* (Orton Society Monographs, No. 2). Pomfret, CT: The Orton Society.

Osgood, C. E., & Hoosain, R. (1974). Salience of the word as a unit in the perception of language. *Perception and Psychophysics, 15,* 168–192.

Packman, L. (1972). Selected oral reading errors and levels of reading comprehension. In H. A. Klein (Ed.), *The quest for competency in teaching reading.* Newark, DE: International Reading Association.

Palmer, J. C., MacLeod, C. M., Hunt, E., & Davidson, J. E. (1981). Some relations between information processing and reading. Unpublished manuscript, University of Washington.

Patrick, G. T. (1899). Should children under ten learn to read and write? *Popular Science Monthly, 54,* 382–392.

Patterson, K. E. (1978). Phonemic dyslexia: Errors of meaning and the meaning of errors. *Quarterly Journal of Experimental Psychology, 30,* 587–601.

Patterson, K. E. (1979). What is right with "deep" dyslexic patients. *Brain and Language, 8,* 111–129.

Patterson, K. E. (1981). Neuropsychological approaches to the study of reading. *British Journal of Psychology, 72,* 151–174.

Pavlidis, G. Th. (1981). Do eye movements hold the key to dyslexia? *Neuropsychologica, 17,* 57–64.

Pearson, P. D., & Johnson, D. D. (1978). *Teaching reading comprehension.* New York: Holt, Rinehart, & Winston.

Penfield, W., & Roberts, L. (1959). *Speech and brain mechanisms.* Princeton, NJ: Princeton University Press.

Perfetti, C. A., Goldman, S., & Hogaboam, T. (1979). Reading skill and the identification of words in discourse context. *Memory and Cognition, 7,* 273–282.

Perfetti, C. A., & Hogaboam, T. (1975a). Relationship between single word decoding and reading comprehension skill. *Journal of Educational Psychology, 67,* 461–469.

Perfetti, C. A., & Hogaboam, T. (1975b, November). *The effects of word experience on decoding speeds of skilled and unskilled readers.* Paper presented at the annual meeting of the Psychonomics Society, Denver.

Perfetti, C. A., & Lesgold, A. M. (1979). Coding and comprehension in skilled reading and implications for reading instruction. In L. B. Resnick & P. A. Weaver (Eds.), *Theory and practice of early reading.* Hillsdale, NJ: Erlbaum.

Perfetti, C. A., & Roth, S. (1981). Some of the interactive processes in reading and their role in reading skill. In A. M. Lesgold & C. A. Perfetti (Eds.), *Interactive processes in reading.* Hillsdale, NJ: Erlbaum.

Pestalozzi, J. H. (1895). *Leonard and Gerard.* Boston: Heath.

Piaget, J. (1950). *The psychology of intelligence.* London: Routledge.

Pichert, J. W., & Anderson, R. C. (1977). Taking different perspectives on a story. *Journal of Educational Psychology, 69,* 309–315.

Pillsbury, W. B. (1897). A study in apperception. *American Journal of Psychology, 8,* 315–393.

Pinter, R. (1913a). Oral and silent reading of fourth grade pupils. *Journal of Educational Psychology, 4,* 333–337.

Pinter, R. (1913b). Inner speech during silent reading. *Psychological Review, 20,* 129–153.

Pirozzolo, F. J. (1979). *The neuropsychology of developmental reading disorders.* New York: Praeger.

Porac, C., & Coran, S. (1981). *Lateral preferences and human behavior.* New York: Springer.

Posner, M. I., Boies, S. J., Eichelman, W. H., & Taylor, R. L. (1969). Retention of physical and name codes of single letters. *Journal of Experimental Psychology Monographs, 79,* 1–16.

Powell, W. R. (1971). The validity of the instructional reading level. In R. E. Liebert (Ed.), *Diagnostic viewpoints in reading.* Newark, DE: International Reading Association.

Pumfrey, P. D. (1976). *Reading tests and assessment techniques.* London: Hodder & Stoughton.

Pumfrey, P. D. (1977). *Measuring reading abilities.* London: Hodder & Stoughton.

Pyrczak, F. (1979). Definitions of measurement terms. In R. Schreimer (Ed.), *Reading tests and teachers: A practical guide.* Newark, DE: International Reading Association.

Quantz, J. O. (1897). Problems in the psychology of reading. *Psychological Monographs, 2,* (1, Whole No. 5).

Quantz, J. O. (1898). Problems in the psychology of reading. *Psychological Review, 5,* 434–436.

Rankin, E. F., & Culhane, J. W. (1969). Comparable cloze and multiple-choice comprehension test scores. *Journal of Reading, 13,* , 193–198.

Rayner, K. (1977). Visual attention in reading: Eye movements reflect cognitive processes. *Memory and Cognition, 5,* 443–448.

Rayner, K., & Pollatsek, A. (1981). Eye movement control during reading: Evidence for direct control. *Quarterly Journal of Experimental Psychology, 31a*, 351–373.

Reder, L. M. (1979). The role of elaborations in memory for prose. *Cognitive Psychology, 11*, 221–234.

Reed, J. C., Rabe, E. F., & Mankinen, M. (1970). Teaching reading to brain damaged children: A review. *Reading Research Quarterly, 5*, 379–401.

Reicher, G. M. (1969). Perceptual recognition as a function of meaningfulness of stimulus material. *Journal of Experimental Psychology, 81*, 275–280.

Reid, D. K., & Hresko, W. P. (1981). *A cognitive approach to learning disabilities*. New York: McGraw-Hill.

Resnick, D. P., & Resnick, L. B. (1977). The nature of literacy: An historical experiment. *Harvard Educational Review, 47*, 370–385.

Roettger, D., Szymczuk, M., & Millard, J. (1979). Validation of a reading attitude scale for elementary students and an investigation of the relationship between attitude and achievement. *Journal of Educational Research, 72*, 138–142.

Rogers, C. D. (1980). Forecasting the instructional reading level. *Reading Improvement, 17*, 94–96.

Rosenshine, B. V. (1980). Skill hierarchies in reading comprehension. In R. J. Spiro, B. C. Bruce, & W. F. Brewer (Eds.), *Theoretical issues in reading comprehension*. Hillsdale, NJ: Erlbaum.

Rosner, J., & Simon, D. P. (1971). The Auditory Analysis Test: An initial report. *Journal of Learning Disabilities, 4*, 40–48.

Ross, A. O. (1976). *Psychological aspects of learning disabilities and reading disorders*. New York: McGraw-Hill.

Rowley, G. (1980). Reading age and associated myths. *Australian Journal of Reading, 3*, 76–85.

Royer, J. M., Hastings, C. N., & Hook, C. (1979). A sentence verification technique for measuring reading comprehension. *Journal of Reading Behavior, 11*, 355–363.

Ruediger, W. C. (1907). The field of distinct vision. *Archives of Psychology, 5*, 1–68.

Rugel, R. P. (1971). Arousal and levels of reading difficulty. *Reading Teacher, 24*, 458–460.

Rummelhart, D. E. (1975). Notes on a schema for stories. In D. G. Brew & A. Collins (Eds.), *Representation and understanding: Studies in cognitive science*. New York: Academic Press.

Rummelhart, D. E. (1977). Understanding and summarizing brief stories. In D. LaBerge & S. J. Samuels (Eds.), *Basic processes in reading: Perception and comprehension*. Hillsdale, NJ: Erlbaum.

Rummelhart, D. E., & Siple, P. (1974). Process of recognizing tachistoscopically presented words. *Psychological Review, 81*, 99–118.

Ryback, D., & Staats, A. W. (1970). Parents as behavior therapy technicians in treating reading deficits (dyslexia). *Journal of Behavior Therapy and Experimental Psychiatry, 1*, 109–119.

Samuels, S. J. (1976). Hierarchical subskills in the reading acquisition process. In J. T. Guthrie (Ed.), *Aspects of reading acquisition*. Baltimore: Johns Hopkins University Press.

Samuels, S. J., LaBerge, D., & Bremer, C. D. (1978). Units of word recognition: Evidence for developmental changes. *Journal of Verbal Learning and Verbal Behavior, 17*, 715–720.

Satz, P. (1976). Cerebral dominance and reading disability: An old problem revisited. In R. M. Knights & D. J. Bakker (Eds.), *The neuropsychology of learning disorders*. Baltimore: University Park Press.

Satz, P. (1977). Laterality: An inferential problem. *Cortex, 13*, 208–212.

Satz, P., & Friel, J. (1978). Predictive validity of an abbreviated screening battery. *Journal of Learning Disabilities, 11*, 347–351.

Schank, R. C. (1982). *Reading and understanding: Teaching from the perspective of artificial intelligence*. Hillsdale, NJ: Erlbaum.

Schell, L. M. (1981). *Diagnostic and criterion-referenced reading tests*. Newark, DE: International Reading Association.

Schneider, W., & Shiffrin, R. M. (1977). Controlled and automatic human information processing: I. Detection, search and attention. *Psychological Review, 84*, 1–66.

Schonell, F. J. (1980). *New Order Graded Word Reading Test*. London: Oliver & Boyd.

Schwartz, R. M. (1980). Levels of processing: The strategic demands of reading comprehension. *Reading Research Quarterly, 15*, 433–450.

Schwartz, S. (1981). Verbal ability, attention and automaticity. In M. F. Friedman, J. P. Das, & N. O'Connor (Eds.), *Intelligence and learning*. New York: Plenum.

Schwartz, S., Griffin, T. M., & Brown, J. W. M. (1983). Power and speed components of individual differences in letter matching. *Intelligence, 7*, 369–378.

Schwartz, S., & Hartley, L. (1984). Effect of noise on cognitive strategies in a sentence–picture comparison task. Unpublished manuscript, University of Queensland.

Schwartz, S., & Johnson, J. H. (1981). *Psychopathology of childhood*. New York: Pergamon Press.

Schwartz, S., & Kirsner, K. (1982). Laterality effects in visual information processing: Hemispheric specialization or the orienting of attention? *Quarterly Journal of Experimental Psychology, 34a*, 61–77.

Schwartz, S., & Wiedel, T. C. (1978). Individual differences in cognition: Relationship between verbal ability and memory for order. *Intelligence, 2*, 353–369.

Seifert, M. (1976). Reading comprehension and the speed of encoding. *Reading Teacher, 30*, 314–315.

Senf, G. M., & Freundl, P. C. (1972). Sequential auditory and visual memory in learning disabled children. *Proceedings of the 80th annual convention of the American Psychological Association, 1*, 511–512.

Shiffrin, R. M., & Schneider, W. (1977). Controlled and automatic human information processing, II: Perceptual learning, automatic attending and a general theory. *Psychological Review, 84*, 127–190.

Silvaroli, N. J. (1976). *Classroom reading inventory*. Dubuque, IA: Brown.

Singer, M. (1976). Context inferences in the comprehension of sentences. *Canadian Journal of Psychology, 30*, 39–46.

Singer, M. H. (1979). Further comment on reading, language and learning. *Harvard Educational Review, 49*, 125–128.

Sipay, E. R. (1964). A comparison of standardized reading scores and functional reading levels. *Reading Teacher, 17*, 265–268.

Sipay, E. R. (1970). *Mastery test*. New York: Macmillan.

Smith, D. E. P. (1976). *A technology of reading and writing (Vol. 1)*. New York: Academic Press.

Smith, D. E. P., & Carrigan, P. M. (1959). *The nature of reading disability*. New York: Harcourt, Brace.

Smith, F. (1973). *Psycholinguistics and reading*. New York: Holt, Rinehart, & Winston.

Smith, F. (1979). Conflicting approaches to reading research and instruction. In L. B. Resnick & P. A. Weaver (Eds.), *Theory and practice of early reading* (Vol. 2). Hillsdale, NJ: Erlbaum.

Smith, J. M., Smith, D. E. P., & Brink, J. R. (1977). *A technology of reading and writing* (Vol. 2). New York: Academic Press.

Southwell, P. R. (1973). The initial teaching alphabet. *Developmental Medicine and Child Neurology, 15*, 794–799.

Spache, G. D. (1972). *Diagnostic reading scales*. New York: CTB/McGraw-Hill.

Spache, G. D. (1981). *Diagnosing and correcting reading disabilities (2nd ed.)*. Boston: Allyn & Bacon.

Speer, O. B., & Lamb, G. S. (1976). First-grade reading ability and fluency in naming verbal symbols. *Reading Teacher, 29*, 572–576.

Sperling, G. (1963). A model for visual memory tasks. *Human Factors, 5,* 19–31.

Spiro, R. J. (1977). Remembering information from text: The "state-of-the-schema" approach. In R. C. Anderson, R. J. Spiro, & W. E. Montague (Eds.), *Schooling and the acquisition of knowledge.* Hillsdale, NJ: Erlbaum.

Spring, C., & Capps, C. (1974). Encoding speed, rehearsal and probed recall of dyslexic boys. *Journal of Educational Psychology, 66,* 780–786.

Stack, D. (1980–81). An ophthalmologist reviews learning disabilities. *Australian Opthalmology Journal, 18,* 63–65.

Stanovich, K. E. (1980). Toward an interactive-compensatory model of individual differences in the development of reading fluency. *Reading Research Quarterly, 16,* 32–71.

Start, K. B., & Wells, B. K. (1972). *The trend of reading standards.* Slough, U.K.: NFER.

Stein, J., & Fowler, S. (1982). Diagnosis of dyslexia by means of a new indicator of eye dominance. *British Journal of Ophthalmology, 66,* 332–336.

Stein, N. L., & Glenn, C. G. (1979). An analysis of story comprehension in elementary school children. In R. O. Freedle (Ed.), *New directions in discourse processing* (Vol. 2). Norwood, NJ: Ablex.

Sternberg, R. J. (1977). *Intelligence, information processing and analogical reasoning: The componential analysis of human abilities.* Hillsdale, NJ: Erlbaum.

Stewart, G., & Andrews, S. (1979). *The Kensington word pool.* Sydney: University of New South Wales.

Sticht, T. G. (1979). Applications of the audread model to reading evaluation and instruction. In L. B. Resnick & P. A. Weaver (Eds.), *Theory and practice of early reading* (Vol. 1). (pp. 209–226). Hillsdale, NJ: Erlbaum.

Sticht, T. G., & Beck, L. J. (1976). *Experimental literacy assessment battery (LAB)* (AFHRL-TT-76-51). Lowry Air Force Base, CO: Air Force Human Resource Laboratory/Technical Training Division.

Tallal, P. (1980). Auditory temporal perception, phonics and reading disabilities in children. *Brain and Language, 9,* 182–191.

Thibadeau, R., Just, M. A., & Carpenter, C. A. (1982). A model of time, course and content of reading. *Cognitive Science, 6,* 157–203.

Thomas, J. L. (1981). *Microcomputers in the schools.* Phoenix: Oryx Press.

Thorndike, E. L. (1923). *Educational psychology: The psychology of learning, Vol. 2.* New York: Columbia University Press.

Thorndyke, P. W. (1977). Cognitive structures in comprehension and memory for narrative discourse. *Cognitive Psychology, 9,* 77–110.

Thurstone, L. L. (1947). *Multiple factor analysis.* Chicago: University of Chicago Press.

Tinker, M. A. (1958). Recent studies of eye movements in reading. *Psychological Bulletin, 55,* 215–231.

Tinker, M. A. (1965). *Bases for effective reading.* Minneapolis: University of Minnesota Press.

Torgeson, J. K. (1977). Memorization processes in reading disabled children. *Journal of Educational Psychology, 69,* 571–578.

Torgeson, J. K., & Goldman, T. (1977). Verbal rehearsal and short term memory in reading disabled children. *Child Development, 48,* 56–60.

Trabasso, T. (1972). Mental operations in language comprehension. In J. Carroll & R. O. Freedle (Eds.), *Language comprehension and the acquisition of knowledge.* Washington, DC: V. H. Winston.

Tracy, R. J., and Rankin, E. F. (1970). Methods of computing and evaluating residual gain scores in the reading program. In R. Farr (Ed.), *Measurement and evaluation of reading.* New York: Harcourt, Brace & World.

Traxler, A. E. (1970). Values and limitations of standardized reading tests. In R. Farr (Ed.), *Measurement and evaluation of reading.* New York: Harcourt, Brace & World.

Tulving, E., & Thompson, D. M. (1973). Encoding specificity and retrieval processes in episodic memory. *Psychological Review, 80,* 352–373.

Tunmer, W. E., & Herriman, M. L. (1983). The development of metalinguistic awareness in children. In W. E. Tunmer, C. Pratt, & M. L. Herriman (Eds.), *Metalinguistic awareness in children: Theory, research and application.* New York: Springer.

Tversky, A. (1975). Pictorial encoding of sentences in sentence–picture verification. *Quarterly Journal of Experimental Psychology, 27,* 405–410.

Umansky, J. A., & Chambers, S. M. (1980). Letters and words in word identification. *Memory and Cognition, 8,* 433–446.

Valtin, R. (1973). Report of research in dyslexia in children. Paper presented at the meeting of the International Reading Association, Denver. (ERIC Document No. ED079713).

Vellutino, F. R. (1978). Toward an understanding of dyslexia: Psychological factors in specific reading disability. In A. L. Benton & D. Pearl (Eds.), *Dyslexia: An appraisal of current knowledge.* New York: Oxford University Press.

Vellutino, F. R. (1979). The validity of perceptual deficit explanations of reading disability: A reply to Fletcher and Satz. *Journal of Learning Disabilities, 12,* 27–34.

Venezky, R. L. (1977). Research on reading processes: A historical perspective. *American Psychologist, 32,* 339–345.

Viitaniemi, E. (1965). Differences in reading between the sexes, I–II. *Education and School (Kasvatus jakoulu), 51,* 122–131 & 173–180.

Vincent, D., & Cresswell, M. (1976). *Reading tests in the classroom.* Windsor, U.K.: NFER.

Vogel, S. A. (1975). *Syntactic abilities in normal and dyslexic children.* Baltimore: University Park Press.

Vygotsky, L. S. (1978). *Mind in society: The development of higher psychological processes.* Cambridge, MA: Harvard University Press.

Wallbrown, J. D., Wallbrown, F. H., Engin, A. W., & Blaha, J. (1975). The prediction of first grade reading achievement with selected perceptual-cognitive tests. *Psychology in the Schools, 12,* 140–149.

Weinschenk, C. (1970). Über die Häufigkeit der kongenitalen legasthenie im zweiten Grund Schuljahr: II. *Psychologische Rundschau, 21,* 44–51.

Wernicke, C. (1874). *Der aphasische Symptomen-Komplex.* Breslau: Cohn & Weigart.

West, R. F., & Stanovich, K. E. (1978). Automatic contextual facilitation in readers of three ages. *Child Development, 49,* 717–727.

Wheeler, D. D. (1970). Processes in word recognition. *Cognitive Psychology, 1,* 59–85.

White, D. R., & Jacobs, E. (1979). The prediction of first-grade reading achievement from WPPSI scores of preschool children. *Psychology in the Schools, 16,* 189–192.

Whitehill, R. P., & Jipson, J. A. (1970). Differential reading program performance of extroverts and introverts. *Journal of Experimental Education, 38,* 93–96.

Wiedel, T. C., & Schwartz, S. (1982). Verbal ability and memory processing speed. *Current Psychological Research, 2,* 247–256.

Williams, J. (1979). Reading instruction today. *American Psychologist, 34,* 917–922.

Willows, D. M. (1978). Individual differences in distraction by pictures in a reading situation. *Journal of Educational Psychology, 70,* 837–847.

Willows, D. M., Borwick, D., & Hayvren, M. (1981). The content of school readers. In G. E. MacKinnon & T. G. Waller (Eds.), *Reading research: Advances in theory and practice* (Vol. 2). New York: Academic Press.

Wong, B. (1978). The effects of directive cues on the organization of memory and recall in good and poor readers. *Journal of Educational Research, 72,* 32–38.

Wong, B., Wong, R., & Foth, D. (1977). Recall and clustering of verbal materials among normal and poor readers. *Bulletin of the Psychonomic Society, 10*, 375–378.

Woodcock, R. W. (1973). *Woodcock reading mastery tests*. Circle Pines, MN: American Guidance Service.

Woodworth, R. S. (1938). *Experimental psychology*. New York: Holt.

Young, A. W., & Ellis, A. W. (1981). Asymmetry in cerebral hemispheric function in normal and poor readers. *Psychological Bulletin, 89*, 183–190.

Ysseldyke, J. E. (1973). Diagnostic-prescriptive teaching: The search for aptitude–treatment interactions. In L. Mann & D. Sabatino (Eds.), *Review of special education* (Vol. 1). Philadelphia: Buttonwood Farms.

Zaidel, E. (1978). Lexical organization in the right hemisphere. In P. A. Buser & A. Rougeul-Buser (Eds.), *Cerebral correlates of conscious experience*. Amsterdam: North Holland.

AUTHOR INDEX

SUBJECT INDEX

Alexia, 20, 21, 32
   See also Dyslexia and Reading, effects of
     brain injury on
Aphasia, 20–21, 32, 38
   See also Cerebral laterality and Reading,
     neuroanatomical and neurophysiologi-
     cal views of
Aptitude by treatment interactions, 189, 192
Auding, 75–76
Auditory Analysis Test, 74
Automatic information processing. *See* Infor-
     mation processing, automatic

Basic Sight Word Test, 65
Botel Reading Inventory, 64, 66

Cerebral laterality, 22–23, 25–28, 32, 38, 184
   See also Aphasia; Dyslexia; and Reading,
     neuroanatomical and neurophysiologi-
     cal views of
   reliability of tests of, 26–27
   validity of tests of, 27–28
Classroom Reading Inventory, 66
Cloze technique, 119, 126, 139, 151–152, 182
   See also GAP and GAPADOL
Clymer–Barrett Pre-Reading Battery, 64, 69
Cognition. *See* Information processing
Competence, new definitions of, 208–209
Competency-based measures. *See* Criterion-
     referenced tests
Componential analysis, 203–205
Comprehension
   definitions of, 85, 87, 99, 153
   individual differences in, 99–104, 108, 110,
     113, 115, 121–122, 127, 135, 138, 141,
     146, 151, 153, 161–162, 165, 209
   measures of, 61–63, 98, 119, 157 (*see also*
     Computers in reading, programs for and

Comprehension (*Cont.*)
   measures of (*Cont.*)
     Sentence Comprehension Test)
   schemas in, 85–86, 101, 106, 108, 169, 182
   scripts in, 182, 200, 206
   semantic context in, 100–101
   story grammars in, 86, 182
   strategies of, 101–103, 135, 153, 206
   subskills of, 86–87, 103–104
   teaching, 176, 181–182, 199–201
Computers in reading
   games for, 116, 216–217
   instruction, 210, 212–217
   interactive testing by, 210–212
   programs for, 9–238
     hardware requirements, 115–116, 221–
     222
     Initialization (INIT), 223–228
     Long-Term Memory Access Speed Test,
     277–293
     Mazes, 22
     Memory-For-Order Test, 293–311
     Sentence Comprehension Test, 263–277
     Tictactoe, 238–246
     Word-Decoding Test, 246–263
Constituent Comparison Model, 154–155
   See also Sentence Comprehension Test,
     rationale for and Sentence verification
     technique
Criterion-referenced tests, 4–6, 40, 44, 48, 54,
     59–61, 65–67, 69
   See also Reading, skills

Decoding. *See also* Information-processing,
     models of decoding
   definitions of, 64–65, 87–88, 98, 113, 152
   individual differences in, 80, 84, 88–95, 98,
     108, 110, 113, 123, 128–129, 135, 138,